To Be a Soldier

THE ARMY'S CAPSTONE DOCTRINAL MANUALS

DEPARTMENT OF THE ARMY

Skyhorse Publishing

Fm-1 The Army published 2005 by Department of the Army.
FM-3 Operations (With Changes) published 2011 by the Department of the Army.
No copyright is claimed on these texts.

First Skyhorse edition 2017.
Compilation and design © Skyhorse Publishing 2017.

All inquiries should be addressed to Skyhorse Publishing,
307 West 36th Street, 11th Floor, New York, NY 10018.

Skyhorse Publishing books may be purchased in bulk at special discounts for sales promotion, corporate gifts, fund-raising, or educational purposes. Special editions can also be created to specifications. For details, contact the Special Sales Department, Skyhorse Publishing, 307 West 36th Street, 11th Floor, New York, NY 10018 or info@skyhorsepublishing.com.

Skyhorse® and Skyhorse Publishing® are registered trademarks of
Skyhorse Publishing, Inc.®, a Delaware corporation.

Visit our website at www.skyhorsepublishing.com.

10 9 8 7 6 5 4 3 2 1

Library of Congress Cataloging-in-Publication Data is available on file.

Cover design by Rain Saukas

Print ISBN: 978-1-5107-2845-5
Ebook ISBN: 978-1-5107-2847-9

Printed in China

FM 1

The Army

June 2005

HEADQUARTERS
DEPARTMENT OF THE ARMY

Foreword

The Army is the primary Landpower arm of our Nation's Armed Forces. It exists to serve the American people, protect enduring national interests, and fulfill the Nation's military responsibilities. FM 1 is one of the Army's two capstone field manuals. It contains our vision for the Army. While the entire manual is important, I would direct your attention to four particular items.

FM 1 establishes the fundamental principles for employing Landpower. The most important of these are the Army's operational concept and the fundamentals that support it. They form the foundation for all Army doctrine. All Soldiers should understand and internalize them.

FM 1 describes the American profession of arms, the Army's place in it, and what it means to be a professional Soldier. Central to this discussion are the Soldier's Creed, Warrior Ethos, and Army Values. These three statements establish the guiding values and standards of the Army profession. To understand Soldiers, you must know about them. To be a Soldier, you must live them.

FM 1 discusses Army contributions to the joint force. As the Armed Forces achieve even greater joint interdependence, the Army will depend more on the other Services and vice versa. For this reason, the Army is currently transforming its units and institutions to enhance our campaign qualities for sustained operations and to achieve greater expeditionary and joint capabilities. It is important for Soldiers and all who support or are associated with the Army to understand these contributions and how the Army is transforming to better meet its obligations to the other Services.

Finally, FM 1 talks about Soldiers, the centerpiece of all Army organizations. Without Soldiers there is no Army. Soldiers of all components and the Army civilians who support them render selfless service to the Nation daily. FM 1 begins and ends with Soldiers because the Army begins and ends with Soldiers. It is they who, together with their leaders, will keep the Army relevant and ready, today and tomorrow.

PETER J. SCHOOMAKER
General, United States Army
Chief of Staff

Field Manual
No. 1

Headquarters
Department of the Army
Washington, DC, 14 June 2005

THE ARMY

Contents

Distribution Restriction: Approved for public release; distribution is unlimited.

*This publication supersedes FM 1, 14 June 2001.

Figures

Acknowledgments

The copyright owners listed here have granted permission to reproduce material from their works. Other sources of quotations, graphics, and material used in vignettes are listed in the Source Notes.

Excerpt from *This Kind of War: A Study in Unpreparedness*, by T.R. Fehrenbach. Macmillan, 1963. Reprinted with permission of Richard Curtis Literary Agency.

Photograph "Capt. Michael Dugan hangs an American flag from a light pole in front of what is left of the World Trade Center..." by Andrew Savulich. ©*New York Daily News* LP.

Quote by Peter J. Schoomaker, "We will not be effective ...." *Military Officer Magazine*, November 2004, vol.II:11. Reprinted with permission of *Military Officer Magazine*.

Photograph accompanying the 724th Transportation Company in Iraq reproduced with permission of the 724th Transportation Company Family Support Group Web site. www.724transco.citymax.com/page/page/1810557.htm.

Preface

FM 1 is one of the Army's two capstone doctrinal manuals. The other is FM 3-0, *Operations*. FM 1's audience includes the Executive Branch; Congress; Office of the Secretary of Defense; Joint Staff; combatant commanders; other Services; officers, noncommissioned officers, and enlisted Soldiers of all Army components; and Army civilians.

FM 1 is prepared under the direction of the Army Chief of Staff. It states what the Army is, what the Army does, how the Army does it, and where the Army is going. It establishes the Army's operational concept and other fundamental principles for employing landpower in support of the National Security, National Defense, and the National Military Strategies. FM 1 delineates the Army's purpose, roles, and functions as established by the Constitution; the Congress, in Title 10, United States Code; and the Department of Defense, in Department of Defense Directive 5100.1. FM 1 is also the Army Chief of Staff's vision for the Army.

To facilitate joint interdependence, Army doctrine supports and is consistent with joint doctrine. FM 1 connects Army doctrine to joint doctrine as expressed in the relevant joint doctrinal publications, especially, Joint Publication 1, *Joint Warfare of the Armed Forces of the United States*, and Joint Publication 3-0, *Doctrine for Joint Operations*. FM 1 also links the National Security, National Defense, and National Military Strategies with the Army's operational doctrine in FM 3-0.

This publication contains copyrighted material.

This publication applies to the Active Army, Army National Guard, and U.S. Army Reserve.

U.S. Army Training and Doctrine Command is the proponent for this publication. The preparing agency is the Combined Arms Doctrine Directorate, U.S. Army Combined Arms Center. Send written comments and recommendations on DA Form 2028 (Recommended Changes to Publications and Blank Forms) directly to Commander, U.S. Army Combined Arms Center and Fort Leavenworth, ATTN: ATZL-CD (FM 1), 201 Reynolds Avenue, Fort Leavenworth, KS 66027-2337. Send comments and recommendations by e-mail to *web-cadd@leavenworth.army.mil*. Follow the DA Form 2028 format or submit an electronic DA Form 2028.

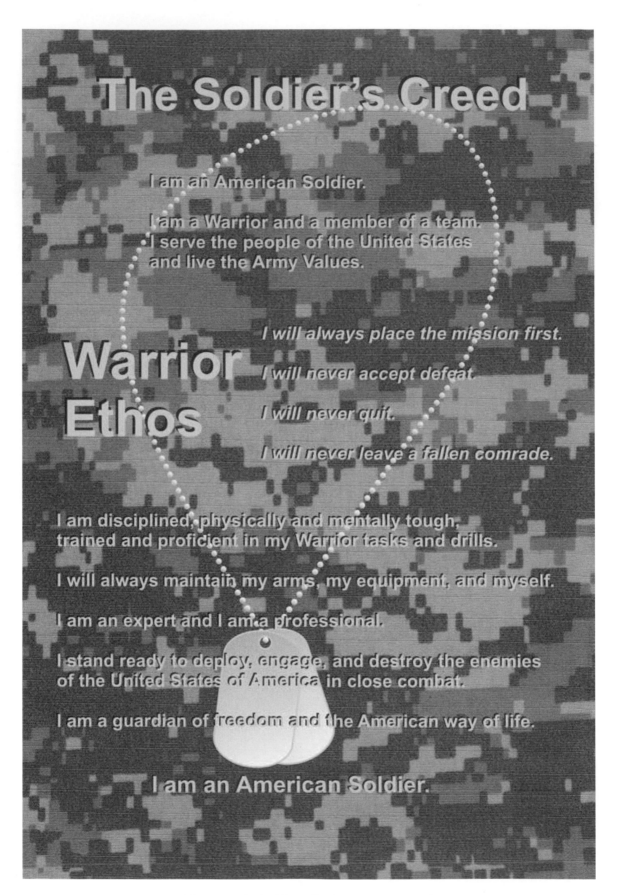

Figure 1-1. The Soldier's Creed

Chapter 1

The Army and the Profession of Arms

...[Y]ou may fly over a land forever; you may bomb it, atomize it, pulverize it and wipe it clean of life—but if you desire to defend it, protect it, and keep it for civilization, you must do this on the ground, the way the Roman legions did, by putting your young men into the mud.

T.R. Fehrenbach
This Kind of War

1-1.   First and foremost, the Army is Soldiers. No matter how much the tools of warfare improve, it is Soldiers who use them to accomplish their mission. Soldiers committed to selfless service to the Nation are the centerpiece of Army organizations. Everything the Army does for the Nation is done by Soldiers supported by Army civilians and family members. Only with quality Soldiers answering the noble call to serve freedom can the Army ensure the victories required on battlefields of today and the future.

1-2.   The Army, a long-trusted institution, exists to serve the Nation. As part of the joint force, the Army supports and defends America's Constitution and way of life against all enemies, foreign and domestic. The Army protects national security interests, including, forces, possessions, citizens, allies, and friends. It prepares for and delivers decisive action in all operations. Above all, the Army provides combatant commanders with versatile land forces ready to fight and win the Nation's wars.

1-3.   The Army's contribution to joint operations is landpower. *Landpower* is the ability—by threat, force, or occupation—to promptly gain, sustain, and exploit control over land, resources, and people. Landpower includes the ability to—

- Impose the Nation's will on adversaries—by force if necessary—in diverse and complex terrain.
- Establish and maintain a stable environment that sets the conditions for a lasting peace.
- Address the consequences of catastrophic events—both natural and man-made—to restore infrastructure and reestablish basic civil services.
- Support and provide a base from which forces can influence and dominate the air and sea dimensions of the joint operational area.

1-4.   While the Army is an integral part of the joint force, the value of its contribution depends on its ability to exercise landpower. Ultimately, Army forces' ability to control land, resources, and people through a sustained presence makes permanent the advantages gained by joint forces.

1-5.   At the dawn of the twentieth century, Secretary of War Elihu Root wrote, "The real object of having an Army is to provide for war." He continued, "The regular [military] establishment in the United States will probably never be by itself the whole machine with which any war will be fought." But Root also knew that the Army does more than fight wars. Even as he wrote, Army forces were establishing civil governments in recently acquired territories in Puerto Rico, the Philippines, and Cuba. After fighting the war with Spain, the Army had reduced its strength. However, it was recruiting Soldiers for counterinsurgency operations in the Philippines. Now, at the beginning of the twenty-first century, Secretary Root's observation remains true. The Army—Regular Army and Reserve Components—continues to provide forces relevant to mission requirements. The Soldiers and Army civilians of these forces are ready for employment on short notice and able to conduct sustained operations when required.

1-6.   Army forces provide combatant commanders the means to deter potential adversaries and shape the strategic environment. Fundamental to deterrence is the credible, demonstrated capability to fight and win in all land environments. Several factors underlie the credibility and capability that make Army forces relevant in any environment. Tough, disciplined Soldiers and imaginative, adaptive leadership are essential components. Rigorous and realistic training, sound doctrine, and modern equipment also contribute. The design and practices of Army institutional structures provide essential support. These same characteristics make Army forces important to establishing relationships with potential multinational partners. The versatile mix of Army organizations provides combatant commanders with the landpower necessary to achieve objectives across the range of military operations.

1-7.   Army forces are ready—well led, well trained, and well equipped. They are prepared to deploy immediately anywhere in the world. Army forces can manage crises. They are ready to conduct prompt force projection and sustained land operations. When deterrence fails or disaster strikes, they can lead or support the unified action required to resolve a situation.

1-8.   Army forces are versatile. In addition to conducting combat operations, Army forces help provide security. They supply many services associated with establishing order, rebuilding infrastructure, and delivering humanitarian support. When necessary, they can direct assistance in reestablishing governmental institutions. Army forces help set the conditions that allow a return to normalcy or a self-sustaining peace.

THE ARMY IN AMERICAN HISTORY

1-9.   The Army traces its heritage to the colonial militias. These were precursors of today's Army National Guard. Citizens answering the call to protect their homes and families began a heritage of selfless service and sacrifice that continues today. Opposition to British colonial policies in the eighteenth century led to war in 1775. After the battles at Lexington and Concord, militia forces from across New England surrounded British forces in Boston. The Continental Congress assumed command of these units as "Troops of the United Provinces of North America" on 14 June 1775.

This date is taken as the Army's birthday. The next day, Congress gave command of all "Continental forces" to George Washington. Washington's forces were the first American military organizations responsible to an authority other than that of the individual colonies or the British Crown. Born in this quest for freedom, the Army has served the Nation in peace and war for over 230 years.

1-10. On 1 January 1776, the national force authorized by Congress came into existence. It was described by Washington in his first general order of the new year as "the new army, which, in every point of View is entirely Continental." The name stuck, and the national forces became known as the Continentals. The Continentals drew strength from strong leadership and selfless patriotism despite shortages of supplies and equipment. Their early hardships and the crucible of Valley Forge molded them into the Army that, with the state militias, kept the spirit of patriotism alive until the long war for independence could be won.

1-11. Thus, from the start, the Army comprised a small national force and the state militias' citizen-Soldiers. In times of emergency, the standing army was enlarged with recruits and augmented by mobilizing the militia and creating volunteer units, initially by state and nationally by the time of the Civil War. This tradition of an Army that combines "full-time" regular Soldiers and citizen-Soldiers serving for short active-service periods is still the cornerstone of Army organization.

1-12. In 1781, with the support of French land and naval forces, the Continental Army defeated the British at Yorktown. This victory secured for the Nation the ideals so eloquently stated in the Declaration of Independence:

WE hold these Truths to be self-evident, that all Men are created equal, that they are endowed by their Creator with certain unalienable Rights, that among these are Life, Liberty, and the pursuit of Happiness....

1-13. Sustained by the selfless service of patriots, the Army continues to protect these same unalienable rights today. Thus, the most meaningful lines of the Declaration of Independence with respect to the Army may not be the first, but the last:

And for the support of this Declaration, with a firm Reliance on the Protection of divine Providence, we mutually pledge to each other our Lives, our Fortunes, and our sacred Honor.

1-14. This sentence reflects the ideals of American civil society and its military. Since it was written, the Army has provided Americans the means to pledge their lives, fortunes, and honor to a noble, selfless cause. Today's young men and women are continuing the Army's vigilant, dedicated, and selfless service to the American people. They are honoring the bond and sacred trust the Army bears as the servant of the Nation. The commitment of today's Soldiers sustains freedom and inspires the next generation to answer the call to duty.

Washington at Newburgh
Establishing the Role of the Military in a Democracy

Following victory at Yorktown in 1781, the Continental Army moved into quarters near Newburgh, New York, to await peace. The national situation was grim. The Continental Congress could not raise the funds to provide pay or pensions to the Soldiers, some of whom had not been paid for several years. Many officers feared that Congress would disband the Army and renege on its promises. By the winter of 1782–83, tension had reached a dangerous level. The future of the Republic was in doubt.

A group of officers determined to use the threat of military action to compel Congress to settle its debts. They attempted to enlist their commander, General George Washington, to lead the plot. He refused every appeal, and the rebellious officers prepared to act without him. On 15 March 1783, Washington entered an officers assembly and warned them of the grave danger inherent in their scheme. He was having little effect until he took a pair of spectacles from his pocket to read.

The officers were astonished. None of them had seen their hero in his eyeglasses. Washington seemed to age before them. But an offhand comment demonstrated the depth of character that had sustained a revolution: "Gentlemen, you will permit me to put on my spectacles, for I have not only grown gray, but almost blind, in the service of my country." The act, the statement, and the power of a leader's example quelled an incipient rebellion.

Washington's selfless leadership and willing subordination instituted the tradition of civilian control of the military—a fundamental tenet of the American military profession.

1-15. The American tradition of subordinating the military to civilian authority dates from the end of the Revolutionary War. This tradition began with a threat to liberty at Newburgh, New York, in 1781. As described in the vignette on page 1-4, a group of Continental Army officers were plotting to compel the Continental Congress to settle debts owed to Soldiers with the threat of force. George Washington took a strong stand against the conspirators and quelled what could have become a military rebellion. His actions stand as an example of the selfless service and willing subordination to civilian authority the Nation expects of American military professionals today.

1-16. After the Revolutionary War, the government reduced the Army to fewer than 100 Soldiers. This action began a recurring pattern of small peacetime forces followed by wartime expansion. This reduction was based on both a distrust of large standing forces and a belief that the Atlantic Ocean would protect the Nation from major foreign threats. Significant federal forces were reconstituted only in response to emergencies, usually to protect citizens on the frontier. The Army did expand significantly to fight the British in the War of 1812. This war was fought primarily with the standing Army, augmented by militia and volunteers. It solidified the Army's reputation of service to the Nation. Although it was again reduced in size after the war, the Army was never again reduced to the extent that it was after the Revolutionary War.

1-17. From the beginning, the Army made major contributions to America's growth. As the Nation expanded westward, Army explorers mapped new territories and extended the frontier. Army engineers built roads and canals and improved navigation on waterways. Army forces kept watch over the frontier, enforcing law and order and providing the security necessary for the Nation's expansion. In 1846, the Army expanded to fight the Mexican War. Afterwards, it again was reduced to a small standing force.

1-18. In the 1860s, the Army and the Nation experienced their most trying period, when both were torn apart by the Civil War. The Army grew dramatically—in size, capability, and technological sophistication—during the four long years of war. Afterwards, the Army was charged with reconstructing the South. Simultaneously, it resumed responsibility for maintaining security on the frontier.

1-19. Changes in military thought and technology accelerated in the second half of the nineteenth century. The hard-won lessons of the Civil War and examples from European wars demonstrated the need to codify a body of professional knowledge and train leaders to apply it. Army leaders, like General William Tecumseh Sherman, acted to meet this need. In 1882, the Army established the School of Application for Cavalry and Infantry at Fort Leavenworth, Kansas. In time, this school became the foundation of the Army's professional education system. Its founding was key to the Army's development as a profession between 1870 and 1910.

1-20. The Spanish-American War of 1898 exposed Army leadership, organizational, logistic, and training deficiencies. The Army overcame these and defeated Spanish forces at opposite ends of the globe. Afterwards, it struggled to assimilate many technological changes. It also became an expeditionary force for a growing world power.

Army forces assumed responsibility for governing the new possessions of Puerto Rico, the Philippines, and Cuba. They continued to protect the border with Mexico as well.

1-21. The Spanish-American War and Philippine Insurrection showed the need for a federal reserve force. This force was created in 1908 and eventually became the Organized Reserve. It was the predecessor of the Army Reserve. The Organized Reserve provided a formal peacetime structure for volunteers. It produced a pool of reserve officers and enlisted Soldiers with medical and other skills.

1-22. The early twentieth century found the Nation and the Army involved in the first of two world wars. These wars transformed them both. A greatly and hastily expanded U.S. Army assured the Allied victory in World War I. The American Expeditionary Forces first saw action at Cantigny. Important victories at Soissons, St. Mihiel, and the Meuse-Argonne followed. The action of the 369th Infantry Regiment described on page 1-7 provides one example of the contributions of the American Expeditionary Forces. These and other victories helped turn the tide on the Western Front and defeat the Central Powers. The Nation had raised, trained, and equipped almost three million Soldiers and deployed them overseas in 18 months.

1-23. World War I also saw developments in land operations that began the evolution to the joint operations of today. Different Army branches were integrated into combined arms operations on a larger scale than ever before. The use of military aircraft led to the awareness of the potential of airpower. Military leaders began to recognize that landpower, airpower, and sea power are interrelated. Large Marine forces served under Army command and Army forces served under Marine commanders for the first time. As important, the Army, under Generals John J. Pershing and Peyton March, learned to mobilize, train, and project power across the Atlantic Ocean. The Regular Army revised its relationship with the Army National Guard as part of that effort. In addition, members of the Organized Reserve were mobilized to provide the many skills needed to sustain a large twentieth-century Army.

1-24. A generation later, World War II challenged the Army to again project landpower across the Atlantic Ocean—and the Pacific as well. The United States recognized an unofficial state of national emergency after the fall of France in June 1940. The National Guard was mobilized and a peacetime draft initiated. All members of the Organized Reserve were called to active duty. To take advantage of technological advances, the Army changed the structure of its organizations, fielding such specialized units as armored divisions, airborne divisions, and special operations forces. To defeat the Axis powers, combat organizations were deployed to North Africa, Europe, Asia, and the Pacific.

1-25. The Army had been greatly reduced during the lean years between the wars. The Great Depression limited available money, equipment, and Soldiers. However, the Army used that time and its education system to develop leaders. This brilliant generation of Army leaders included such generals as Marshall, MacArthur, Arnold, Eisenhower, Bradley, and Patton. These leaders were able to mobilize, train, and equip a force that grew to 89 divisions by 1945. Organized Reserve officers formed the leadership cadre for most of these divisions.

Meuse-Argonne, 26 September–1 October 1918

The 369th Infantry fought valiantly in the Meuse-Argonne as part of the French 161st Division. Attacking behind a fiery barrage, the 369th Infantry assaulted successive German trench lines and captured the town of Ripont. On 29 September, the regiment stormed powerful enemy positions and took the town of Sechault. Despite heavy casualties, the 369th, called "Hell Fighters" by the French and Germans, relentlessly continued the attack at dawn. Raked by enemy machine guns, they assaulted in the woods northeast of Sechault, flanking and overwhelming enemy machine gun positions. The "Let's Go!" elan and indomitable fighting spirit of the 369th Infantry was illustrated throughout the battle. Their initiative, leadership, and gallantry won for their entire regiment the French Croix de Guerre.

1-26. Twice in 25 years, America's regulars and citizen-Soldiers had answered the call to duty. During World War II, the Army's ranks swelled to meet unprecedented challenges of global magnitude. It formed a decisive force that helped sustain freedom and democracy throughout the world. The sacrifices of millions of American Soldiers of two generations helped establish the United States as a global power. At the end of World War II, Army forces were stationed around the world. They were governing occupied countries, assisting in reconstruction programs, and securing new borders against new foes.

1-27. World War II did not end the threat to freedom. The Soviet Union also emerged from the war as a global power, and the Chinese Communists drove the Nationalists from the Chinese mainland in 1949. These developments resulted in a continuing state of tension that persisted for five decades. Army forces were involved in worldwide commitments. For the first time, Americans accepted the need to maintain a large standing army in peacetime. However, the belief that strategic nuclear weapons would prove decisive in future conflict led to resource scarcity for the Army until the 1960s.

1-28. Even so, the strategic environment was also dangerous from a conventional perspective. Between 1950 and 1989, Army forces served in many small but important actions. These included an intervention in the Dominican Republic in 1965 and combat operations in Grenada in 1983. The Multinational Force and Observers mission in the Sinai began in 1982. The major conflicts of this period, in Korea and Vietnam, were limited in terms of objectives and scope to prevent escalation into nuclear warfare. Limited in scope did not mean that either of these conflicts were "small wars." Both involved Army forces in large-scale conventional operations.

1-29. Operations in Vietnam entailed significant counterinsurgency operations as well. Soldiers fought with honor, many times overcoming great odds to prevail. This protracted conflict sorely challenged the Army. However, the lessons learned served as a catalyst to revitalize it. Following this conflict, the Army launched key initiatives to create the all-volunteer force; refocus doctrine, training, and leader development; and modernize its equipment.

1-30. The 1970s and 1980s were a challenging time of rebuilding. The Army's focus returned to fighting a large-scale conventional war in Europe. However, budgets for military spending remained tight until the 1980s. Then the Army began modernizing its equipment with such systems as the Abrams tank and Bradley fighting vehicle. Army doctrine was refined as well. Ground tactics that had not changed much since the mid-1950s gave way to the Active Defense and then to AirLand Battle. In addition, innovations in both individual and collective training brought Soldiers and their leaders to a proficiency seldom seen in any army. These Soldiers, trained and ready, secured the frontiers of freedom in Korea and central Europe.

1-31. The Cold War ended with the fall of the Berlin Wall in 1989. The dissolution of the Warsaw Pact, collapse of the Soviet Union, and reunification of Germany brought changes for the military. The United States faced a strategic environment containing no peer competitor. There was no clear-cut threat against which to prepare a defense. The strategic environment was increasingly volatile, uncertain, complex, and ambiguous. The Army had to prepare to deter unknown adversaries, defeat ill-defined enemies, and control unfamiliar situations. Instead of focusing on prevailing in major combat operations, the Army was required to balance its capabilities. However, the desire for a "peace dividend" again resulted in smaller Army budgets during the 1990s.

1-32. The last decade of the twentieth century found Army forces reassuring partners and deterring aggression in critical regions. In December 1989, Army forces intervened to establish a U.S.-recognized government in Panama. After the intervention, Army Reserve civil affairs and military police units remained to restore order. In 1991, Army forces ejected the Iraqi Army from Kuwait in an unprecedented 100-hour ground offensive that followed an equally unprecedented joint air offensive. This operation occurred during the post-Cold War force reduction. It required mobilizing many National Guard and Army Reserve units. To ensure regional stability and bolster respect for human rights, Army forces participated in several North Atlantic Treaty Organization and United Nations peacekeeping operations. These included missions in Somalia, Haiti, and the Balkans.

1-33. The twenty-first century brought new threats to the United States. These took the form of ideologies and networks hostile to the American way of life. Today finds Army forces committed worldwide in the War on Terrorism. After the attacks of 11 September 2001, Army forces contributed to successful major combat operations in Afghanistan and Iraq. These operations removed two repressive regimes. In Afghanistan, Army and joint forces carried the fight to the sponsors and organizers of the 11 September attacks. In both countries, Army forces' sustained operations established the conditions for unprecedented national elections. The Army continues to contribute most of the forces for the stability and reconstruction operations in these two countries. Today, Army forces are acting in a new strategic environment, one in which the Nation is waging a complex, protracted conflict. In this environment, peace is the exception; combat and extended operations are routine.

1-34. Throughout its history, the Army has demonstrated respect for enduring principles and institutional characteristics in its service to the Nation. Among the first are the primacy of the Constitution, the rule of law, and military subordination to civilian authority. Among the second are maintaining the ability to mobilize rapidly to support the Nation's interests, integrating new technology, and quickly adapting to and learning to win in changing environments and circumstances. The Army's rich history inspires today's Soldiers as members of a proud and noble profession. It links this generation of Soldiers to those of past generations who answered the call to duty.

A HISTORIC CHALLENGE

> *The Army used to have all the time in the world and no money; now we've got all the money and no time.*
>
> General George C. Marshall

1-35. Besides evoking inspiration and ancestral linkage, history also bears lessons. In the immediate aftermath of the Cold War, there was a widespread and apparently reasonable expectation of a "peace dividend." There also appeared to be time for the Army to methodically transform the force. The "new world order" was supposed to be one of fewer conflicts. Threats to the United States were expected to decrease. These assumptions affected defense planning and budgeting. Both the size and readiness of the Army decreased.

1-36. The attacks of 11 September 2001 exposed the realities of the current security environment. The United States is now engaged in a protracted global war against enemies fighting with unconventional means. The more extreme of them value human life differently and reject any accommodation. These realities make clear that, to ultimately succeed in the War on Terrorism, the Army must rebalance its capabilities and capacities. The Army is using this strategic opportunity to transform itself. It is undergoing its most profound restructuring in more than 50 years. Combat capabilities and capacities designed to defeat a peer competitor are being converted to those better able to sustain protracted operations across the range of military operations. At the same time, the Army is applying increased resources to meet the needs of combatant commanders today and posturing itself for tomorrow's challenges.

1-37. This is not the first time the Army has made such a force correction. Throughout its history, increases in size and modernization efforts to meet national challenges have been followed by decreases in strength and resources after the crisis. For example, after World War I, the Army received barely enough resources to experiment with new technologies, let alone integrate them into the force. Thus, the eve of World War II found the Army in a race against time as it created a mechanized force and built the combat organizations needed to defeat peer competitors on opposite ends of the globe.

1-38. Today the Army finds itself in a similar situation. The threat is here and now, and it is global in scope. This time, however, the Army is making the best use of existing Army capabilities while expanding capacities where needed. World War II required a large Army to match the capacities of peer competitors. The War on Terrorism requires an Army with diverse capabilities to meet a different kind of adversary. The Army is rapidly rebalancing its capabilities and capacities to effectively meet this challenge.

1-39. But there is a significant difference between the challenges before World War II and those of today. During World War II, the homeland was safe from major attacks. While there was a threat of sabotage, the Axis powers could neither project a major force to North America nor strike it from the air. Today's security environment is different. Weapons of mass destruction and those able to produce catastrophic effects are small enough to smuggle into the homeland. America's adversaries are actively seeking those weapons. The United States must find and defeat those adversaries before they procure and use them. A second difference is the nature of the adversary. America's adversaries during World War II were nation states. Their sources of power could be located and destroyed. Once this was accomplished, the war ended. Today's enemies include nonstate organizations. Their members and power sources are hard to find and defeat. New enemies may appear with little warning. This situation makes it impossible to determine when the War on Terrorism will end. It places a premium on operational flexibility and adaptability—attributes of Army forces with balanced capabilities. It requires Army forces to sustain a consistently high readiness level. There will be no time to "ramp up" to meet a crisis. Maintaining this readiness level while fighting the War on Terrorism requires a long-term commitment—of both resources and will—by the Nation as well as the Army. These differences form the basis of today's challenge.

THE AMERICAN PROFESSION OF ARMS

1-40. The purpose of any profession is to serve society by effectively delivering a necessary and useful specialized service. To fulfill those societal needs, professions—such as, medicine, law, the clergy, and the military—develop and maintain distinct bodies of specialized knowledge and impart expertise through formal, theoretical, and practical education. Each profession establishes a unique subculture that distinguishes practitioners from the society they serve while supporting and enhancing that society. Professions create their own standards of performance and codes of ethics to maintain their effectiveness. To that end, they develop particular vocabularies, establish journals, and sometimes adopt distinct forms of dress. In exchange for holding their membership to high technical and ethical standards, society grants professionals a great deal of autonomy. However, the profession of arms is different from other professions, both as an institution and with respect to its individual members.

1-41. Institutionally, the consequences of failure in the profession of arms—for both individual members of the Armed Forces and the Nation—are more dire than those in any other. Most professions serve individual clients. The military serves a collective client, the Nation. Its actions impact broadly in extent and consequences: the recovery of a community devastated by natural disaster, the defeat of enemy forces, or the security of the Nation. Therefore, failure of the military profession would have catastrophic consequences. American military professionals work, study, and train throughout their careers to ensure the military profession will not fail in the call to duty.

1-42. Individual members of the profession of arms are distinguished from those of other professions by the "unlimited liability" they assume in their oaths of office. While members of some professions engage in dangerous tasks daily, only members of the Armed Forces can be ordered to place their lives in peril anywhere at any time. The obligations they undertake, risking life and well-being for the greater good, are in many ways extraordinary.

1-43. The profession of arms is global. Most nations maintain armies. American Soldiers consider soldiers of most other nations to be peers. They consider each other members of a community born of similar experiences, military cultures, and values. However, the American profession of arms is distinguished in three ways:

- Service to the Constitution.
- Officer and noncommissioned officer professionalism.
- Proficiency in integrating technology.

1-44. Members of the American military profession swear to support and defend a document, the Constitution of the United States—not a leader, people, government, or territory. That solemn oath ties military service directly to the founding document of the Nation. It instills a nobility of purpose within each member of the Armed Forces and provides deep personal meaning to all who serve. The profession holds common standards and a code of ethics derived from common moral obligations undertaken in its members' oaths of office. These unite members of all the Services in their common purpose: defending the Constitution and protecting the Nation's interests, at home and abroad, against all threats.

1-45. All branches of government contribute to providing for the common defense. Under the Constitution, Congress, representing the people, has authority "to raise and support Armies...[and] To provide and maintain a Navy." Congress also makes statutes applicable to the land and naval forces and appropriates funds for their missions. The Constitution designates the President as Commander in Chief of the Armed

Forces. Once the Congress has approved the use of force, the President directs that use. The judicial branch interprets laws passed by Congress as they apply to the Armed Forces and the authority of the President as Commander in Chief. Thus, the military is responsible to the legislative, executive, and judicial branches of the government in their separate functions.

1-46. A final aspect that distinguishes the American profession of arms is the professionalism of its officers and noncommissioned officers. Both are given considerable authority early in their careers. Both are expected to exercise initiative to identify and resolve unforeseen circumstances. Both are developed through a series of schools that equips them for greater responsibilities as they are promoted. This combination of professional development and experience in making decisions within general guidelines rather than rigid rules develops flexible and self-aware leaders. It has resulted in an agile institution able to conduct decentralized operations and obtain extraordinary results. The accompanying vignette contains one example of this kind of military professional, Sergeant First Class Paul R. Smith.

1-47. In the past two decades, the American military has advanced technologically at an unprecedented rate. More importantly, it has integrated technology into combined arms and joint operations beyond the militaries of most other nations. The identity of the American profession of arms is joint in nature and essence. It encompasses specialized knowledge of land, maritime, aerospace, and special operations that it applies through unified action.

1-48. The American profession of arms has three dimensions: physical, intellectual, and moral.

1-49. The profession of arms is *physical* because warfare is physical. The joint force applies violent measures to destroy assets and personnel essential to adversaries' interests. The physical dimension includes deploying forces over vast distances and moving them through complex environments. Doing this requires considerable energy. Doing it well without adverse unintended consequences requires considerable skill and training. Extraordinary physical strength is necessary to endure the violence and friction attendant to military operations.

1-50. The profession of arms is *intellectual* because the body of expertise required to employ joint forces in military operations is extensive and detailed. From the strategic perspective, this expertise is exercised in concert with the other instruments of national power: diplomatic, informational, and economic. From the operational and tactical perspectives, military professionals exercise their expertise against intelligent adversaries actively seeking to defeat them in life-and-death situations.

1-51. The intellectual dimension also encompasses two cultural aspects of the profession. The first is internal: it pertains to knowledge of the military's values-based culture (addressed in the next section). The second is external: it pertains to the need to adapt to varying environments with different cultural and political values. Military professionals must be culturally aware—sensitive to differences and the implications those differences have on the operational environment.

(U.S. Army photo)

Professionalism in Combat—Beyond the Call of Duty

His Soldiers considered Sergeant First Class Paul R. Smith a strict disciplinarian and tough trainer. Smith's experiences during the Persian Gulf War of 1991 impressed on him the importance of strong leadership and training to standard. As a platoon sergeant, he lived that conviction, training his platoon tirelessly. When deployed to Kuwait before Operation Iraqi Freedom, Smith vowed to do all it took to bring his Soldiers home.

On 4 April 2003, near the Baghdad airport, Smith's combat engineer unit was attacked by a company-sized enemy force. Realizing the threat to his unit, Smith personally engaged the enemy with hand grenades and antitank weapons. Then he organized the evacuation of three wounded Soldiers from a damaged armored personnel carrier. Concerned that the enemy would overrun their defenses, Smith moved under withering fire to a .50 caliber machine gun mounted on the damaged vehicle. With total disregard for himself, he engaged the attackers from an exposed position, ordering the Soldier feeding ammunition to his weapon to stay down. After firing over three cans of ammunition, Smith was mortally wounded. However, his courageous actions helped repel the enemy attack, resulting in as many as 50 enemy killed and the safe withdrawal of many wounded Soldiers.

The only casualty from his platoon that day was Sergeant First Class Smith. He was awarded the Medal of Honor for his selfless, coura-geous action. Many Soldiers of his platoon, "his boys," believe they re-turned home because of their platoon sergeant's unceasing efforts to prepare them for combat and his selfless service above and beyond the call of duty on 4 April 2003.

1-52. The *moral* dimension of the profession of arms lies in the fact that war is ultimately fought for ideas. Ideas motivate combatants. It is only in the moral dimension—when opponents understand and believe that they are defeated—that victory is complete. While the use of force is sometimes necessary for the common good, the authority to wield it carries a moral responsibility of the greatest magnitude. The morality of applying force in a just cause derives from ancient ethical and religious standards. The moral and ethical tenets of the Constitution and the Declaration of Independence form the basis of the military's professional ideals. The Law of Land Warfare, Uniform Code of Military Justice, and Code of Conduct give structure to its moral standards.

1-53. Included in the moral dimension is civilian control of the military. The Armed Forces do not wage war in their own name or under their own authority. Under the Constitution, the decision to use military force belongs to the American people (acting through Congress) and the President (acting under their authority). Once the Nation, through its elected representatives, decides to authorize military action, it relies on the professionalism of its military leaders to ensure the judicious application of violence.

1-54. Doing the right thing for the right reason and with the right intention is always challenging. But this challenge is even more difficult during the fast-moving, ambiguous, and deadly chaos of combat. It is only slightly less so under the stressful conditions of providing humanitarian assistance. Military leaders are responsible for ensuring proper moral and ethical conduct of their Soldiers. They influence character development and foster correct actions through role-modeling, teaching, and coaching. Besides influencing moral behavior, the moral realm for military leaders includes maintaining popular support, cooperation among multinational partners, and Soldiers' loyalty.

1-55. The imperative to master these dimensions of the profession of arms is the basis of the physical, intellectual, and moral aspects of professional military education and leader development. Military leaders continuously cultivate expertise in their Service's capabilities. Through study and practice, they seek to better understand how to integrate that knowledge into joint operations. They strive to be expert practitioners of the art and science of warfare. Military professionals personally commit to a career-long process of learning, teaching, evaluating, and adapting. They are constantly mastering changing security environments, technologies, and military techniques.

THE ARMY IN THE PROFESSION OF ARMS

1-56. The Army profession is nested within the American profession of arms. The larger profession comprises the professions of the individual Services: the Army, Air Force, Navy, Marine Corps, and Coast Guard. The value of the Army's contribution depends on its ability to dominate its operational sphere—the conduct of prompt and sustained operations on land. The Army organizes its forces and educates and trains its leaders to apply landpower. Army leaders maintain and advance the body of knowledge that guides land operations. This specialized knowledge contributes to further developing a comprehensive knowledge of joint operations. The Army's culture expresses its traditions and history, norms of conduct, and guiding values and standards. These have evolved over two centuries of operations in peace and war, of shared hardships and triumphs.

TRADITIONS AND HISTORY

1-57. The Army's culture has its roots in its traditions and history. The Army cherishes its past and nourishes its institutional memory through ceremonies and traditions. Its organizations preserve their unit histories and display them in unit distinctive insignia ("crests"), patches, and mottos. Such traditions reinforce morale and the distinctiveness of the Army's contributions within the profession of arms. The Army's rich and honorable history of service to the Nation reminds Soldiers of who they are, the cause they serve, and their ties to those who have gone before them.

NORMS OF CONDUCT

1-58. The Army's culture promotes certain norms of conduct. For example, discipline is central to its professional identity. Soldiers, who manage violence under the stress and ambiguity of combat, require the highest level of individual and organizational discipline. Likewise, because Soldiers must face the violence of combat, they require the stiffening of discipline to help them do their duty. General George S. Patton Jr. summarized the need for discipline as follows:

> *Discipline is based on pride in the profession of arms, on meticulous attention to details, and on mutual respect and confidence. Discipline must be a habit so engrained that it is stronger than the excitement of battle or the fear of death.*

1-59. Army norms of conduct also demand adherence to the laws, treaties, and conventions governing the conduct of war to which the United States is a party. The law of war seeks both to legitimatize and limit the use of military force and prevent employing violence unnecessarily or inhumanely. For Soldiers, this is more than a legal rule; it is an American value. For Americans, each individual has worth. Each is a person endowed with unalienable rights.

GUIDING VALUES AND STANDARDS

1-60. The Army is a values-based organization. It upholds principles that are grounded in the Constitution and inspire guiding values and standards for its members. These principles are best expressed by the Army Values, Soldier's Creed, and Warrior Ethos. (See figure 1-1, page iv, and figure 1-2, page 16.) Derived from the obligations of the oaths of office, they express the professional competence required of Soldiers and affirm long-standing values within the Army's culture.

1-61. The Army Values are the basic building blocks of a Soldier's character. They help Soldiers judge what is right or wrong in any situation. The Army Values form the very identity of the Army, the solid rock on which everything else stands, especially in combat. They are the glue that binds together the members of a noble profession.

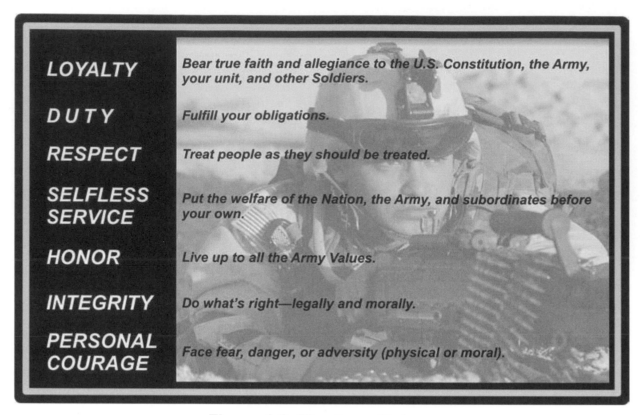

Figure 1-2. The Army Values

1-62. The Soldier's Creed captures the spirit of being a Soldier and the dedication Soldiers feel to something greater than themselves. It outlines the fundamental obligations of Soldiers to their fellow Soldiers, their unit, and the Army itself. In fact, the Soldier's Creed extends beyond service as a Soldier; it includes commitment to family and society. It begins with an affirmation of who Soldiers are and what they do:

> *I am an American Soldier. I am a Warrior and a member of a team.*
> *I serve the people of the United States and live the Army Values.*

Embedded in the Soldier's Creed is the Warrior Ethos—the very essence of what it means to be a Soldier:

- *I will always place the mission first.*
- *I will never accept defeat.*
- *I will never quit.*
- *I will never leave a fallen comrade.*

1-63. The Warrior Ethos describes the frame of mind of the professional Soldier. It proclaims the selfless commitment to the Nation, mission, unit, and fellow Soldiers that all Soldiers espouse. When internalized, it produces the will to win. The accompanying vignette portrays the actions of two Soldiers that epitomize the Warrior Ethos.

(U.S. Army photo)

(U.S. Army photo)

Master Sergeant Gary Gordon

Sergeant First Class Randall Shughart

Warrior Ethos—"I Will Never Leave a Fallen Comrade."

During a raid in Mogadishu in October 1993, Master Sergeant Gary Gordon and Sergeant First Class Randall Shughart, leader and member of a sniper team with Task Force Ranger in Somalia, were providing precision and suppressive fires from helicopters above two helicopter crash sites. Learning that no ground forces were available to rescue one of the downed aircrews and aware that a growing number of enemy were closing in on the site, Gordon and Shughart volunteered to be inserted to protect their critically wounded comrades. Their initial request was turned down because of the danger of the situation. They asked a second time; permission was denied. Only after their third request were they inserted.

Gordon and Shughart were inserted one hundred meters south of the downed chopper. Armed with only their personal weapons, the two non-commissioned officers fought their way to the downed fliers through intense small arms fire, a maze of shanties and shacks, and the enemy converging on the site. After Gordon and Shughart pulled the wounded from the wreckage, they established a perimeter, put themselves in the most dangerous position, and fought off a series of attacks. The two warriors continued to protect their comrades until they had depleted their ammunition and were themselves fatally wounded. Their actions saved the life of an Army pilot.

1-64. At its core, the Warrior Ethos is the refusal to accept failure and instead overcome all obstacles with honor. The Warrior Ethos moves Soldiers to fight through all conditions to victory, no matter how long it takes and how much effort is required. Army leaders develop and sustain it through discipline, realistic training, commitment to the Army Values, and pride in the Army's heritage.

1-65. The Army Values, Soldier's Creed, and Warrior Ethos are mutually dependent. A Soldier cannot follow one while ignoring the others. Together they guide the personal conduct of every Soldier. They place requirements on individual Soldiers beyond those necessary in civil professions. By taking an oath to defend the Constitution, Soldiers accept a set of responsibilities that other citizens do not. For example, Soldiers agree to limit their freedom to come and go in order to be available on short notice as readiness demands. Soldiers also subordinate certain freedoms of expression to the needs of security and disciplined organizations.

1-66. Soldiers show their commitment to the Army's guiding values and standards by willingly performing their duty at all times and subordinating their personal welfare to that of others without expecting reward or recognition. Conversely, the Army is committed to developing values-based leadership and seeing to the well-being of Soldiers and their families. Soldiers with patriotism, pride in their profession, commitment to the Army and its values, and belief in the essential purposes of the military provide the inner strength of cohesive units. They enable the Army to attain its service ideal. Developing these attributes is a major goal of Army leadership.

LEADERSHIP

> *The American soldier is a proud one and he demands professional competence in his leaders. In battle, he wants to know that the job is going to be done right, with no unnecessary casualties. The noncommissioned officer wearing the chevron is supposed to be the best soldier in the platoon and he is supposed to know how to perform all the duties expected of him. The American soldier expects his sergeant to be able to teach him how to do his job. And he expects even more from his officers.*
>
> General of the Army Omar N. Bradley

1-67. The Army defines *leadership* as influencing people—by providing purpose, direction, and motivation—while operating to accomplish the mission and improving the organization. The Army leadership framework comprises values, attributes, skills, and actions—summarized by the shorthand expression, *BE-KNOW-DO*.

1-68. Army leadership begins with character, the values and attributes that shape what the leader must *BE*. Army leaders must demonstrate exemplary conduct in their professional and personal lives. They adopt and internalize the Army Values and develop the requisite mental, physical, and emotional attributes of a warrior. Additionally, the ambiguous nature of the operational environment requires Army leaders to know themselves and deal with circumstances as they are, not as they want them to be.

1-69. Interpersonal, conceptual, technical, and tactical skills constitute what a leader must *KNOW*. Army leadership demands competence in a diverse range of human activities that expand in complexity in positions of greater responsibility. Army leaders maintain and advance the body of knowledge that guides land operations.

1-70. In the new security environment, cultural awareness has become one of the most important knowledge areas for Army leaders. Army leaders develop their knowledge of major world cultures and learn how those cultures affect military operations. The Army's rich mix of Soldiers' backgrounds and cultures is a natural enabler of cultural awareness. Effective Army leaders get to know their Soldiers; in doing so, they increase their awareness of different perspectives. This knowledge helps them become more self-aware and adaptive.

1-71. But character and knowledge—while absolutely necessary—are not enough. Leadership demands action—the self-discipline to *DO* what feels or is known to be right. Army leaders must act in both immediate conditions, which may be complex and dangerous, and over the long term, where the effects of decisions may not be readily apparent. Army leaders exercise influencing actions to motivate and mentor subordinates. They execute operating actions to conduct operations. And they perform improving actions to continually develop and increase the proficiency of their units, their Soldiers, and themselves. Leadership is a lifelong learning process for Army leaders, but action is its essence.

1-72. Today's security environment demands more from Army leaders than ever before. Army leaders must not only be able to lead Soldiers but also influence other people. They must be able to work with members of other Services and governmental agencies. They must win the willing cooperation of multinational partners, both military and civilian. But ultimately, the Army demands self-aware and adaptive leaders who can compel enemies to surrender in war and master the circumstances facing them in peace. Victory and success depend on the effectiveness of these leaders' organizations. Developing effective organizations requires hard, realistic, and relevant training.

TRAINING

1-73. Army forces train every day. After the War of 1812, Secretary of War John C. Calhoun articulated the sole purpose of a peacetime army—to prepare for war. But in today's security environment, the Nation is engaged in a protracted war—the War on Terrorism. The Army no longer considers itself a peacetime army preparing for war. Today peace is the exception. Deployments, including combat operations, are normal. To prepare Soldiers and units to operate in this new strategic context, the Army is training them for ongoing operations and preparing for other possible contingencies simultaneously.

1-74. The threats facing the Nation require the Army to provide a continuous supply of relevant and ready landpower to combatant commanders and civil authorities. To accomplish this, the Army follows a structured progression of unit readiness known as the operational readiness cycle. It consists of three phases: reset/train, ready, and available. The operational readiness cycle begins with a redeployed unit and produces combat ready, available forces. These forces are trained, equipped, resourced, and ready for deployment to fulfill the combatant commanders' operational requirements when needed.

1-75. The Army trains to meet the gravest military threat to the Nation's security—fighting a peer or near-peer competitor—because this capability is fundamental to strategic deterrence. But gone are the days when the Army could focus training only on major combat operations. Today the Army must train Soldiers and units to fight insurgents and other irregular threats while executing multiple operations worldwide. The complexities of the strategic environment demand a balanced training focus. Leaders and units must be prepared to expect the unexpected. Organizations must be adaptable and flexible. Both leaders and organizations must be able to accomplish missions throughout the range of military operations and at locations distributed throughout the operational area. Focusing training on capabilities at one end of the range of military operations and neglecting those on the opposite end is unacceptable. It would create an asymmetry for adversaries to exploit. Training that produces balanced capabilities is essential to remaining relevant and ready. Units and leaders must be prepared to operate under any conditions and in any environment.

1-76. Increasingly, Army forces have little time to train before deploying. To increase readiness for no-notice expeditionary operations, the Army is modifying its training model to coincide with the new operational readiness cycle. The Army is moving from an "alert-train-deploy" training model to a "train-alert-deploy-employ" model. Furthermore, the Army has modified training and education to provide key skills and knowledge Soldiers require. Lessons learned from recent operations are quickly incorporated into systems and training scenarios at home stations, mobilization stations, and combat training centers. Training conditions on ranges and other facilities reflect the current security environment. Language, cultural awareness, and regional expertise education and training are included.

1-77. Army training includes a system of techniques and standards that allow Soldiers and units to determine, acquire, and practice necessary skills. This allows them to maintain a high level of warfighting readiness. Candid after action reviews and repeated application of skills under changing conditions reinforce training and readiness standards. The Army is also applying significant resources to ensure training enhances Soldier and unit effectiveness. It is incorporating operational lessons learned into all its systems and training scenarios at mobilization stations and combat training centers. Additionally, it is assigning veterans with current operational experience to key joint positions and as instructors and doctrine developers. These practices and the Army's training system helps Army leaders develop quality Soldiers and lethal units with relevant skills, ready for conditions in today's operational environment.

DOCTRINE

1-78. Doctrine is the concise expression of how Army forces contribute to campaigns, major operations, battles, and engagements. It is a guide to action, not hard and fast rules. Doctrine provides a common frame of reference across the Army. It helps standardize operations, facilitating readiness by establishing common ways of accomplishing military tasks. Standardization means that Soldiers transferring between units do not need to learn new ways to perform familiar tasks.

1-79. Doctrine facilitates communication among Soldiers, contributes to a shared professional culture, and serves as the basis for curricula in the Army education system. The Army is a learning organization. It has evolved with the Nation through societal changes, technological advancements, and ever changing international circumstances. It continually revises its doctrine to account for changes, incorporating new technologies and lessons from operations. It improves education and training processes to provide Soldiers with the most challenging and realistic experience possible. It aims to impart to Soldiers and units the individual and collective skills, knowledge, and attributes required to accomplish their missions.

1-80. Doctrine links theory, history, experimentation, and practice. Its objective is to foster initiative and creative thinking. Doctrine encapsulates a larger body of knowledge and experience. It provides an authoritative statement about how military forces conduct operations and a common lexicon with which to describe them. Doctrine furnishes the intellectual tools with which to diagnose unexpected requirements. It also provides a menu of practical options based on experience from which self-aware and adaptive Army leaders can create their own solutions quickly and effectively.

SUMMARY

> *...[Y]ours is the profession of arms—the will to win, the sure knowledge that in war there is no substitute for victory; that if you lose, the nation will be destroyed; that the very obsession of your public service must be Duty—Honor—Country.*
>
> General of the Army Douglas MacArthur

1-81. The profession of arms involves the disciplined use of legally sanctioned force to defend the security of the Nation, its ideals, and its way of life. Nested in the profession of arms and providing the Nation's major source of landpower is the Army, whose members are educated, trained, and organized to win. The Army's culture encompasses the traditions, norms of conduct, and ideals that have evolved since its inception in 1775.

1-82. The Army's most important guiding values and standards are written in the Army Values, Soldier's Creed, and Warrior Ethos. These instill in every Soldier the will to win and make great personal sacrifices—sometimes the ultimate sacrifice—in selfless service to the Nation. In answering the call to duty, Soldiers voluntarily limit certain rights to become disciplined, competent practitioners of the art and science of war. In so doing, they guarantee the Nation's security.

1-83. For over two centuries, the Army has served the Nation in peace and war. It has adapted repeatedly and successfully to changing conditions and situations. As technologies and conditions change, the Army will continue to develop leaders and train Soldiers to contribute landpower to joint operations. Above all, however, the Army will continue to provide versatile land forces ready to fight and win the Nation's wars. These forces—both the Regular Army and the Reserve Components—will remain relevant and ready to defend America's Constitution against all enemies, foreign and domestic.

Chapter 2

The Strategic Environment and Army Organization

Our Nation's cause has always been larger than our Nation's defense. We fight, as we always fight, for a just peace, a peace that favors human liberty. We will defend the peace against threats from terrorists and tyrants. We will preserve the peace by building good relations among the great powers. And we will extend the peace by encouraging free and open societies on every continent.

President George W. Bush

2-1.   The United States possesses unprecedented and unequaled strength and influence in the world. Sustained by faith in the principles of liberty and the value of a free society, this position comes with unparalleled responsibilities, obligations, and opportunities. The Nation's leaders have decided to use this strength to promote a balance of power that favors freedom both at home and abroad.

2-2.   This is a time of opportunity and challenge for America. The Nation will work, both at home and internationally, to translate this moment of influence into decades of peace, prosperity, and liberty. The National Security Strategy is based on a distinctly American internationalism that reflects the union of the Nation's values and interests. Its aim is to help make the world not just safer but better.

2-3.   To shape the international environment, the United States wields strength and influence through the instruments of national power—diplomatic, informational, military, and economic. The National Security Strategy articulates how the President intends to use these instruments to accomplish three goals in pursuit of making the world safer and better:

- Political and economic freedom.
- Peaceful relations with other states.
- Respect for human dignity.

Together these national security goals provide the foundation of U.S. national security policies.

THE NATIONAL SECURITY ENVIRONMENT

2-4.   Globalization and the information revolution continue to change the way the Nation engages the international environment. Combined with the compression of time and distance, these phenomena affect all instruments of national power. The world's open economic system of interdependent global markets, global communications systems, and ubiquitous media presence have broadened security responsibilities beyond military concerns. Both national and international security require integrating many nonmilitary disciplines, including such areas as economic and political health. To a greater degree than ever, diplomatic, informational, and economic factors affect national security. At the strategic level, an adversary's power is no longer reckoned only in terms of its military capabilities. It is now assessed more comprehensively, in terms of its interconnected political, military, economic, social, informational, and infrastructure systems.

2-5.   The end of the Cold War did not make the world more stable. Instead, it exposed points of stress worldwide where American interests might be threatened. Threats to American security and interests have become more varied. They are harder to anticipate and more difficult to combat than ever before. A growing number of borderless threats complicate the strategic environment, making its challenges less predictable. Some of these threats are sponsored or given passive support by states. They include extremist movements, narcotics trafficking, and organized crime. Typically, they are long-term, continuous threats that cannot be eliminated in short, limited actions. Instead, they require continuous engagement and the extended application of all instruments of national power.

2-6.   Today the Nation is fighting the War on Terrorism. In this war, adversaries are not only foreign states but also extremists employing irregular means. These adversaries seek to erode American power, influence, and resolve. They threaten the security of American society, endangering its freedoms and way of life. This war is fueled by an ideology that promotes intractable hatred of the democratic ideal, especially in its Western manifestations. It is likely to endure in some form for the foreseeable future.

2-7.   The Army is at war in this uncertain, unpredictable environment. It is prepared to conduct sustained operations throughout a period of protracted conflict in which the familiar distinction between war and peace does not exist. More notably, this war is the first severe, long-term test of the all-volunteer Army. The need to conduct sustained operations over a number of years may be the most significant aspect of the early twenty-first century security environment.

2-8.   In the aftermath of 11 September 2001, it is inadequate to focus defenses only on threats by other states and known enemies. The strategic environment requires the Army to respond to unconventional and asymmetric threats too. The most prominent are followers of extremist ideologies. The protection afforded by geographic distance has decreased, while the potential for attacks on civilian, military, and economic targets has increased. The threat of an attack with weapons of mass destruction or other means of causing catastrophic effects adds urgency to operations against these enemies. The current trend toward regional and global integration may render interstate war less likely. However, the stability and legitimacy of the conventional political order in regions vital to the United States are increasingly under pressure.

2-9. New adversaries, methods, and capabilities now challenge the United States, its interests, and its partners and friends in strategically significant ways. Persistent and emerging challenges to the United States include the following:

- *Traditional challenges* through established and well-known forms of military competition and conflict.
- *Irregular challenges* by state and nonstate sources using unconventional methods.
- *Catastrophic challenges* from terrorists and rogue states threatening the use of weapons of mass destruction or other means of causing catastrophic effects.
- *Disruptive challenges* from competitors developing, possessing, and employing breakthrough technologies to gain an advantage in a particular operational domain.

In many operations, these challenges may overlap, occur simultaneously, or offer no easily discernible transition from one to another.

2-10. The National Security, National Defense, and National Military Strategies recognize traditional threats from other states and known adversaries. However, old security and deterrence concepts based on advanced warnings developed through traditional intelligence approaches do not fit the new strategic environment. In today's security environment, the Nation's overwhelming conventional and nuclear military superiority does not deter many emerging threats, especially followers of extremist ideologies who are willing to destroy themselves to achieve their aims.

2-11. Certain threats are nonstate entities, loosely organized networks of independent cells bound by beliefs or criminal activity rather than a hierarchical structure. They have a minimal physical presence, are difficult to target, and feel no moral obligation to limit collateral damage. These enemies often employ irregular methods—such as, terrorism, insurgency, and civil war—to erode U.S. power. Some seek to acquire weapons of mass destruction or other means of causing catastrophic effects. Because the United States can dominate conventional combat, some adversary states have allied themselves with terrorist and criminal groups that use more elusive, asymmetric methods. These include using unconventional means of coercion against friendly civilians and multinational partners rather than attempting traditional challenges against U.S. forces.

2-12. Nonstate threats are elusive. They may seek to undermine the American technological advantages by concealing themselves in complex environments. Multidimensional geography (natural, man-made, or subterraneous) and a society (with its associated social and political domains) can provide a convenient operational base and safe haven for adversaries. Complex environments degrade the conventional military advantages of speed and knowledge. They hinder development of an accurate, comprehensive intelligence picture and may preclude standoff precision strikes. They may limit Army commanders' ability to freely determine the time and place for engaging adversaries. Successful operations in such environments require integration and simultaneous application of multiple governmental and nongovernmental capabilities.

2-13. Traditional strategic threats (those possessing nuclear weapons or pursuing breakthrough technological capabilities) have not disappeared. Threats from nuclear armed states and states with large, modernizing conventional forces remain. Some of these are in Asia, where they can threaten neighbors and supply others with nuclear weapons. Breakthrough technologies include such advanced capabilities as cybernetic warfare, directed-energy weapons, and genetically engineered pathogens and toxins. These weapons are asymmetric in that they are difficult to engage militarily and can produce major disruptive and catastrophic effects. To preempt such challenges, the Army is developing and maintaining favorable relationships with armies of regional powers. Such relationships facilitate mutual understanding of issues and values. While they do not preclude misunderstandings, such relationships provide a basis for resolving differences. They reduce the likelihood of competitors becoming adversaries.

2-14. These diverse threats require combatant commanders to shape the security environment to a greater extent than ever. The Army's ability to conduct stability and reconstruction operations provides an important tool for doing this. The Army plays a vital role in terms of security cooperation and engagement. These operations are both military and humanitarian in nature. Around the world, Army forces are cooperating with the armies of established and emerging democracies to create a better and more secure future. Simultaneously, they are meeting current threats and preparing for future challenges.

2-15. In order to counter these challenges, the Army is increasing its versatility and flexibility, pursuing iterative solutions, and developing a sophisticated understanding of the new environment and its implications. Army forces are committed to global requirements beyond those associated with the War on Terrorism. They are operating to counter challenges ranging from the traditional to potentially catastrophic. Army forces provide the bulk of the landpower component of the military instrument of national power. They deter potential adversaries, reassure allies and friends, and assist when disaster strikes. The versatility of Army forces and their readiness to deploy on short notice make them relevant throughout the range of military operations.

NATIONAL MILITARY STRATEGY FORMULATION

*This nation can afford to be strong—it cannot afford to be weak. We
shall do what is needed to make and to keep us strong.*

President John F. Kennedy

2-16. The President is responsible for national security. The National Security Council helps the President determine how best to employ the instruments of national power to achieve national goals. The National Security Council coordinates the efforts of all governmental agencies to execute a synchronized strategy that most effectively uses all the instruments. The Department of Defense—under the leadership of the Secretary of Defense—prepares the National Defense Strategy. It synchronizes Defense Department support of the National Security Strategy.

2-17. The Chairman of the Joint Chiefs of Staff is the principal military advisor to the President, National Security Council, and Secretary of Defense. The chairman prepares the National Military Strategy in consultation with the Secretary of Defense, Joint Chiefs of Staff, and combatant commanders. The National Military Strategy contains the advice of the chairman and the Joint Chiefs of Staff on the role of the Armed Forces in implementing the National Security and National Defense Strategies. The chairman, on behalf of the Secretary of Defense, directs combatant commanders to develop theater security cooperation plans as well as war and contingency plans.

NATIONAL MILITARY OBJECTIVES

2-18. The Armed Forces of the United States execute the National Military Strategy within the context of the National Security and National Defense Strategies. The National Military Strategy establishes the following interrelated military objectives:

- Protect the United States against external attacks and aggression.
- Prevent conflict and surprise attack.
- Prevail against adversaries.

These objectives guide military contributions to national defense and ultimately to the accomplishment of the national security goals.

2-19. Executing the National Military Strategy requires military forces with an expeditionary capability. It stresses fast, flexible power projection to eliminate threats before they reach the United States. It relies on versatile military forces able to deal with the breadth and scope of the security environment's challenges. The National Military Strategy also requires significant actions to shape the security environment to support achieving the national security goals. These actions include engagement, deterrence, and security cooperation operations. Ultimately, however, achieving the national security goals requires the Armed Forces to deter—and, if necessary, defeat—adversaries on land, in space, in the air, and at sea. Success in these endeavors requires landpower.

THE ARMY'S STATUTORY OBLIGATIONS

The Congress shall have Power To lay and collect Taxes, Duties, Imposts and Excises, to pay the Debts and provide for the common Defence and general Welfare of the United States; ...

To raise and support Armies, but no Appropriation of Money to that Use shall be for a longer Term than two Years;

To provide and maintain a Navy;

To make Rules for the Government and Regulation of the land and naval Forces;

To provide for calling forth the Militia to execute the Laws of the Union, suppress Insurrections and repel Invasions;

To provide for organizing, arming, and disciplining, the Militia, and for governing such Part of them as may be employed in the Service of the United States, ...

Constitution of the United States, article 1, section 8

2-20. Under its Constitutional responsibility to raise and support armies, Congress establishes statutory obligations governing the roles and responsibilities of the Department of the Army. These are contained in Title 10 of the United States Code. (See figure 2-1.)

Subject to the authority, direction, and control of the Secretary of Defense...the Secretary of the Army is responsible for...the Department of the Army, including the following functions:

- Recruiting.
- Organizing.
- Supplying.
- Equipping (including research and development).
- Training.
- Servicing.
- Mobilizing.
- Demobilizing.

- Administering (including the morale and welfare of personnel).
- Maintaining.
- The construction, outfitting, and repair of military equipment.
- The construction, maintenance, and repair of buildings, structures, and utilities, and the acquisition of real property....

Title 10, U.S. Code, Section 3013 (b)

Figure 2-1. Title 10 functions

2-21. More specifically, Department of Defense Directive 5100.1 lists the primary statutory functions of the Army: organize, equip, and train forces for the conduct of prompt and sustained combat operations on land. Additionally, it requires Army forces to be capable of conducting air and missile defense, space and space-control operations, and joint amphibious and airborne operations. Army forces are also required to support special operations forces, operate land lines of communication, and conduct other civil programs prescribed by law.

2-22. Title 10 charges the Army with administrative control (ADCON) of Army forces assigned to combatant commands. ADCON entails providing administrative (legal, personnel, and finance) and logistic support to these forces. When designated an executive agent, the Army also enters into inter-Service, interagency, and intergovernmental agreements for certain responsibilities. These may include—

- Civil engineering support.
- Common-user land transportation.
- Disaster assistance.
- Force protection.
- Mortuary services.
- Detainee operations.
- Bulk petroleum management.

Title 10 also includes combatant commanders' responsibilities and authorities. Two of these overlap the military departments' Title 10 functions: joint training and directive authority for logistics. Title 10 functions and the diverse set of missions assigned by the President and combatant commanders link the Army's enduring roles to its vision and mission.

THE ARMY VISION

2-23. The Army vision expresses how the Army intends to meet the challenges of the security environment. (See figure 2-2.)

Relevant and Ready Landpower in Service to the Nation

*The **Nation** has **entrusted** the Army with preserving its **peace** and **freedom**, defending its **democracy,** and providing **opportunities** for its Soldiers to **serve** the country and personally develop their skills and citizenship. Consequently, we are and will continuously strive to remain among the most respected institutions in the United States. To fulfill our solemn obligation to the Nation, we must remain the preeminent land power on earth—**the ultimate instrument of national resolve**; strategically dominant on the ground where **our Solders' engagements are decisive**.*

Dr. Francis J. Harvey
Secretary of the Army
April 2005

Figure 2-2. The Army vision

2-24. The organization and training of its forces, innovation and adaptability of its leaders, and design and practices of its institutional support structures will keep the Army relevant to the challenges posed by the complex global security environment. The Army will be ready to promptly provide combatant commanders with the capabilities—principally well-led, well-trained, and well-equipped forces—required to achieve all operational objectives. To realize this vision, the Army is positioning itself for the security environment in which it will operate for the foreseeable future. It is transforming its mindset, capabilities, effectiveness, efficiency, training, education, leadership, and culture. Throughout this transformation, the American Soldier will remain the Army's primary focus—the centerpiece of Army organizations. Chapter 4 describes how the Army will achieve its vision.

THE ARMY MISSION

It is the intent of Congress to provide an Army that is capable, in conjunction with the other armed forces, of—

(1) preserving the peace and security, and providing for the defense, of the United States, the Territories, Commonwealths, and possessions, and any areas occupied by the United States;

(2) supporting the national policies;
(3) implementing the national objectives; and
(4) overcoming any nations responsible for aggressive acts that imperil the peace and security of the United States.

Title 10, U.S. Code, Section 3062 (a)

2-25. Title 10 of the United States Code states the purpose of Congress in establishing the Army and its guidance on how the Army is to be organized, trained, and equipped. Title 10 states that the Army includes land combat and service forces, and organic aviation and water transport. Army forces are to be organized, trained, and equipped primarily for prompt and sustained combat incident to operations on land. The Army is responsible for preparing the land forces necessary to effectively prosecute war except as otherwise assigned. It is also responsible, in accordance with integrated joint mobilization plans, for its expansion to meet the needs of war.

2-26. The Army exists to serve the American people, protect enduring national interests, and fulfill the Nation's military responsibilities. Specifically, the Army mission is to provide to combatant commanders the forces and capabilities necessary to execute the National Security, National Defense, and National Military Strategies. Army forces provide the capability—by threat, force, or occupation—to promptly gain, sustain, and exploit comprehensive control over land, resources, and people. This landpower capability compliments the other Services' capabilities. Furthermore, the Army is charged to provide logistic and other executive agent functions to enable the other Services to accomplish their missions. The Army is organized to accomplish this mission.

THE ORGANIZATION OF THE ARMY

Battles are won by the infantry, the armor, the artillery, and air teams, by soldiers living in the rains and huddling in the snow. But wars are won by the great strength of a nation—the soldier and the civilian working together.

General of the Army Omar N. Bradley

2-27. Soldiers are the centerpiece of Army organizations. Professional Soldiers— warriors well trained, well equipped, and well led—serve as the ultimate expression of what the Army provides to the Nation and the joint force. They are the engine behind Army capabilities. However, the Army is more than a collection of individuals. It is a complex institution comprising many diverse types of organizations. Its Soldiers are both "full-time" Regulars and Reserve Component citizen-Soldiers. Army civilians are members of the force as well, serving in leadership and support functions at all levels. The Army is all these people and organizations, united by a common purpose in service to the Nation. In addition, civilian contractors augment Army organizations, providing specialized support that sustains readiness and operations.

2-28. Army forces are engaged in the Nation's numerous global commitments of today and preparing for the uncertainties of tomorrow. Nearly half the Soldiers on active duty are deployed or forward-stationed in more than 120 countries. They are accompanied by Army civilians and contractors. In addition to conducting combat operations, these Soldiers secure the homeland by deterring aggression and supporting friends and allies. The Army's organization supports mobilizing, training, deploying, and sustaining Soldiers at home and abroad.

FUNCTIONAL ORGANIZATION

2-29. Soldiers and Army civilians serve in two functionally discrete entities known as the institutional Army and the operational Army.

Institutional Army

2-30. The institutional Army exists to support accomplishing the Army's Title 10 functions. Institutional organizations provide the foundation necessary to design, raise, train, equip, deploy, sustain, and ensure the readiness of all Army forces. (See figure 2-3.) For example, institutional organizations include the training base that provides military skill development and professional education to Soldiers, members of the other Services, and multinational students. The institutional Army includes the schools, Soldier training centers, and combat training centers that develop and maintain individual and collective skills. These centers and schools also preserve the doctrine, research, and learning activities of the Army's professional knowledge base.

- Accessions.
- Training.
- Doctrine development.
- Human resource management.
- Medical support and health sustainment.
- Civil engineer and infrastructure support.

- Acquisition and procurement activities.
- Organic industrial facilities.
- Laboratories and research centers.
- Hospitals and clinics.
- Corps of Engineers districts.

Figure 2-3. Sample institutional Army functions and facilities

2-31. The institutional Army provides the infrastructure and capabilities needed to rapidly expand the Army and deploy its forces. It synchronizes Army acquisition and force development efforts with the national industrial capabilities and resources needed to provide equipment, logistics, and services. It also manages reach-back resources, capabilities at home station that deployed units access to support their operations. These include everything from databases and staff support to contracted services. Reach-back capabilities reduce strategic lift requirements and the size of in-theater logistic operations (the "footprint"). The institutional Army provides vital support to joint campaigns and Army operations.

Operational Army

2-32. The operational Army provides essential landpower capabilities to combatant commanders. For most of the twentieth century, the operational Army was organized around the division. Field armies and corps were groups of divisions and supporting organizations. Brigades, regiments, and battalions were divisional components. This structure served the Army and the Nation well. However, to remain relevant and ready, the operational Army is transforming from a division-based to a brigade-based force. This more agile "modular force" is organized and trained to fight as part of the joint force. Modular organizations can be quickly assembled into strategically responsive force packages able to rapidly move wherever needed. They can quickly and seamlessly transition among types of operations better than could their predecessors. Modular organizations provide the bulk of forces needed for sustained land operations in the twenty-first century. In addition to conventional modular forces, the Army will continue to provide the major special operations force capabilities (both land and air) in support of the U.S. Special Operations Command's global mission.

COMPONENTS

2-33. In addition to functional distinctions, the Army is described in terms of components. Each component is characterized by the source and role of its units and people. There are three components: the Regular Army and two Reserve Components, the Army National Guard and Army Reserve. All components include Army civilians as well as officers, noncommissioned officers, and enlisted Soldiers.

Regular Army

2-34. The Regular Army is a federal force consisting of full-time Soldiers and Army civilians. Both are assigned to the operational and institutional organizations engaged in the day-to-day Army missions. Congress annually determines the number of Soldiers the Army can maintain in the Regular Army.

Army National Guard

2-35. The Army National Guard has a dual mission that includes federal and state roles. In its federal role, the National Guard provides trained units able to mobilize quickly for war, national emergencies, and other missions. In its state role, it prepares for domestic emergencies and other missions as required by state law. National Guard Soldiers serve as the first military responders within states during emergencies. National Guard units are commanded by their state executive (usually the governor) unless they are mobilized for a federal mission. Members of the National Guard exemplify the state militia traditions of citizens answering the call to duty. Their selfless service, like that of Sergeant Christian P. Engeldrum described in the following vignette, reflects America's values and inspires others to the noble calling that serves freedom.

Citizen Soldier—Selfless Service

In 2004, Sergeant Christian P. Engeldrum deployed to Iraq with B Company, 1st Battalion, 69th Infantry, New York Army National Guard. This was not the first time Engeldrum had fought in Iraq; he had served there with the 82d Airborne Division during Operation Desert Storm. After leaving the Regular Army, Engeldrum became a New York City police officer and later a firefighter.

Engeldrum experienced 11 September 2001 first hand. As a member of the New York City Fire Department, he was a first responder to the attack on the World Trade Center. His organization, Ladder Company 61, arrived as the first tower collapsed. Later, he helped raise the first flag at Ground Zero on a lamp post. Engeldrum had completed his military service obligation but was outraged by the attacks of 11 September and joined the Army National Guard.

On 29 November 2004, B Company was attacked while engaged in a convoy in the northwest part of Baghdad. Engeldrum's vehicle detonated an improvised explosive device, which destroyed the vehicle and killed Engeldrum and two other Soldiers. This citizen-Soldier, four times the volunteer, had given his life for his country. By his example of selfless service, Sergeant Christian Engeldrum demonstrated what it means to answer the call to duty.

Army Reserve

2-36. The Army Reserve is the Army's primary federal reserve force. It is a complementary force consisting of highly trained Soldiers and units able to perform a vast range of missions worldwide. Their primary role is to provide the specialized units, capabilities, and resources needed to deploy and sustain Army forces at home and overseas. The Army Reserve is also the Army's major source of trained individual Soldiers for augmenting headquarters staffs and filling vacancies in Regular Army units. The Army Reserve provides a wide range of specialized skills required for consequence management, foreign army training, and stability and reconstruction operations. Many of its Soldiers are civilian professionals.

ARMY CIVILIANS AND CONTRACTORS

2-37. Army civilians and contractors support the Army's ability to mobilize, deploy, employ, and sustain Army forces at home and abroad. In recent years, an increasing number of Army civilians and contractors have been supporting Soldiers on the battlefield, employing their technical expertise under hazardous conditions. They provide critical capabilities that supplement Soldier skills.

Army Civilians

2-38. Army civilians are full-time federal employees with skills and competencies that encompass many functional areas and occupational series. Army civilians perform technical and administrative tasks that free Soldiers for training and for operational and institutional missions. Army civilians are integral, vital team members of all three components.

Contractors

2-39. Civilian contractors work to support Army forces in garrison locations and on the battlefield. Unlike Army civilians, contractors are hired for specific tasks and for a specific duration. They provide professional skills and perform technical and administrative tasks that allow Soldiers to focus on their primary missions. They are an important part of the Army team.

WELFARE AND READINESS

2-40. The challenge of serving a Nation at war highlights the importance of providing for the physical, material, mental, and spiritual well-being of Soldiers, Army civilians, and their family members. Their welfare is linked to readiness and the Army's sustained viability as an all-volunteer force. Army leaders will never take for granted the personal sacrifices made by Soldiers and their families. These include facing the hardships of war and extended periods of separation. In the case of Reserve Component Soldiers, they include concerns over continued employment and advancement in their civilian jobs as well. Additionally, the Army recognizes the importance of civilian employer support of Reserve Component Soldiers. Employers make sacrifices to support mobilized citizen-Soldiers. Their continued support is essential to the immediate and long-term readiness required to win the War on Terrorism.

2-41. Ultimately, the Army is a team comprising many people: Soldiers and Army civilians, regular and reserve; the citizens who support them; retirees, veterans, and family members. All are vital to the Army's success. These team members are drawn together by shared values and experiences, sacrifice, and selfless service to the Nation. All subordinate their own welfare to a higher calling. Dedicated, well-prepared people—Soldiers and those who support them—provide the leadership and skills necessary to ensure success in any complex military operation. It is they who translate the Army vision into decisive capabilities.

SUMMARY

2-42. Today the Nation is at war, facing enemies that endanger its freedoms and way of life. At the same time, the Army is also undergoing its most profound transformation since World War II. The War on Terrorism will likely continue in some form for the foreseeable future. This protracted conflict against implacable enemies is occurring in a security environment that is dangerous, volatile, uncertain, complex, and ambiguous. To meet today's challenges, the Army is engaged in a continuous, adaptive cycle of innovation and experimentation informed by experience. This effort is improving the forces and capabilities the Army is providing today and ensuring that it is well postured for tomorrow.

2-43. America is strong and a bastion of freedom. Its citizens are a free people and, to a great extent, its strength flows from that freedom. America has abundant resources and a dynamic and productive population. It wields enormous political power and has the world's largest economy. But without a strong military to protect its enduring interests, America's freedom would be at risk. National power remains relative and dynamic. Because of this, the military provides the President with flexible forces that can operate across the range of military operations.

2-44. The Army's commitment to the Nation is certain and unwavering. All members of the Army—the Soldiers and Army civilians of all components—serve to accomplish the Army mission and meet its vision. They are guided by the compelling requirement to defend America's Constitution and way of life. The Army has defended the Nation and served the cause of freedom against all enemies and various forms of extremism for well over two centuries. It will continue to remain vigilant in these fundamental tasks.

This page intentionally left blank.

Chapter 3

Army Forces in Unified Action

3-1. Over the last century, warfare became increasingly complex. Army organizations changed from the large, predominantly infantry divisions of World War I to today's brigade-based combined arms teams. The way the Army fights evolved from a single-Service to a joint focus. As technology increased weapons ranges and enabled the application of airpower and sea power to land operations, the context for Army operations evolved from Service independence through joint interoperability to joint interdependence. *Joint interdependence* is the purposeful combination of Service capabilities to maximize their total complementary and reinforcing effects while minimizing their relative vulnerabilities. Army forces exploit joint interdependence to dominate land combat. Today's Army forces routinely participate in unified action, integrating their operations with those of joint, interagency, and multinational partners.

UNIFIED ACTION

3-2. Joint doctrine defines *unified action* as a broad generic term that describes the wide scope of actions (including the synchronization of activities with governmental and nongovernmental agencies) taking place within combatant commands, subordinate unified commands, or joint task forces under the overall direction of the commanders of those commands. Army forces provide the bulk of landpower resources for unified action. Combatant commanders and subordinate joint force commanders integrate joint force operations with interagency activities.

3-3. Regardless of the task or nature of the threat, combatant commanders use land, air, sea, space, and special operations forces to achieve strategic and operational objectives. They synchronize their efforts with those of interagency and multinational partners when possible. They establish theater strategies and provide strategic guidance and operational focus to subordinates. They organize joint forces, designate operational areas, and direct campaigns. Their aim is to achieve unity of effort among many diverse agencies in today's complex operational environment.

JOINT OPERATIONS

3-4. The Armed Forces (Army, Marine Corps, Navy, Air Force, and Coast Guard, and their associated special operations forces) provide globally responsive assets for joint operations to support combatant commanders' theater strategies. These theater strategies support the National Security, National Defense, and National Military Strategies.

3-5. The President exercises authority and control over the Army through a single chain of command with two distinct branches. The first branch runs from the President through the Secretary of Defense to the combatant commanders. It controls the operational Army, the fighting force, for missions assigned to combatant commands. The second branch is used for purposes other than operational direction of forces. It principally controls the institutional Army, whose organizations raise, train, and equip Army forces. It runs from the President through the Secretary of Defense to the Secretary of the Army. The Chairman of the Joint Chiefs of Staff directs the Joint Staff for the Secretary of Defense. The chairman is not in a chain of command but may be in the channel of communications between the Secretary of Defense and combatant commanders. The chairman normally conveys orders issued by the President by authority and direction of the Secretary of Defense.

3-6. Each Service retains responsibility for administration and logistic support (called administrative control—ADCON) of forces it allocates to a joint force. The Secretary of the Army exercises this responsibility through the Army Chief of Staff and the Army service component commander assigned to each combatant command. The Army service component commander is responsible for the preparation and administrative support of Army forces assigned or attached to the combatant command.

3-7. A formal chain of command exists within each combatant command. Combatant commanders establish their chains of command according to their preferences and the needs of the command. The Secretary of Defense specifies the degree of control that combatant commanders exercise over their forces. When necessary to execute a mission, combatant commanders can establish a command structure using any of the following options: a subordinate unified command, joint task force, functional component command, Service component command, or single-Service force. Some Army headquarters may provide the nucleus for the establishment of either joint task forces or functional component commands.

3-8. Army forces do not fight alone; they fight as part of a joint team. *Joint operations* involve forces of two or more Services under a single joint force commander. Effective joint integration does not demand joint commands at all echelons but does require an understanding of joint interdependence at all echelons. Joint interdependence combines Army forces' strengths with those of other Service forces. The combination of multiple and diverse joint force capabilities creates military effects more potent than the effects produced by any Service alone.

INTERAGENCY ACTIVITIES

3-9. The instruments of national power—diplomatic, informational, military, and economic—complement and reinforce each other. Army forces enhance their effectiveness through close coordination with interagency partners. By understanding the capabilities of other agencies, senior- and midlevel commanders can add diplomatic, informational, and economic depth to their military efforts. Conversely, U.S. military capabilities allow other agencies to interact with foreign powers from a position of strength and security. Synchronizing military power with other instruments of national power substantially improves the joint force's strategic capabilities.

3-10. The links among the instruments of national power require Army commanders to consider how all capabilities and agencies can contribute to accomplishing the mission. Interagency coordination forges a vital link between military operations and nonmilitary organization activities. These may include governmental agencies of the United States, host nations, and partner nations. It may also include regional and international nongovernmental organizations. Theater strategies routinely incorporate the capabilities of the entire U.S. interagency network.

MULTINATIONAL OPERATIONS

3-11. Although the United States acts unilaterally when necessary, it normally pursues its national interests through multinational operations—those conducted by alliances and coalitions. An *alliance* is the result of formal agreements (treaties) between two or more nations for broad, long-term objectives that further the common interests of the members. Alliance members strive to field compatible military systems and establish common procedures. They develop contingency plans to integrate their responses to potential threats. A *coalition* is an ad hoc arrangement between two or more nations for common action. A coalition is normally formed for a focused, limited-scope purpose. Alliances and coalitions increase the quantity and skills of available forces and allow the participants to share the cost of operations. They may enhance the perceived legitimacy of U.S. strategic aims. In some cases, the military forces of other nations contribute vital capabilities to the multinational force. For example, the infantry strength of the Army of the Republic of Korea is indispensable to the Combined Forces Command, which defends the Korean peninsula.

HOW ARMY FORCES FIGHT

3-12. The Army's operational concept is the core statement of its doctrine. It drives the way the Army fights its engagements, battles, and major operations. The operational concept shapes Army tactics, techniques, procedures, organizations, support, equipment, and training. From its operational concept, the Army develops its operational doctrine, contained in FM 3-0, *Operations*. The Army's operational concept is not static. It evolves, shaped by the Nation's requirements for landpower, the operational environment, and emerging capabilities.

3-13. Today's operational concept is distinct from future concepts. The Army Training and Doctrine Command develops future concepts and publishes them in its 525-series publications. These documents forecast landpower requirements anticipated between ten and twenty years in the future. Once validated, they provide the basis for developing doctrine, organizations, and systems. In contrast, the operational concept discussed below forms the foundation for current doctrine and applies to operations today.

3-14. Four fundamentals—combined arms, joint interdependence, full spectrum operations, and mission command—underlie the operational concept. *Combined arms* involves the complementary application of the different Army branches. *Joint interdependence* describes the complementary use of Army forces with those of other

Services as part of the joint force. *Full spectrum operations* combine offensive, defensive, stability and reconstruction, and civil support operations. *Mission command* is the Army's preferred method for commanding and controlling forces. These fundamentals define the way the Army executes operations.

OPERATIONAL CONCEPT

3-15. The Army's operational concept is seizing, retaining, and exploiting the initiative with speed, shock, surprise, depth, simultaneity, and endurance. The operational concept depends on flexible combinations of Army capabilities (combined arms) and joint capabilities (joint interdependence) integrated across the full spectrum of operations through mission command.

3-16. *Initiative*, in its operational sense, is setting or dictating the terms of action throughout an operation. The side with the initiative determines the nature, tempo, and sequence of actions. Initiative is decisive if retained and exploited. In any operation, a force has the initiative when it is controlling the situation rather than reacting to circumstances. The counterpart to operational initiative is individual initiative, the willingness to act in the absence of orders or when existing orders no longer fit the situation.

3-17. *Speed* is the ability of land forces to act rapidly. Rapid maneuver dislocates the enemy force and exposes its elements before they are prepared or positioned. Rapid action preempts threats to security. It reduces suffering and loss of life among noncombatants or victims of disaster by restoring order and essential services. At the strategic level, speed gives Army forces their expeditionary quality. Speed allows Army forces to keep the initiative. It contributes to their ability to achieve shock and surprise.

3-18. *Shock* is the application of violence of such magnitude that the enemy force is stunned and helpless to reverse the situation. It entails the use of overwhelming force at the decisive time and place. When circumstances limit the use of violence, as in some stability and reconstruction operations, the perceived ability to deliver decisive force is as important as its actual use. In noncombat operations, shock stems from employing enough military force to dissuade possible adversaries from hostile action.

3-19. *Surprise* involves the delivery of a powerful blow at a time and place for which the adversary is unprepared. With the exception of some humanitarian relief missions, surprise always magnifies the effects of landpower. When combined with shock, it reduces friendly casualties and ends opposition swiftly.

3-20. *Depth,* a function of space and reach, is the ability to operate across the entire area of operations. It includes the ability to act in the information environment as well as the physical domain. Depth may involve subordinate elements of a force executing operations in locations distributed throughout the area of operations. In stability and reconstruction operations, depth includes the ability to deliver relief, perform reconstruction tasks, or achieve deterrence at multiple sites. It increases opportunities to influence the population.

3-21. *Simultaneity,* a function of time, confronts opponents with multiple actions occurring at once. Multiple actions overload adversaries' control systems and overstretch their resources. In stability and reconstruction operations, the ability to handle multiple events at the same time increases opportunities to influence the population. Simultaneity is at the heart of how the Army operates: Army forces conduct offensive, defensive, and stability and reconstruction operations at the same time throughout a campaign.

3-22. *Endurance* is the ability to survive and persevere over time. Swift campaigns, however desirable, are the exception. To succeed, Army forces frequently conduct operations for protracted periods. Endurance stems from the ability to generate, protect, and sustain a force, regardless of how far away it is deployed, how austere the environment, or how long the combatant commander requires landpower. It involves anticipating requirements and preparing to make the most effective use of available resources. At the strategic level, endurance gives Army forces their campaign quality.

COMBINED ARMS AND JOINT INTERDEPENDENCE

3-23. Combined arms is a function both of organizational design and temporary association for particular missions. To achieve combined arms, commanders merge elements of different branches—armor, infantry, artillery, civil affairs, combat engineering, and many others—into highly integrated tactical organizations. The strengths of each branch complement and reinforce those of the others, making combined arms teams stronger than the sum of their elements. For example, the brigade combat team has organic elements of many different branches, including, military police, intelligence, infantry, artillery, logistics, and engineers. When deployed, specialized units are added or removed according the needs of the mission. Within the brigade, the commander constantly adjusts the organization of battalion task forces and company teams into different combinations of specialties to achieve the best balance. Well-trained combined arms teams dominate close combat. Army forces using combined arms win against all types of enemies and prevail in stability and reconstruction operations.

3-24. Joint interdependence is combined arms raised to the joint force level. It reinforces and complements the effects of Army combined arms operations and makes Army forces many times more effective than they would be otherwise. Joint interdependence enables the operational concept. Joint force capabilities provide additional mobility, intelligence, fires, protection, and logistics throughout the land area of operations. Flexible combinations of Service forces break the enemy force into pieces unable to complement or reinforce each other, shattering its coherence. Tough, resilient enemies rarely succumb to a single swift action. Ultimately, land forces must maneuver against and destroy them in close combat. Continuous, sustained Army operations, fully supported by joint capabilities, erode the resolve of remaining enemies. Joint interdependence makes the landpower of the joint force the most effective in history, particularly when measured in terms of capabilities per deployed Soldier.

3-25. Combined arms and joint interdependence make land forces more effective in stability and reconstruction operations. Army special operations forces—such as, civil affairs, psychological operations, and special forces A-teams—operate with conventional Army forces, often cooperating with other governmental agencies. Conventional brigades may be task-organized for security, reconstruction, and services. Although combat is less likely during stability and reconstruction operations, the Army's requirement for joint support does not diminish. Medical and logistic operations, for example, depend on responsive air support and, when feasible, movement on inland waterways. This support is especially important when areas of operations are noncontiguous.

FULL SPECTRUM OPERATIONS

3-26. Army forces employ landpower throughout the range of military operations. Effective employment of landpower requires securing and maintaining the initiative and combining types of operations. During joint campaigns overseas, Army forces execute a simultaneous and continuous combination of offensive, defensive, and stability and reconstruction operations as part of integrated joint, interagency, and multinational teams. Concurrently with overseas campaigns, Army forces within the United States and its territories combine offensive, defensive, and civil support operations to support homeland security. (See figure 3-1.) Strategically, the ability to conduct offensive, defensive, and stability and reconstruction operations in overseas campaigns while supporting homeland security domestically is central to full spectrum operations. Domestic operations provide Army capabilities to support homeland security directly. Overseas campaigns contribute to homeland security by taking the fight to the enemy.

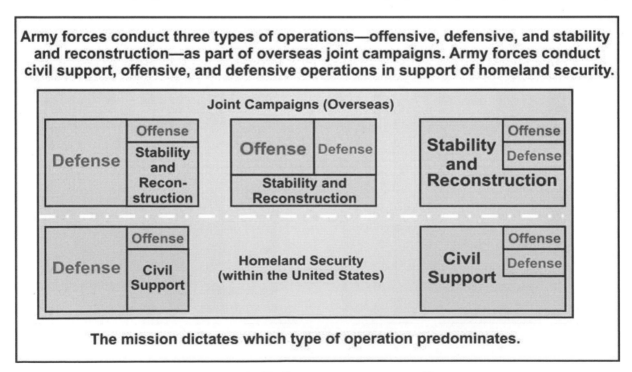

Figure 3-1. Full spectrum operations

3-27. *Offensive* operations carry the fight to the enemy by closing with and destroying enemy forces, seizing territory and vital resources, and imposing the commander's will on the enemy. They focus on seizing, retaining, and exploiting the initiative. This active imposition of landpower makes the offense the decisive type of military operation, whether undertaken against irregular forces or the armed forces of a nation state. In addition, the physical presence of land forces and their credible ability to conduct offensive operations enable the unimpeded conduct of stability and reconstruction operations.

3-28. *Defensive* operations counter enemy offensive operations. They defeat attacks, destroying as many attackers as necessary. Defensive operations preserve control over land, resources, and populations. They retain terrain, guard populations, and protect key resources. Defensive operations also buy time and economize forces to allow the conduct of offensive operations elsewhere. Defensive operations not only defeat attacks but also create the conditions necessary to regain the initiative and go on the offensive or execute stability and reconstruction operations.

3-29. *Stability and reconstruction* operations sustain and exploit security and control over areas, populations, and resources. They employ military capabilities to reconstruct or establish services and support civilian agencies. Stability and reconstruction operations involve both coercive and cooperative actions. They may occur before, during, and after offensive and defensive operations; however, they also occur separately, usually at the lower end of the range of military operations. Stability and reconstruction operations lead to an environment in which, in cooperation with a legitimate government, the other instruments of national power can predominate.

3-30. Within the United States and its territories, Army forces support *homeland security* operations. Homeland security operations provide the Nation strategic flexibility by protecting its citizens and infrastructure from conventional and unconventional threats. Homeland security has two components. The first component is *homeland defense*. If the United States comes under direct attack or is threatened by hostile armed forces, Army forces under joint command conduct offensive and defensive missions as part of homeland defense. The other component is *civil support*, which is the fourth type of Army operation.

3-31. *Civil support* operations address the consequences of man-made or natural accidents and incidents beyond the capabilities of civilian authorities. Army forces do not conduct stability and reconstruction operations within the United States; under U.S law, the federal and state governments are responsible for those tasks. Instead, Army forces conduct civil support operations when requested, providing Army expertise and capabilities to lead agency authorities.

3-32. The skills Army forces require to conduct one type of operation complement those required to conduct other types of operations. For example, the perceived ability of Army forces to attack and destroy enemies contributes to success in stability and reconstruction operations by deterring potential threats. Conversely, stability and reconstruction operations reduce the chance of offensive and defensive requirements by influencing civilians to not support enemy efforts. Defensive capabilities are employed in such homeland security missions as protecting key infrastructure during a crisis. The discipline, physical stamina, and unit cohesion developed during training for offensive and defensive operations prepare Soldiers and units to deal effectively with the ambiguities and complexities of stability and reconstruction operations and civil support operations.

MISSION COMMAND

3-33. *Mission command* is the Army's preferred method for commanding and controlling forces. The distribution, speed, and simultaneity of integrated joint operations and the design of the modular force mandate conducting operations with mission command. A climate of mission command allows Army forces to adapt and succeed despite the chaos of combat. Successful mission command rests on the following elements: commander's intent, subordinates' initiative, mission orders, and resource allocation. Under mission command, commanders provide subordinates with a mission, their commander's intent and concept of operations, and resources adequate to accomplish the mission. Higher commanders empower subordinates to make decisions within the commander's intent. They leave details of execution to their subordinates and require them to use initiative and judgment to accomplish the mission. Higher commanders expect subordinates to identify and act on unforeseen circumstances, whether opportunities or threats, while synchronizing their operations with those of adjacent unit commanders. Seizing, retaining, and exploiting the operational initiative requires subordinate commanders and leaders to exercise individual initiative and higher commanders to give them authority to do so. Training subordinates under mission command develops disciplined initiative and skilled judgment. It also gives commanders the confidence to delegate them the necessary authority during operations. Mission command enables commanders to use the unprecedented agility and flexibility of the modular force to take advantage of the chaos of war. It allows Army forces to rapidly adapt to changes in the situation and exercise initiative within the commander's intent to accomplish the mission.

LANDPOWER IN FULL SPECTRUM OPERATIONS

3-34. Overcoming the enemy's will is the objective of combat operations; physical destruction of enemy forces, when necessary, is only a means to this end. Breaking the enemy's will signals victory but does not end a campaign. Americans fight for a better peace. Security must be established, services restored, and the foundation for lasting change set. During and after major combat operations, Army forces contribute to joint, interagency, and multinational efforts to exploit the opportunities military victory provides and provide strategic permanence to the otherwise temporary effects of combat.

3-35. Decisive resolution of conflicts normally occurs on land. Of the Armed Forces' capabilities, landpower is unique because only land forces can occupy, control, and protect vital areas. People and resources—the participants, supporters, and objectives of land operations—can only be controlled or protected by land forces. Effective employment of landpower is never purely destructive, nor is it totally benign or unobtrusive. Employing landpower requires using the appropriate level of force—for example, peaceful persuasion and long-term stabilizing presence, localized raids, or overwhelming physical destruction.

3-36. Offensive and defensive land operations have immediate and severe effects on people, institutions, and infrastructure. Concurrent stability and reconstruction operations are normally needed to sustain the integrity of noncombatants' society. Effective stability and reconstruction operations protect the society's essential infrastructure, institutions, and basic needs. In some cases, stability and reconstruction operations alter factors or institutions to promote security and effect permanent changes. They enable the fastest possible return to a stable environment. Land forces may undertake stability and reconstruction operations to prevent or contain conflicts. In doing so, they sometimes have to conduct offensive and defensive operations. In many cases, stability and reconstruction operations include communicating the clear understanding that Army forces can and will counter any threat with the force required. In other words, combat capabilities underwrite stability and reconstruction operations.

3-37. The deployment of ground forces into a region and the approach they take to the population immediately affect the population's daily life, perceptions, and politics— for better or worse, depending on the viewpoint of the inhabitants. This effect occurs even without a shot being fired. It is especially true within the United States and its territories, where law and civil authority carefully circumscribe the use of military force.

3-38. Employing landpower effectively in joint campaigns requires combining types of operations and transitioning between them. While one type of operation normally predominates during each campaign phase, other types also occur. For example, after the Baathist regime collapsed and its military forces were destroyed during Operation Iraqi Freedom, the coalition campaign transitioned from one where offensive operations predominated to one characterized by stability and reconstruction operations. To counter the various insurgent groups that emerged afterwards, coalition forces again transitioned; they began to conduct offensive and defensive missions simultaneously with stability and reconstruction operations. The stability and reconstruction operations now included counterinsurgency. Simultaneous combinations of types of operations and transitions between them characterize full spectrum operations. They will be typical of the use of landpower in future campaigns. The skills required to transition between types of operations are special and critical for Army units. Mastering them requires the Army to develop Soldiers and leaders with not only combat expertise but also imagination and flexibility.

EXPEDITIONARY CAMPAIGNS

3-39. A *campaign* is a series of related military operations aimed at accomplishing a strategic or operational objective within a given time and space. Campaigns are inherently joint operations. Expeditionary campaigns that involve land operations almost always require Army forces. During campaigns, deployed Army forces normally conduct simultaneous offensive, defensive, and stability and reconstruction operations throughout the area of operations. The predominant type of operation and its relationship to other types of operations vary according to the joint force commander's design.

3-40. At the outset of a campaign, the joint force commander typically needs forces to respond promptly to a crisis. The Army provides rapidly deployable units able to operate in any environment—from complex urban areas to remote, austere wilderness regions. If a decisive conclusion to combat operations does not occur swiftly, the Army provides land forces with greater combat power and the endurance needed to conduct sustained operations. Campaigns that are predominantly stability and reconstruction in character may require landpower for years, as operations in the Sinai and Balkans demonstrate. The capability to conduct sustained joint-enabled land operations—the Army's campaign quality—gives Army forces their ability to preserve the gains of joint operations where necessary. This allows employment of other instruments of national power to achieve strategic objectives.

3-41. Commanders seek to win decisively as quickly as possible. However, fighting strong or resilient enemies, or facing relief or humanitarian circumstances that cannot be resolved quickly, requires the staying power only land forces provide. Army forces remain on the ground until the job is done. Army forces make permanent the effects of joint operations.

ENHANCING JOINT INTERDEPENDENCE

3-42. The challenges of the security environment, complexity of unified action, and capabilities required to conduct full spectrum operations make joint interdependence imperative. Joint interdependence extends combined arms synergy into the joint realm. It is more than interoperability, the assurance that Service forces can work together smoothly. It is even more than integration to improve their collective efficiency and effectiveness. Joint interdependence purposefully combines Service capabilities to maximize their complementary and reinforcing effects while minimizing their vulnerabilities.

3-43. Fundamentally, joint interdependence means each Service depends on the others and on the joint force for key capabilities. It is based on recognition that the Armed Forces fight as one team of joint, interagency, and multinational partners. Several conditions are essential for joint interdependence. Joint force commanders must establish clear command relationships among force components; clearly stating supporting and supported relationships among joint force elements is particularly important. Commanders must also determine measures that allow unity of effort with interagency and multinational partners. Commanders at all levels must realize that assured access to partners' capabilities does not require command authority over them. Joint interdependence requires confidence that the supporting force will provide its capabilities where and when needed; conversely, commitment to delivering those capabilities to the supported force is also essential. Joint interdependence rests on trust among military professionals. For Soldiers, it means their Warrior Ethos obligations apply to their joint, interagency, and multinational partners.

3-44. At the strategic level, joint interdependence allows each Service to divest itself of redundant functions that another Service provides better. Doing this reduces unnecessary duplication of capabilities among the Services. It achieves greater efficiency in all areas of expertise. Interdependence allows the Army to focus on developing capabilities that only land forces can provide. Likewise, relying on the Army for land-related capabilities allows the other Services to achieve greater efficiencies in their respective domains.

3-45. Joint interdependence requires joint training. Organizations that operate together must train together. The Army's joint training opportunities continue to improve as it works with U.S. Joint Forces Command and the other Services to further develop a joint training capability. The planning, scenarios, connectivity, and overall realism of joint training are enhancing the joint operations skills of Army commanders and Soldiers. The Army is also learning from the strategic environment. The Nation's adversaries are elusive and adaptive. They seek refuge in complex terrain, sometimes harbored by failed or failing states. They often leverage such new and easy-to-obtain technologies as the Internet and satellite communications. The Army is incorporating these conditions into deployment scenarios, training, and education to enhance its joint warfighting proficiency. In pursuit of joint interdependence, the Army is considering joint operations at the outset when designing capabilities and establishing training requirements. Joint training and education help Soldiers and Army leaders learn about the other Services' cultures, responsibilities, and relationships. This knowledge, combined with experience in the joint environment, is enhancing Soldiers' and Army leaders' contributions to joint interdependence.

3-46. The Army's modular force combines an *expeditionary* capability, the ability to promptly deploy combined arms forces worldwide, and a *campaign* quality, the ability to sustain operations long enough to achieve the desired end state. Army forces' expeditionary capability and campaign quality allow them to contribute decisive, sustained landpower to joint, interagency, and multinational operations in any environment. An ever present challenge is to reconcile the Army's staying power—the ability to conduct long-term operations—with its strategic agility—the ability to promptly deploy forces of appropriate size and strength over vast distances to anywhere in the world. Army forces are postured, both at home and abroad, to demonstrate their agility and readiness to quickly execute expeditionary operations anytime, anywhere.

SUMMARY

3-47. Combatant commanders are responsible for winning wars and commanding the joint forces that fight them; however, the Army is responsible for providing the bulk of the landpower needed to achieve those victories, set the conditions for an enduring peace, and sustain those conditions as long as needed to achieve that peace. The campaign quality and joint and expeditionary capabilities of Army forces offer the President and combatant commanders diverse options for security cooperation, crisis response, and warfighting. The Army's campaign quality is expressed in its ability to conduct sustained operations on land with a variety of units for as long as it takes to accomplish the Nation's political objectives. Its expeditionary capability is seen in its versatile organizations able to promptly deploy and operate in austere environments across the range of military operations. The campaign quality and expeditionary capability of Army forces make them relevant to today's operational environment and ready to meet any challenge to the Nation's security or well-being.

Chapter 4

The Way Ahead

The condition of the Army today can only be understood when one considers where we have been and where we are going.... The changes in the world have made us realize that to ultimately be successful in the Global War on Terror, we must transform our capabilities. We will not be ready and relevant in the 21st Century unless we become much more expeditionary, more joint, more rapidly deployable and adaptive, as well as enhance our capability to be successful across the entire range of military operations from major combat to the condition of stability.

Dr. Francis J. Harvey
Secretary of the Army

4-1.   The strategic environment, national guidance, and operational requirements demand that today's Army forces conduct operations of a type, tempo, and duration that differ significantly from those of the past. The late twentieth century required a force able to execute a fixed number of deliberate war plans and prepared to provide small forces for infrequent contingencies. The twenty-first century requires a force able to conduct sustained operations against several ongoing contingencies while remaining prepared to execute a number of deliberate war plans. Sustained operations and readiness to meet both old and new threats will be normal for the foreseeable future. This situation requires changes in both structure and mindset. The Army is rapidly transforming itself to meet both requirements.

4-2.   The War on Terrorism has given the Army a strategic opportunity to reshape itself. It is leveraging its wartime focus to build campaign quality Army forces with joint and expeditionary capabilities. It is shedding inefficient processes and procedures designed for peacetime and reexamining institutional assumptions, organizational structures, paradigms, policies, and procedures. This ongoing transformation is producing a better balance of capabilities. When complete, Army forces will be able to deploy more promptly and sustain operations longer to exercise decisive landpower across the range of military operations. The Army's goal is to transform itself into a more responsive, effective expeditionary force capable of sustained campaigning anywhere in the world. Meanwhile, it continues to sustain operational support to combatant commanders and maintain the quality of the all-volunteer force.

FUTURE OPERATING ENVIRONMENT CHALLENGES

4-3.   The Army is preparing today to meet the four types of challenges outlined in chapter 2:

- Traditional.
- Irregular.
- Catastrophic.
- Disruptive.

4-4.   To address *traditional* challenges, the Army is extending its mastery of major combat operations. It is maintaining the ability to counter today's conventional threats while preparing for tomorrow's antiaccess environments. The ability to prevail in major combat operations is a crucial responsibility and primary driver of capabilities development. Many capabilities required for major combat operations apply across the range of military operations. Those capabilities include—

- Strategic and operational mobility.
- Advanced information systems to support command, control, intelligence, surveillance, and reconnaissance.
- Precision weaponry.
- Force protection.
- Sustainment.

4-5.   The Army is broadening and deepening its ability to counter *irregular* challenges. However, because the Nation cannot afford two armies, the Army is meeting this requirement by increasing the versatility and agility of the same forces that conduct conventional operations. In many situations, the combination of traditional and irregular threats presents the most demanding challenges to military effectiveness. This combination requires Soldiers and units able to transition between the operations required to counter conventional and irregular threats.

4-6.   Preempting catastrophic threats includes deterring the use of or destroying weapons of mass destruction. To accomplish these tasks, the Army is continuously enhancing its expeditionary capability. It is increasing its ability to rapidly project forces and decisively maneuver them over both global and theater distances. It is seeking minimal reliance on predictable, vulnerable deployment transition points (intermediate staging bases) or ports of entry.

4-7.   To prepare for disruptive challenges, the Army is maintaining and improving a range of capabilities, minimizing the potential for single-point strategic surprise and failure. It is also developing intellectual capital to power a culture of innovation and adaptability, the Army's most potent response to disruptive threats.

4-8.   While preparing for irregular, disruptive, and catastrophic challenges, the Army is retaining its ability to dominate land operations in traditional conflicts. American land forces clearly occupy a commanding position in the world with respect to defeating traditional military challenges. The Army must retain a superior position, particularly in the face of modernizing armies that might challenge U.S. partners and interests. Failure to maintain a qualitative edge over these traditional threats would promote instability and create vulnerabilities that adversaries might attempt to exploit.

4-9.   While technology will be crucial to achieving greater operational agility and precision lethality, the human dimension will continue to be the critical element of war. The Soldier will remain the centerpiece of Army organizations. As the complexity of operations increases, well-trained, innovative, and disciplined Soldiers and leaders will become more important than ever. Recruiting, training, educating, and retaining of Soldiers is vital to maintaining landpower dominance in all forms of conflict.

ARMY TRANSFORMATION

4-10. Transformation describes the process by which the current force is becoming the future force. (See figure 4-1.) It occurs as the Army incorporates new capabilities into its force structure and trains Soldiers to use them. The future force is what the Army continuously seeks to become. It will be strategically responsive and joint interdependent. It will be capable of precision maneuver and able to dominate adversaries and situations across the range of military operations envisioned in the future security environment. The future force will be lighter, more lethal and agile, and optimized for versatility. It will be capable of seamlessly transitioning among the different types of military operations.

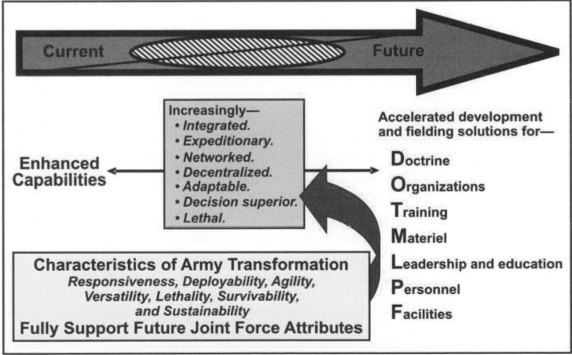

Figure 4-1. Current to future force

4-11. Army transformation is more than materiel solutions. Adaptive and determined leadership, innovative concept development and experimentation, and lessons learned from recent operations produce corresponding changes to doctrine, organizations, training, materiel, leadership and education, personnel, and facilities (DOTMLPF). DOTMLPF is a problem-solving construct for assessing current capabilities and managing change. Change is achieved through a continuous cycle of adaptive innovation, experimentation, and experience. Change deliberately executed across DOTMLPF elements enables the Army to improve its capabilities to provide dominant landpower to the joint force.

4-12. The Army Campaign Plan is the authoritative basis that sets into action the Army's transformation strategies. It provides specific objectives, assigns responsibilities for execution, and synchronizes resources. It directs the planning, preparation, and execution of Army operations and Army transformation within the context of the Nation's ongoing strategic commitments. These commitments and resource availability dictate the synchronization and pace of change. The Army Campaign Plan also sustains operational support to combatant commanders and maintains the quality of the all-volunteer force.

THE ARMY'S TRANSFORMATION STRATEGIES

4-13. The Army's comprehensive restructuring combines four interrelated strategies. These strategies are centered on forces, people, quality of life, and infrastructure. Together, they enable the Army mission: Provide to combatant commanders the forces and capabilities necessary to execute the National Security, National Defense, and National Military Strategies. The Army's transformation strategies are—

- **Forces**. Provide relevant and ready landpower to combatant commanders to meet the full range of global commitments.
- **People**. Train and equip Soldiers as world-class warriors, and develop competent, flexible, and adaptive leaders able to meet twenty-first century challenges.
- **Quality of life**. Attain a quality of life and well-being for Army people that match the quality of the service they provide.
- **Infrastructure**. Establish and maintain the infrastructure and the information network required to develop, generate, train, and sustain operational forces for their global mission.

These interrelated strategies unify the Army's transformation effort. Properly implemented, they will produce an Army able to meet everything asked of it.

ESSENTIALS OF ARMY TRANSFORMATION

4-14. The Army Campaign Plan establishes eight campaign objectives that enable the Army to achieve its transformation strategies. (See figure 4-2.) These objectives are clearly defined, measurable, decisive, and attainable goals.

4-15. The Army is undertaking a significant shift in emphasis and priorities with respect to its near- and midterm focus and resourcing. This shift is driven by a reassessment of the strategic and operational environments. It is also driven by the

Army's responsibility to provide relevant and ready landpower to combatant commanders now and in the future.

- **Support global operations**. Organize, train, equip, and sustain a campaign capable joint, expeditionary Army to provide relevant and ready landpower to combatant commanders.

- **Adapt and improve total Army capabilities**. Organize Army forces into modular, capabilities-based unit designs to enable rapid force packaging and deployment, and sustained land combat.

- **Optimize Reserve Component contributions**. Transform Reserve Component force structure and continuum of service paradigms to optimize Reserve Component capabilities and provide relevant and ready forces and Soldiers to combatant commanders.

- **Sustain the right all-volunteer force**. Recruit and retain competent, adaptive, and confident Soldiers and Army civilians to meet immediate and long-range multicomponent personnel and family readiness requirements.

- **Adjust the global footprint**. Adjust Army stationing and support infrastructure in accordance with integrated global presence and basing strategy to better execute the National Defense Strategy and support operational deployments and sustained operational rotations.

- **Build the future force**. Develop future force capabilities to meet future landpower requirements of the combatant commanders.

- **Adapt the institutional Army**. Transform the institutional Army and associated processes to responsively execute Title 10 responsibilities to sustain a campaign quality Army with joint, expeditionary capabilities.

- **Develop a joint, interdependent logistic structure**. Create an integrated logistic capability responsible for end-to-end sustainment to joint force commanders across the range of military operations.

Figure 4-2. Army campaign objectives

TRANSFORMING TODAY

We will not be effective and relevant in the 21st century unless we become much more agile but with the capacity for a long-term, sustained level of conflict. Being relevant means having a campaign-quality Army with joint expeditionary capability. It must be an Army not trained for a single event like a track athlete, but talented across a broad spectrum like a decathlete.

General Peter J. Schoomaker

4-16. To respond to the contemporary strategic challenges, the Army has accelerated its transformation. During times of peace, change is generally slow and deliberate, conducted at a pace supported by limited resources. In wartime, however, change must occur faster to strengthen operational forces and provide the best available resources to deployed Soldiers. Thus, Army transformation is not an end in itself; it contributes to accomplishing today's missions as well. To improve its ability to provide forces and capabilities to combatant commanders, the Army is undergoing its most profound restructuring in over 50 years. Key aspects of the transformation already affecting the current force include the following:

- Resetting, restructuring, rebalancing, and stabilizing the force.
- Integrating component technology of the future combat systems.
- Developing networked information systems.
- Modernizing institutional Army processes.

RESETTING THE FORCE

4-17. Operations in Iraq and Afghanistan are placing tremendous demands on Army equipment and Soldiers. As a result, the Army has initiated a program to reset units returning from deployment. Resetting refers to actions taken to prepare redeploying units for future missions. Resetting units is not a one-time event, for either the Army as a whole or individual units. It is required for all units, regardless of component, every time they return from a deployment. The reset program consists of five elements. Each addresses different unit deployment requirements:

- Units and Soldiers are provided training in essential tasks incorporating lessons learned from the operational environment.
- Soldiers and leaders receive individual training and professional development.
- Pre-positioned equipment and ammunition stocks are adjusted.
- If necessary, units are reorganized into the appropriate modular design. Resetting units are not left in legacy designs.
- Overall unit readiness is returned to Army standards.

Through its reset program, the Army is simultaneously supporting current global commitments and transforming itself for future challenges.

4-18. Two programs geared for both redeployed and deployed units complement the reset program: the rapid fielding initiative and the rapid equipping force program. These programs are designed to quickly integrate combat systems and equipment for Soldiers into the current force.

4-19. The *rapid fielding initiative* is designed to fill Soldier and unit equipment requirements by quickly fielding commercial, off-the-shelf technology rather than waiting for standard acquisition programs to address shortages. Soldiers receive individual equipment, such as, body armor and ballistic goggles. Units receive equipment based on operational lessons learned, such as, grappling hooks and fiber-optic viewers. Soldiers and units of all components are equipped to a common standard.

4-20. The *rapid equipping force program* uses commercial and field-engineered solutions to quickly meet operational needs. It provides both simple and sophisticated equipment. Examples range from lock shims that open padlocks nondestructively to robotic sensors that explore caves, tunnels, wells, and other confined spaces.

4-21. These programs are directly aligned with the Army's people and force transformation strategies. They reflect how the Army cares for its people and prepares units for upcoming training and deployments. They also position the Army to be more responsive to emerging threats and contingencies.

RESTRUCTURING THE FORCE

4-22. The Army is restructuring from a division-based to a brigade-based force—the modular force. Modular force brigades are strategically flexible. The major combat and support capabilities a brigade needs for most operations are organic to its structure. This modular organization simplifies providing force packages to meet operational requirements. It also increases brigades' tactical independence. It enhances integration with Army, joint, other-Service, and multinational forces. This organizational transformation is making the operational Army more powerful and responsive.

4-23. Transforming to the modular force will increase Regular Army combat capability to as many as 48 combined arms brigade combat teams. It will increase the size of the Army's overall pool of available maneuver organizations to no fewer than 77 brigade combat teams. Having a larger pool of available brigade-based forces will enable the Army to generate forces in a predictable rotation. This enlarged force pool will also give Soldiers and units more time between deployments. Further, this stabilization will allow higher quality training and better support to combatant commanders.

4-24. The modular force includes five types of multifunctional support brigades that complement and reinforce brigade combat teams: aviation, battlefield surveillance, maneuver enhancement, fires, and sustainment. These brigades are also organized as combined arms units. Each accomplishes a broad function, such as, protection in the case of maneuver enhancement brigades. In addition, theater-level single-function commands or brigades (such as, Army air and missile defense commands) provide additional capabilities for the campaign quality modular force.

REBALANCING THE FORCE

4-25. The skills and organizations required for operations against today's threats are different from those of the recent past. The twentieth century required an Army with a large capacity focused on combat capabilities. Today's operational environment requires an Army with more diverse capabilities as well as the capacity for sustained operations. The Army is developing these diverse capabilities through a process called rebalancing.

4-26. Rebalancing involves retraining Soldiers and converting organizations to produce more Soldiers and units with high-demand skills. It will result in a substantial increase in infantry capabilities, with similar increases in military police, civil affairs, military intelligence, and other critical skills. It will also relieve stress on the relatively small pool of Soldiers and units currently possessing these high-demand skills. Additionally, rebalancing increases the Army's ability to conduct sustained stability and reconstruction operations.

4-27. The Army has already begun rebalancing the Regular Army and Reserve Components. The objective is to prepare the Regular Army to be able to execute the first 30 days of an operation without augmentation from the Reserve Components. This is increasing Army capabilities available for the first 30 days of an operation. Ultimately, rebalancing the force will realign the specialties of more than 100,000 Soldiers.

STABILIZING THE FORCE

4-28. The Army is now assigning Soldiers to brigades for longer periods. This policy increases combat readiness and cohesion as it reduces turnover and eliminates repetitive training requirements. With Soldiers and families moving less frequently, more Soldiers are available to train or fight on any given day. This initiative is a major step in transitioning the Army from an individual replacement system to a unit replacement system. It allows Soldiers to train, deploy, fight, and redeploy together. Unit replacement lessens the strain of the high operational tempo and creates greater stability in the lives of Soldiers and their families.

INTEGRATING COMPONENT TECHNOLOGY OF FUTURE COMBAT SYSTEMS

4-29. Also key to Army transformation is the fielding of future combat system technologies. These form the foundation for long-term Army transformation. The future combat systems are not platforms; they are a family of networked land- and air-based maneuver and supporting systems built around Soldiers. Networked future combat system capabilities will integrate sensors and information systems. They will also include manned and unmanned reconnaissance and surveillance systems. This network will improve commanders' situational understanding. Future combat system-equipped units will have superior joint interoperability and be more rapidly deployable and survivable than current force units.

4-30. The operational Army is benefiting from future combat system programs today. The Army is integrating component technologies into the current force as they become available. It is not waiting until all future combat system elements are completely developed. This strategy allows the operational force to use the best equipment and latest technological enhancements available. In addition, the experience gained in using these technologies is helping improve future force decisions. A continuous cycle of innovation, experimentation, experience, and change is improving the Army's ability to provide dominant and sustained landpower to combatant commanders. It is getting newly developed technology to Soldiers faster then previously envisioned.

DEVELOPING NETWORKED INFORMATION SYSTEMS

4-31. Also important to Army transformation is providing networked information systems down to the lowest level, including individual Soldiers. These networked systems support command, control, intelligence, surveillance, and reconnaissance. They are transforming how Army leaders make decisions and operate. They are improving commanders' connectivity within the collaborative information environment necessary for joint operations. Networked systems will contribute to information superiority by providing leaders access to online knowledge sources and interconnecting people and systems independent of time, location, or Service. Disciplined information sharing over this network will improve commanders' situational understanding. This collaboration will facilitate the human art of command and ultimately shorten commanders' decision cycles, contributing to decision superiority.

MODERNIZING INSTITUTIONAL ARMY PROCESSES

4-32. The institutional Army is reengineering its business, force-generation, and training practices to improve its support of the operational Army and other Services. Initiatives include eliminating irrelevant policies, processes, and practices. Other improvements include increasing institutional agility by developing a joint, end-to-end logistic structure and fostering a culture of innovation. The institutional Army is seeking to improve effectiveness and identify efficiencies that free people and money to better support the operational Army.

CHANGING ARMY CULTURE

4-33. When large, complex organizations pursue transformational change, a key measure of success is leaders' ability to reorient peoples' attitudes and actions. For Army leaders, these people include Soldiers, Army civilians, and families. The Army is changing policies, training, and behavior to create a culture that embraces the operational and organizational challenges of a turbulent security environment.

4-34. The Army's success in changing its culture will be a significant measure of its success in transforming itself. This cultural change will build on the existing Army culture and beliefs as expressed in the Army Values and Soldier's Creed. This effort has four major dimensions:

- Inculcate a culture of innovation.
- Realize the implications of joint, expeditionary warfare.

- Commit to the ideals of the Warrior Ethos.
- Promote resiliency.

INCULCATE A CULTURE OF INNOVATION

4-35. The Army's practice of learning and changing continually while performing its mission has historical roots. Since the 1980s, the Army has been a national leader in anticipating and leading change. Its deliberate study of technical and professional developments, focused collection and analysis of data from operations and training events, free-ranging experimentation, and transforming processes have made it a model of effective innovation. Army leaders are continuing to foster creative thinking. They are challenging inflexible ways of thinking, removing impediments to institutional innovation, and underwriting the risks associated with bold change.

4-36. Innovation seeks engagement by all Soldiers. Engagement fosters and improves communication among Soldiers and leaders throughout the force. It tests new ideas, concepts, and ways of conducting operations. Engagement includes methodically collecting and analyzing data and conducting informed discussions. It experiments with new ideas and creates opportunities to learn from critics. Army leaders are seeking to innovate radically. They want to move beyond incremental improvements to transformational changes. They continue to identify and test the best practices in industrial and commercial enterprises, the other Services, and foreign military establishments. They review history for insights and cautions. Consistent with security, they share information and ideas across organizational, public, private, and academic boundaries.

4-37. Engagement begins with a flexible doctrine adaptable to changing circumstances. The Army is enhancing its doctrine to address enemies who deliberately avoid predictable operating patterns. It is incorporating lessons learned from ongoing operations to equip Soldiers for today's security environment and prepare them for tomorrow's. Doctrine cannot predict the precise nature and form of asymmetric engagements; however, it can forecast the kinds of knowledge and organizational qualities necessary for victory. The Army is applying its intellectual and physical resources to refine its doctrine to accomplish that task. Effective doctrine fosters initiative and creative thinking. In so doing, it helps adaptive and flexible leaders make good decisions and stimulate a culture of innovation.

REALIZE THE IMPLICATIONS OF JOINT, EXPEDITIONARY WARFARE

4-38. Recent adversaries have achieved strategic surprise by operating against the United States from remote locations. Other adversaries may seek refuge in similar formidable environments. Thus, future conflicts are likely to involve joint, expeditionary operations. These conflicts will be characterized by rapid deployments with little to no notice, contingency operations in austere theaters, and incomplete planning information. Operations are likely to involve fighting for information rather than fighting with information against adaptive and creative adversaries. Future force organizations are designed to prevail under these circumstances.

4-39. However, victory in future conflicts requires more than redesigned organizations, materiel, and facilities. The Army is also changing its mindset to better cope with the implications of an uncertain and ambiguous security environment. Joint, expeditionary warfare places a premium on adapting to the unique circumstances of each campaign. Operational success depends on flexible employment of Army capabilities and different combinations of joint and interagency capabilities. No military force in history has had the range of capabilities available to today's joint force. However, there is no standard formula that fits every operation. Land warfare will always generate unexpected opportunities and sudden risks.

4-40. It is important that Soldiers have the training and experience to recognize what tactics and techniques might fit a particular situation. It is equally important that they have the imagination to recognize and initiative to adapt to new conditions and unforeseen events. It is therefore critical to view themselves through enemy eyes. To accomplish this, the modular force will include a "red-teaming" capability. Red team-trained personnel will actively participate during planning to ensure proper consideration of both conventional and asymmetric threats. Other red team personnel will be available to review plans and address commanders' areas of concern. Red team personnel are one resource commanders will be able to use to increase their Soldiers' self-awareness and knowledge of adversaries.

4-41. Although planning provides a necessary forecast for any operation, it cannot predict the actual course of events. The operational environment of the early twenty-first century requires Soldiers and units to adapt and execute in order to win. The Army is enhancing its training, education, and Soldier and leader development programs to develop the flexible, adaptive mindset needed to prevail in joint, expeditionary operations.

COMMIT TO THE IDEALS OF THE WARRIOR ETHOS

4-42. The Army prepares every Soldier to be a warrior. Army training seeks to replicate the stark realities of combat. The Army has changed its training systems to reflect the conditions of the current operational environment and better prepare Soldiers for them. The goal is to build Soldiers' confidence in themselves and their equipment, leaders, and fellow Soldiers.

4-43. Mental and physical toughness underpin the beliefs established in the Soldier's Creed. Army leaders develop them in all Soldiers. The Warrior Ethos inspires the refusal to accept failure and conviction that military service is much more than a job. It generates an unfailing commitment to win. The Warrior Ethos defines who Soldiers are and what Soldiers do. It is derived from the Army Values and reinforces a personal commitment to service.

4-44. Commitment to the ideals of the Warrior Ethos is deeply embedded in the Army's culture. The Warrior Ethos instills a "mission first–never quit" mental toughness in Soldiers. Training as tough as combat reinforces the Warrior Ethos. Soldiers who demonstrate it are promoted. Soldiers combine the Warrior Ethos with initiative, decisiveness, and mental agility to succeed in the complex, often irregular, environments in which they operate. Soldiers and leaders who exemplify the Warrior Ethos accomplish the mission regardless of obstacles.

PROMOTE RESILIENCY

4-45. To complement the "mission first–never quit" spirit of the Warrior Ethos, the Army is emphasizing the importance of resiliency. Resiliency enables Soldiers to thrive in ambiguous, adverse situations. It allows units to respond aggressively to changes and setbacks. Resilient Soldiers overcome the stress, confusion, friction, and complexity of the environment to accomplish the mission. They are mentally prepared to deal with uncertainty. They can absorb the effects of unexpected developments without stopping or losing their orientation. Tough, realistic training develops Soldiers and leaders comfortable with uncertainty. This self-confidence produces a willingness to innovate and accept risk. Resiliency—underpinned by the ideals of the Warrior Ethos—allows Army forces to exploit adversaries less capable of dealing with ambiguity.

BALANCING RISKS

4-46. Before 11 September 2001, the absence of a peer competitor shaped the Army's strategic investment decisions. The Army's investment strategy accepted risks in numerous current force procurement areas to allow investment in the future force. After 11 September, the War on Terrorism changed Army requirements dramatically. The Army had to "buy back" many of the deferred capabilities required for current operations. Doing this has reduced operational risk and improved Army forces' firepower, force protection, mobility, and sustainability. While these decisions have produced dramatic, immediate improvements for Soldiers and increased current force capabilities, the monetary costs have been substantial.

4-47. To reduce the risks associated with fighting the War on Terrorism, the Army has made deliberate choices in several areas. These include allocating resources, assigning missions to its units and components, altering stationing, and procuring new weapons and equipment. These decisions accommodate urgent wartime needs and have better enabled Soldiers to accomplish their missions. The months and years ahead will challenge the Army to balance current and future investments to keep risk at moderate levels as it executes current requirements and prepares for future challenges.

WHAT DOES NOT CHANGE: THE HUMAN DIMENSION

Above all, we must realize that no arsenal or no weapon in the arsenals of the world is so formidable as the will and moral courage of free men and women.

President Ronald Reagan

4-48. As the Army moves into the future, two things will not change—the primacy of Soldiers and Army Values. Appropriately, this manual begins and ends with Soldiers. Well-trained Soldiers are fundamental to realizing any improvements in technology, techniques, or strategy. It is Soldiers who use technology, execute techniques, and accomplish strategies. It is they who bear the hardships of combat, adapt to the demands of complex environments, and accomplish the mission. Their collective proficiency and willingness to undergo the brutal test of wills that is combat remains the ultimate test of Army forces.

4-49. American Soldiers—exemplifying the Army Values of *loyalty, duty, respect, selfless service, honor, integrity,* and *personal courage*—remain the centerpiece of Army organizations. The Army will continue to recruit, train, equip, and retain physically fit, mentally tough, high-quality Soldiers. It is quality people that make the Army what it is—the world's premier landpower force. An example of what quality Soldiers do—day in and day out—is in the story of the 724th Transportation Company deployed in support of Operation Iraqi Freedom. (See page 4-14.)

SUMMARY

4-50. The Nation has entrusted the Army with preserving its peace and freedom, defending its democracy, and providing opportunities for its Soldiers to serve their country and develop their skills and citizenship. To fulfill its solemn obligation to the Nation, the Army will continue to be the preeminent landpower on earth—the ultimate instrument of national resolve.

4-51. The Army will remain a values-centered, doctrine-based profession of Soldiers, rooted in the fundamental principles expressed in the Declaration of Independence and Constitution of the United States. George Washington's moral courage and selfless leadership preserved the ideal of civilian control of the military. Washington's actions at Newburgh show what selfless service to the Nation means—enduring personal sacrifice for the greater common good and rejecting personal gain that comes at the Nation's expense. Today's Soldiers continue his legacy of sacrifice and selfless service.

4-52. The Army's proud history and traditions point to countless men and women who have been and are committed to defending the American way of life. They are citizens who answered the call to duty. Many made the ultimate sacrifice. Today's Soldiers, bound together through the trials of service and combat, hold fast to the professional standards embodied in the Army Values and Warrior Ethos. In so doing, they will continue to inspire the Nation and the next generation that answers the call to duty.

(724th Transportation Company Family Readiness Group)

724th Transportation Company in Iraq

The 724th Transportation Company, an Army Reserve unit, mobilized on 8 November 2003 and deployed for Operation Iraqi Freedom on 18 February 2004. They served in Iraq until February 2005. On 327 missions, they traveled more than 728,000 miles and delivered nearly 9 million gallons of fuel. That much fuel would have supplied a World War II field army for more than three weeks.

The 724th spent most of its time in the Sunni Triangle, the most dangerous part of Iraq. Delivering fuel was a dangerous mission. Every convoy was a combat operation. The mission of 9 April 2004 was particularly memorable. It was the anniversary of the fall of Baghdad. A 724th convoy carrying fuel to al Asad was attacked as it traveled a four-mile stretch along Alternate Supply Route Husky. Insurgents subjected the convoy to a gauntlet of fire from built-up areas dominated by two- and three-story houses and narrow side streets. Nearly 200 enemy fighters engaged the convoy with rocket-propelled grenades, command-detonated improvised explosive devices, machine guns, and assault rifles. The Soldiers of the 724th responded as American Soldiers have done for over 200 years; they fought through and accomplished the mission. Specialist Jeremy Church, driving the lead vehicle, distinguished himself by engaging targets with his rifle and treating his wounded lieutenant without stopping the vehicle. He was awarded the Silver Star for exemplary courage under fire.

The 724th Transportation Company is typical of the many units that have served and are now serving in the War on Terrorism. The action of 9 April 2004 was not an exceptional occurrence. Similar engagements happened every day. The Soldiers of the 724th responded as all Soldiers do—in a selfless, professional manner. However, the 724th Transportation Company was exceptional because what Soldiers do in service to the Nation is exceptional.

Source Notes

This section lists sources by page number. Where material appears in a paragraph, both the page number and paragraph number are listed. Boldface indicates titles of vignettes.

1-1   "[Y]ou may fly over a land...": T.R. Fehrenbach, *This Kind of War: A Study in Unpreparedness* (New York: MacMillan, 1963), 427.

1-1   1-5. "The real object...": House, *Annual Reports of the War Department, Fiscal Year Ended June 30, 1899, Report of the Secretary of War,* 56th Congress, 1st session, 1899, Document 2, 45–46.

1-3   1-10. "the new army...": John C. Fitzpatrick, ed., *The Writings of George Washington from the Original Manuscript Sources, 1745–1799*, vol. 4, October, 1775–April, 1776 (Washington DC: Government Printing Office, 1931), 202.

1-4   **Washington at Newburgh—Establishing the Role of the Military in a Democracy**: The American Soldier, 1775, Center for Military History Prints and Posters, The American Soldier, Set No. 3. [Online]. Available http://www.army. mil/cmh/art/P-P/As-3/1775.htm. "Gentlemen, you will permit me...": John C. Fitzpatrick, ed., *The Writings of George Washington from the Original Manuscript Sources, 1745–1799*, vol. 26, January 1, 1783–June 10, 1783 (Washington DC: Government Printing Office, 1938), 222n38. This note also describes Washington's actions at the officers assembly.

1-7   **Meuse-Argonne, 26 September–1 October 1918**: DA Poster 21-49, Hell Fighters! Let's Go! Vignette based on a Center for Military History account. [Online]. Available http://www.army.mil/cmh/art/P-P/USAIA/harlem.htm

1-9   "The Army used to have ...": George C. Marshall, *Warrior's Words: A Quotation Book*, comp. Peter G. Tsouras, (London: Arms and Armour Press, 1992), 265. Marshall said this in 1942.

1-13   **Professionalism in Combat—Beyond the Call of Duty**: Based on the Medal of Honor citation and media reports. Photo by U.S. Army.

1-15   "Discipline is based on pride...": Third Army Letter of Instruction No. 2, 3 Apr 1944. See George S. Patton Jr., *War As I Knew It* (Boston: Houghton-Mifflin, 1947, reprinted 1975), 403.

1-17   **Warrior Ethos—"I will Never Leave a Fallen Comrade."**: Based on the account in Mark Bowden, "Black Hawk Down," chapter 8, *Philadelphia Inquirer* (Nov 23, 1997) and official sources. Photos by U.S. Army.

1-18   "The American soldier is a proud one...": Omar N. Bradley, "American Military Leadership," *Army Information Digest* 8, no. 2 (Feb 1953): 5.

1-21   "Yours is the profession of arms,...": Douglas MacArthur, Speech at West Point, 12 May 1962.

2-1 "Our Nation's cause has always been larger...": George W. Bush, Speech at West Point graduation, 1 June 2002, *Weekly Compilation of Presidential Documents,* vol. 38, April–June 2002, (Washington, DC: U.S. Government Printing Office, 2002), 945.

2-4 "This Nation can afford to be strong...": President John F. Kennedy, Special Message to Congress on the Defense Budget 28 Mar 1961, *Public Papers of the Presidents of the United States: John F. Kennedy, Containing the Public Messages, Speeches, and Statements of the President, January 20 to December 31, 1961* (Washington, DC: U.S. Government Printing Office, 1962), 231.

2-8 "Battles are won by the infantry,...": Omar N. Bradley, Department of the Army Pamphlet 600-65, *Leadership Statements and Quotes* (Washington, DC: U.S. Government Printing Office, 1985), 4.

2-11 **Citizen Soldier—Selfless Service**: Based on information from various media reports. Photograph "Capt. Michael Dugan hangs an American flag from a light pole in front of what is left of the World Trade Center..." by Andrew Savulich. ©*New York Daily News* LP. Photo of Sergeant Engeldrum by the 1-69 Infantry, New York Army National Guard.

4-1 "The condition of the Army today...": Francis J. Harvey and Peter J. Schoomaker, "Statement before the House Armed Services Committee, Washington, DC, February 9, 2005," [Online]. Available http://www.army.mil/leaders/leaders/sa/testimony/20050209HASC.html.

4-6 "We will not be effective ...": Peter J. Schoomaker, Tom Philpot, "The Army's Challenge,". *Military Officer Magazine* 2, no. 11 (November 2004):62.

4-12 "Above all, we must realize..." Ronald W. Reagan, Inaugural Address, *Weekly Compilation of Presidential Documents,* vol. 17, no. 4, Monday, January 26, 1981, *Inauguration of President Ronald Reagan* (Washington, DC: U.S. Government Printing Office, 1981), 4.

4-14 **724th Transportation Company in Iraq**: Based on information provided by the 88th Regional Readiness Command, 506 Roeder Circle, Fort Snelling, MN 55111: The information came from the following sources: Silver Star citation for Specialist Jeremy Church, 724th Transportation Company unit history, and interviews by the 88th Regional Readiness Command public affairs office. Photograph by permission of the 724th Transportation Company Family Readiness Group Web site. www.724transco.citymax.com/page/page/1810557.htm

References

These are the sources quoted or paraphrased in this publication. Military publications are listed by title.

"2004 Army Transformation Roadmap." Washington, DC: Office of the Deputy Chief of Staff, Army Operations, Army Transformation Office. 2004.

"Army Posture Statement." Washington, DC: Office of the Chief of Staff, Army. 2005.

"Army Strategic Planning Guidance." 2005. An overview of the "Army Strategic Planning Guidance was disseminated by the Army Strategic Communications office as, "The Way Ahead: Our Army at War."

Bowden, Mark. "Black Hawk Down," Chapter 8. *Philadelphia Inquirer*. November 23, 1997.

Bradley, Omar N. "American Military Leadership." *Army Information Digest* 8, no. 2 (February 1953): 5–6.

Brownlee, Les, and Peter J. Schoomaker. "Serving a Nation at War: A Campaign Quality Army with Joint and Expeditionary Capabilities." *Parameters* (Summer 2004), 4–23. This article was disseminated by the Army Strategic Communications office as an Army white paper, "Serving a Nation at War: A Campaign Quality Army with Joint and Expeditionary Capabilities."

Department of Defense Directive 5100.1 *Functions of the Department of Defense and Its Major Components*. 1 Aug 2002.

Department of the Army Pamphlet 600-65. *Leadership Statements and Quotes*. 1 Nov 1985.

Fehrenbach, T.R. *This Kind of War: A Study in Unpreparedness*. New York: MacMillan, 1963.

Field Manual 3-0. *Operations*. 14 Jun 2001.

Field Manual 6-0. *Mission Command: Command and Control of Army Forces*. 11 Aug 2003.

Field Manual 22-100. *Army Leadership*. 31 Aug 1999.

Fitzpatrick, John C., ed. *The Writings of George Washington from the Original Manuscript Sources, 1745–1799*. 39 vols. Washington, DC: Government Printing Office, 1931–1944.

Harvey, Francis J. and Peter J. Schoomaker "Statement Before the House Armed Services Committee, Washington, DC, February 9, 2005." [Online]. Available http://www.army.mil/leaders/leaders/sa/testimony/20050209 HASC.html.

Joint Publication 1. *Joint Warfare of the Armed Forces of the United States.* 14 Nov 2000.

Joint Publication 3-0. *Doctrine for Joint Operations.* 10 Sep 2001.

Kennedy, John F. *Public Papers of the Presidents of the United States: John F. Kennedy, Containing the Public Messages, Speeches, and Statements of the President, January 20 to December 31, 1961.* Washington, DC: U.S. Government Printing Office, 1962.

National Defense Strategy of the United States of America. Washington, DC: U.S. Government Printing Office, 2005.

National Military Strategy of the United States of America. Washington, DC: U.S. Government Printing Office, 2005.

National Security Strategy of the United States of America. Washington, DC: U.S. Government Printing Office, 2002.

"Our Army at War—Relevant and Ready…Today and Tomorrow: A Game Plan for Advancing Army Objectives in FY 05 and Beyond: Thinking Strategically." Washington, DC: Office of the Chief of Staff, Army. 28 Oct 2004. Letter of transmittal dated 1 Nov 2004.

Patton, George S., Jr. *War As I Knew It.* Boston: Houghton Mifflin, 1947. Reprint, 1975.

Philpot, Tom. "The Army's Challenge." *Military Officer Magazine* 11, no.2. (November 2004): 60–66.

Tsouras, Peter G., comp. *Warrior's Words: A Quotation Book.* London: Arms and Armour Press, 1992.

U.S. House. *Annual Reports of the War Department, Fiscal Year Ended June 30, 1899, Report of the Secretary of War.* 56th Congress, 1st session, 1899. Document 2.

Weekly Compilation of Presidential Documents. Vol. 17, No. 4, Monday, January 26, 1981, *Inauguration of President Ronald Reagan.* Washington, DC: U.S. Government Printing Office, 1981.

Weekly Compilation of Presidential Documents. Vol. 38, April–June 2002. Washington, DC: U.S. Government Printing Office, 2002.

Weighley, Russell E. *History of the United States Army.* New York: MacMillan Company, 1967.

By Order of the Secretary of the Army:

PETER J. SCHOOMAKER
General, United States Army
Chief of Staff

Official

SANDRA R. RILEY
Administrative Assistant to the
Secretary of the Army
0513905

DISTRIBUTION:
Active Army, Army National Guard, and U.S. Army Reserve: To be distributed in accordance with the initial distribution number 110510G, requirements for FM 1.

This page intentionally left blank.

> *The Army is a strategic instrument of national policy that has served our country well in peace and war for over two centuries.*

Call to Duty—the American Soldier in Service to our Nation.

FM 3-0

OPERATIONS

FEBRUARY 2008

DISTRIBUTION RESTRICTION:
Approved for public release; distribution is unlimited.

HEADQUARTERS
DEPARTMENT OF THE ARMY

*Foreword

Change 1 of FM 3-0 reflects our intention to take advantage of a "Campaign of Learning" across our Army to adapt our concepts, doctrine, and processes more frequently than in the past.

Most of what was published in 2008 endures. Our emphasis remains on developing leaders and Soldiers for full-spectrum operations. We continue to highlight both defeat and stability mechanisms and to stress that we live in an era of persistent conflict.

To these enduring themes, we add several new and important ideas:

- The future operational environment will be characterized by *hybrid threats:* combinations of regular, irregular, terrorist, and criminal groups who decentralize and syndicate against us and who possess capabilities previously monopolized by nation states. These hybrid threats create a more **competitive security environment**, and it is for these threats we must prepare.

- We replace the command and control warfighting function with **mission command**. This change emphasizes both "art" and "science" but places emphasis on the role of commanders in their responsibilities in full-spectrum operations with joint, interagency, intergovernmental, and multinational partners. Mission command highlights the trust, collaboration, initiative, and co-creation of context necessary among leaders in decentralized operations. It mandates that systems and processes must support and enable the leader's responsibility to understand, visualize, decide, direct, lead, and assess.

- Consistent with recent changes in FM 5-0, we add *design* as a leader's cognitive tool to seek to understand complex problems before attempting to solve them. *Design* allows the leader to understand and visualize before deciding and directing.

- We "unburden" the term information operations and regroup tasks under two headings: inform and influence activities (IIA) and cyber/electromagnetic activities. This change allows us to "see ourselves" better both now and into the future.

- We delete the Tennessee chart. This chart portrayed the spectrum of conflict (stable peace to general war) and operational themes (peace operations to irregular war to major combat operations). For a time, it contributed to our understanding of full-spectrum operations. However, it inadvertently established a false dichotomy regarding whether we must prepare for irregular warfare or for major combat operations. In the next revision of FM 3-0, we will sharpen our language regarding full-spectrum operations. We will emphasize our Army's capability to conduct both *combined arms maneuver* and *wide area security*—the former necessary to gain the initiative and the latter necessary to consolidate gains and set conditions for stability operations, security force assistance, and reconstruction. We must be capable of both and often simultaneously. That's what defines us as truly capable of full-spectrum operations. Moreover, in a competitive security environment, the kinds of threats we will confront in executing these two broad responsibilities are likely to be increasingly indistinguishable.

For this document to mean anything, it must come alive in classrooms, training centers, and officer and noncommissioned officer professional developments. Learn from it, adhere to it, and continue to help us adapt it to the complex and competitive security environments in which we operate.

Victory Starts Here!

MARTIN E. DEMPSEY
General, U.S. Army
Commanding General
U.S. Army Training and Doctrine Command

Operations

1. Change 1 to FM 3-0, 27 February 2008, is updated to align with FM 2-0, FM 5-0, and FM 3-28.

2. This change modifies the Army operational concept to emphasize mission command, the civil support tasks, and the discussion of operational art.

3. This change replaces the command and control element of combat power and warfighting function with mission command.

4. This change eliminates chapter 7, Information Superiority, and relocates the discussion of information-related tasks; intelligence, surveillance, and reconnaissance; and knowledge management to other chapters. Chapter 7 in this change is now titled Operational Art.

5. This change adds an addendum to appendix D summarizing the changes.

6. Significant changes are marked with an asterisk at the beginning of the discussion (*).

Remove Old Pages	Insert New Pages
pages Foreword through 7-16	pages Foreword through 7-16
page 8-7	page 8-7
	pages D-7 through D-9
Source Notes-1 through Index-16	Source Notes-1 through Index-7

7. File this transmittal sheet in front of the publication for reference purposes.

DISTRUBUTION RESTRICTION: Approved for public release; distribution is unlimited.

By order of the Secretary of the Army:

GEORGE W. CASEY, JR.
General, United States Army
Chief of Staff

Official:

JOYCE E. MORROW
Administrative Assistant to the
Secretary of the Army
1102004

DISTRIBUTION:
Active Army, the Army National Guard, and the U.S. Army Reserve: To be distributed in accordance with the initial distribution number 110512, requirements for FM 3-0.

Field Manual
No. 3-0

Headquarters
Department of the Army
Washington, DC, 27 February 2008

OPERATIONS

Contents

Distribution Restriction: Approved for public release; distribution is unlimited.

*This publication supersedes FM 3-0, 14 June 2001.

22 February 2011

Figures

Tables

**This publication is available at
Army Knowledge Online (AKO) (www.us.army.mil)
and the Reimer Digital Library (RDL) at
(www.adtdl.army.mil)**

Preface

FM 3-0 is one of the Army's two capstone doctrinal publications; the other is FM 1, *The Army*. FM 3-0 presents overarching doctrinal guidance and direction for conducting operations. The seven updated chapters that make up this edition of *Operations* constitute the Army's view of how it conducts prompt and sustained operations on land and sets the foundation for developing the other fundamentals and tactics, techniques, and procedures detailed in subordinate field manuals. FM 3-0 also provides operational guidance for commanders and trainers at all echelons and forms the foundation for Army Education System curricula:

- Chapter 1 establishes the context of land operations in terms of a global environment of persistent conflict, the operational environment, and unified action. It discusses the Army's expeditionary and campaign capabilities while emphasizing that it is Soldiers and leaders who remain the Army's most important advantage. *Change 1 adds a brief discussion of hybrid threats and implications for Army operations.*

- Chapter 2 describes a spectrum of conflict extending from stable peace to general war. From that spectrum, it establishes five operational themes into which various joint operations fit. This chapter helps Army leaders to understand and differentiate between the requirements of diverse joint operations such as peacekeeping and counterinsurgency. It shapes supporting doctrine for each operational theme. *Change 1 eliminates some graphics used to illustrate the continuum of operations. It also expands and clarifies the discussion of major combat operations.*

- Chapter 3 is the most important chapter in the book; it describes the Army's operational concept—full spectrum operations. Full spectrum operations seize, retain, and exploit the initiative and achieve decisive results through combinations of four elements: offense, defense, and stability or civil support. It establishes mission command as the preferred method of exercising battle command. *Change 1 moves the discussion of mission command from the section within the operational concept to chapters 4, 5, and 6 to consolidate and emphasize mission command. The discussion of stability operations now includes security force assistance. Change 1 also modifies the discussion of civil support tasks from three tasks to four to conform to the newly published Army field manual on civil support operations, FM 3-28.*

- Chapter 4 addresses combat power, the means by which Army forces conduct full spectrum operations. It replaces the older battlefield operating systems ("BOS") with six warfighting functions, bound by leadership and employing information as the elements of combat power. Combined arms and mutual support are the payoff. *Change 1 replaces the command and control element of combat power and warfighting function with mission command. The discussion of the intelligence warfighting function now includes sections moved from the old chapter 7. This chapter defines mission command warfighting function. The mission command warfighting function now includes a discussion of inform and influence and cyber/electromagnetic activities. These activities and others replace the previously discussed "information tasks" deleted from the old "information superiority" chapter.*

- Chapter 5 reviews the principles of command and control and their affects on the operations process—plan, prepare, execute, and assess. The emphasis is on commanders and the central role that they have in battle command. Commanders understand, visualize, describe, direct, lead, and continually assess. *Change 1 provides a rewritten chapter 5 that discusses the commander and defines mission command. Chapter 5 discusses the four commander's tasks under mission command. It discusses how the commander drives the operations process and how the commander understands, visualizes, describes, directs, leads, and assesses operations. Chapter 5 describes how the commander builds teams, and how the commander leads inform and influence activities.*

- Chapter 6 discusses operational art, including operational design and the levels of war. Operational art represents the creative aspect of operational-level command. It is the expression of informed vision across the levels of war. *Change 1 provides a new chapter 6 on the science of control. It discusses the three staff tasks under mission command, which are conducting the operations process, conducting knowledge management and information management, and conducting inform and influence and cyber/electromagnetic activities.*

- Chapter 7 is about information superiority, particularly the five Army information tasks, purpose, and staff responsibility. *Change 1 eliminates the chapter on information superiority. It is now an updated discussion of the previous chapter 6. It provides an updated discussion of operational art to emphasize design (as discussed in FM 5-0).*

- Chapter 8 discusses the requirement for Army forces in joint campaigns conducted across intercontinental distances. It frames the challenges created by the requirement for Army forces in terms of strategic and operational reach. *Change 1 retains chapter 8 without other substantial change.*

Four appendixes complement the body of the manual. The principles of war and operations are in appendix A. Command and support relationships are in appendix B. A brief description of modular force is in appendix C. A discussion of the purpose of doctrine in the Army is in appendix D. *This appendix includes a chapter-by-chapter summary of the important changes, including those made in change 1, to FM 3-0.* It also includes tables listing new, modified, and rescinded terms for which this manual is the proponent.

Army doctrine is consistent and compatible with joint doctrine. FM 3-0 links landpower doctrine to joint operations doctrine as expressed in joint doctrinal publications, specifically, JP 3-0, *Doctrine for Joint Operations*. FM 3-0 also uses text and concepts developed with North Atlantic Treaty Organization partners.

The principal audience for FM 3-0 is the middle and senior leadership of the Army, officers in the rank of major and above who command Army forces in major operations and campaigns or serve on the staffs that support those commanders. It is also applicable to the civilian leadership of the Army.

FM 3-0 uses joint terms where applicable. Most terms with joint or Army definitions are in both the glossary and the text. *Glossary references*: Terms for which FM 3-0 is the proponent publication (the authority) have an asterisk in the glossary. *Text references*: Definitions for which FM 3-0 is the proponent publication are in boldfaced text. These terms and their definitions will be in the next revision of FM 1-02. For other definitions in the text, the term is italicized and the number of the proponent publication follows the definition.

"Adversaries" refers to both enemies and adversaries when used in joint definitions.

"Opponents" refers to enemies and adversaries.

FM 3-0 applies to the Active Army, Army National Guard/Army National Guard of the United States, and U.S. Army Reserve unless otherwise stated.

This manual contains copyrighted material.

Headquarters, U.S. Army Training and Doctrine Command, is the proponent for this publication. The preparing agency is the Combined Arms Doctrine Directorate, U.S. Army Combined Arms Center. Send written comments and recommendations on a DA Form 2028 (Recommended Changes to Publications and Blank Forms) to Commander, U.S. Army Combined Arms Center and Fort Leavenworth, ATTN: ATZL-MCK-D (FM 3-0), 300 McPherson Avenue, Fort Leavenworth, KS 66027-2337; by e-mail to leav-cadd-web-cadd@conus.army.mil; or submit an electronic DA Form 2028.

Acknowledgments

The copyright owners listed here have granted permission to reproduce material from their works. Other sources of quotations are listed in the source notes.

On War, by Carl von Clausewitz, edited and translated by Michael Howard and Peter Paret. Reproduced with permission of Princeton University Press. Copyright © 1984.

*Introduction to Change 1, FM 3-0

This is change 1 to the fifteenth edition of the Army's capstone operations manual. FM 3-0, *Operations*, initiated a comprehensive change in Army doctrine by capturing the experience of Soldiers over 7 years of combat and using it to change the way the Army conceptualized operations. It established full spectrum operations—simultaneous offensive, defensive, stability, or civil support operations—as the central tenet of how the Army applies its capabilities. The Army's operational concept of full spectrum operations remains valid.

As in 2008, the Army continues to operate in Afghanistan and Iraq, as well as in other operations worldwide. The Army's experience illustrates that the United States cannot accurately predict the nature, location, or duration of the next conflict. The operational environment remains extremely fluid, with continually changing coalitions, alliances, partnerships, and actors. It is unforgiving of leaders who are overly dependent on technology or are incapable of acting independently amid uncertainty and complexity.

Change 1 to FM 3-0 reflects an evolving understanding of the impact of what is now 9 years of persistent conflict on how the Army operates. FM 3-0 emphasizes people over technology, focusing on initiative and responsibility at lower levels of command. Understanding the operational environment, as well as the problem to be solved, requires a methodology that expands beyond the military decisionmaking process. The emergence of hybrid threats has added to the uncertainty of the operational environment. Additionally, creating teams among modular forces to work closely with joint, interagency, intergovernmental, and multinational assets is critical to mission success. When working with host-nation partners, teamwork requires more personal cooperation than military command. Finally, the ability to convey clear and succinct messages to target audiences is often as important as the ability to deliver lethal combat power.

As a result, the traditional framework of command and control that the Army relied on for many years is no longer adequate to ensure success in full spectrum operations. The traditional framework assumed—

- Only higher echelons would work with joint, interagency, intergovernmental, and multinational agencies and assets.
- A high level of understanding of the operational environment and the problems to be solved.
- Relatively stable organizations with fixed structures that ensured teamwork and cohesion.
- Informing and influencing various audiences were primarily a government, not a military, function.
- Technological solutions were needed to solve complex problems.
- Smaller, more capable forces would know enough about the enemy to apply combat power precisely and effectively.
- The higher the echelon, the greater the understanding of the operational environment.

More importantly, the traditional framework failed to stress that the commander is the most important actor in operations. Commanders, in their relationships with the population or with joint, interagency, intergovernmental, and multinational partners, drive mission accomplishment.

Commanders must be capable of acting independently amid uncertainty, complexity, and ambiguity. The operational environment will place a premium on decentralization of authority and on the distribution of combined arms capabilities that enable leaders to develop the situation through action, consistent with their commander's intent. It also requires commanders who are comfortable with risk and who can command effectively when their networks are degraded. To assist commanders and leaders, the Army recognizes that doctrine requires a change that better defines the art of command and the science of control in full spectrum operations.

Change 1 to FM 3-0 recognizes the primacy of commanders and leaders in military operations. Thus, mission command replaces the command and control warfighting function as the means for leaders to integrate the other warfighting functions, while focusing on the command of people in operations instead of processes and technological solutions. Concurrently, mission command provides a methodology to create a more thorough understanding of the operational environment and of the problems to be addressed. Within mission command, commanders build teams and establish themes and messages to drive processes and procedures. Mission command enables an operationally adaptive force that anticipates transitions; accepts risks to create opportunities; informs friendly and joint, interagency, intergovernmental, and multinational partners; and influences neutrals, adversaries, and enemies. The ultimate outcome results in successful full spectrum operations.

In addition to replacing the command and control warfighting function with mission command, change 1 of FM 3-0 also accounts for changes in the operational environment. These changes include—

- Updating the operational environment to address hybrid threats.
- Adding security force assistance to the discussion of civil security under stability operations.
- Restructuring the civil support tasks by adding chemical, biological, radiological, nuclear, and high-yield explosives (CBRNE) consequence management as the fourth civil support task.
- Revising chapter 7, Operational Art, to match the discussion of design in FM 5-0.
- Updating the continuum of operations to eliminate the intermediate points, adding the role and nature of deterrence, and eliminating figure 2-2, the spectrum of conflict and operational themes (known as the Tennessee chart), and figure 3-4, examples of combining the elements of full spectrum operations within operational themes.
- Replacing the five information tasks with inform and influence and cyber/electromagnetic activities.

The demands placed on leaders have expanded dramatically in an era of persistent conflict among populations. The need to empower them with skills, knowledge, resources, and freedom of action is critical to success. Mission command provides a means for both senior and junior leaders to create a more thorough understanding of the operational environment and of the problems to be addressed. It highlights the initiative necessary for success in today's operational environment. Mission command emphasizes the commander in operations. It encourages collaboration and dialog among commanders and leaders as a means of developing an environment of mutual trust and understanding that enables agile and adaptive organizations to succeed in full spectrum operations.

Introduction

This is the fifteenth edition of the Army's capstone operations manual. Its lineage goes back to the first doctrine written for the new American Army, Baron von Steuben's 1779 *Regulations for the Order and Discipline of the Troops of the United States*. Today, as with each previous version of *Operations*, FM 3-0 shapes all of Army doctrine, while influencing the Army's organization, training, materiel, leadership and education, and Soldier concerns. But its contents are not truly capstone doctrine until Army forces internalize it. This requires education and individual study by all Army leaders. And it requires more: Army leaders must examine and debate the doctrine, measuring it against their experience and strategic, operational, and tactical realities. They must also recognize that while FM 3-0 can inform them of how to think about operations, it cannot provide a recipe for what to do on the battlefield.

Always dynamic, Army doctrine balances between the Army's current capabilities and situation with its projected requirements for future operations. At the same time, Army doctrine forecasts the immediate future in terms of organizational, intellectual, and technological developments. This requirement is particularly challenging for this edition of FM 3-0. The Army is heavily committed in conflicts in Afghanistan and Iraq and to countering terrorism worldwide. How long this will remain the case remains unknown. Therefore, this edition promulgates doctrine for Army operations in those conflicts. However, America's strategic requirements remain global. FM 3-0 does not focus exclusively on current operations, regardless of how pressing their requirements. The Army's experience makes it clear that no one can accurately predict the nature, location, or duration of the next conflict. So this doctrine also addresses the needs of an Army responsible for deploying forces promptly at any time, in any environment, against any adversary. This is its expeditionary capability. Once deployed, the Army operates for extended periods across the spectrum of conflict, from stable peace through general war. This is its campaign capability.

This edition of FM 3-0 reflects Army thinking in a complex period of prolonged conflicts and opportunities. The doctrine recognizes that current conflicts defy solution by military means alone and that landpower, while critical, is only part of each campaign. Success in future conflicts will require the protracted application of all the instruments of national power—diplomatic, informational, military, and economic. Because of this, Army doctrine now equally weights tasks dealing with the population—stability or civil support—with those related to offensive and defensive operations. This parity is critical; it recognizes that 21st century conflict involves more than combat between armed opponents. While defeating the enemy with offensive and defensive operations, Army forces simultaneously shape the broader situation through nonlethal actions to restore security and normalcy to the local populace.

Soldiers operate among populations, not adjacent to them or above them. They often face the enemy among noncombatants, with little to distinguish one from the other until combat erupts. Killing or capturing the enemy in proximity to noncombatants complicates land operations exponentially. Winning battles and engagements is important but alone is not sufficient. Shaping the civil situation is just as important to success. Informing the public and influencing specific audiences are central to mission accomplishment. Within the context of current operations worldwide, stability operations are often as important as—or more important than—offensive and defensive operations. Department of Defense policy states:

> *Stability operations are a core U.S. military mission that the Department of Defense shall be prepared to conduct with proficiency equivalent to combat operations. The Department of Defense shall be prepared to: (1) Conduct stability operations activities throughout all phases of conflict and across the range of military operations, including in combat and non-combat environments.*

DODI 3000.05

Because of this, full spectrum operations—simultaneous offensive, defensive, and stability or civil support operations—is the primary theme of this manual. This continues a major shift in Army doctrine that began with FM 3-0 (2001) and now is embedded in joint doctrine as well. Stability and civil support operations cannot be something that the Army conducts in "other than war" operations. Army forces must address the civil situation directly and continuously, combining tactical tasks directed at noncombatants with tactical tasks directed against the enemy. These tasks have evolved from specialized ancillary activities—civil-military operations—into a central element of operations equal in importance to the offense and defense—stability and civil support. The nature of the mission determines the appropriate weighting and combination of tasks.

The emergence of full spectrum operations drives key changes in capstone doctrine. The Army established full spectrum operations in FM 3-0 (2001), shifting sharply from an "either-or" view of combat and other operations to an inclusive doctrine that emphasized the essentiality of nonlethal actions with combat actions. This edition of FM 3-0 continues that development. In FM 3-0 (2001), stability operations were "other" joint missions stated in an Army context. The current edition describes stability operations as tactical tasks applicable at all echelons of Army forces deployed outside the United States. In addition, civil support operations are also defined as tactical-level tasks, similar to stability tasks but conducted in the very different operational environment of the United States and its territories.

The impact of the information environment on operations continues to increase. What Army forces do to achieve advantages across it—information superiority—significantly affects the outcome of operations. Consequently, FM 3-0 revises how the Army views information operations and staff responsibility for associated Army information tasks. Other changes include replacing the battlefield operating systems with the warfighting functions and adding the spectrum of conflict with related operational themes.

Chaos, chance, and friction dominate land operations as much today as when Clausewitz wrote about them after the Napoleonic wars. In this environment, an offensive mindset—the predisposition to seize, retain, and exploit the initiative to positively change the situation—makes combat power decisive. The high quality of Army leaders and Soldiers is best exploited by allowing subordinates maximum latitude to exercise individual and small-unit initiative. Tough, realistic training prepares leaders for this, and FM 3-0 prescribes giving them the maximum latitude to accomplish the mission successfully. This requires a climate of trust in the abilities of superior and subordinate alike. It also requires leaders at every level to think and act flexibly, constantly adapting to the situation. Subordinates' actions are guided by the higher commander's intent, but not circumscribed by excessive control. This is a continuing tension across the Army, aggravated by advanced information systems that can provide higher commanders with the details of lower echelon operations. The temptation for senior leaders to micromanage subordinates is great, but it must be resisted.

Despite the vital importance of nonlethal action to change the civil situation, FM 3-0 recognizes that the Army's primary purpose is deterrence, and should deterrence fail, decisively winning the Nation's wars by fighting within an interdependent joint team. America is at war and should expect to remain fully engaged for the next several decades in a persistent conflict against an enemy dedicated to U.S. defeat as a nation and eradication as a society. This conflict will be waged in an environment that is complex, multidimensional, and rooted in the human dimension. This conflict cannot be won by military forces alone; it requires close cooperation and coordination of diplomatic, informational, military, and economic efforts. Due to the human nature of the conflict, however, landpower will remain important to the military effort and essential to victory. FM 3-0 considers the nature of today's enemies as well as a wide range of other potential threats. It contains doctrine that seeks nothing less than victory for the United States—now and in the future.

As with all previous Army capstone doctrine, this doctrine provides direction for the Army and reflects its progress through the years. Like the manual that emerged from Valley Forge, it reflects the lessons learned from combat experience and addresses strategic, operational, and tactical realities. Baron von Steuben's doctrine allowed for the creation of forces capable of standing against the British Army, the world's best, by giving the Continental Army the skills necessary to win. Then, as now, success depended on the determination of well-trained Soldiers, the quality of their small-unit leadership, and the abilities of their commanders.

Chapter 1

The Operational Environment

Military operations occur within a complex framework of environmental factors that shape their nature and affect their outcomes. These operations require commanders who understand the strategic and operational environments and their relevance to each mission. This understanding includes specific traits of the particular operational environment to each mission and how essential elements of the environment shape how Army forces conduct operations. This chapter discusses the operational environment as the basis for understanding the Army's doctrine for the conduct of land operations. It addresses these operations, emphasizing the Army's expeditionary and campaign qualities and the integral role of Army forces in unified actions—joint, interagency, and multinational undertakings that execute campaigns and major operations.

INSTABILITY AND PERSISTENT CONFLICT

1-1.   An *operational environment* is a composite of the conditions, circumstances, and influences that affect the employment of capabilities and bear on the decisions of the commander (JP 3-0). While they include all enemy, adversary, friendly, and neutral systems across the spectrum of conflict, they also include an understanding of the physical environment, the state of governance, technology, local resources, and the culture of the local population. This doctrine pertains in an era of complex global, regional, and local change leading to both opportunities and risks. The risk component of this change manifests in certain trends that drive instability and a continuing state of persistent conflict. ***Persistent conflict* is the protracted confrontation among state, nonstate, and individual actors that are increasingly willing to use violence to achieve their political and ideological ends.** Some important trends that affect ground force operations in an era of persistent conflict include—

- Globalization.
- Technology.
- Demographic changes.
- Urbanization.
- Resource demands.
- Climate change and natural disasters.
- Proliferation of weapons of mass destruction and their effects.
- Failed or failing states.

1-2.   Experts predict globalization will continue to support the exportation of terrorism worldwide. Interdependent economies have enabled great wealth. The benefits of this wealth remain concentrated in the hands of a few while many bear the risks of failure. This unequal distribution of wealth often creates *have* and *have-not* conditions that can spawn conflict. This dichotomy appears between developed nations in the northern hemisphere and developing nations to their south and in the southern hemisphere. By 2015, experts project that up to 2.8 billion people—almost exclusively in economic have-not areas in developing nations—will live below the poverty level. These people are more vulnerable to recruitment by extremist groups. Globalization has also contributed to the rise of nonstate actors to economic, informational, and even military and diplomatic positions rivaling or exceeding those of states. The decline in state power and influence makes diplomatic interaction more difficult and complex. Globalization has already left several states behind, and more nations will lag in the increasing tempo of globalization. As a result, their populations will both suffer and become more apt to embrace radical ideologies to express their frustration and increase their desire, if not ability, to share in global prosperity.

1-3.   Globalization has enabled a greater diffusion of technology. Often, adversaries use innovations—that improve the quality of life and livelihood—to destroy lives. It would seem that technology evolved with an asymmetric advantage of developed nations. They have greater access to research facilities to develop and innovate. Technology also gives nations access to the industrial base. These nations can then mass-produce advanced products and widely distribute them at relatively low costs. The low cost of products, their user-friendly design, and their availability in a global economy makes advanced technology accessible to unstable states as well as extremist organizations. The revolution and proliferation of benefits derived from integrating multidisciplinary nano- and bio-technologies and smart materials potentially promises to improve living conditions. However, nations will not always have these products available at the pace and in the quantities necessary to make them and their benefits as universally available as desired. Such disparity can create another source of friction between the haves and have-nots. Moreover, the proliferation, falling costs, and availability of technologically advanced products—especially expanded information technologies using mobile, wireless, and global fiber-optic networks—enable nonstate adversaries to acquire them.

1-4.   Population growth in the developing world will increase opportunities for instability, radicalism, and extremism. Populations of some less-developed countries will almost double by 2020, most notably in Africa, the Middle East, and South and Southeast Asia. The *youth bulge* created by this growth will be vulnerable to antigovernment and radical ideologies, worsening governance challenges. Middle class populations will grow as well. They will demand improved quality-of-life benefits and more resources to go with their increased wealth. Inability or inequity to distribute wealth will intensify tensions between haves and have-nots. It will likely escalate calls for changes in how to share wealth globally.

1-5.   By 2015, well over half the world's population will live in urban centers, and by 2030, up to 60 percent will live in cities. Many cities are already huge; 15 have populations in excess of 10 million. Eight of these megacities lie near known geological fault lines that threaten natural disaster. These megacities increasingly assume the significance of nation-states, posing similar governance and security concerns. Their urban growth appears more pronounced in developing regions in which states are already more prone to failure. Organized crime and extremist ideological and cultural enclaves flourish in urban terrain, overwhelming and supplanting local governance apparatus. Chronic unemployment, overcrowding, pollution, uneven resource distribution, and poor basic services such as sanitation and health care add to population dissatisfaction and increase the destructive allure of radical ideologies.

1-6.   Demand for energy, water, and food for growing populations will increase competition and, potentially, conflict. Resources—especially water, gas, and oil—are finite. By 2030, energy consumption will probably exceed production. Current sources, investment, and development of alternatives likely will not bridge the gap. A shift to cleaner fuels such as natural gas will find about 60 percent of known reserves concentrated in Russia, Iran, and Qatar. Demand for water doubles every 20 years. By 2015, 40 percent of the world's population will live in water-stressed countries, increasing the potential for competition over a resource that has already led to conflict in the past. The demand for food will increase in direct proportion to the growth in population, but increases in food production will depend upon adequate energy and water resources.

1-7.   Natural disasters will compound already difficult conditions in developing countries. They will cause humanitarian crises, driving regionally destabilizing population migrations and raising potential for epidemic diseases. Desertification occurs at nearly 50–70 thousand square miles per year. Increased consumption of resources, especially in densely populated areas, will increase air, water, and land pollution. Depletion reduces natural replenishment sources as well as intensifies the effects of natural disasters, having increasingly greater impacts on more densely populated areas. Over 15 million people die each year from communicable diseases; these numbers may grow exponentially as urban densities increase.

1-8.   Proliferation of weapons of mass destruction and their effects will increase the potential for catastrophic attacks. These attacks will destabilize and undercut the confidence that spurs global economic development. The threat of the use of weapons of mass destruction is as real as it is deadly. Over 1,100 identified terrorist organizations exist. Some of them, most notably Al Qaeda, actively seek weapons of mass destruction. Since 1993, 662 reported incidents of unauthorized activities surrounding nuclear and radioactive materials occurred. These incidents involved quantities of enriched uranium from military and civilian reactors exceeding 3,700 tons, enough to produce thousands of nuclear weapons. Additionally, some nuclear nations now share technology as a means to earn money and secure influence. For small countries and terrorist organizations, biological weapons convey a similar status as nuclear weapons. Laboratories can easily and cheaply produce many biological and chemical agents. Wider Internet access has made the technologies and processes of developing weapons of mass destruction and their effects readily available to potential adversaries. Further, some states may pursue these programs to ensure their security and prevent forced regime change.

1-9.   Governments of nation-states face increasingly greater challenges in providing effective support to their growing populations. Security, economic prosperity, basic services, and access to resources strain systems designed in an industrial age. Additionally, these governments are unprepared to increase openness intellectually or culturally to address an information age. Compounding this inability to adapt, nation-state governments find themselves pitted against who have made the shift and are already exploiting it to gain support of local populaces. These adversaries can include criminal organizations, extremist networks, private corporate enterprises, and increasingly powerful megacities. Stability, not the form of governance, will be paramount. The problem of failed or failing states can result in new safe havens in which adversaries can thrive.

INFLUENCES ON THE OPERATIONAL ENVIRONMENT

1-10. The operational environment of the future will be complicated by globalization, population growth, inadequate resources, climate change, inadequate governance, and the spread of lethal weapons. The driving trends discussed in paragraphs 1-1 through 1-9 create a useable forecast of persistent conflict. The international nature of commercial and academic efforts could also have dramatic impacts. The complexity of the operational environment will push future operations to occur across the spectrum of conflict.

1-11. The operational environment of the future will be an arena in which operational goals are attained or lost by not only the use of highly lethal force but also by how quickly units can establish and maintain a state of stability. The operational environment will remain a dirty, frightening, physically and emotionally draining one. Death and destruction will result from environmental conditions creating humanitarian crisis as well as conflict itself. The high lethality and range of advanced weapons systems and tendency of enemies to operate among the population will increase the risk to combatants and noncombatants dramatically. All enemies, state or nonstate, regardless of technological or military capability, will likely use every political, economic, informational, and military measure at their disposal. In addition, the operational environment will expand to areas historically immune to battle, including the continental United States and the territory of multinational partners, especially urban areas. In fact, the operational environment will probably include areas not defined by geography, such as cyberspace. Computer network attacks will span borders, enabling antagonists to hit anywhere, anytime. With the exception of cyberspace, units will conduct all operations among the people and will measure outcomes in terms of effects on populations.

1-12. The operational environment will become extremely fluid. With continually changing coalitions, alliances, partnerships, and actors, interagency and joint operations will have to adjust to the intricate range of players occupying the environment. International news organizations using new information and communications technologies will no longer depend on states to access the area of operations and will more greatly sway how the public views operations. News organizations will have satellites or their own unmanned aerial reconnaissance platforms from which to monitor the scene. Secrecy will be difficult to maintain, making operations security more vital than ever. Finally, complex cultural, demographic, and physical environmental factors will be present, adding to the fog of war. Such factors include humanitarian crises, ethnic and religious differences, and complex and urban terrain, which often become major centers of gravity and a haven for potential threats. The operational environment will remain interconnected, dynamic, and extremely volatile.

THE CHANGING NATURE OF THE THREAT

1-13. Threats are nation-states, organizations, people, groups, or conditions that can damage or destroy life, vital resources, or institutions. States, nations, transnational actors, and nonstate entities will continue to challenge and redefine the global distribution of power, the concept of sovereignty, and the nature of warfare. Preparing for and managing these threats requires employing all instruments of national power—diplomatic, informational, military, and economic. Threats fit a range of four major categories: traditional, irregular, catastrophic, and disruptive. While helpful in describing threats the Army will most likely face, these categories or challenges do not define the nature of the adversary. In fact, adversaries may combine any and all of these challenges to achieve a desired effect against the United States.

1-14. Traditional threats emerge from states employing recognized military capabilities and forces in understood forms of military competition and conflict. In the past, the United States optimized its forces for this challenge. Currently the United States possesses the world's preeminent conventional and nuclear forces, but this status is not guaranteed. Many nations maintain powerful conventional forces, and not all are friendly to the United States. Some potentially hostile adversaries possess weapons of mass destruction. Although these adversaries may not actively seek armed confrontation and will actively avoid U.S. military strength, their activities can provoke regional conflicts that threaten U.S. interests. Deterrence therefore remains the first aim of the joint force. Should deterrence fail, and some evidence shows that deterrence is less able to accomplish this goal, the United States strives to maintain capabilities to overmatch any combination of enemy conventional and unconventional forces.

1-15. Irregular threats are those posed by an opponent employing unconventional, asymmetric methods and means to counter traditional U.S. advantages. A weaker enemy often uses irregular warfare to exhaust the U.S. collective will through protracted conflict. Irregular warfare includes such means as terrorism, insurgency, and guerrilla warfare. Economic, political, informational, and cultural initiatives usually accompany and may even be the chief means of irregular attacks on U.S. influence.

1-16. Catastrophic threats involve the acquisition, possession, and use of chemical, biological, radiological, and nuclear weapons, also called weapons of mass destruction, and their effects. Possession of these weapons gives an enemy the potential to inflict sudden and catastrophic effects. The proliferation of related technology has made this threat more likely than in the past.

1-17. Disruptive threats involve an enemy using new technologies that reduce U.S. advantages in key operational domains. For example, U.S. forces depend on battlefield networks to generate combined arms effects. An advanced cybernetic attack may degrade or usurp automated systems, leaving no means of identifying the problem and making countermeasures ineffective. Disruptive threats can employ such different methods and technology that the target fails to understand the nature of the threat. The allied exploitation of the German ENIGMA code machines provides an example. Because the Germans could not conceive that human intellect and computer technology could break their top codes, they enacted countermeasures to every possible threat except the one that occurred.

1-18. Adversaries seek to create an advantage over U.S. forces by combining traditional, irregular, catastrophic, and disruptive capabilities. These combined threats change the nature of the conflict, enabling adversaries to use capabilities for which the United States is least prepared. Adversaries seek to interdict U.S. forces attempting to enter any area of crisis. If U.S. forces successfully gain entry, adversaries often engage them in complex terrain and urban environments to offset U.S. advantages. Methods used by adversaries include dispersing their forces into small, mobile combat teams—combined only when required to strike a common objective—and becoming invisible by blending in with the local population.

1-19. U.S. forces expect threats to use the environment and rapidly adapt. Extremist organizations adopt state-like qualities using the media, technology, and their position within a state's political, military, and social infrastructures to their advantage. Their operations grow more sophisticated, combining conventional, unconventional, irregular, and criminal tactics. They focus on creating conditions of instability, seek to alienate legitimate forces from the population, and employ global networks to expand local operations. Threats employ advanced information operations and use violence indiscriminately.

1-20. Future conflicts will much more likely to be fought *among* the people instead of *around* the people. This fundamentally alters how Soldiers can apply force to achieve success in a conflict. Enemies will increasingly seek populations within which to hide for protection, preparation, and refuge. They use populations as protection against the proven attack and detection means of U.S. forces, in preparation for attacks against communities, and as refuge from U.S. strikes against their bases. War remains a battle of wills—a contest for dominance over people. The essential struggle of the future conflict will occur where people live and will require U.S. security dominance to extend across the population.

*THE EMERGENCE OF HYBRID THREATS

1-21. The term hybrid threat has recently evolved to capture the seemingly increased complexity of operations and the multiplicity of actors involved. While the existence of innovative enemies is not new, today's hybrid threats demand that U.S. forces prepare for a range of possible threats simultaneously. The conditions associated with persistent conflict can form a very capable hybrid threat. In either case, close combat is as violent as major combat operations, even when the opponent is an irregular force.

1-22. **A *hybrid threat* is the diverse and dynamic combination of regular forces, irregular forces, criminal elements, or a combination of these forces and elements all unified to achieve mutually benefitting effects.** Hybrid threats combine regular forces governed by international law, military tradition, and custom with unregulated irregular forces that act with no restrictions on violence or their targets. These forces could include militias, terrorists, guerillas, and criminals. Such forces combine their abilities to use and transition between regular and irregular tactics and weapons. These abilities enable hybrid threats to capitalize on perceived vulnerabilities making them particularly effective.

1-23. These forces may cooperate in the context of pursuing their own organizational objectives. For example, criminal elements may steal parts for a profit while at the same time compromising the readiness of an adversary's combat systems. Militia forces may defend their town with exceptional vigor as a part of a complex defensive network. Hybrid threats may use the media, technology, and their position within a state's political, military, and social infrastructures to their advantage. Hybrid threats creatively adapt, combining sophisticated weapons, command and control, cyber activities, and combined arms tactics to engage U.S. forces when conditions are favorable. Their tactics will often shift. By using insurgent, criminal, and cyber activities, they create instability and hamper U.S. forces and allies. Additionally, hybrid threats use global networks to influence perceptions of the conflict and shape global opinion.

OPERATIONAL AND MISSION VARIABLES

1-24. The operational environment includes physical areas—the air, land, maritime, and space domains. It also includes the information that shapes the operational environment as well as enemy, adversary, friendly, and neutral systems relevant to that joint operation. The operational environment for each campaign or major operation differs and evolves as each campaign or operation progresses. Army forces use operational variables to understand and analyze the broad environment in which they are conducting operations. They use mission variables to focus analysis on specific elements of the environment that apply to their mission.

OPERATIONAL VARIABLES

1-25. Military planners describe the operational environment in terms of operational variables. Operational variables are those broad aspects of the environment, both military and nonmilitary, that may differ from one operational area to another and affect campaigns and major operations. Operational variables describe not only the military aspects of an operational environment but also the population's influence on it. Joint planners analyze the operational environment in terms of six interrelated operational variables: political, military, economic, social, information, and infrastructure. To these variables, Army doctrine adds two more: physical environment and time. As a set, Soldiers often abbreviate these operational variables as PMESII-PT.

1-26. The variables humanize the operational environment. Since land forces operate among populations, understanding human variables is crucial. They help describe each operation's context for commanders and other leaders. Understanding these variables helps commanders appreciate how the military instrument complements the other instruments of national power. Comprehensive analysis of the variables usually occurs at the joint level; Army commanders continue analysis to improve their understanding of their environment. The utility of the operational variables improves with flexible application; complicated human societies defy precise categorization. Whenever possible, commanders and staffs employ specialists in each variable to improve analysis.

Political

1-27. The political variable describes the distribution of responsibility and power at all levels of governance. Political structures and processes enjoy varying degrees of legitimacy with populations from local through international levels. Formally constituted authorities and informal or covert political powers strongly influence events. Political leaders can use ideas, beliefs, actions, and violence to enhance their power and control over people, territory, and resources. Many sources of political motivation exist. These may include charismatic leadership; indigenous security institutions; and religious, ethnic, or economic communities. Political opposition groups or parties also affect the situation. Each may cooperate differently with U.S. or multinational forces. Understanding the political circumstances helps commanders and staffs recognize key organizations and determine their aims and capabilities.

1-28. Understanding political implications requires analyzing all relevant partnerships—political, economic, military, religious, and cultural. This analysis captures the presence and significance of external organizations and other groups, including groups united by a common cause. Examples include private security organizations, transnational corporations, and nongovernmental organizations that provide humanitarian assistance.

1-29. A political analysis also addresses the effect of will. Will is the primary intangible factor; it motivates participants to sacrifice to persevere against obstacles. Understanding what motivates key groups (for example, political, military, and insurgent) helps commanders understand the groups' goals and willingness to sacrifice to achieve their ends.

1-30. The political variable includes the U.S. domestic political environment. Therefore, mission analysis and monitoring the situation includes an awareness of national policy and strategy.

Military

1-31. The military variable includes the military capabilities of all armed forces in a given operational environment. For many states, an army is the military force primarily responsible for maintaining internal and external security. Paramilitary organizations and guerrilla forces may influence friendly and hostile military forces. Militaries of other states not directly involved in a conflict may also affect them. Therefore, analysis should include the relationship of regional land forces to the other variables. Military analysis examines the capabilities of enemy, adversary, host-nation, and multinational military organizations. Such capabilities include—

- Equipment.
- Manpower.
- Doctrine.
- Training levels.
- Resource constraints.
- Leadership.
- Organizational culture.
- History.
- Nature of civil-military relations.

Understanding these factors helps commanders estimate actual capabilities of each armed force. Analysis focuses on each organization's ability to field and use capabilities domestically, regionally, and globally.

Economic

1-32. The economic variable encompasses individual and group behaviors related to producing, distributing, and consuming resources. Specific factors may include the influence of—

- Industrial organizations.
- Trade.
- Development (including foreign aid).
- Finance.

- Monetary policy and conditions.
- Institutional capabilities.
- Geography.
- Legal constraints (or the lack of them) on the economy.

1-33. While the world economy continues to grow more interdependent, local economies differ. These differences significantly influence political choices, including individuals' decisions to support or subvert the existing order. Many factors create incentives or disincentives for individuals and groups to change the economic status quo. These may include—

- Technical knowledge.
- Decentralized capital flows.
- Investment.
- Price fluctuations.
- Debt.
- Financial instruments.
- Protection of property rights.
- Existence of black market or underground economies.

Thus, indicators measuring potential benefits or costs of changing the political-economic order may enhance how commanders understand the social and behavioral dynamics of friendly, adversary, and neutral entities.

Social

1-34. The social variable describes societies within an operational environment. A society is a population whose members are subject to the same political authority, occupy a common territory, have a common culture, and share a sense of identity. Societies are not monolithic. They include diverse social structures. Social structure refers to the relations among groups of persons within a system of groups. It includes institutions, organizations, networks, and similar groups. (FM 3-24 discusses socio-cultural factors analysis and social network analysis.)

1-35. Culture comprises shared beliefs, values, customs, behaviors, and artifacts that society members use to cope with their world and with one another. Societies usually have a dominant culture but may have many secondary cultures. Different societies may share similar cultures, but societal attributes change over time. Changes may occur in any of the following areas:

- Demographics.
- Religion.
- Migration trends.
- Urbanization.
- Standards of living.
- Literacy and nature of education.
- Cohesiveness and activity of cultural, religious, or ethnic groups.

Social networks, social status and related norms, and roles that support and enable individuals and leaders require analysis. This analysis should also address societies outside the operational area whose actions, opinions, or political influence can affect the mission.

1-36. People base their actions on perceptions, assumptions, customs, and values. Cultural awareness helps identify points of friction within populations, build rapport, and reduce misunderstandings. It can improve the commander's insight into individual and group intentions and enhance the unit's effectiveness. However, U.S. forces require training in cultural awareness before deploying to an unfamiliar operational environment and continuous updating while deployed. Commanders develop their knowledge of the societal aspects within their areas of operations to a higher level of cultural awareness. This level allows them to understand how their operations affect the population and prepares them to meet local leaders face-to-face.

Information

1-37. Joint doctrine defines the *information environment* as the aggregate of individuals, organizations, and systems that collect, process, disseminate, or act on information (JP 3-13). The environment shaped by information includes leaders, decisionmakers, individuals, and organizations. The global community's access and use of data, media, and knowledge systems occurs in the information shaped by the operational environment. Commanders use information activities to shape the operational environment as part of their operations.

1-38. Media representatives significantly influence the information that shapes the operational environment. Broadcast and Internet media sources can rapidly disseminate competing views of military operations worldwide. Media coverage influences U.S. political decisionmaking, U.S. popular opinion, and multinational sensitivities. Adversaries often use media coverage to further their aims by controlling and manipulating how audiences perceive a situation's content and context.

1-39. Global telecommunications networks now provide immense amounts of information. Observers and adversaries have unprecedented access to multiple information sources, as the public disclosure of thousands of classified U.S. documents in 2010 demonstrated. They often attempt to influence and counter opinion by providing their own interpretation of events. Televised news and propaganda reach many people. However, in developing countries, information still flows by less sophisticated means such as messengers and graffiti. Commanders need to understand the nature of information flow within their area of operations and apply the best available methods to communicate with the local populace.

Infrastructure

1-40. Infrastructure comprises the basic facilities, services, and installations needed for a society to function. Degrading infrastructure affects the entire operational environment. Infrastructure includes technological sophistication—the ability to conduct research and development and apply the results to civil and military purposes.

1-41. Not all segments of society view infrastructure in the same way. Improvements viewed by some as beneficial may be perceived as a threat by others. For example, introducing cellular networks can help a local economy but may offend influential and conservative local leaders who view it as permitting access to licentious material. Actions affecting infrastructure require a thorough analysis of possible effects.

Physical Environment

1-42. The physical environment includes the geography and manmade structures in the operational area. The following factors affect the physical environment:

- Manmade structures, particularly urban areas.
- Climate and weather.
- Topography.
- Hydrology.
- Natural resources.
- Biological features and hazards.
- Other environmental conditions.

Enemies understand that less complex and open terrain often exposes their military weaknesses. Therefore, they may try to counteract U.S. military advantages by operating in urban or other complex terrain and during adverse weather conditions.

Time

1-43. Time proves a significant consideration in military operations. Analyzing it as an operational variable focuses on how an operation's duration might help or hinder each side. This has implications at every planning level. Enemies with a limited military capability usually view protracted conflict as advantageous to them. They avoid battles and only engage when conditions work overwhelmingly to their favor. This is a strategy of exhaustion. Such a strategy dominated the American Revolution and remains effective today.

The enemy concentrates on surviving and inflicting friendly and civilian casualties over time. Although the military balance may not change, this creates opportunities to affect how domestic and international audiences view the conflict. Conversely, the enemy may attempt to mass effects and achieve decisive results in a short period.

MISSION VARIABLES

1-44. The operational variables directly relate to campaign planning. That does not mean that they are not valuable at the tactical level; they are fundamental to understanding the operational environment to plan at any level, in any situation. The degree to which each operational variable provides useful information depends on the situation and echelon. For example, social and economic variables often receive close analysis as part of enemy and civil considerations at brigade and higher levels. They may affect the training and preparation of small units. However, they may not be relevant to a small-unit leader's mission analysis. That leader may only be concerned with such questions as "Who is the tribal leader for this village?" "Is the electrical generator working?" "Does the enemy have antitank missiles?"

1-45. Upon receipt of a warning order or mission, Army tactical leaders narrow their focus to six mission variables. Mission variables are those aspects of the operational environment that directly affect a mission. They outline the situation as it applies a specific Army unit. The mission variables consist of mission, enemy, terrain and weather, troops and support available, time available, and civil considerations (METT-TC). Army leaders use these categories of relevant information for mission analysis to synthesize operational variables and tactical-level information with local knowledge about conditions relevant to their mission. (Chapter 5 expands the discussion of the mission variables.)

1-46. Army forces interact with people at many levels. In general, anyone in any operational area can qualify as an enemy, an adversary, a supporter, or a neutral. One reason land operations are complex is that all four categories intermix, often with no easy means to distinguish one from another:

- An *enemy* **is a party identified as hostile against which the use of force is authorized.** An enemy is also called a combatant and is treated as such under the law of war.
- An *adversary* is a party acknowledged as potentially hostile to a friendly party and against which the use of force may be envisaged (JP 3-0). Adversaries include members of the local populace who sympathize with the enemy.
- A *supporter* **is a party who sympathizes with friendly forces and who may or may not provide material assistance to them.**
- A *neutral* **is a party identified as neither supporting nor opposing friendly or enemy forces.**

1-47. Incorporating the analysis of the operational variables into METT-TC emphasizes the operational environment's human aspects. This emphasis is most obvious in civil considerations, but it affects the other METT-TC variables as well. Incorporating human factors into mission analysis requires critical thinking, collaboration, continuous learning, and adaptation. It also requires analyzing local and regional perceptions. Many factors influence perceptions of the enemy, adversaries, supporters, and neutrals. These include—

- Language.
- Culture.
- Geography.
- History.
- Education.
- Beliefs.
- Perceived objectives and motivation.
- Media reporting and analysis.
- Personal experience.

UNIFIED ACTION

1-48. *Unified action* is the synchronization, coordination, and/or integration of the activities of governmental and nongovernmental entities with military operations to achieve unity of effort (JP 1). It involves the application of all instruments of national power, including actions of other government agencies and multinational military and nonmilitary organizations. Combatant commanders play a pivotal role in unified actions; however, subordinate commanders also integrate and synchronize their operations directly with the activities and operations of other military forces and nonmilitary organizations in their area of operations. Department of Defense and other government agencies may refer to unified action as being joint, interagency, intergovernmental, multinational, or a combination of these parts.

1-49. Unified action includes joint integration. Joint integration extends the principle of combined arms to operations conducted by two or more Service components. The combination of diverse joint force capabilities generates combat power more potent than the sum of its parts. Joint integration does not require joint command at all echelons. It does, however, require joint interoperability at all levels. Army mission accomplishment links to the national strategic end state through campaigns and major operations.

CAMPAIGNS AND JOINT OPERATIONS

1-50. Joint planning integrates military power with other instruments of national power to achieve the desired military end state. (The *end state* is the set of required conditions that defines achievement of the commander's objectives [JP 3-0].) This planning connects the strategic end state to campaign design and ultimately to tactical missions. Joint force commanders use campaigns and joint operations to translate their operational-level actions into strategic results. Campaigns are always joint operations. (See paragraph 7-12 for more on campaign.)

1-51. Campaigns exploit the advantages of interdependent Service capabilities through unified action. U.S. forces need coordinated, synchronized, and integrated action to reestablish civil authority after joint operations end, even when combat is not required. Effective joint and Army operations require all echelons to perform extensive collaborative planning and understand joint interdependence.

JOINT INTERDEPENDENCE

1-52. Joint interdependence is the purposeful reliance by one Service's forces on another Service's capabilities to maximize the complementary and reinforcing effects of both. Army forces operate as part of an interdependent joint force. Joint capabilities make Army forces more effective than if they operated alone. Combinations of joint capabilities defeat enemy forces by shattering their ability to operate as a coherent, effective whole. Acting with other instruments of national power, joint forces also work to reduce the level of violence and establish security. (Table 1-1 lists areas of joint interdependence that directly enhance Army operations.)

Table 1-1. Areas of joint interdependence

Area	Characteristic
Joint command and control	Integrated capabilities that— • Gain information superiority through improved, fully synchronized, integrated intelligence, surveillance, and reconnaissance; knowledge management; and information management. • Share a common operational picture. • Improve the ability of joint force and Service component commanders to conduct operations.
Joint intelligence	Integrated processes that— • Reduce unnecessary redundancies in collection asset tasking through integrated intelligence, surveillance, and reconnaissance. • Increase processing and analytic capability. • Facilitate collaborative analysis. • Provide global intelligence production and dissemination. • Provide intelligence products that enhance situational understanding by describing and assessing the operational environment.

Area	Characteristic
Joint information operations capabilities	Integrated capabilities, including— • Special technical operations. • Electronic warfare platforms and personnel. • Reachback to strategic assets.
Joint fires	Integrated fire control networks that allow joint forces to deliver coordinated fires from two or more Service components.
Joint air operations	Air and Naval forces able to— • Maneuver aircraft to positions of advantage over the enemy beyond the reach of land forces. • Gain and maintain air superiority that extends the joint force's area of influence by providing freedom from attack as well as freedom to attack. • Support operational and tactical maneuver with lethal and nonlethal fires.
Joint air and missile defense	A comprehensive joint protection umbrella that— • Begins with security of ports of debarkation. • Enables uninterrupted force flow against diverse antiaccess threats. • Extends air and missile defense to multinational partners.
Joint force projection	Strategic and operational lift capabilities and automated planning processes that facilitate strategic responsiveness and operational agility.
Joint sustainment	Deliberate, mutual reliance by each Service component on the sustainment capabilities of two or more Service components. It can reduce redundancies or increase the robustness of operations without sacrificing effectiveness.
Joint space operations	Access to national imagery, communications, satellite, and navigation capabilities that enhance situational awareness and support understanding of the operational environment.

1-53. The other Services rely on Army forces to complement their capabilities. (Table 1-2 lists Army capabilities that enhance other Service component operations.)

Table 1-2. Army capabilities that complement other Services

Security and control of terrain, people, and resources, including—
• Governance over an area or region.
• Protection of key infrastructure and facilities from ground threats.
Land-based ballistic missile defense, including defense against cruise missiles and counterrocket, counterartillery, and countermortar capabilities.
Chemical, biological, radiological, and nuclear operations.
Support to interagency reconstruction efforts, including provision of essential services to an affected population.
Denial of sanctuary through ground maneuver, enabling attack from the air.
Discriminate force application within populated areas.
Inland sustainment of bases and of forces operating from those bases.
Land operations against enemy air and sea bases.
Detainee and enemy prisoner of war operations.
Intelligence support.

1-54. Joint forces also rely on Army forces for support and services as designated in—
• Title 10, United States Code.
• Other applicable U.S. laws.
• Department of Defense directives and instructions.
• Inter-Service agreements.

- Multinational agreements.
- Other applicable authorities and Federal regulations.

This support and other support directed by combatant commanders are broadly defined as "Army support to other Services."

INTERAGENCY COORDINATION AND COOPERATION WITH OTHER ORGANIZATIONS

1-55. Interagency coordination is inherent in unified action. Within the context of Department of Defense involvement, *interagency coordination* is the coordination that occurs between elements of Department of Defense, and engaged US Government agencies for the purpose of achieving an objective (JP 3-0). In addition, unified action involves synchronizing joint or multinational military operations with activities of other government agencies, intergovernmental organizations, nongovernmental organizations, and contractors. During civil support operations, unified action includes state and local government agencies. It occurs at every level—tactical, operational, and strategic.

Civilian Organizations

1-56. Commanders must understand the respective roles and capabilities of civilian organizations in unified action. Other agencies of the Federal government work with the military and are part of a national chain of command under the President of the United States. While this does not guarantee seamless integration, it does provide a legal basis for cooperation. Although experience and professional cultures differ widely, organizations need to recognize and capitalize on the inherent professionalism of each other to develop the teamwork necessary for the campaign.

1-57. Most civilian organizations are not under military control. Nor does the U.S. ambassador or a United Nations commissioner control them. Civilian organizations have different organizational cultures and norms. Some may be willing to work with Army forces; others may not. Thus, personal contact and trust building are essential. Command emphasis on immediate and continuous coordination encourages effective cooperation. Commanders should establish liaison with civilian organizations to integrate their efforts as much as possible with joint and Army operations. Civil affairs units typically establish this liaison.

1-58. Civilian organizations bring resources and capabilities that can help establish host-nation civil authority and capabilities. However, civilian organizations may arrive well after military operations have begun. Therefore, joint and Army forces prepare to establish and maintain order if host-nation authorities cannot do so. Successfully performing these tasks can help secure a lasting peace and facilitate the timely withdrawal of U.S. military forces.

1-59. Army forces provide sustainment and security for civilian organizations when directed, since many of these organizations lack these capabilities. Army forces often provide this support to state and local agencies during civil support operations. (Table 1-3 lists examples of civilian organizations.)

Contractors

1-60. A *contractor* is a person or business that provides products or services for monetary compensation. A contractor furnishes supplies and services or performs work at a certain price or rate based on the terms of a contract (FM 3-100.21). Contracted support includes traditional goods and services support, but may also include interpreter communications, infrastructure, and other related support. In military operations, contractors often provide—

- Life support.
- Construction and engineering support.
- Weapons systems support.
- Security.
- Other technical services.

(FM 3-100.21 contains doctrine for contractors accompanying deployed forces.)

Table 1-3. Definitions and examples of civilian organizations

Category	Definition	Examples
Other government agency	Within the context of interagency coordination, a non Department of Defense agency of the United States Government (JP 1).	• Department of State • Central Intelligence Agency • Federal Bureau of Investigation • National Security Agency • U.S. Agency for International Development
Intergovernmental organization	An organization created by a formal agreement (for example, a treaty) between two or more governments. It may be established on a global, regional, or functional basis for wide-ranging or narrowly defined purposes. Formed to protect and promote national interests shared by member states (JP 3-08).	• United Nations • European Union • North Atlantic Treaty Organization • Organization for Security and Cooperation in Europe • African Union
Nongovernmental organization	A private, self-governing, not-for-profit organization dedicated to alleviating human suffering; and/or promoting education, health care, economic development, environmental protection, human rights, and conflict resolution; and/or encouraging the establishment of democratic institutions and civil society (JP 3-08).	See the United Nations Web site (www.un.org) to research accredited nongovernmental organizations.

MULTINATIONAL OPERATIONS

1-61. *Multinational operations* is a collective term to describe military actions conducted by forces of two or more nations, usually undertaken within the structure of a coalition or alliance (JP 3-16). In multinational operations, all parties agree to the commitment of forces, even if the resources each invests differ. While each nation has its own interests, all nations bring value to the operation. Each national force has distinct capabilities, and each usually contributes to the operation's legitimacy in terms of international or local acceptability.

1-62. An *alliance* is the relationship that results from a formal agreement (for example, treaty) between two or more nations for broad, long-term objectives that further the common interests of the members (JP 3-0). Military alliances, such as the North Atlantic Treaty Organization (NATO), allow partners to establish formal, standard agreements. For example, U.S. forces operate within a highly developed multinational command structure to maintain the armistice on the Korean peninsula. Alliance members strive for interoperability. They field compatible military systems, establish common procedures, and develop contingency plans to meet potential threats.

1-63. A *coalition* is an ad hoc arrangement between two or more nations for common action (JP 5-0). Nations usually form coalitions for focused, short-term purposes. A *coalition action* is a multinational action outside the bounds of established alliances, usually for single occasions or longer cooperation in a narrow sector of common interest (JP 5-0). Coalition actions may be conducted under the authority of a United Nations resolution. Since coalition actions are not structured around formal treaties, a preliminary understanding of the requirements for operating with a specific foreign military may occur through peacetime military engagement. (Paragraph 2-16 defines peacetime military engagement.)

1-64. Agreement among the multinational partners establishes the level of command authority vested in a multinational force commander. The President retains command authority over U.S. forces. Most nations have similar restrictions. However, in certain circumstances, it may be prudent or advantageous to place Army forces under the operational control of a multinational commander. Often, multinational forces have complex lines of command. To compensate for limited unity of command, multinational partners concentrate on achieving unity of effort. Consensus building, rather than direct command authority, is often the key element of successful multinational operations.

1-65. An Army officer assigned to command a multinational force faces many complex demands. These include dealing with cultural issues, different languages, interoperability challenges, national caveats on the use of respective forces, and sometimes underdeveloped command and control. Multinational force commanders must address different national procedures, restrictions, intelligence sharing, and theater sustainment functions. Another command challenge is the multinational commander's limited ability to choose or replace subordinates. Nations assign their contingent leaders. They answer to their national chains of command as well as to the multinational force commander. Every multinational operation differs. Commanders analyze the mission's peculiar requirements to exploit the multinational force's advantages and compensate for its limitations. (FM 6-22 discusses leadership considerations for multinational operations.)

1-66. Multinational sustainment requires detailed planning and coordination. Each nation normally provides a national support element to sustain its deployed forces. However, integrated multinational sustainment may improve efficiency and effectiveness. When directed, an Army theater sustainment command can provide logistic and other support to a multinational force. Integrating the support requirements of several national forces, often spread over considerable distances and across international boundaries, is challenging. Nonetheless, multinational partners can provide additional resources to address the sustainment challenges. For example, a multinational partner may provide a secure intermediate staging base near the operational area. Commanders prefer deploying and employing forces from an intermediate staging base over making a forcible entry from a distant base. This is especially true when the staging base offers a mature infrastructure.

1-67. During multinational operations, U.S. forces establish liaison with assigned multinational forces as soon as possible. Army forces exchange specialized liaison personnel based on mission requirements. Fields requiring specialized liaison may include aviation, fire support, engineer, intelligence, and civil affairs. Exchanging liaison fosters a common understanding of missions and tactics, facilitates a transfer of information, and enhances mutual trust and confidence.

1-68. Missions assigned to multinational units should reflect the capabilities and limitations of each national contingent. Some significant factors include—

- Relative size and mobility.
- Intelligence collection assets.
- Long-range fires capabilities.
- Special operations forces capabilities.
- Organic sustainment capabilities.
- Ability to contribute to theater air and missile defense.
- Training for operations in special environments.
- Willingness and ability to cooperate directly with troops of other nationalities.
- Preparation for defensive operations involving weapons of mass destruction.

1-69. When assigning missions, commanders consider the special skills, language, and rapport forces have with the local population as well as multinational partners' national sensitivities. Multinational commanders may assign host-nation forces home defense or police missions, such as sustainment area and base security. They may entrust air defense, coastal defense, or a special operation to a single member of the multinational force based on that force's capabilities. Commanders consider multinational force capabilities, such as mine clearance, that may exceed U.S. capabilities. (JP 3-16 and FM 3-16 contain doctrine for multinational operations.)

1-70. Since persistent conflict affects a diverse range of international interests, it requires coalitions of nations joined in common cause to defeat a universal foe. All leaders use their patience, understanding, and a willingness to subordinate self to the common good when working within a coalition. Each nation will bring distinct capabilities, strengths, and limitations to future coalitions, and Army forces must be able to operate within them. These coalitions will not always have the same partners, and even when they do, the relative commitments of the partners will vary—sometimes even over time within the same conflict.

THE NATURE OF LAND OPERATIONS

War is thus an act of force to compel our enemy to do our will.

Carl von Clausewitz
On War[1]

1-71. Modern conflict occurs in many domains; however, landpower normally solidifies the outcome, even when it is not the decisive instrument. **Landpower is the ability—by threat, force, or occupation—to gain, sustain, and exploit control over land, resources, and people**. Landpower includes the ability to—

- Impose the Nation's will on an enemy, by force if necessary.
- Establish and maintain a stable environment that sets the conditions for political and economic development.
- Address the consequences of catastrophic events—both natural and manmade—to restore infrastructure and reestablish basic civil services.
- Support and provide a base from which joint forces can influence and dominate the air and maritime domains of an operational environment.

1-72. Several attributes of the land environment affect the application of landpower. These include—

- The requirement to deploy and employ Army forces rapidly.
- The requirement for Army forces to operate for protracted periods.
- The nature of close combat.
- Uncertainty, chance, friction, and complexity.

ARMY FORCES—EXPEDITIONARY AND CAMPAIGN CAPABILITIES

1-73. The initial operations in Afghanistan and Iraq modeled rapid, effective combat operations. U.S. forces rapidly destroyed or dispersed large enemy forces with little friendly loss. However, these operations also demonstrated that the duration and character of military campaigns is unpredictable. Future conflicts will include incomplete planning information, rapid deployments with little or no notice, and sustained operations in austere theaters. Joint, expeditionary warfare focuses on achieving decisive effects. It places a premium on promptly deploying landpower and constantly adapting to each campaign's distinct circumstances as it changes. But swift campaigns, however desirable, are the exception. Whenever objectives involve controlling populations or dominating terrain, campaign success usually requires employing landpower for protracted periods. Therefore, the Army combines expeditionary and campaign qualities to contribute decisive, sustained landpower to unified actions.

1-74. Expeditionary capability is the ability to promptly deploy combined arms forces worldwide into any operational environment and operate effectively upon arrival. Expeditionary operations require the ability to deploy quickly with little notice, shape conditions in the operational area, and operate immediately on arrival. Uncertainty as to the operational area, the possibility of an austere environment, and the need to match forces to available lift drive expeditionary capabilities.

1-75. Expeditionary capabilities assure friends, allies, and foes that the Nation can and will deploy necessary Army forces to the right place at the right time. Forward deployed units, forward positioned capabilities, peacetime military engagement, and force projection—from anywhere in the world—all contribute to expeditionary capabilities. Expeditionary capabilities enable the Army to respond rapidly under unknown conditions to areas with complex and austere operational environments prepared to fight not only on arrival but also through successive operations. Fast deploying and expandable Army forces introduce operationally significant land forces into a crisis on short notice, providing preemptive options to deter, shape, fight, and win if deterrence fails, and to sustain these options for the duration necessary to achieve success. Forces with expeditionary capability are organized and equipped to be modular, versatile, and rapidly deployable with agile institutions capable of supporting them. Rapidly deployed expeditionary force packages provide immediate options for seizing or retaining the operational initiative. With their

---

[1] © 1984. Reproduced with permission of Princeton University Press.

modular capabilities, these forces can be swiftly deployed, employed, and sustained for extended operations without an unwieldy footprint. These forces are tailored for the initial phase of operations, easily task-organized, and highly self-sufficient. Army installations worldwide serve as support platforms for force projection, providing capabilities and information on demand.

1-76. Expeditionary capabilities are more than physical attributes; they begin with a mindset that pervades the force. Soldiers with an expeditionary mindset stand ready to deploy on short notice. They have confidence that they can accomplish any mission. They are mentally and physically prepared to deploy anywhere in the world at any time in any environment against any adversary. Leaders with an expeditionary mindset adapt. They possess the individual initiative needed to accomplish missions through improvisation and collaboration. They prepare mentally to operate within different cultures in any environment. An expeditionary mindset requires developing and empowering adaptive thinkers at all levels, from tactical to strategic.

1-77. Campaign capability is the ability to sustain operations as long as necessary to conclude operations successfully. Forces resolve many conflicts only by altering the conditions that prompted the conflict. This requires combat power and time. The Army's campaign capability extends its expeditionary capability well beyond deploying combined arms forces that are effective upon arrival. This capability enables forces to conduct sustained operations for as long as necessary, adapting to unpredictable and often profound changes in the operational environment as the campaign unfolds. Army forces are organized, trained, and equipped for endurance. Their endurance stems from the ability to create, protect, and sustain landpower—regardless of how far away they deploy, how austere the environment, or how long the combatant commander requires it. It includes taking care not only of Soldiers but also of their families throughout the complete cycle of deployment, employment, and redeployment. Campaign capability involves anticipating requirements across the entire Army and effectively using all available resources—deployed or not. Finally, campaign capability draws on iterative and continuous learning based on operational experience. This requirement extends to training at all echelons, from individual Soldier skills to operational-level collective tasks.

1-78. Campaigning requires a mindset and vision that complements expeditionary requirements. Soldiers understand that no matter how long they are deployed, the Army will take care of them and their families. They are confident that the loyalty they pledge to their units will be returned to them, no matter what happens on the battlefield or in what condition they return home. Tactical leaders understand the effects of protracted land operations on Soldiers and adjust the tempo of operations whenever circumstances allow. Senior commanders plan effective campaigns and major operations. They provide the resources needed to sustain operations, often through the imaginative use of joint capabilities.

1-79. The Army's preeminent challenge is to balance expeditionary agility and responsiveness with the endurance and operational adaptability needed to complete a campaign successfully, no matter what form it eventually takes. Landpower is a powerful complement to the global reach of American airpower and sea power. Prompt deployment of landpower gives joint force commanders options—for either deterrence or decisive action. Once deployed, landpower may be required for months or years. The initially deployed Army force will evolve constantly as the operational environment changes. Operational success depends on flexible employment of Army capabilities together with varying combinations of joint and interagency capabilities.

CLOSE COMBAT

1-80. Only on land do combatants come face-to-face with one another. Thus, the capability to prevail in close combat is indispensable and unique to land operations. It underlies most Army efforts in peace and war. **Close combat is warfare carried out on land in a direct-fire fight, supported by direct, indirect, and air-delivered fires.** Distances between combatants may vary from several thousand meters to hand-to-hand fighting. Close combat is required when other means fail to drive enemy forces from their positions. In that case, Army forces close with them and destroy or capture them. The outcome of battles and engagements depends on Army forces' ability to prevail in close combat. No other form of combat requires as much of Soldiers as it does.

1-81. In urban operations, close combat is frequent. **An *urban operation* is a military operation conducted where manmade construction and high population density are the dominant features**. The complexity of urban terrain and density of noncombatants reduce the effectiveness of advanced sensors and long-range and air-delivered weapons. Thus, a weaker enemy often attempts to negate Army advantages by engaging Army forces in urban environments. Operations in large, densely populated areas require special considerations. From a planning perspective, commanders view cities as both topographic features and dynamic entities containing hostile forces, local populations, and infrastructure. (JP 3-06 and FM 3-06 address these and other aspects of urban operations.)

UNCERTAINTY, CHANCE, AND FRICTION

> *Everything in war is very simple, but the simplest thing is difficult. The difficulties accumulate and end by producing a kind of friction that is inconceivable unless one has experienced war.... This tremendous friction, which cannot, as in mechanics, be reduced to a few points, is everywhere in contact with chance, and brings about effects that cannot be measured, just because they are largely due to chance.*
>
> Carl von Clausewitz
> *On War*[2]

1-82. Uncertainty, chance, and friction have always characterized warfare. On land, they are commonplace. Many factors inherent in land combat combine to complicate the situation. These include—

- Adverse weather.
- Chaos and confusion of battle.
- Complexity.
- Lack of accurate intelligence.
- Errors in understanding or planning.
- Fatigue.
- Misunderstanding among multinational partners.
- An adaptive and lethal enemy.
- Difficult terrain.
- Personality clashes.
- Civilian population.

1-83. Chance further complicates land operations. Things such as weather and other unforeseen events are beyond the control of a commander. For example, in December 1989, an ice storm at Fort Bragg, North Carolina, delayed deployment of some elements of the force invading Panama in Operation Just Cause. In addition to chance occurrences, enemy commanders have their own objectives and time schedules. These often lead to unforeseen encounters. Both enemy and friendly actions often produce unintended consequences. Resulting consequences can further complicate a situation or lead to opportunities.

1-84. Several factors can reduce the effects of uncertainty, chance, and friction. Good leadership, flexible organizations, and dependable technology can lessen uncertainty. Timely, accurate intelligence may reduce the factors affected by chance. And a simple plan combined with continuous coordination might moderate the effects of friction. However, even when operations are going well, commanders make decisions based on incomplete, inaccurate, and contradictory information under adverse conditions. Determination is one means of overcoming friction; experience is another. High morale, sound organization, effective mission command networks and systems, and well-practiced drills all help forces overcome adversity. Uncertainty, chance, and friction also affect the enemy, so commanders should look forward and exploit all opportunities. To achieve tactical, operational, and strategic success, commanders understand the operational environment, effective decisions, and flexibility in spite of adversity.

COMPLEXITY

1-85. Future operational environments will be complex. While this does not necessarily equal a more dangerous environment, Soldiers can expect to encounter more complicated situations than ever before. The nature of land operations has expanded from a nearly exclusive focus on lethal combat with other armies to a complicated mixture of lethal and nonlethal actions directed at enemies, adversaries, and the local population, itself often a complicated mix. The enemy often follows no rules, while Army forces apply U.S. laws and international conventions to every conflict. The operational environment is saturated with information, with almost universal access to telecommunications and the Internet. The media will be ubiquitous. Action and message can no longer remain separate parts of operations because perception is so important to success. False reports, propaganda, rumors, lies, and inaccuracies spread globally faster than military authorities can correct or counter them, forcing Soldiers to cope with the consequences. Senior commanders and political leaders share tactical information in real time. Army forces work with and around various agencies and organizations—governmental, intergovernmental, nongovernmental, and commercial—and usually within a multinational military framework. U.S. forces are the most advanced in the world. They have access to joint capabilities from the lowest echelons equaling unmatched combat power but at a cost in simplicity. Army forces will fight and operate in complex terrain and in cyberspace. These and many other factors increase the complexity of operations and stress every dimension of the Army's capabilities, especially the strength and depth of Army leaders.

SOLDIERS

1-86. Regardless of the importance of technological capabilities, it really comes down to Soldiers who accomplish the mission. Today's dangerous and complex security environment requires Soldiers—men and women of character. Their character and competence represent the foundation of a values-based, trained, and ready Army. Soldiers train to perform tasks while operating alone or in groups. Soldiers and leaders develop the ability to exercise mature judgment and initiative under stress. The Army requires agile and adaptive leaders able to handle the challenges of full spectrum operations in an era of persistent conflict. Army leaders must remain—

- Competent in their core proficiencies.
- Broad enough to operate across the spectrum of conflict.
- Able to operate in joint, interagency, intergovernmental, and multinational environments and use other capabilities in accomplishing their objectives.
- Culturally astute and able to use this awareness and understanding to conduct operations innovatively.
- Courageous enough to see and exploit opportunities in the challenges and complexities of the operational environment.
- Grounded in Army Values and the Warrior Ethos.

THE LAW OF WAR AND RULES OF ENGAGEMENT

1-87. Commanders at all levels ensure their Soldiers operate in accordance with the law of war. The *law of war*—also called the law of armed conflict—is that part of international law that regulates the conduct of armed hostilities (JP 1-02). It is the customary and treaty law applicable to the conduct of warfare on land and to relationships between belligerents and neutral states. The law of war includes treaties and international agreements to which the United States is a party, as well as applicable customary international law. The purposes of the law of war are to—

- Protect both combatants and noncombatants from unnecessary suffering.
- Safeguard certain fundamental human rights of persons who become prisoners of war, the wounded and sick, and civilians.
- Make the transition to peace easier.

(FM 27-10 contains doctrine on the law of war.)

1-88. *Rules of engagement* are directives issued by competent military authority that delineate the circumstances and limitations under which United States forces will initiate and/or continue combat engagement with other forces encountered (JP 1-04). Rules of engagement always recognize a Soldier's inherent right of self-defense. Properly developed rules of engagement fit the situation and are clear, reviewed for legal sufficiency, and included in training. The joint staff and combatant commanders develop rules of engagement. The President and Secretary of Defense review and approve them. Rules of engagement vary between operations and may change during an operation. Adherence to them ensures Soldiers act consistently with international law, national policy, and military regulations.

1-89. The disciplined and informed application of lethal and nonlethal action is a critical contributor to successful Army operations and strategic success. All warfare, but especially irregular warfare, challenges the morals and ethics of Soldiers. An enemy may feel no compulsion to respect international conventions and indeed may commit atrocities with the aim of provoking retaliation in kind. Their propaganda will distort then exploit any loss of discipline on the part of Soldiers and their media will then magnify it. The ethical challenge rests heavily on small-unit leaders who maintain discipline and ensure that the conduct of Soldiers remains within ethical and moral boundaries. There are compelling reasons for this. First, humane treatment of detainees encourages enemy surrender and thereby reduces friendly losses. Conversely, nothing emboldens enemy resistance like the belief that U.S. forces will kill or torture prisoners. Second, humane treatment of noncombatants reduces their antagonism toward U.S. forces and may lead to valuable intelligence. Third, leaders make decisions in action fraught with consequences. If they lack an ethical foundation, those decisions become much, much harder. Finally, Soldiers must live with the consequences of their conduct. Every leader shoulders the responsibility that their subordinates return from a campaign not only as good Soldiers, but also as good citizens with pride in their service to the Nation.

1-90. The Soldier's Rules in AR 350-1 distill the essence of the law of war. They outline the ethical and lawful conduct required of Soldiers in operations. (Table 1-4 lists the Soldier's Rules.)

Table 1-4. The Soldier's Rules

- **Soldiers fight only enemy combatants.**
- **Soldiers do not harm enemies who surrender. They disarm them and turn them over to their superior.**
- **Soldiers do not kill or torture any personnel in their custody.**
- **Soldiers collect and care for the wounded, whether friend or foe.**
- **Soldiers do not attack medical personnel, facilities, or equipment.**
- **Soldiers destroy no more than the mission requires.**
- **Soldiers treat civilians humanely.**
- **Soldiers do not steal. Soldiers respect private property and possessions.**
- **Soldiers should do their best to prevent violations of the law of war.**
- **Soldiers report all violations of the law of war to their superior.**

MEETING THE CHALLENGES OF FULL SPECTRUM OPERATIONS

1-91. Contemporary operations challenge the Army in many ways. The U.S. Army has always depended upon its ability to learn and adapt. Today's complex environment requires organizations and Soldiers that can adapt equally quickly and well. To adapt, organizations constantly learn from experience (their own and that of others) and apply new knowledge to each situation. Flexibility and innovation are at a premium, as are creative and adaptive leaders. As knowledge increases, the Army will continuously adapt its doctrine, organization, training, materiel, leadership and education, personnel, and facilities.

1-92. The Army must be effective across the entire spectrum of conflict, from stable peace, through insurgency, to general war. Units need to adapt quickly and to shift with little effort from a focus on one portion of the spectrum of conflict to focus on another. The Service must recognize and implement changes that once required years within unit deployment cycles. Technology, having vastly increased the lethality of the industrial age battlefield, assumes even more importance and requires greater and more rapid innovation in tomorrow's conflicts. Response to enemy developments cannot consume months and Soldiers' lives. Leaders now field solutions across the force in weeks. They carefully analyze the enemy's counteraction in order to negate it and retain the initiative.

1-93. Army forces prepare by learning about the country in which they plan to operate. Forces must understand the culture, security forces, government, and, as necessary, tribal leaders of that country. This includes understanding the order of the relevant hierarchies and structures of the local society. Such understanding can assist forces in addressing factors that may lead to instability. Army forces can then establish conditions to empower those members of society who have been marginalized and marginalize those members of society who have been wrongly empowered.

1-94. Leaders prepare by maintaining proficiency in their core competencies, staying broad-minded enough to operate across the spectrum of conflict, and adapting whenever necessary. Such leaders operate in joint, interagency, intergovernmental, and multinational environments leveraging political, economic, and informational efforts to accomplish military objectives. And most importantly, leaders require an offensive mindset that focuses on the enemy and is opportunistic; they can see opportunities in challenges and act on them.

1-95. Effective training builds the cornerstone of operational success. Through training, Soldiers, leaders, and units achieve the tactical and technical competence that builds confidence and allows them to conduct successful operations across the spectrum of conflict. The Army trains its forces using training doctrine that sustains its expeditionary and campaign excellence. Focused training prepares Soldiers, leaders, and units to deploy, fight, and win. This same training prepares Soldiers to create stable environments. Achieving this competence requires specific, dedicated training on offensive, defensive, and stability or civil support tasks. The Army trains Soldiers and units daily in individual and collective tasks under challenging, realistic conditions. Training continues in deployed units to sustain skills and to adapt to changes in the operational environment.

1-96. The United States' responsibilities envelop the globe; therefore, Army forces train to operate in any environment. Army training develops confident, competent, and agile leaders and units. Training management, including mission-essential task list development, links training with missions. Commanders focus their training time and other resources on tasks linked to their mission. Because Army forces face diverse threats and mission requirements, senior commanders adjust their training priorities based on the likely operational environment. As units prepare for deployment, commanders adapt training priorities to address tasks required by actual or anticipated operations. (FM 7-0 describes training management.)

1-97. Army training includes a system of techniques and standards that allow Soldiers and units to determine, acquire, and practice necessary skills. Candid assessments, after action reviews, and applying lessons learned and best practices produce quality Soldiers and versatile units ready for all aspects of the situation. The Army's training system prepares Soldiers and leaders to employ Army capabilities adaptively and effectively in today's varied and challenging conditions.

1-98. Through training, the Army prepares Soldiers to win. Training builds teamwork and cohesion within units. It recognizes that Soldiers ultimately fight for one another and their units. Training instills discipline. It conditions Soldiers to operate within the law of war and rules of engagement. Training prepares unit leaders for the harsh reality of land combat. It emphasizes the fluid and disorderly conditions inherent in land operations.

1-99. Within these training situations, commanders emphasize mission command. To employ mission command successfully during operations, units must understand, foster, and frequently practice its principles during training. (Chapter 5 discusses mission command.)

SUMMARY

1-100. Successful mission accomplishment requires understanding the operational environment, the role of the Army in unified action, and how Soldiers, leaders, and units accomplish missions through full spectrum operations. Army forces conduct prompt and sustained operations as part of a joint force to conclude hostilities and establish conditions favorable to the host nation, the United States, and their multinational partners. Today's operational environments are complex and require continuous learning and adaptation. Commanders use experience, applied judgment, and various analytic tools to gain the situational understanding necessary to make timely decisions to maintain the initiative and achieve decisive results. The more commanders understand their operational environment, the more effectively they can employ forces.

Chapter 2

The Continuum of Operations

The continuum of operations frames the application of landpower. It includes the spectrum of conflict and operational themes. The spectrum of conflict is an ascending scale of violence ranging from stable peace to general war. Operational themes give commanders a way to characterize the dominant major operation underway in an area of operations. The themes also provide overlapping categories for grouping types of operations from the land force perspective. The continuum of operations thus links the operational environment, discussed in chapter 1, with the Army's operational concept—full spectrum operations—discussed in chapter 3.

THE SPECTRUM OF CONFLICT

2-1.   The spectrum of conflict is the backdrop for Army operations. The spectrum of conflict uses violence as a discriminator on an ascending scale that ranges from stable peace to general war. On the left hand of the spectrum, stable peace represents an operational environment characterized by the absence of militarily significant violence (see paragraph 2-3). On the right hand of the spectrum, general war describes an environment dominated by interstate and intrastate violence (see paragraph 2-6).

2-2.   Military power cannot, by itself, restore or guarantee stable peace. It must, however, establish global, regional, and local conditions that allow the other instruments of national power—diplomatic, informational, and economic—to exert their full influence. For example, the Nation's air, land, and sea power deter threats posed by hostile powers by holding their homeland and vital interests at risk. This creates avenues for diplomacy to resolve disputes. Multinational forces may separate warring factions to stop a civil war that threatens regional peace. Their actions allow international aid organizations to reach masses of refugees and an international commission to seek some sort of equitable settlement. On a local level, an Army task force suppresses terrorism and lawlessness so other government agencies can work freely with host-nation officials to restore self-sustaining governance. In each case, achieving stable peace requires expertise and capabilities beyond those developed in the military force. Every use of military force to restore stable peace requires the other three instruments of national power. Conversely, diplomatic, informational, and economic efforts to restore a stable peace usually do not work unless backed by effective military power—military power with global reach and endurance. In every campaign and major operation, success (as characterized by a stable peace) depends on unified action involving concerted efforts by multinational military and civilian partners.

STABLE PEACE

2-3.   Stable peace is characterized by the absence of militarily significant violence. International actors (such as states, corporations, and nongovernmental organizations) limit their activities to peaceful interaction in politics, economics, and other areas of interest. Peaceful interaction may include intense competition as well as cooperation and assistance. While tensions do exist, all recognize that they can best achieve their interests by means other than violence.

UNSTABLE PEACE

2-4.   When one or more parties threaten or use violence to accomplish their objectives, stable peace degenerates into unstable peace. Unstable peace may also result when violence levels decrease after violent conflict. In some cases, outside powers may apply force to limit conflict. Preventing a return to violent conflict may require peace operations. (See paragraphs 2-33 through 2-43.) Sometimes stable peace is not immediately achievable. At those times, the goal of conflict termination aims to establish conditions in which peace operations can prevent conflict from recurring. Doing this allows the instruments of national power to work toward stable peace.

INSURGENCY

2-5. Joint doctrine defines an *insurgency* as the organized movement of subversion and violence by a group or movement that seeks to overthrow or force change of a governing authority. Insurgency can also refer to the group itself (JP 3-24). This condition of politically motivated conflict involves significant intrastate or interstate violence but usually stays short of large-scale operations by opposing conventional forces. Insurgencies often include widespread use of irregular forces and terrorist tactics. An insurgency may develop in the aftermath of general war or through degeneration of unstable peace. Insurgencies may also emerge on their own from chronic social or economic conditions. In addition, some conflicts, such as the Chinese Revolution, have escalated from protracted insurgencies into general wars. Intervention by a foreign power in an insurgency may increase the threat to regional stability.

GENERAL WAR

2-6. General war is armed conflict between major powers in which the belligerents have used all their resources, and the national survival of a major belligerent is in jeopardy. Diplomatic and economic channels have broken down. Violence has reached a level that will only end by the exhaustion, defeat, or destruction of the military capabilities of one or more antagonists. At its extreme, general war includes the unlimited use of nuclear, biological, and chemical weapons, possibly leading to the destruction of entire societies. Any conflict may escalate or decline depending upon a host of factors. General war usually involves nation-states and coalitions; however, civil wars may reach this level of violence. In general war, large and heavily armed conventional forces fight for military supremacy by conducting major combat operations. These operations aim to defeat the enemy's armed forces and eliminate the enemy's military capability. Although dominated by large-scale conventional operations, these conflicts often include guerrilla and unconventional warfare. To illustrate, Soviet partisans waged unconventional warfare against German lines of communications during World War II. The Vietcong conducted guerrilla warfare throughout the Vietnam War, even as the North Vietnamese Army fought conventional battles against U.S. and South Vietnamese forces.

ARMY FORCES AND THE SPECTRUM OF CONFLICT

2-7. Army forces operate anywhere on the spectrum of conflict. In each case, achieving the end state requires reducing the violence level and establishing conditions that advance U.S. national strategic goals. Commanders conduct a series of operations intended to establish conditions conducive to a stable peace. Some situations require applying massive force in major combat operations to eliminate a threat; others involve applying military power to reduce an insurgency to a size that host-nation forces can defeat. Regardless, the goal aims to move conditions to a lower level of violence; however, avoiding intermediate levels is desirable. When impossible, commanders seek to move the situation through them to stable peace as quickly as time permits.

2-8. Today's operational environment requires Army forces to continuously evaluate and adapt their tactics to ensure that they have the desired results. Recent experience demonstrates the difficulty and cost of fighting terrorists and insurgents while supporting reconstruction efforts. These experiences and a study of other conflicts have revealed insights guiding the Army's effort to prepare for future operations:

- All major operations combine offensive, defensive, and stability elements executed simultaneously at multiple echelons.
- The operational environment evolves over time and changes due to military operations.
- Operations conducted during one phase of a campaign or major operation directly affect subsequent phases. Commanders should conduct current operations in a manner that establishes the conditions necessary for future operations—and ultimately allows the other instruments of national power to secure a stable peace.

- Major operations are conducted not only to defeat the enemy but also to restore a stable peace. The military plays a large role in this effort, even after major combat operations have ended. Restoring a stable peace after a violent conflict may take longer and be more difficult than defeating enemy forces.
- In any campaign or major operation, changing conditions require Army forces to adapt their tactics, techniques, and procedures to the operational environment. To be successful, leaders must develop learning organizations that collect and share best practices and lessons learned.

OPERATIONAL THEMES

2-9. Army forces conduct major operations to defeat an enemy and to establish conditions necessary to achieve the national strategic end state. (Paragraph 7-12 defines major operations.) Examples of major operations include Operation Cobra (the breakout from the Normandy beachhead during World War II) and Operation Chromite (the amphibious landing at Inchon during the Korean War).

2-10. Conflict intensity varies over time and among locations; therefore, it is difficult to precisely describe a major operation's character. In fact, the character of most major operations will likely evolve. All major operations comprise many smaller operations conducted simultaneously. These also may vary with time. Nevertheless, leaders can establish a theme for each major operation, one that distinguishes it from other operations with different characteristics. Major combat operations, for instance, differ distinctly from counterinsurgency operations; both differ from peace operations. Different themes usually demand different approaches and force packages, although some activities apply to all.

2-11. **An *operational theme* describes the character of the dominant major operation being conducted at any time within a land force commander's area of operations. The operational theme helps convey the nature of the major operation to the force to facilitate common understanding of how the commander broadly intends to operate.** Operational themes have implications for task-organization, resource allocation, protection, and tactical task assignment. They establish a taxonomy for understanding the joint and Army major operations and relationships among them.

2-12. Grouping military operations with common characteristics under operational themes allows Army forces to develop doctrine for each theme rather than for a multitude of joint operations. (See table 2-1, page 2-4.) However, this taxonomy does not limit when commanders may use a type of operation. Forces routinely conduct some operations listed under one operational theme within major operations characterized by another. For example, units can conduct noncombatant evacuation operations during counterinsurgency, or a unit can support an insurgency during major combat operations. Such situations do not change the broader character of the major operation. The operational themes emphasize the differences among the various types of joint operations. These differences are usually greater for land forces (including special operations forces) than for the other Services.

2-13. Each operational theme corresponds broadly to a range along the spectrum of conflict. Commanders describe their desired end state as how they envision the conditions of the operational environment when the operation ends. Often, this envisions either a condition of stable peace or at least a condition in which civilian organizations can build toward a stable peace with a sustainable military commitment. A stable peace may include any or all of the following: a safe and secure populace, a legitimate central government, a viable market economy, and an effective rule of law. Lacking involvement by civilian organizations, none of these goals is sustainable. To ensure progress toward the end state, higher level commanders continuously assess the overall campaign and their subordinates' operations. They adjust the type of operation as each campaign phase unfolds. This adjustment affects their focus, resource allocation, and directed tasks. Commanders visualize how they prepare to transition between operational themes as the operation progresses. They pursue avenues for increased cooperation with civilian agencies, handing over activities to civilian direction as soon as conditions permit.

Table 2-1. Examples of joint military operations conducted within operational themes

Peacetime military engagement	Limited intervention	Peace operations	Irregular warfare
• Multinational training events and exercises • Security assistance • Joint combined exchange training • Recovery operations • Arms control • Counterdrug activities	• Noncombatant evacuation operations • Strike • Raid • Show of force • Foreign humanitarian assistance • Consequence management • Sanction enforcement • Elimination of weapons of mass destruction	• Peacekeeping • Peace enforcement • Peacemaking • Peace building • Conflict prevention	• Foreign internal defense • Support to insurgency • Counterinsurgency • Combating terrorism • Unconventional warfare
Note: Major combat operations usually involve a series of named major operations, such as Operation Desert Storm, each involving significant offensive and defensive operations and supporting air, land, sea, and special operations.			

2-14. The transition between operational themes requires careful planning and continuous assessment. For example, at the conclusion of major combat operations, the campaign may evolve to irregular warfare or peace operations. While the scope of their defeat may induce an enemy to accept occupation and peace enforcement without a period of irregular warfare, commanders plan for a potential insurgency and prepare accordingly. Shifting from one operational theme to another often requires adjustments to the composition of the force. These adjustments apply not only to task-organizing the force but also to deploying and redeploying units, establishing new bases, and dismantling bases no longer needed. In particular, a change in operational theme may require modification to the mission-essential task lists and additional training for both deploying units and units in theater. Responsibilities between military commanders and other government officials may also change. For example, the ambassador may become the senior U.S. Government official as opposed to the joint force commander.

2-15. Soldiers should not confuse operational themes with tactical tasks or activities. Operational themes are too general to be assigned as missions. Rather, they describe the major operation's general characteristics, not the details of its execution. The theme of a major operation may change for various reasons such as—

- Planned phases.
- Changes caused by friendly, enemy, or neutral activity.
- Revised political guidance.
- Unexpected opportunities.

PEACETIME MILITARY ENGAGEMENT

2-16. *Peacetime military engagement* **comprises all military activities that involve other nations and are intended to shape the security environment in peacetime. It includes programs and exercises that the United States military conducts with other nations to shape the international environment, improve mutual understanding, and improve interoperability with treaty partners or potential coalition partners. Peacetime military engagement activities are designed to support a combatant commander's objectives within the theater security cooperation plan.** Peacetime military engagement encourages regional stability. These activities may be long term, such as training teams and advisors assisting land forces, or short term, such as multinational exercises. Combat is not envisioned, although terrorist attacks against deployed forces are always possible. Policy, regulations, and security cooperation plans, rather than doctrine, typically govern peacetime military engagement activities. Units usually conduct bilaterally but can involve multiple nations. Examples of joint operations and activities that fall under peacetime military engagement include the following:

- Multinational training events and exercises.
- Security assistance.
- Joint combined exchange training.
- Recovery operations.
- Arms control.
- Counterdrug activities.

Multinational Training Events and Exercises

2-17. Combatant commanders support many multinational training events and exercises. These exercises have many purposes, including—

- Demonstrating military capabilities to potential aggressors.
- Improving interoperability.
- Establishing or improving military-to-military ties with another nation.

Security Assistance

2-18. The security assistance program is an important instrument of U.S. foreign and national security policy. It contributes to—

- Deterrence.
- Promoting regional stability.
- Guaranteeing the United States access to vital overseas military facilities.
- Increasing host-nation military capabilities, thus reducing unilateral U.S. military requirements.
- Enhancing weapons standardization and interoperability to support multinational force compatibility. (AR 34-1 governs multinational force compatibility.)
- Supporting the U.S. defense industrial base.

2-19. Security assistance includes various supporting programs for foreign military logistic, financial, and military education assistance. For example, the international military education and training program is part of security assistance. It also includes U.S. military teams sent to multinational partners to assist in training. (AR 12-1 governs security assistance. Also, see FM 3-07.1 for a discussion on security force assistance.)

Joint Combined Exchange Training

2-20. *Joint combined exchange training* is a program conducted overseas to fulfill US forces training requirements and at the same time exchange the sharing of skills between US forces and host nation counterparts. Training activities are designed to improve US and host nation capabilities (JP 3-05). Army forces routinely participate in exchange programs, often at the small-unit level. Special operations forces use this program to improve their regional expertise while contributing to a combatant commander's theater security cooperation plan. (JP 3-05 addresses joint combined exchange training.)

Recovery Operations

2-21. *Recovery operations* are operations conducted to search for, locate, identify, recover, and return isolated personnel, human remains, sensitive equipment, or items critical to national security (JP 3-50). (JP 3-50 and FM 3-50.1 contain doctrine on personnel recovery.)

Arms Control

2-22. Combatant commanders support multinational arms control agreements concerning prohibited weapons and illegal arms trafficking. They also provide forces and control means to block the sale or transfer of arms to terrorists or other criminals as the Secretary of Defense directs. Such actions may be unilateral or multinational.

Counterdrug Activities

2-23. *Counterdrug activities* are those measures taken to detect, interdict, disrupt, or curtail any activity that is reasonably related to illicit drug trafficking. This includes, but is not limited to, measures taken to detect, interdict, disrupt, or curtail activities related to substances, materiel, weapons, or resources used to finance, support, secure, cultivate, process, or transport illegal drugs (JP 3-07.4). (See JP 3-07.4 for doctrine on counterdrug activities.)

LIMITED INTERVENTION

2-24. Units execute a limited intervention to achieve an end state that is clearly defined and limited in scope. Units impose corresponding limitations on the supporting operations and size of the forces involved. These operations may be phased but are not intended to become campaigns. Although limited interventions are confined in terms of end state and forces, their execution may be lengthy. Joint task forces usually conduct limited interventions. The most common types of limited interventions include—

- Noncombatant evacuation operations.
- Strikes.
- Raids.
- Shows of force.
- Foreign humanitarian assistance.
- Consequence management.
- Sanction enforcement.
- Elimination of weapons of mass destruction.

Noncombatant Evacuation Operations

2-25. *Noncombatant evacuation operations* are operations directed by the Department of State or other appropriate authority, in conjunction with the Department of Defense, whereby noncombatants are evacuated from foreign countries when their lives are endangered by war, civil unrest, or natural disaster to safe havens or to the United States (JP 3-0). (JP 3-68 contains doctrine for noncombatant evacuation operations.)

Strike

2-26. A *strike* is an attack to damage or destroy an objective or a capability (JP 3-0). While units conduct strikes as part of tactical operations, in limited interventions, a joint force (apart from a campaign or major operation) conducts them. An example of a strike conducted as a limited intervention is Operation El Dorado Canyon, executed in 1986. It consisted of a series of air strikes on targets inside Libya.

Raid

2-27. A *raid* is an operation to temporarily seize an area in order to secure information, confuse an adversary, capture personnel or equipment, or to destroy a capability. It ends with a planned withdrawal upon completion of the assigned mission (JP 3-0). Units routinely conduct raids as part of tactical operations but sometimes as separate joint operations. The latter is characterized as a limited intervention. (FM 3-90 contains doctrine on tactical-level raids.)

Show of Force

2-28. A *show of force* is an operation designed to demonstrate US resolve that involves increased visibility of US deployed forces in an attempt to defuse a specific situation that, if allowed to continue, may be detrimental to US interests or national objectives (JP 3-0). Deployed forces back up U.S. promises and commitments and increase its regional influence. Although military in nature, show of force operations often serve both diplomatic and military purposes. These operations can influence other governments to respect U.S. interests.

Foreign Humanitarian Assistance

2-29. *Foreign humanitarian assistance* consists of Department of Defense activities, normally in support of the United States Agency for International Development or Department of State, conducted outside the United States, its territories, and possessions to relieve or reduce human suffering, disease, hunger, or privation (JP 3-29). This list includes hostile activities waged against noncombatants. Activities such as genocide, crimes against humanity, and war crimes constitute examples of manmade suffering in which the population need U.S. intervention. Non-Department of Defense agencies may refer to such intervention as mass atrocity response operations. Foreign humanitarian assistance provided by U.S. forces is limited in scope and duration. It supplements or complements the efforts of the host-nation civil authorities or agencies that may have the primary responsibility for providing foreign humanitarian assistance. The multinational relief operation sent to Indonesia after the December 2004 tsunami illustrates a natural disaster response. (JP 3-29 contains doctrine for foreign humanitarian assistance.) The U.S. response to Serbian actions against Kosovar Albanians in the Serbian province of Kosovo in 1999 illustrates a manmade disaster response.

Consequence Management

2-30. *Consequence management* involves actions taken to maintain or restore essential services and manage and mitigate problems resulting from disasters and catastrophes, including natural, man-made, or terrorist incidents (JP 3-28). (JP 3-41 contains doctrine on chemical, biological, radiological, nuclear, and high-yield explosives consequence management.)

Sanction Enforcement

2-31. *Sanction enforcement* comprises operations that employ coercive measures to interdict the movement of certain types of designated items into or out of a nation or specified area (JP 3-0). Depending on the geography, sanction enforcement normally involves some combination of air and surface forces. The enforcement of United Nations sanctions against Iraq prohibited cargo originating from Iraq without an authorization letter from the United Nations.

Elimination of Weapons of Mass Destruction

2-32. Operations to eliminate weapons of mass destruction systematically locate, characterize, secure, disable, or destroy a state or nonstate actor's weapons of mass destruction and related capabilities. Elimination operations are one of eight joint mission areas—offensive operations, elimination operations, interdiction operations, active defense, passive defense, weapons of mass destruction consequence management, security cooperation, and threat reduction. These areas make up the three pillars (nonproliferation, counterproliferation, and consequence management) of combating weapons of mass destruction. (JP 3-40 contains doctrine on combating weapons of mass destruction.)

PEACE OPERATIONS

2-33. *Peace operations* is a broad term that encompasses multiagency and multinational crisis response and limited contingency operations involving all instruments of national power with military missions to contain conflict, redress the peace, and shape the environment to support reconciliation and rebuilding and facilitate the transition to legitimate governance. Peace operations include peacekeeping, peace enforcement, peacemaking, peace building, and conflict prevention efforts (JP 3-07.3). Army forces conduct the following types of peace operations:

- Peacekeeping.
- Peace enforcement.
- Peacemaking.
- Peace building.
- Conflict prevention.

2-34. Peace operations aim to keep violence from spreading, contain violence that has occurred, and reduce tension among factions. Accomplishing these objectives creates an environment in which forces use other instruments of national power to reduce the level of violence to stable peace. Peace operations are usually interagency efforts. They require a balance of military and diplomatic resources. (JP 3-07.3 and FM 3-07 contain doctrine for peace operations.)

Peacekeeping

2-35. *Peacekeeping* consists of military operations undertaken with the consent of all major parties to a dispute, designed to monitor and facilitate implementation of an agreement (cease fire, truce, or other such agreement) and support diplomatic efforts to reach a long-term political settlement (JP 3-07.3). Peacekeeping operations follow a truce or cease fire. They seek to interpose a peaceful third party between belligerents, allowing diplomacy an opportunity to resolve the conflict. Units only use force for self-defense in a peacekeeping operation.

Peace Enforcement

2-36. *Peace enforcement* involves the application of military force, or the threat of its use, normally pursuant to international authorization, to compel compliance with resolutions or sanctions designed to maintain or restore peace and order (JP 3-07.3). They may include the enforcement of sanctions and restoration of order. These operations try not to destroy or defeat an adversary, but to use force or threat of force to establish a safe and secure environment so that peace building can succeed.

Peacemaking

2-37. *Peacemaking* is the process of diplomacy, mediation, negotiation, or other forms of peaceful settlements that arranges an end to a dispute and resolves issues that led to it (JP 3-07.3). The military does not have the lead, but military leaders normally provide military expertise in negotiating the military aspects of a peace agreement.

Peace Building

2-38. *Peace building* involves stability actions, predominately diplomatic and economic, that strengthen and rebuild governmental infrastructure and institutions in order to avoid a relapse into conflict (JP 3-07.3). Peace building provides the reconstruction and societal rehabilitation after a conflict thereby offering hope to the host-nation populace. Stability operations promote reconciliation, strengthen and rebuild civil infrastructures and institutions, build confidence, and support economic reconstruction to prevent a return to conflict. The ultimate measure of success in peace building is political, not military.

Conflict Prevention

2-39. Conflict prevention consists of actions taken before a predictable crisis to prevent or limit violence, deter parties, and reach an agreement before armed hostilities begin. Conflict prevention often involves diplomatic initiatives. It also includes efforts designed to reform a country's security area of operations and make it more accountable to civilian control. Conflict prevention may require deploying forces to contain a dispute or prevent it from escalating into hostilities. (JP 3-07.3 contains doctrine on conflict prevention.)

Considerations for Peace Operations

2-40. In a war-torn nation or region, peace operations ease the transition to a stable peace by supporting reconciliation and rebuilding. Units often conducted peace operations under international supervision. U.S. forces may conduct peace operations under the sponsorship of the United Nations, another intergovernmental organization, as part of a coalition, or unilaterally.

2-41. Units often conduct peace operations in complex, ambiguous, and uncertain environments. The operational environment for a peace operation may include any or all of the following characteristics:

- Hybrid threats.
- Failing or failed states.
- Absence of the rule of law.
- Terrorism and terrorist organizations.

- Gross violations of human rights.
- Collapse of civil infrastructure.
- Presence of dislocated civilians.

2-42. Army forces in peace operations strive to create a safe and secure environment, primarily through stability operations. Army forces use their offensive and defensive capabilities to deter external and internal adversaries from overt actions against each other. Establishing security and control enables civilian agencies to address the underlying causes of the conflict and create a self-sustaining peace. Army forces provide specialized support to other government agencies as necessary.

2-43. Peace operations require opposing parties to cooperate with the international community. In most peace operations, this comes voluntarily. However, peace enforcement involves the threat or use of military force to compel cooperation. Successful peace operations also require support from the local populace and host-nation leaders. The likelihood of combat declines, and, when it occurs, it is usually at the small-unit level. Units involved in peace operations prepare for sudden engagements, even while executing operations to prevent them. Commanders emphasize the use of information activities, particularly information used to inform and influence various opposing audiences in the area of operations. Peace operations require perseverance to achieve the desired end state.

IRREGULAR WARFARE

2-44. *Irregular warfare* **is a violent struggle among state and nonstate actors for legitimacy and influence over a population**. This broad form of conflict has insurgency, counterinsurgency, and unconventional warfare as the principal activities. Irregular forces are normally active in these conflicts. However, conventional forces may also be heavily involved, particularly in counterinsurgencies.

2-45. Irregular warfare differs from conventional operations dramatically in two aspects. First, it is warfare among and within the people. Actors wage the conflict not for military supremacy but for political power. Military power can contribute to the resolution of this form of warfare, but it is not decisive. Effectively applying military forces can establish the conditions for the other instruments of national power to exert their influence. Secondly, irregular warfare also differs from conventional warfare by its emphasis on the indirect approach. (Chapter 6 discusses indirect approach.) Irregular warfare avoids a direct military confrontation. Instead, it combines irregular forces and indirect, unconventional methods (such as terrorism) to subvert and exhaust the opponent. Often irregular warfare offers the only practical means for a weaker opponent to engage a powerful military force. Irregular warfare seeks to defeat the opponent's will through steady attrition and constant low-level pressure. In some instances, it targets the population and avoids conventional forces. This approach creates instability. It severely challenges civil authority to fulfill its first responsibility—providing security.

2-46. Special operations forces conduct most irregular warfare operations. Sometimes conventional forces support them; other times special operations forces operate alone. However, if special operations forces and host-nation forces cannot defeat unconventional and irregular threats, conventional Army forces may assume the lead role. The joint operations grouped under irregular warfare include the following:
- Foreign internal defense.
- Support to insurgency.
- Counterinsurgency.
- Combating terrorism.
- Unconventional warfare.

Foreign Internal Defense

2-47. *Foreign internal defense* is the participation by civilian and military agencies of a government in any of the action programs taken by another government or other designated organization to free and protect its society from subversion, lawlessness, insurgency, terrorism, and other threats to its security (JP 3-22). The categories of foreign internal defense operations are indirect support and direct support.

Indirect Support

2-48. Indirect support emphasizes host-nation self-sufficiency. It builds strong national infrastructures through economic and military capabilities. Examples include security assistance programs, multinational exercises, and exchange programs. Indirect support reinforces host-nation legitimacy and primacy in addressing internal problems by keeping U.S. military assistance inconspicuous.

Direct Support

2-49. Direct support uses U.S. forces to assist the host-nation population or military forces directly. Direct support includes operational planning assistance, civil affairs activities, intelligence and communications sharing, logistics, and training of local military forces. It may also involve limited combat operations, usually in self-defense.

Considerations for Foreign Internal Defense

2-50. Foreign internal defense involves all instruments of national power. Primarily a series of programs, it supports friendly nations operating against or threatened by hostile elements. Foreign internal defense promotes regional stability by helping a host nation respond to its population's needs while maintaining security. Participating Army forces normally advise and assist host-nation forces while refraining from combat operations.

2-51. Foreign internal defense is a significant mission for selected Army special operations forces. However, it requires joint planning, preparation, and execution to integrate and focus the efforts of all Service and functional components. These missions are approved by the President, limited in scope and duration, and accomplished to support legitimate host-nation forces.

2-52. Foreign internal defense operations often respond to growing insurgencies. Most of these activities help a host nation prevent an active insurgency from developing further. If an insurgency already exists or preventive measures fail, foreign internal defense focuses on using host-nation security forces and other resources to eliminate, marginalize, or assimilate insurgent elements. The United States provides military support to host-nation counterinsurgency efforts, recognizing that military power alone cannot achieve lasting success. Host-nation and U.S. actions promote a secure environment with programs that eliminate causes of insurgencies. Military support to a threatened government balances security with economic development to enhance or reestablish stability. (JP 3-22 and FM 3-05.202 contain doctrine for foreign internal defense.)

Support to Insurgency

2-53. Army forces may support insurgencies against regimes that threaten U.S. interests. Normally, Army special operations forces provide the primary U.S. land forces. These forces' training, organization, and regional focus make them well suited for these operations. Conventional Army forces that support insurgencies provide logistic and training support but normally do not conduct offensive or defensive operations.

Counterinsurgency

2-54. *Counterinsurgency* consists of comprehensive civilian and military efforts taken to defeat an insurgency and to address any core grievances (JP 3-24). In counterinsurgency, host-nation forces and their partners operate to defeat armed resistance, reduce passive opposition, and establish or reestablish the host-nation government's legitimacy. Counterinsurgency is the dominant joint operation in Operations Iraqi Freedom and Enduring Freedom. (FM 3-24 discusses counterinsurgency.)

2-55. Insurgents try to persuade the populace to accept the insurgents' goals or force political change. When persuasion does not work, insurgents use other methods to achieve their goals. These may include intimidation, sabotage and subversion, propaganda, terror, and military pressure. Sometimes insurgents attempt to organize the populace into a mass movement. At a minimum, they aim to make effective host-nation governance impossible. Some insurgencies are transnational. Other situations involve multiple insurgencies underway in one area at the same time. Counterinsurgency becomes more complex in these situations.

2-56. While each insurgency is distinct, similarities among them exist. Insurgencies occur more often in states with a lack of national cohesion or with weak, inefficient, unstable, or unpopular governments. Internal conflicts may be racial, cultural, religious, or ideological. Additional factors, such as corruption and external agitation, may also fuel an insurgency. Successful insurgencies develop a unifying leadership and organization and an attractive vision of the future. Usually only insurgencies able to attract widespread, popular support pose a real threat to state authority.

2-57. Most operations in counterinsurgencies occur at the small-unit level—squad, platoon, or company. However, larger operations also occur. Commanders prepare with a consistent, long-range plan to defeat an insurgency. They carefully assess the negative effects of violence on the populace and strictly adhere to the rules of engagement. Operations reflect and promote the host-nation government's authority, thus undermining insurgent attempts to establish an alternative authority. Such operations also reduce the tendency of the population to view the insurgents as an occupying force.

2-58. Larger units, such as brigades and divisions, provide direction and consistency to Army operations in their areas of operations and mass resources and forces to make operations more effective. They also respond to any threat large enough to imperil the smaller units distributed throughout the areas of operations. Lower echelons can then operate across larger areas (against rural insurgencies) or among greater populations (against urban insurgencies).

Combating Terrorism

2-59. *Combating terrorism* is actions, including antiterrorism and counterterrorism, taken to oppose terrorism throughout the entire threat spectrum (JP 3-26). *Terrorism* is the calculated use of unlawful violence or threat of unlawful violence to inculcate fear; [it is] intended to coerce or to intimidate governments or societies in the pursuit of goals that are generally political, religious, or ideological (JP 3-07.2). An enemy who cannot defeat conventional Army forces may resort to terrorism. Terrorist attacks can create disproportionate effects on conventional forces. Their effect on societies can be even greater. Terrorist tactics may range from individual assassinations to employing weapons of mass destruction.

Counterterrorism

2-60. *Counterterrorism* is actions taken directly against terrorist networks and indirectly to influence and render global and regional environments inhospitable to terrorist networks (JP 3-26). Special operations forces conduct counterterrorism. This can include strikes and raids against terrorist organizations and facilities outside the United States and its territories. Although counterterrorism is a specified mission for selected special operations forces, conventional Army forces may also contribute. Commanders who employ conventional forces against terrorists are conducting offensive operations, not counterterrorism operations.

Antiterrorism

2-61. *Antiterrorism* is defensive measures used to reduce the vulnerability of individuals and property to terrorist acts, to include limited response and containment by local military and civilian forces (JP 3-07.2). It is a protection task. All forces consider antiterrorism during all operations. Commanders take the security measures to accomplish the mission and protect their forces against terrorism. They make every reasonable effort to minimize their forces' vulnerability to violence and hostage taking. Typical antiterrorism actions include—

- Completing unit and installation threat and vulnerability assessments.
- Training in antiterrorism awareness.
- Establishing special reaction teams and protective services at installations and bases.
- Ensuring that antiterrorism measures protect personnel, physical assets, and information, including high-risk personnel and designated critical assets.

- Establishing civil-military partnerships for weapons of mass destruction crises and consequence management.
- Developing terrorist threat and incident response plans that include managing the force protection condition system.
- Establishing appropriate policies based on the threat and force protection condition system.

(JP 3-07.2 contains doctrine for antiterrorism.)

Unconventional Warfare

2-62. *Unconventional warfare* is a broad spectrum of military and paramilitary operations, normally of long duration, predominantly conducted through, with, or by indigenous or surrogate forces who are organized, trained, equipped, supported, and directed in varying degrees by an external source. It includes, but is not limited to, guerrilla warfare, subversion, sabotage, intelligence activities, and unconventional assisted recovery (JP 3-05). Within the U.S. military, conduct of unconventional warfare is a highly specialized special operations force mission. Special operations forces may conduct unconventional warfare as part of a separate operation or within a campaign. During Operation Enduring Freedom, special operations forces and other government agencies conducted unconventional warfare within the joint campaign to topple the Taliban regime.

2-63. Conventional Army forces may support unconventional warfare. For example, during Operation Iraqi Freedom, conventional forces supported Joint Task Force-North by securing bases in the joint special operations area. (JP 3-05 contains doctrine on unconventional warfare conducted by Army special operations forces.)

MAJOR COMBAT OPERATIONS

2-64. *Major combat operations differ from the other operational themes due to the extreme violence inherent in their conduct. Major combat operations employ all available combat power (directly and indirectly) to destroy an enemy's military capability, thereby decisively altering the military conditions within the operational environment. Major combat operations dominate campaigns during general war. Combat between large formations characterizes these operations. Major combat operations conducted by U.S. forces are always joint operations, although an Army headquarters may form the base of a joint force headquarters. These operations typically entail high tempo, high resource consumption, and numerous casualties. Joint doctrine does not specify types of operations unique to major combat operations. However, the joint force may conduct—

- Forcible entry operations (see paragraph **Error! Reference source not found.**).
- Air operations to gain and maintain air supremacy.
- Naval operations to eliminate threats to movement of forces and resources.
- Space operations to ensure space supremacy.
- Land operations to seize and control enemy population, military, and manufacturing areas.
- Joint conventional and unconventional operations in combination to overthrow a hostile regime.

2-65. Major combat operations usually involve intense combat between the uniformed armed forces of nation-states. Hybrid threats may have the capability to engage in major combat, although their capacity to wage protracted major combat operations will be less than that of a developed nation-state. Even then, major combat operations tend to blur with other operational themes. Within the theater of war, other joint task forces may conduct counterinsurgency and limited intervention. For example, in Vietnam both the United States and North Vietnam deployed their national armed forces. Although major battles occurred, the United States characterized much of the war as counterinsurgency operations.

2-66. Civil wars, particularly within a developed nation, often include major combat operations. The American Civil War, the Russian Revolution, and Yugoslavia's collapse all involved recurring, high-intensity clashes between armies. Even in less developed regions, civil war leads to massive casualties among combatants and noncombatants alike. Insurgencies can develop into civil wars, particularly when external powers back both the government and the insurgents.

2-67. Not all major combat operations are protracted. Joint operations may capitalize on superior military capability to quickly overwhelm a weaker enemy. Examples include the following:

- The coup de main in Panama in 1989.
- The forcible entry of Grenada in 1983.
- The major combat operations against Iraq in 1991 and 2003.

2-68. Successful major combat operations defeat or destroy the enemy's armed forces and seize terrain. Commanders assess them in terms of numbers of military units destroyed or rendered combat ineffective, the level of enemy resolve, and the terrain objectives seized or secured. Major combat operations are the operational theme for which doctrine, including the principles of war, was originally developed.

SUMMARY

2-69. Commanders use the spectrum of conflict to describe the level of violence in terms of an ascending scale marked by graduated steps. Army forces operate anywhere across the spectrum of conflict, from peacetime military engagement in areas of stable peace to major combat operations during general war. In each case, the objective aims to establish conditions that advance U.S. goals. The operational themes group types of military operations according to common characteristics. Operational themes establish a taxonomy for understanding the many kinds of joint operations and the relationships among them. Commanders convey the overall character of a major operation, including the principles that govern it, by its operational theme. The operational theme varies during a campaign or major operation. Although many tactical activities apply to all, different themes demand different approaches.

This page intentionally left blank.

Chapter 3

Full Spectrum Operations

The foundations for Army operations are contained in its operational concept—full spectrum operations. The goal of full spectrum operations is to apply landpower as part of unified action to defeat the enemy on land and establish conditions that achieve the joint force commander's end state. The complexity of today's operational environments requires commanders to combine offensive, defensive, and stability or civil support tasks to reach this goal. Commanders direct the application of full spectrum operations to seize, retain, and exploit the initiative and achieve decisive results.

THE OPERATIONAL CONCEPT

3-1. The Army's operational concept is the core of its doctrine. All Soldiers must uniformly know and understand the operational concept. The operational concept frames how Army forces, operating as part of a joint force, conduct operations. It describes how Army forces adapt to meet the distinct requirements of land operations. The concept is broad enough to describe operations now and in the near future. It is flexible enough to apply in any situation worldwide.

3-2. The Army's operational concept is *full spectrum operations:* **Army forces combine offensive, defensive, and stability or civil support operations simultaneously as part of an interdependent joint force to seize, retain, and exploit the initiative, accepting prudent risk to create opportunities to achieve decisive results. They employ synchronized action—lethal and nonlethal—proportional to the mission and informed by a thorough understanding of all variables of the operational environment. Mission command that conveys intent and an appreciation of all aspects of the situation guides the adaptive use of Army forces**. (See figure 3-1 and chapter 5.)

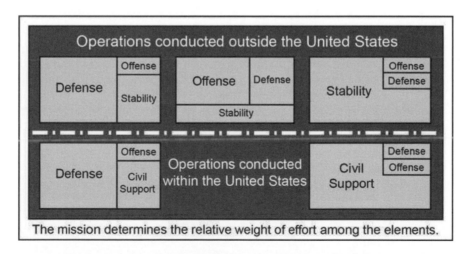

Figure 3-1. Full spectrum operations—the Army's operational concept

3-3. Full spectrum operations require continuous, simultaneous combinations of offensive, defensive, and stability or civil support tasks. In all operations, commanders seek to seize, retain, and exploit the initiative while synchronizing their actions to achieve the best effects possible. Operations conducted outside the United States and its territories simultaneously combine three elements—offense, defense, and stability. Within the United States and its territories, operations combine the elements of civil support, defense, and offense to support civil authority. Army forces operate using mutually supporting lethal and nonlethal capabilities.

3-4. Army forces use offensive and defensive operations to defeat the enemy on land. They simultaneously execute stability or civil support operations to interact with the populace and civil authorities. In most domestic operations, Army forces perform only civil support tasks. However, an extreme emergency, such as an attack by a hostile foreign power, may require simultaneous combinations of offensive, defensive, and civil support tasks. Stability tasks typically dominate peace operations, peacetime military engagement, and some limited interventions. For example, foreign humanitarian assistance operations involve primarily stability tasks with minor defensive tasks and no offensive element.

3-5. Full spectrum operations begin with the commander's concept of operations. This single, unifying idea provides direction for the entire operation. Based on a specific idea of how to accomplish the mission, commanders refine the concept of operations during planning. They adjust it throughout the operation as subordinates develop the situation or conditions change. Often, subordinates acting on the higher commander's intent develop the situation in ways that exploit unforeseen opportunities. Mission command requires commanders to convey a clear commander's intent and concept of operations. This becomes essential in full spectrum operations, where the complexity and chaos of ground operations often compel subordinate commanders to make difficult decisions in unforeseen circumstances. Therefore, mission command is an essential complement to full spectrum operations. (Chapter 5 discusses mission command.)

3-6. No set formula exists for applying landpower. Each campaign and major operation requires an original design and flexible execution. Army forces must be able to operate as part of a joint or multinational force anywhere across the spectrum of conflict. They also must vary combinations of the elements of full spectrum operations appropriate to the situation. The concept of operations combines and weights these elements as the situation requires.

3-7. Full spectrum operations involve continuous interaction between friendly forces and multiple groups in the operational area. In addition to enemy forces and the local populace, Soldiers work with multinational partners, adversaries, civil authorities, business leaders, and other civilian agencies. This interaction has a simple concept but complex application. For example, enemies and adversaries may consist of multiple competing elements. Civil authorities range from strategic-level leaders to local government officials to religious leaders. Populations may include people of differing tribes, ethnic groups, and nationalities. Within the United States and its territories, the roles and responsibilities of Army forces and civil authorities substantially differ from their roles and responsibilities overseas. For that reason, Army forces conduct civil support operations domestically and stability operations overseas, even though stability and civil support operations have many similarities.

3-8. The operational concept addresses more than combat between armed opponents. Army forces conduct operations amid populations. This requires Army forces to defeat the enemy and simultaneously shape civil conditions. Offensive and defensive tasks defeat enemy forces; stability tasks shape civil conditions. Winning battles and engagements is important but alone may not be decisive. Shaping civil conditions (in concert with civilian organizations, civil authorities, and multinational forces) is just as important to campaign success. In many joint operations, stability or civil support often prove more important than the offense and defense.

3-9. The emphasis on different elements of full spectrum operations changes with echelon, time, and location. In an operation dominated by stability, part of the force might be conducting simultaneous offensive and defensive tasks. Within the United States, civil support operations may be the only activity actually conducted. In short, no single element is always more important than the others. Rather, *simultaneous combinations* of the elements, which commanders constantly adapt to conditions, are the key to successful land operations.

3-10. Operations today require versatile, adaptive units and tough, flexible leadership. These qualities develop first and foremost from training that prepares individuals and units for challenging operational environments. Managing training for full spectrum operations challenges leaders at all echelons. Training for offensive and defensive tasks develops discipline, endurance, unit cohesion, and tolerance for uncertainty. It prepares Soldiers and units to address ambiguities and complexities inherent in stability and civil support operations as well. However, operational experience demonstrates that forces trained exclusively for offensive and defensive tasks are not as proficient at stability tasks as those trained specifically for stability are. For maximum effectiveness, stability and civil support tasks require dedicated training, similar to training for offensive and defensive tasks. Likewise, forces involved in protracted stability or civil support operations require intensive training to regain proficiency in offensive or defensive tasks before engaging in large-scale combat operations. Effective training reflects a balance among the elements of full spectrum operations that produces and sustains proficiency in all of them. Commanders adjust their emphasis by developing their core mission-essential task list. (FM 7-0 discusses training management.)

INITIATIVE

3-11. All Army operations aim to seize, retain, and exploit the initiative and achieve decisive results. *Operational initiative* **is setting or dictating the terms of action throughout an operation**. Initiative gives all operations the spirit, if not the form, of the offense. It originates in the principle of the offensive. The principle of the offensive goes beyond attacking. It embodies seizing, retaining, and exploiting the initiative as the surest way to achieve decisive results. It requires positive action to change both information and the situation on the ground. Risk and opportunity are intrinsic in seizing the initiative. To seize the initiative, commanders evaluate and accept prudent risks. Opportunities never last long. Unless commanders willingly accept risk and then act, the enemy will likely close the window of opportunity and exploit friendly inaction. Once Army forces seize the initiative, they exploit the created opportunities. Initiative requires constant effort to control tempo while maintaining freedom of action. The offensive mindset, with its focus on initiative, is central to the Army's operational concept and guides all leaders in the performance of their duty. It emphasizes opportunity created by action through full spectrum operations, whether offensive, defensive, stability, or civil support.

3-12. In combat operations, commanders force the enemy to respond to friendly action. In the offense, it is about taking the fight to the enemy and never allowing enemy forces to recover from the initial shock of the attack. In the defense, it is about preventing the enemy from achieving success and then counterattacking to seize the initiative. The object is not just to kill enemy personnel and destroy their equipment. Combat operations aim to force the enemy to react continuously and finally to be driven into untenable positions. Retaining the initiative pressures enemy commanders into abandoning their preferred options, accepting too much risk, or making costly mistakes. As enemy mistakes occur, friendly forces seize opportunities and create new avenues for an exploitation. The ultimate goal is to break the enemy's will through relentless pressure.

3-13. In stability and civil support operations, initiative is about improving civil conditions and applying combat power to prevent the situation from deteriorating. Commanders identify nonmilitary but critical objectives to achieving the end state. Such objectives may include efforts to ensure effective governance, reconstruction projects that promote social well-being, and consistent actions to improve public safety. All of these contribute to retaining and exploiting the initiative in stability operations. An enemy insurgent, for example, cannot allow stability efforts to succeed without serious consequences and must react. As the enemy reacts, Army forces maintain the initiative by modifying their own lethal and nonlethal actions, forcing the enemy to change plans and remain on the defensive. Army forces retain the initiative by anticipating both enemy actions and civil requirements and by acting positively to address them. In civil support, Army forces take action to restore normalcy. Soldiers work closely with their civilian counterparts to remedy the conditions threatening lives, property, and domestic order. In some situations, rapid and determined action by Army forces becomes the stimulus that prompts a demoralized civilian community to begin recovery.

3-14. Seizing, retaining, and exploiting the initiative depends on *individual initiative*—**the willingness to act in the absence of orders, when existing orders no longer fit the situation, or when unforeseen opportunities or threats arise**. Military history contains many instances where a subordinate's action or inaction significantly affected the tactical, operational, or even strategic situation. When opportunity occurs, it is often fleeting. Subordinate leaders need to act quickly, even as they report the situation to their commanders. Individual initiative is a key component of mission command. Full spectrum operations depend on subordinate commanders exercising individual initiative and higher commanders giving them the authority to do so. (Chapter 5 discusses mission command.)

SIMULTANEITY AND SYNCHRONIZATION

3-15. Simultaneously executing the elements of full spectrum operations requires the synchronized application of combat power. *Synchronization* is the arrangement of military actions in time, space, and purpose to produce maximum relative combat power at a decisive place and time (JP 2-0). It is the ability to execute multiple related and mutually supporting tasks in different locations at the same time, producing greater effects than executing each in isolation. Synchronization is a means, not an end. Commanders balance it with agility and initiative; they never surrender the initiative for the sake of synchronization. Rather, they synchronize activities to best facilitate mission accomplishment. Excessive synchronization can lead to over control, which limits the initiative of subordinates.

3-16. Simultaneity means doing multiple things at the same time. It requires the ability to conduct operations in depth and to integrate them so that their timing multiplies their effectiveness. Commanders consider their entire area of operations, the enemy, information activities necessary to shape the operational environment, and civil conditions. Then they mount simultaneous operations that immobilize, suppress, or shock the enemy. Such actions nullify the enemy's ability to conduct synchronized, mutually supporting actions. Army forces increase the depth of their operations through combined arms, advanced information systems, and joint capabilities. Because Army forces conduct operations across large areas, the enemy faces many potential friendly actions. Executing operations in depth is equally important in stability operations; commanders act to keep threats from operating outside the reach of friendly forces. In civil support operations and some stability operations, depth includes conducting operations that reach all citizens in the area of operations, bringing relief as well as hope. (Chapter 6 discusses depth at the operational level.)

LETHAL AND NONLETHAL ACTIONS

3-17. An inherent, complementary relationship exists between using lethal force and applying military capabilities for nonlethal purposes. Though each situation requires a different mix of violence and constraint, lethal and nonlethal actions used together complement each other and create dilemmas for opponents. Lethal actions are critical to accomplishing offensive and defensive missions. However, nonlethal actions are also important contributors to full spectrum operations, regardless of which element dominates. Finding ways to accomplish the mission with an appropriate mix of lethal and nonlethal force remains an important consideration for every commander. Commanders analyze the situation carefully to achieve a balance between lethal and nonlethal actions.

Lethal Actions

3-18. Offensive and defensive operations place a premium on employing the lethal effects of combat power against the enemy. In these operations, speed, surprise, and shock are vital considerations. Historically, the side better able to combine them defeats its opponent rapidly while incurring fewer losses. Such victories create opportunities for an exploitation. In some operations, the effects of speed, surprise, and shock are enough to collapse organized resistance. Such a collapse occurred in the offensive phase of Operation Iraqi Freedom in 2003.

3-19. Speed is swiftness of action. It allows a force to act before the enemy is ready or before the situation deteriorates further. Speed requires being able to adjust operations quickly to dynamic conditions. It increases opportunities to exploit momentary tactical advantages and expand them to retain and exploit the initiative. Wherever possible, Army forces exploit their advantages in command and control, tactical mobility, and joint capabilities to operate at a higher tempo than the enemy. Delegating decisionmaking authority to subordinates through mission command allows commanders to increase the speed of decisionmaking and execution in most situations. Rapid friendly action may surprise the enemy and create opportunities.

3-20. Surprise is achieved by acting at a time, acting in a place, or using methods to which the enemy cannot effectively react or does not expect. Speed contributes to surprise. So does executing operations simultaneously and in depth. Exploiting advantages gained through security, military deception, and aggressive intelligence, surveillance, and reconnaissance operations contributes to surprise. Surprise is essential when executing offensive missions that complement stability operations (such as a raid). It mitigates the effectiveness of enemy early warning networks within the local populace.

3-21. Shock results from applying overwhelming violence. Combat power applied with enough speed and magnitude to overwhelm the enemy produces it. Shock slows and disrupts enemy operations. Usually transient, but while it lasts, shock may paralyze the enemy's ability to fight. Sometimes the psychological effects of threatening to use overwhelming violence can also produce shock. Shock is often greater when created with asymmetric means. Joint forces create opportunities to increase it by using capabilities against which the enemy has limited defense. Surprise and speed magnify the effects of shock.

Nonlethal Actions

3-22. Army forces employ a variety of nonlethal means in stability and civil support operations. Stability operations often involve using military capabilities to perform such tasks as restoring essential services. Civil support operations are characterized by providing constructive support to civil authorities. However, demonstrating the potential for lethal action (by actions such as increased military presence in an area) often contributes to maintaining order during stability and some civil support operations. Other examples include such actions as pre-assault warnings and payments for collateral damage.

3-23. Friendly and enemy forces continuously struggle for information advantages while conducting operations in the physical domains. Friendly information actions shape the operational environment by attacking the enemy's command and control system, defending against electronic attacks, and protecting friendly information. Increasingly sophisticated capabilities allow Army forces to identify, disrupt, and exploit enemy communications (including networks). These actions may keep the enemy from massing combat power effectively or synchronizing combined arms operations. Commanders may use electromagnetic means alone or with maneuver and lethal fires.

3-24. Nonlethal actions in combat include a wide range of intelligence-gathering, disruptive, and other activities. Effective maneuver and fires require timely, accurate intelligence and effective mission command networks and systems. The threat of detection often compels the enemy to limit or cease operations. This inaction allows friendly forces to seize the initiative. Interference with enemy command and control through nonlethal means can also limit enemy effectiveness and increase its exposure to attack.

3-25. The United States continues to develop nonlethal weapons that allow commanders to apply force without killing or crippling an enemy. These weapons provide options in situations that restrict the use of lethal force or when enemy fighters intermix with noncombatants. Furthermore, nonlethal means can mitigate the indirect effects on noncombatants of lethal actions directed against the enemy.

3-26. Stability and civil support operations emphasize nonlethal, constructive actions by Soldiers working among noncombatants. Civil affairs personnel have a major role. In stability operations, they work with and through host-nation agencies and other civilian organizations to enhance the host-nation government's legitimacy. Commanders use inform and influence activities shaped by intelligence to inform, influence, and persuade the local populace within limits prescribed by U.S. law. They also integrate inform and influence activities with stability tasks to counter false and distorted information and propaganda.

3-27. Nonlethal, constructive actions can persuade the local populace to withhold support from the enemy and provide information to friendly forces. Loss of popular support presents the enemy with two bad choices: stay and risk capture or depart and risk exposure to lethal actions in less populated areas. Commanders focus on managing the local populace's expectations and countering rumors. However, they recognize that their Soldiers' actions, positive and negative, most strongly sway the populace's perception of Army forces.

3-28. The moral advantage provided by the presence of well-trained, well-equipped, and well-led forces can be a potent nonlethal capability. It creates fear and doubt in the minds of the enemy and may deter adversaries. This effect is important in many stability-dominated operations. Even though stability operations emphasize nonlethal actions, the ability to engage potential enemies with decisive lethal force remains a sound deterrent. Enemy commanders may curtail their activities and avoid combat if they perceive Army forces as highly capable and willing to use precise, lethal force. This permits Army forces to extend the scope and tempo of nonlethal actions.

THE ELEMENTS OF FULL SPECTRUM OPERATIONS

3-29. Full spectrum operations require simultaneous combinations of four elements—offense, defense, and stability or civil support. Figure 3-2 lists the elements of full spectrum operations, the primary tasks associated with them, and the purposes of each element. Each primary task has numerous associated subordinate tasks. When combined with who (unit), when (time), where (location), and why (purpose), the primary tasks become mission statements.

Offensive Operations	*Defensive Operations*
Primary Tasks: <ul><li>Movement to contact</li><li>Attack</li><li>Exploitation</li><li>Pursuit</li></ul> **Purposes:** <ul><li>Dislocate, isolate, disrupt, and destroy enemy forces</li><li>Seize key terrain</li><li>Deprive the enemy of resources</li><li>Develop intelligence</li><li>Deceive and divert the enemy</li><li>Create a secure environment for stability operations</li></ul>	**Primary Tasks:** <ul><li>Mobile defense</li><li>Area defense</li><li>Retrograde</li></ul> **Purposes:** <ul><li>Deter or defeat enemy offensive operations</li><li>Gain time</li><li>Achieve economy of force</li><li>Retain key terrain</li><li>Protect the populace, critical assets, and infrastructure</li><li>Develop intelligence</li></ul>
Stability Operations	*Civil Support Operations*
Primary Tasks: <ul><li>Civil security (including security force assistance)</li><li>Civil control</li><li>Restore essential services</li><li>Support to governance</li><li>Support to economic and infrastructure development</li></ul> **Purposes:** <ul><li>Provide a secure environment</li><li>Secure land areas</li><li>Meet the critical needs of the populace</li><li>Gain support for host-nation government</li><li>Shape the environment for interagency and host-nation success</li></ul>	**Primary Tasks:** <ul><li>Provide support for domestic disasters</li><li>Provide support for domestic chemical, biological, radiological, nuclear, and high-yield explosives incidents</li><li>Provide support for domestic civilian law enforcement agencies</li><li>Provide other designated support</li></ul> **Purposes:** <ul><li>Save lives</li><li>Restore essential services</li><li>Maintain or restore law and order</li><li>Protect infrastructure and property</li><li>Maintain or restore local government</li><li>Shape the environment for interagency success</li></ul>

*Figure 3-2. The elements of full spectrum operations

OFFENSIVE OPERATIONS

3-30. *Offensive operations* **are combat operations conducted to defeat and destroy enemy forces and seize terrain, resources, and population centers. They impose the commander's will on the enemy**. In combat operations, the offense is the decisive element of full spectrum operations. Against a capable, adaptive enemy, the offense is the most direct and sure means of seizing, retaining, and exploiting the initiative to achieve decisive results. Executing offensive operations compels the enemy to react, creating or revealing weaknesses that the attacking force can exploit. Successful offensive operations place tremendous pressure on defenders, creating a cycle of deterioration that can lead to the enemy's disintegration. This was the case in early 2003 in Iraq, when coalition operations led to the collapse of the Iraqi military and ultimately the Baathist regime of Saddam Hussein.

3-31. While strategic, operational, or tactical considerations may require defending, defeating an enemy at any level eventually requires shifting to the offense. Even in the defense, seizing and retaining the initiative requires executing offensive operations at some point. The more fluid the battle, the truer this is.

3-32. Effective offensive operations capitalize on accurate intelligence regarding the enemy, terrain and weather, and civil considerations. Commanders maneuver their forces to advantageous positions before making contact. However, commanders may shape conditions by deliberately making contact to develop the situation and mislead the enemy. In the offense, the decisive operation is a sudden, shattering action against an enemy weakness that capitalizes on speed, surprise, and shock. If that operation does not destroy the enemy, operations continue until enemy forces disintegrate or retreat to where they no longer pose a threat. (Chapter 5 discusses decisive, shaping, and sustaining operations.)

Primary Offensive Tasks

3-33. At the operational level, offensive operations defeat enemy forces that control important areas or contest the host-nation government's authority. The joint force conducts operations throughout its operational area. Army forces attack using ground and air maneuver to accomplish objectives that conclude the campaign or move it to a subsequent phase. In expeditionary campaigns and major operations, operational maneuver includes deploying land forces to positions that facilitate joint force offensive action. U.S. forces can conduct operational-level offensives in counterinsurgency to eliminate insurgent sanctuaries. Counterinsurgencies usually combine offensive and stability tasks to achieve decisive results.

3-34. In offensive operations, a force often transitions from one offensive task to another without pausing. For example, an attack can lead to an exploitation and then pursuit, or to an exploitation followed by another attack as enemy forces rally. Army forces perform the following primary offensive tasks. (FM 3-90 discusses them in detail.)

Movement to Contact

3-35. A movement to contact develops the situation and establishes or regains contact. It also sets favorable conditions for subsequent tactical actions. Forces executing this task seek to make contact with the smallest friendly force feasible. On contact, the commander has five options: attack, defend, bypass, delay, or withdraw. Movements to contact include search and attack and cordon and search operations.

Attack

3-36. An attack destroys or defeats enemy forces, seizes and secures terrain, or both. Attacks require maneuver supported by direct and indirect fires. They may be either decisive or shaping operations. Attacks may be hasty or deliberate, depending on the time available for planning and preparation. Commanders execute hasty attacks when the situation calls for immediate action with available forces and minimal preparation. They conduct deliberate attacks when they have more time to plan and prepare. Success depends on skillfully massing the effects of all the elements of combat power.

Exploitation

3-37. An exploitation rapidly follows a successful attack and disorganizes the enemy in depth. Exploitations seek to expand an attack to the point where enemy forces have no alternatives but to surrender or flee. Commanders of exploiting forces receive the greatest possible latitude to accomplish their missions. They lead with great aggressiveness, initiative, and boldness. Exploitations may be local or major. Local exploitations take advantage of tactical opportunities, foreseen or unforeseen. Division and higher headquarters normally conduct major exploitations using mobile forces to transform tactical success into a pursuit.

Pursuit

3-38. A pursuit is designed to catch or cut off a hostile force attempting to escape with the aim of destroying it. Pursuits often follow successful exploitations. However, they can develop at any point when enemy forces start to disintegrate or disengage. Pursuits occur when the enemy fails to organize a defense and attempts to disengage. If it becomes apparent that enemy resistance has broken down entirely and enemy forces are fleeing, a force can transition to a pursuit from any type of offensive or defensive operation. Pursuits require speed and decentralized control.

Purposes of Offensive Operations

3-39. Seizing, retaining, and exploiting the initiative is the essence of the offense. Offensive operations seek to throw enemy forces off balance, overwhelm their capabilities, disrupt their defenses, and ensure their defeat or destruction by synchronizing and applying all the elements of combat power. The offensive operation ends when it destroys or defeats the enemy, reaches a limit of advance, or approaches culmination. Army forces conclude an offense in one of four ways: consolidating gains through stability operations, resuming the attack, transitioning to the defense, or preparing for future operations. Army forces conduct offensive operations for the following purposes. (FM 3-90 discusses these purposes in detail.)

Dislocate, Isolate, Disrupt, and Destroy Enemy Forces

3-40. Well-executed offensive operations dislocate, isolate, disrupt, and destroy enemy forces. If destruction is not feasible, offensive operations compel enemy forces to retreat. Offensive maneuver seeks to place the enemy at a positional disadvantage. This allows friendly forces to mass overwhelming effects while defeating parts of the enemy force in detail before the enemy can escape or get reinforcements. When required, friendly forces close with and destroy the enemy in close combat. Ultimately, the enemy surrenders, retreats in disorder, or is eliminated altogether.

Seize Key Terrain

3-41. Offensive maneuver may seize terrain that provides the attacker with a decisive advantage. The enemy either retreats or risks defeat or destruction. If enemy forces retreat or attempt to retake the key terrain, they are exposed to fires and further friendly maneuver.

Deprive the Enemy of Resources

3-42. At the operational level, offensive operations may seize control of major population centers, seats of government, production facilities, and transportation infrastructure. Losing these resources greatly reduces the enemy's ability to resist. In some cases, Army forces secure population centers or infrastructure and prevent irregular forces from using them as a base or benefitting from the resources that they develop.

Develop Intelligence

3-43. Enemy deception, concealment, and security may prevent friendly forces from developing necessary intelligence. Commanders conduct some offensive operations to develop the situation and discover the enemy's intent, disposition, and capabilities.

Deceive and Divert the Enemy

3-44. Offensive operations distract enemy intelligence, surveillance, and reconnaissance. They may cause the enemy to shift reserves away from the friendly decisive operation.

Create a Secure Environment for Stability Operations

3-45. Stability operations cannot occur if significant enemy forces directly threaten or attack the local populace. Offensive operations destroy or isolate the enemy so stability operations can proceed. Offensive operations against insurgents help keep them off balance. These actions may force insurgents to defend their bases, thus keeping them from attacking.

DEFENSIVE OPERATIONS

3-46. **Defensive operations are combat operations conducted to defeat an enemy attack, gain time, economize forces, and develop conditions favorable for offensive or stability operations**. The defense alone normally cannot achieve a decision. However, it can set conditions for a counteroffensive operation that lets Army forces regain the initiative. Defensive operations can also establish a shield behind which stability operations can progress. Defensive operations counter enemy offensive operations. They defeat attacks, destroying as much of the attacking enemy as possible. They also preserve control over land, resources, and populations. Defensive operations retain terrain, guard populations, and protect critical capabilities against enemy attacks. Commanders can use defensive operations to gain time and economize forces so offensive tasks can be executed elsewhere.

3-47. Successful defensive operations share the following characteristics: preparation, security, disruption, massed effects, and flexibility. Successful defenses are aggressive. Commanders use all available means to disrupt enemy forces. They disrupt attackers and isolate them from mutual support to defeat them in detail. Isolation includes extensive use of cyber/electromagnetic activities. Defenders seek to increase their freedom of maneuver while denying it to attackers. Defending commanders use every opportunity to transition to the offense, even if temporarily. As attackers' losses increase, they falter and the initiative shifts to the defenders. These situations are favorable for counterattacks. Counterattack opportunities rarely last long; defenders strike swiftly when the attackers culminate. Surprise and speed complement shock and allow counterattacking forces to seize the initiative and overwhelm the attackers.

3-48. Conditions may not support immediate offensive operations during force projection. In those cases, initial-entry forces defend while the joint force builds combat power. Initial-entry forces should include enough combat power to deter, attack, or defend successfully.

Primary Defensive Tasks

3-49. At the operational level, an enemy offensive may compel joint forces to conduct major defensive operations. Such operations may require defeating or preventing attacks across international borders, defeating conventional attacks, or halting an insurgent movement's mobilization. Operational defenses may be executed anywhere in the operational area. The following primary tasks are associated with the defense. Defending commanders combine these tasks to fit the situation. (FM 3-90 discusses them in detail.)

Mobile Defense

3-50. In a mobile defense, the defender withholds a large portion of available forces for use as a striking force in a counterattack. Mobile defenses require enough depth to let enemy forces advance into a position that exposes them to counterattack. The defense separates attacking forces from their support and disrupts the enemy's command and control. As enemy forces extend themselves in the defended area and lose momentum and organization, the defender surprises and overwhelms them with a powerful counterattack.

Area Defense

3-51. In an area defense, the defender concentrates on denying enemy forces access to designated terrain for a specific time, limiting their freedom of maneuver and channeling them into killing areas. The defender retains terrain that the attacker must control in order to advance. Friendly forces draw the enemy force into a series of kill zones where they attack and destroy the enemy from mutually supporting positions, largely by fires. Commanders commit most of the defending force to defending positions while keeping the rest in reserve. They use the reserve to preserve the integrity of the defense through reinforcement or counterattack.

Retrograde

3-52. Retrograde involves organized movement away from the enemy. This includes delays, withdrawals, and retirements. Retrograde operations gain time, preserve forces, place the enemy in unfavorable positions, or avoid combat under undesirable conditions.

Mobile and Static Elements in the Defense

3-53. All three primary defensive tasks use mobile and static elements. In mobile defenses, static positions help control the depth and breadth of the enemy penetration and retain ground from which to launch counterattacks. In area defenses, commanders closely integrate mobile patrols, security forces, sensors, and reserves to cover gaps among defensive positions. In retrograde operations, some units conduct area or mobile defenses along with security operations to protect other units executing carefully controlled maneuver or movement rearward. Mobile elements maneuver constantly to confuse the enemy and prevent an enemy exploitation. Static elements fix, disrupt, turn, or block the attackers and gain time for other forces to pull back.

Purposes of Defensive Operations

3-54. Defending forces await the enemy's attack and counter it. Waiting for the attack is not a passive activity. Commanders conduct aggressive security operations and intelligence, surveillance, and reconnaissance. Such actions locate enemy forces and deny them information. Defenders engage enemy forces with fires, spoiling attacks, and security operations to weaken them before they reach the main battle area. Commanders use combined arms and joint capabilities to attack enemy vulnerabilities and seize the initiative. Army forces conduct defensive operations for the following purposes. (FM 3-90 discusses these purposes in detail.)

Deter or Defeat Enemy Offensive Operations

3-55. The primary purpose of the defense is to deter or defeat enemy offensive operations. Successful defenses stall enemy actions and create opportunities to seize the initiative. Defensive operations may deter potential aggressors if they believe that breaking the friendly defense would be too costly.

Gain Time

3-56. Commanders may conduct a defense to gain time. Such defensive operations succeed by slowing or halting an attack while allowing friendly reserves enough time to reinforce the defense. Delaying actions trade space for time to improve defenses, expose enemy forces to joint attack, and prepare counterattacks.

Achieve Economy of Force

3-57. The defense is also used to achieve economy of force. Astute use of terrain, depth, and security operations allows friendly forces to minimize resources used defensively. This allows commanders to concentrate combat power for offensive operations.

Retain Key Terrain

3-58. The mission of many defensive operations is to retain key terrain. Units use mobile and area defense to prevent enemy forces from occupying key terrain. Control of key terrain can sway the outcome of the battle or engagement, depending on which side controls it. In operations dominated by stability tasks, friendly bases become key terrain.

Protect the Populace, Critical Assets, and Infrastructure

3-59. Defense of the local populace and vital assets supports stability operations and allows Army forces to receive greater support from the host nation. Army forces protect military and civilian areas that are important to success and provide indirect support to operations worldwide. Achieving this purpose begins with defenses around lodgments and bases, ensuring freedom of action. This protection especially applies to counterinsurgency operations where some facilities have significant economic and political value as opposed to tactical military importance.

Develop Intelligence

3-60. As with the offense, defensive operations may develop intelligence. The more successful the defense, the more Army forces learn about the enemy. Forces may conduct a particular phase or task within a defense (for example, a covering force mission) to satisfy commander's critical information requirements about the enemy's direction of attack and main effort.

STABILITY OPERATIONS

3-61. *Stability operations* is an overarching term encompassing various military missions, tasks, and activities conducted outside the United States in coordination with other instruments of national power to maintain or reestablish a safe and secure environment, provide essential governmental services, emergency infrastructure reconstruction, and humanitarian relief (JP 3-0). Forces can conduct stability operations to support a host-nation or interim government or as part of an occupation when no government exists. Stability operations involve both coercive and constructive military actions. They help to establish a safe and secure environment and facilitate reconciliation among local or regional adversaries. Stability operations can also help establish political, legal, social, and economic institutions and support the transition to legitimate local governance. Stability operations must maintain the initiative by pursuing objectives that resolve the causes of instability. (See paragraphs 3-11 through 3-14.) Stability operations cannot succeed if they only react to enemy initiatives.

3-62. Stability operations require transparency and credibility. Transparency and credibility enhance coordination, integration, and synchronization among host-nation elements, other government agencies, and Army forces. The degree to which the host nation cooperates is fundamental. Commanders publicize their mandate and intentions. Within the limits of operations security, they make the populace aware of the techniques used to provide security and control. Actions on the ground reinforced by a clear and consistent message produce transparency. This transparency reinforces credibility. Credibility reflects the populace's assessment of whether the force can accomplish the mission. Army forces require the structure, resources, and rules of engagement appropriate to accomplishing the mission and discharging their duties swiftly and firmly. They must leave no doubt as to their capability and intentions.

3-63. Civil affairs activities enhance the relationship between military forces and civil authorities in areas with military forces. They involve applying civil affairs functional specialty skills to areas normally under the responsibility of civil government. These operations involve establishing, maintaining, influencing, or exploiting relations between military forces and all levels of host-nation government agencies. These activities are fundamental to executing stability tasks. Civil affairs personnel, other Army forces, personnel from other government agencies, or a combination of all three perform these tasks.

3-64. Civil affairs units and personnel develop detailed civil considerations assessments. These include information about infrastructure, civilian institutions, and the attitudes and activities of civilian leaders, populations, and organizations. These assessments may reveal that a viable host-nation government does not exist or is incapable of performing its functions. In such cases, Army forces may support or exercise governmental authority until the host nation establishes a host-nation civil authority. (JP 3-57 and FMs 3-05.40 and 3-05.401 contain civil affairs doctrine.)

Primary Stability Tasks

3-65. Army forces perform five primary stability tasks. (FM 3-07 discusses these tasks in detail.) The combination of tasks conducted during stability operations depends on the situation. In some operations, the host nation can meet most or all of the population's requirements. In those cases, Army forces work with and through host-nation authorities. Commanders use civil affairs activities to mitigate how the military presence affects the populace and vice versa. Conversely, Army forces operating in a failed state may need to support the well-being of the local populace. That situation requires Army forces to work with civilian agencies to restore basic capabilities. Again, civil affairs activities prove essential in establishing trust between Army forces and civilian organizations required for effective, working relationships.

3-66. Stability operations may be necessary to develop host-nation capacities for security and control of security forces, a viable market economy, the rule of law, and an effective government. Army forces develop these capabilities by working with the host nation. They aim to build a stable, civil situation sustainable by host-nation assets without Army forces. Security, the health of the local economy, and the capability of self-government interrelate. Without security, the local economy falters. A functioning economy provides employment and reduces the dependence of the population on the military for necessities. Security and economic stability precede an effective and stable government.

3-67. Stability operations require the absence of major threats to friendly forces and the populace. As offensive operations clear areas of hostile forces, part of the force secures critical infrastructure and populated areas. Establishing civil security and essential services are implied tasks for commanders during any combat operation. Commanders should act to minimize and relieve civilian suffering. However, if a unit becomes decisively engaged in combat operations, stability tasks should not divert it from its mission.

3-68. Commanders plan to minimize the effects of combat on the populace. They promptly inform their higher headquarters of civilian requirements and conditions that require attention. As units establish civil security, the force returns territory to civil authorities' control when feasible. Transitions to civil authority require coordinating and integrating civilian and military efforts. Unified action is crucial. Properly focused, effectively executed stability tasks prevent population centers from degenerating into civil unrest and becoming recruiting areas for opposition movements or insurgencies.

Civil Security

3-69. Civil security involves protecting the populace from external and internal threats. Ideally, Army forces defeat external threats posed by enemy forces that can attack population centers. Simultaneously, they assist host-nation police and security elements as the host nation maintains internal security against terrorists, criminals, and small, hostile groups. In some situations, no adequate host-nation capability for civil security exists. Then, Army forces provide most civil security while developing host-nation capabilities. For the other stability tasks to work effectively, civil security is required. As soon as the host-nation security forces can safely perform this task, Army forces transition civil security responsibilities to them.

3-70. *Army doctrine defines *security force assistance* as the unified action to generate, employ, and sustain local, host-nation, or regional security forces in support of a legitimate authority (FM 3-07). Security force assistance is a stability task conducted across the spectrum of conflict or in any of the operational themes. Normally, it comprises a part of a larger security sector reform effort; however, security force assistance is not tied to reform but to building partner capacity.

3-71. *Three general situations exist in which security force assistance may occur: an internally focused bilateral relationship, an externally focused bilateral relationship, and a multilateral relationship. Consequently, security force assistance supports the appropriate partner's plans. When security force assistance supports a host nation, it also supports that host nation's strategy. If security force assistance supports a host nation's externally focused efforts, it must support the host nation's national security strategy. Security force assistance may support regional security forces, such as those of the African Union or the Organization of American States. In these cases, security force assistance supports that organization's plans. (See FM 3-07.1 for details on security force assistance.)

Civil Control

3-72. Civil control regulates selected behavior and activities of individuals and groups. This control reduces risk to individuals or groups and promotes security. Civil control channels the population's activities to allow provision of security and essential services while coexisting with a military force conducting operations. A curfew is an example of civil control.

Restore Essential Services

3-73. Army forces establish or restore the most basic services and protect them until a civil authority or the host nation can provide them. Normally, Army forces support civilian and host-nation agencies. When the host nation cannot perform its role, Army forces may provide the basics directly. Essential services include the following:
- Providing emergency medical care and rescue.
- Preventing epidemic disease.
- Providing food and water.
- Providing emergency shelter.
- Providing basic sanitation (sewage and garbage disposal).

Support to Governance

3-74. Stability operations establish conditions that enable actions by civilian and host-nation agencies to succeed. By establishing security and control, stability operations provide a foundation for transitioning authority to civilian agencies and eventually to the host nation. Once this transition is complete, commanders focus on transferring control to a legitimate civil authority according to the desired end state. Support to governance includes the following:

- Developing and supporting host-nation control of public activities, the rule of law, and civil administration.
- Maintaining security, control, and essential services through host-nation agencies. This includes training and equipping host-nation security forces and police.
- Supporting host-nation efforts to normalize the succession of power (elections and appointment of officials).

Support to Economic and Infrastructure Development

3-75. Support to economic and infrastructure development helps a host nation develop capability and capacity in these areas. It may involve direct and indirect military assistance to national, regional, and local entities.

Purposes of Stability Operations

3-76. Although Army forces focus on achieving the military end state, they ultimately need to establish conditions where the other instruments of national power are preeminent. Stability operations focus on creating those conditions. Paragraphs 3-77 through 3-81 discuss the purposes of stability operations. (See FM 3-07 for a discussion on stability operations.)

Provide a Secure Environment

3-77. A key stability task is providing a safe, secure environment. This involves isolating enemy fighters from the local populace and protecting the population. By providing security and helping host-nation authorities control civilians, Army forces begin separating the enemy from the general population. Inform and influence activities complement physical isolation by persuading the populace to support an acceptable, legitimate host-nation government. This isolates the enemy politically and economically.

Secure Land Areas

3-78. Effective stability operations, together with host-nation capabilities, help secure land areas. Areas of population unrest often divert forces that may be urgently needed elsewhere. In contrast, stable areas may support bases and infrastructure for friendly forces, allowing a commitment of forces elsewhere.

Meet the Critical Needs of the Populace

3-79. Often, stability operations must meet the critical needs of the populace. Army forces can provide essential services until the host-nation government or other agencies can do so.

Gain Support for Host-Nation Government

3-80. Successful stability operations ultimately depend on the legitimacy of the host-nation government— its acceptance by the populace as the governing body. All stability operations are conducted with that aim.

Shape the Environment for Interagency and Host-Nation Success

3-81. Stability operations shape the environment for interagency and host-nation success. They do this by providing the security and control necessary for host-nation and interagency elements to function, and supporting them in other key functions.

Stability Operations and Department of State Post-Conflict Technical Sectors

3-82. The stability tasks are linked to the Department of State post-conflict reconstruction and stabilization technical sectors. Normally, Army forces act to support host-nation and other civilian agencies. However, when the host nation cannot provide basic government functions, Army forces may be required to do so directly. The Department of State organizes conditions related to post-conflict stability into five sectors. (See figure 3-3.) Paragraphs 3-83 through 3-89 discuss the Army stability tasks that support these sectors.

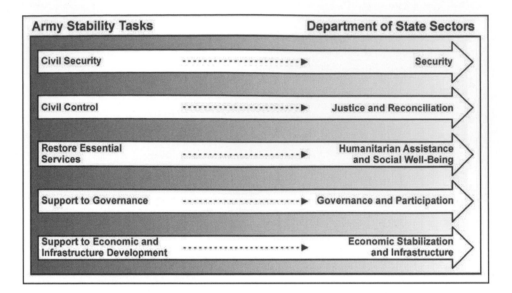

Figure 3-3. Stability tasks and Department of State technical sectors

Security

3-83. Army forces conduct operations to establish and maintain a safe and secure environment, whenever possible together with host-nation forces. They provide public order and safety and protect individuals, infrastructure, and institutions. Typically, offensive, defensive, and stability tasks all support this sector. Civil security and civil control are associated stability tasks. Initially, Army forces have the lead for this sector. Army operations should complement and be concurrent with other agencies' actions. Army forces hand over responsibility to host-nation agencies and assume a supporting role as these agencies develop the needed capabilities.

3-84. The first aim in the security sector is to limit adversaries' influence and isolate the populace from the enemy. Army forces use several methods to isolate the enemy. Isolation in some stability operations is indirect; it aims to redirect, compel, and influence the populace away from supporting adversaries and toward supporting the host-nation government. Concurrently, Army forces secure the support of populations in unstable areas. If the enemy poses a significant military threat, forces engaged in stability operations defend themselves and the populace from attacks. Army forces may conduct offensive operations to physically isolate, defeat, or destroy forces that threaten the stability mission. Security is the foremost condition; it underpins all other sectors.

Justice and Reconciliation

3-85. Establishing public order and safety and providing for social reconciliation are this sector's objectives. The host nation aims to establish self-sustaining public law and order that operates according to internationally recognized standards and respects human rights and freedoms.

Humanitarian Assistance and Social Well-Being

3-86. Army forces work to reduce human suffering, disease, and privation. This sector includes programs conducted to relieve or reduce the results of conditions that seriously threaten life or that can result in great damage to or loss of property. These conditions may be endemic or result from natural or manmade disasters.

Governance and Participation

3-87. This sector focuses on restoring or creating effective government institutions. These efforts involve strengthening host-nation governance and rebuilding government infrastructure. This sector also requires developing institutions that achieve sustainable peace and security, foster a sense of confidence, and support conditions for economic reconstruction. Army forces mainly strive to create an environment conducive to stable governance. Civilian agencies oversee areas such as the following:

- Reestablishing the administrative framework.
- Supporting development of a national constitution.
- Supporting political reform.
- Reforming or establishing fair taxation.

Economic Stabilization and Infrastructure

3-88. Infrastructure restoration begins with meeting the needs of the populace. It continues by restoring economic production and distribution. Army forces meet the basic needs of the populace by reconstituting the following:

- Power.
- Transportation.
- Communications.
- Health and sanitation.
- Firefighting.
- Mortuary services.
- Environmental control.

3-89. Once the basic infrastructure functions, efforts shift to stabilizing the economy. Economic stabilization consists of the following:

- Restoring employment opportunities.
- Initiating market reform.
- Mobilizing domestic and foreign investment.
- Supervising monetary reform and rebuilding public structures.

Use of Force in Stability Operations

3-90. When using force, precision is as important in stability missions as applying massed, overwhelming force is in offensive and defensive operations. Commanders at every level emphasize that in stability operations, violence not precisely applied is counterproductive. Speed, surprise, and shock are vital considerations in lethal actions; perseverance, legitimacy, and constraint are vital considerations in stability and civil support operations.

3-91. The presence of armed Soldiers operating among the local populace causes tension. Discipline and strict adherence to the rules of engagement are essential but not sufficient to reassure the population. In addressing the populace's apprehension, commanders balance protecting the force, defeating enemy forces, and taking constructive action throughout the area of operations. They also stress cultural awareness in training and preparing for operations. Cultural awareness makes Soldiers more effective when operating in a foreign population and allows them to use local culture to enhance the effectiveness of their operations.

3-92. In peace operations, commanders emphasize impartiality in the use of force in addition to credibility and transparency. Impartiality is not neutrality. Impartiality does not imply that Army forces treat all sides equally. Commanders use force against threats in accordance with the rules of engagement. Fair treatment of the local populace improves the prospects for lasting peace, stability, and security.

CIVIL SUPPORT OPERATIONS

3-93. *Civil support* is Department of Defense support to US civil authorities for domestic emergencies, and for designated law enforcement and other activities (JP 3-28). Civil support includes operations that address the consequences of natural or manmade disasters, accidents, terrorist attacks, and incidents in the United States and its territories. Army forces conduct civil support operations when the size and scope of events exceed the capabilities or capacities of domestic civilian agencies. Usually the Army National Guard is the first military force to respond on behalf of state authorities. In this capacity, it functions under authority of Title 32, United States Code, or while serving on state active duty. The National Guard is suited to accomplish these missions; however, the scope and level of destruction may require states to request assistance from Federal authorities. (FM 3-28 provides a more complete overview of civil support operations.)

*Primary Civil Support Tasks

3-94. U.S. law carefully limits actions that military forces, particularly Regular Army units, can conduct in the United States and its territories. The Posse Comitatus Act, for example, prohibits Soldiers on Federal active duty from enforcing the law outside of Federal military installations. Because the Posse Comitatus Act does not apply to state National Guard forces, Soldiers under state control have law enforcement authorities that Regular Army and Army Reserve units do not have. (FM 3-28 provides extensive discussion on legal considerations for civil support.)

3-95. The operational environment within the United States differs so much from that outside the United States that civil support operations have become their own element of full spectrum operations. The purposes of civil support and stability operations are similar, but operational variables will radically differ. For example, units conduct civil support operations to support Federal and state agencies. These agencies are trained, resourced, and equipped more extensively than similar agencies involved in stability operations overseas. In civil support operations, the military is not in charge; civilians from these agencies set the priorities and Army forces coordinate and synchronize their efforts closely with them. Another example occurs with multinational participation. In stability operations, multinational participation is typical; in civil support operations, it is the exception.

3-96. Army civil support operations consist of four primary tasks:
- Provide support for domestic disasters.
- Provide support for domestic chemical, biological, radiological, nuclear, and high-yield explosives (CBRNE) incidents.
- Provide support for domestic civilian law enforcement agencies.
- Provide other designated support.

*Provide Support for Domestic Disasters

3-97. Policies issued by the Federal government provide a comprehensive, tiered approach for disaster response and govern the support Army forces provide in response to natural and manmade disasters. In the event of disaster, Army forces support civil authorities with essential services, including—
- Emergency route clearance.
- Search and rescue support.
- Emergency medical care and medical evacuation.
- Support to medical agencies to detect and prevent serious diseases.
- Distribution of food and water
- Emergency shelter construction and support.
- Sanitation support (sewage and garbage disposal).
- Delivery of personnel and supplies to severely affected areas.

3-98. Any major disaster will reduce the state and local governments' capacities. Army forces support Federal and state officials to help restore and return control of local services to civil authorities as rapidly as possible. When tasked, Army forces may provide additional support to government agencies at all levels until they can carry out their responsibilities without Army assistance. This support includes communications support, surveillance, critical infrastructure protection, and logistic assistance. In dire situations, and as authorized by law, Army forces may enforce the law (see paragraphs 3-102 and 3-103).

Provide Support for Domestic Chemical, Biological, Radiological, Nuclear, and High-Yield Explosives Incidents

3-99. The most dangerous threats to the homeland come from terrorist groups armed with weapons of mass destruction (WMD). After an attack with WMD, Federal, military, and state National Guard forces provide specialized capabilities and general-purpose forces to support response and recovery operations in the event of an attack involving CBRNE. These incidents combine disaster response and support to civilian law enforcement within a deadly operational environment.

3-100. Not every biological threat is from terrorists, or even manmade. A pandemic occurs when a new disease emerges for which people have little or no immunity and for which no vaccine immediately exists. "Pandemic influenza" refers to an influenza virus that infects humans across a large area and proves very difficult to contain. The word "pandemic" confuses many people, particularly those who equate it with mass casualties. Influenza outbreaks are always serious because the virus may mutate into something more lethal as it spreads. Army support to pandemic response is both internal and external. Internally, Army installations take all applicable force health protection measures to maintain the combat readiness of the force. Externally, Army forces respond to lead Federal and state agencies requests for support in dealing with the disease.

3-101. Other outbreaks of infectious disease may prove more serious than a contagious influenza. These include animal diseases, such as hoof-and-mouth disease, and crop infestations caused by fungus, bacteria, or viruses. In these incidents, the Army provides support when requested by government agencies such as the Department of Agriculture. Although technically not pandemics, these incidents could entail significant support from the Department of Defense and National Guard.

Provide Support for Domestic Civilian Law Enforcement Agencies

3-102. This task applies to the use of military assets to support any civilian agency charged with enforcing the laws within the United States and its territories. Army forces support civilian law enforcement under Constitutional and statutory restrictions and corresponding directives and regulations. When authorized and directed, Army forces provide support to Federal, state, and local law enforcement officers. The governor of each state may call out the National Guard of that state to enforce laws. In extreme cases, and when directed by the President, Federal military forces maintain law and order. Army leaders must understand the statutes governing the use of military assets for civilian law enforcement. By understanding these statutes, Soldiers can avoid violating laws while accomplishing desired objectives.

3-103. Support may be direct or indirect. Direct support requires Soldiers to enforce the law (apprehend, arrest, stop and search, and so on). Normally, the National Guard Soldiers acting under State authority rather than Regular Army or U.S. Army Reserve Soldiers provide direct support. Except in extraordinary circumstances, the Posse Comitatus Act prevents Federal troops, to include National Guard troops in Federal status, from providing anything other than indirect support. Indirect support tasks Soldiers to provide assistance and equipment to civilian law enforcement officers, but grants them no authority to enforce the law. Since 2001, the importance of indirect support to civilian law enforcement agencies by Federal and National Guard military forces has increased commensurate with critical requirements for homeland security. The missions that Army forces may receive include—

- Support border security with equipment and personnel.
- Support counterdrug efforts at the national and state level.
- Provide law enforcement support in the aftermath of a disaster.
- Provide support to civilian law enforcement during a civil disturbance.
- Provide equipment and training to civilian law enforcement officers.
- Augment airport security measures.

Provide Other Designated Support

3-104. This task includes pre-planned, routine, and periodic support not related to disasters or emergencies. Most often, this support applies to major public events and consists of participatory support, special transportation, and additional security. These events are national special security events such as the Olympics, an inauguration, or a state funeral. Some missions may involve specific support requested by a

Federal or state agency to augment their capabilities due to labor shortages or a sudden increase in demands. Such support may extend to augment critical government services by Soldiers as authorized by the President and directed by the Secretary of Defense. Missions may include—

- Participation in major public sporting events.
- Critical infrastructure protection.
- Wildland firefighting.
- Providing military equipment and Soldiers to community events.

Purposes of Civil Support Tasks

3-105. Army forces execute civil support tasks to save lives, restore essential services, maintain or restore law and order, protect infrastructure and property, maintain or restore local government, and shape the environment for interagency success.

Save Lives

3-106. The first priority in civil support operations is to save lives. Immediately following a manmade or natural disaster, the first military forces to arrive focus on rescue, evacuation, and consequence management.

Restore Essential Services

3-107. In any major disaster, citizens suffer and may die because it disrupts most, if not all, essential services. This disruption leads to tremendous suffering and the spread of disease. Restoring essential services is crucial to saving lives over the long term and providing the first step to recovery.

Maintain or Restore Law and Order

3-108. When authorized, Army forces assist Federal, state, and local authorities with law enforcement. Often the Army provides support under crisis conditions when events overwhelm civil capacity. In other cases, the Army provides personnel and equipment to support ongoing law enforcement activities, such as control of U.S. borders. In all instances, Army forces use lethal force in accordance with rules for the use of force and only as a last resort.

Protect Infrastructure and Property

3-109. In the aftermath of a disaster or civil disturbance, Army forces frequently secure public and private property. This allows civilian law enforcement to focus on dealing with criminal behavior.

Maintain or Restore Local Government

3-110. In a disaster, local government may be unable to carry out its normal functions. Army forces provide essential services and communications support to local government officials until they can resume their normal functions.

Shape the Environment for Interagency Success

3-111. Success in civil support operations is measured by the success of civilian officials in carrying out their responsibilities. Civil support helps government officials meet their responsibilities to the public, ultimately without assistance from military forces.

Civil Support Operations and Homeland Security

3-112. Army forces conduct civil support operations as part of homeland security. Homeland security provides the Nation with strategic flexibility by protecting its citizens, critical assets, and infrastructure from conventional and unconventional threats. It includes three missions. (JP 3-28 discusses these missions in detail.)

Homeland Defense

3-113. Homeland defense protects the United States from direct attack or a threat by hostile armed forces. In the event of such an attack, Army forces under joint command conduct offensive and defensive operations against the enemy while providing civil support to Federal authorities. A defensive task routinely conducted in homeland defense protects critical assets and key infrastructure during crises. The ability to conduct offensive operations, though maintained primarily as a potential, is also present.

Civil Support

3-114. Civil support includes the key tasks of providing support in response to disaster and supporting law enforcement (as discussed in paragraphs 3-97 and 3-102). Unless the United States is attacked, Army forces conduct civil support operations exclusive of the offense and defense.

Emergency Preparedness Planning

3-115. In emergency preparedness planning, the Department of Homeland Security examines a wide range of threats and plans for manmade and natural disasters and incidents. The Department of Defense supports emergency preparedness planning. When necessary, these plans are executed as civil support operations.

COMBINING THE ELEMENTS OF FULL SPECTRUM OPERATIONS

3-116. Within the concept of operations, the proportion and role of offensive, defensive, and stability or civil support tasks vary based on several factors. Changes in the nature of the operation, the tactics used, and where the environment falls on the spectrum of conflict affect the mix and focus. Some combinations may be sequential, such as a mobile defense followed by a counteroffensive, but many occur simultaneously. During major combat operations, a division may attack in one area, defend in another, and focus on stability tasks in a third. Offensive and defensive operations may be complemented with stability tasks and vice versa at any point of a campaign. Simultaneous combinations are also present in operational themes dominated by stability. A peace operation, for example, may include a mix of several elements. One force may conduct a raid against hostile forces (offense), while a second secures an important airport (defense), and a third provides sanitary and secure facilities to dislocated civilians (stability). In homeland security, civil support is often the only element executed, although forces may plan for defense.

3-117. Differing combinations of the elements of full spectrum operations generally characterize each operational theme. The combinations vary according to the conditions and requirements for each phase of a campaign or major operation. Commanders determine the weight of effort by considering the primary tasks and purposes for each element within the operational theme and which will be decisive. This allows commanders to translate their design into tactical actions. (FM 5-0 discusses design.)

3-118. Conducting full spectrum operations involves more than simultaneous execution of all its elements. It requires commanders and staffs to consider their units' capabilities and capacities relative to each element. Commanders consider their missions, decide which tactics to use, and balance the elements of full spectrum operations while preparing their concept of operations. They determine which tasks the force can accomplish simultaneously, if phasing is required, what additional resources it may need, and how to transition from one element to another. At the operational level, this requires looking beyond the current operation and prioritizing each element for the next phase or sequel.

3-119. The transition between elements of full spectrum operations requires careful assessment, prior planning, and unit preparation as commanders shift their combinations of full spectrum operations. Commanders first assess the situation to determine which primary tasks are applicable and the priority for each. For example, a division assigns a brigade combat team an area of operations and the tasks of eliminating any enemy remnants, securing a dam, and conducting stability operations following a joint offensive phase. The brigade commander determines that the brigade will conduct three tasks: (1) conduct an area defense of the dam, (2) control the civil population in the area while excluding all civilians from the area of the dam, and (3) conduct movements to contact in various objective areas, specifically search and attack operations. Simultaneously, the brigade staff begins planning for the next phase in which civil security, civil control, and assisting the local authorities with essential services will become priorities, while continuing to defend the dam. Reconnaissance and surveillance, inform and influence activities, area and route security operations, and protection are continuous. The commander assigns tasks to subordinates, modifies the brigade task organization, replenishes, and requests additional resources if required. Depending on the length of operations, the higher headquarters may establish unit training programs to prepare units for certain tasks.

3-120. When conditions change, commanders adjust the combination of the elements of full spectrum operations in the concept of operations. When an operation is phased, these changes are included in the plan. The relative weight given to each element varies with the actual or anticipated conditions. It is reflected in tasks assigned to subordinates, resource allocation, and task organization. Full spectrum operations is not a phasing method. Commanders consider the concurrent conduct of each element—offense, defense, and stability or civil support—in every phase of an operation. Figure 3-4 (based on a similar figure in JP 3-0) illustrates combinations and weighting of the elements of full spectrum operations across the phases of a campaign. The phases are examples. An actual campaign may name and array phases differently. (JP 3-0 discusses the campaign phases.)

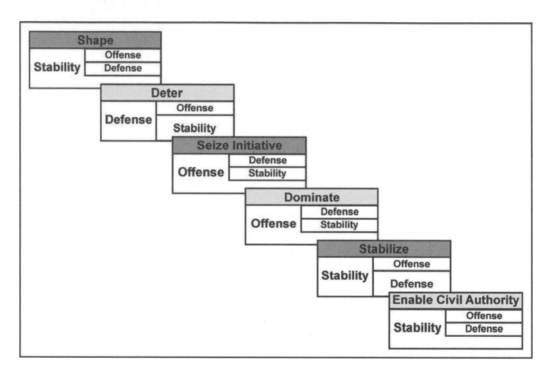

Figure 3-4. Example of combining the elements of full spectrum operations in a notional campaign

3-121. Seizing, retaining, and exploiting the initiative requires commanders to interpret developments and shift the weight of effort throughout their operations to achieve decisive results. As they do this, the forces and priorities they assign to each element of full spectrum operations change. Throughout an operation, commanders constantly adapt and perform many tasks simultaneously. Commanders change tactics, modify their mission command methods, change task organization, and adjust the weight placed on each element of full spectrum operations to keep the force focused on accomplishing the mission. They base these decisions on the situation, available resources, and the force's ability to execute multiple, diverse tasks. Commanders' assessments should consider the progress of ongoing operations, changes in the situation, and how the rules of engagement affect the force's effectiveness in each element. Commanders not only assess how well a current operation is accomplishing the mission but also how its conduct is shaping the situation for subsequent missions.

3-122. Applying tactical and operational art in full spectrum operations involves knowing when and if simultaneous combinations are appropriate and feasible. Every operation does not require offensive tasks; stability or civil support may be the only elements executed. Nonetheless, commanders and staffs always consider each element of full spectrum operations and its relevance to the situation. An element may be unnecessary, but it is the commander who determines that. Not every echelon or unit necessarily executes simultaneous full spectrum operations. Division and higher echelon operations normally combine three elements simultaneously. Brigade combat teams may focus exclusively on a single element when attacking or defending, shifting priority to another element as the plan or situation requires. Battalion and smaller units often execute the elements sequentially based on their capabilities and the situation. However, simultaneous execution of offensive, defensive, and stability tasks at lower echelons often occurs in irregular warfare and peace operations. Sometimes the force available lacks resources for executing simultaneous combinations of offensive, defensive, and stability tasks. In these cases, commanders inform the higher headquarters of the requirement for additional forces. Regardless of the situation, commanders assess the risk to units and mission accomplishment. Combining elements of full spectrum operations requires the following:

- A clear concept of operations that establishes the role of each element and how it contributes to accomplishing the mission.
- Flexible mission command networks and systems.
- Clear situational understanding.
- Aggressive intelligence gathering and analysis.
- Aggressive security operations.
- Units that can quickly change their task organization.
- An ability to respond quickly.
- Responsive sustainment.
- Combat power applied through combined arms, including applicable joint capabilities. (See chapter 4.)

SUMMARY

3-123. The Army's operational concept, full spectrum operations, describes how Army forces conduct operations. The complex nature of the operational environment requires commanders to simultaneously combine offensive, defensive, and stability or civil support tasks to accomplish missions domestically and abroad. Each element of full spectrum operations includes a basic set of tasks and related purposes. Commanders direct the application of full spectrum operations to seize, retain, and exploit the initiative and achieve decisive results.

This page intentionally left blank.

Chapter 4

Combat Power

This chapter discusses combat power and how Army forces use the warfighting functions to generate combat power. The eight elements of combat power include the six warfighting functions—mission command, movement and maneuver, intelligence, fires, sustainment, and protection—multiplied by leadership and complemented by information. This chapter introduces mission command, which replaces the former term command and control. Commanders use combined arms to increase the effects of combat power through complementary and reinforcing capabilities. Army forces achieve combined arms through force tailoring, task organization, and mutual support.

THE ELEMENTS OF COMBAT POWER

4-1. Full spectrum operations require continuously generating and applying combat power, often for extended periods. **_Combat power_ is the total means of destructive, constructive, and information capabilities that a military unit or formation can apply at a given time. Army forces generate combat power by converting potential into effective action.**

4-2. *Commanders conceptualize capabilities in terms of combat power. Combat power has eight elements: leadership, information, mission command, movement and maneuver, intelligence, fires, sustainment, and protection. Commanders apply leadership and information through, and multiply the effects of, the other six elements of combat power. The Army collectively describes these six—mission command, movement and maneuver, intelligence, fires, sustainment, and protection—as the warfighting functions. Commanders apply combat power through the warfighting functions using leadership and information. (See figure 4-1.)

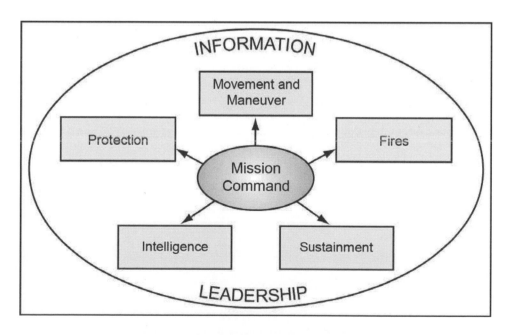

Figure 4-1. The elements of combat power

4-3.   Commanders ensure Army forces have enough potential combat power to combine the elements of full spectrum operations in ways appropriate to conditions. Every unit—regardless of type—either generates or maintains combat power. All contribute to operations. Ultimately, Army forces combine elements of combat power to defeat the enemy and master situations.

4-4.   Commanders balance the ability to mass lethal and nonlethal actions with the need to deploy and sustain the units that produce those actions. They balance accomplishing the mission quickly with being able to project and sustain the force. Generating and maintaining combat power throughout an operation is essential to success. Commanders tailor force packages to maximize the capability of the initial-entry force. Follow-on units increase endurance and ability to operate in depth. Many factors contribute to generating combat power:

- Employing reserves.
- Focusing joint support.
- Rotating committed forces.
- Staging sustainment assets to preserve momentum and synchronization.

4-5.   Commanders achieve success by applying superior combat power. Combat power is not a numerical value. Planners can estimate it but not quantify it. Combat power is always relative. It has meaning only in relation to conditions and enemy capabilities. It is relevant solely at the point in time and space where applied. In addition, how an enemy generates and applies combat power may fundamentally differ from that of Army forces. Planners take an inordinate risk when they assume that enemy capabilities mirror those of friendly capabilities. Before an operation, combat power is unrealized potential. Through leadership, commanders transform this potential information to integrate and enhance action. Commanders also apply information through the warfighting functions to shape the operational environment and complement action. Combat power becomes decisive when applied by skilled commanders leading well-trained Soldiers and units.

LEADERSHIP

4-6.   Commanders apply leadership through the warfighting functions. Leadership is the multiplying and unifying element of combat power. Confident, competent, and informed leadership intensifies the effectiveness of all other elements of combat power by formulating sound operational ideas and assuring discipline and motivation in the force. Good leaders inspire and elicit success. Effective leadership can compensate for deficiencies in all the warfighting functions because it is the most dynamic element of combat power. The opposite is also true; poor leadership can negate advantages in warfighting capabilities. The Army defines *leadership* as the process of influencing people by providing purpose, direction, and motivation, while operating to accomplish the mission and improve the organization (FM 6-22). An Army leader, by virtue of assumed role or assigned responsibility, inspires and influences people to accomplish organizational goals. Army leaders motivate people to pursue actions, focus thinking, and shape decisions for the greater good of the organization. They instill in Soldiers the will to win. Army doctrine describes essential leadership attributes (character, presence, and intellect) and competencies (lead, develop, and achieve). These attributes and competencies mature through lifelong learning. (FM 6-22 contains Army leadership doctrine.)

4-7.   Leaders influence not only Soldiers but other people as well. Commanders embrace their leadership skills when dealing with civilians in any conflict or disaster. Face-to-face contact with people in the area of operations encourages cooperation between civilians and Soldiers. Army leaders work with members of other Services and civilian organizations. These leaders strive for the willing cooperation of multinational military and civilian partners. The Army requires self-aware, adaptive leaders who can both defeat the enemy in combat and master complexities of operations dominated by stability or civil support.

4-8.   Leadership in today's operational environment is often the difference between success and failure. Leaders provide purpose, direction, and motivation in all operations. Through training and by example, leaders develop cultural awareness in Soldiers. This characteristic improves Soldiers' ability to cope with the ambiguities of complex environments. Leadership ensures Soldiers understand the purpose of operations and use their full capabilities. In every operation, Army leaders clarify purpose and mission, direct operations, and set the example for courage and competence. They hold their Soldiers to the Army Values and ensure their Soldiers comply with the law of war.

INFORMATION

4-9.   Information is a powerful tool in the operational environment. Information has become as important as lethal action in determining the outcome of operations. Every engagement, battle, and major operation requires complementary inform and influence activities to inform a global audience, to influence audiences, and to affect morale within the operational area. It also requires cyber/electromagnetic activities as a weapon against enemy command and control information systems and other cyber capabilities. Commanders use information to understand, visualize, describe, and direct the warfighting functions. They also depend on data and information to increase the effectiveness of the warfighting functions.

4-10. Since information shapes the perceptions of the civilian population, it also shapes much of the operational environment. All parties in a conflict—enemy forces, adversaries, and neutral and friendly populations—use information to convey their message to various audiences. Information is critical in stability operations where the population influences its success. The five stability tasks are essential for success. Without complementary inform and influence activities that explain these actions to the population, success may prove unattainable. Information must be proactive as well as reactive. An enemy adeptly manipulates information and combines message and action effectively. Countering enemy messages with factual and effective friendly messages can influence civilians as much as the physical actions of Soldiers can. The effects of each warfighting function should complement information objectives (the message) while information objectives stay consistent with Soldiers' actions.

4-11. The joint force continues to modernize information systems. These improvements provide leaders with the information necessary to enhance and focus the warfighting functions. Leadership based on relevant information enables the commander, at all levels, to make informed decisions on how best to apply combat power. Ultimately, this creates opportunities to achieve decisive results. The computer-displayed common operational picture is one example. It provides commanders with improved situational awareness by merging a lot of information into displays that Soldiers can understand at a glance. Information disseminated by information systems allows leaders to make better decisions quickly. The common operational picture lets Army forces use lethal and nonlethal actions more effectively than the enemy can. For example, accurate intelligence disseminated quickly by information systems allows friendly forces to maneuver around enemy engagement areas while massing the effects of combat power at the decisive place and time. This reduces friendly casualties and may allow a small force to defeat a larger enemy force.

WARFIGHTING FUNCTIONS

4-12. Commanders use the warfighting functions to help them exercise command and to help them and their staffs exercise control. A **warfighting function is a group of tasks and systems (people, organizations, information, and processes) united by a common purpose that commanders use to accomplish missions and training objectives.** Decisive, shaping, and sustaining operations combine all the warfighting functions to generate combat power. Additionally, all warfighting functions possess scalable capabilities to mass lethal and nonlethal effects. No warfighting function is exclusively decisive, shaping, or sustaining. The Army's warfighting functions are fundamentally linked to the joint functions.

*MISSION COMMAND

4-13. The **mission command warfighting function develops and integrates those activities enabling a commander to balance the art of command and the science of control.** Formerly described as the command and control warfighting function, this function adapts and captures what the Army has learned in a decade of war. These lessons include—

- The changing roles and responsibilities of leaders in distributed and increasingly decentralized operations.
- The requirement for leaders at every echelon to co-create the context for operations.

- The importance of teaming and collaborating with joint, international, interagency, and multinational partners.
- The need for leaders to anticipate and manage transitions during the course of a campaign.

(Chapter 5 defines mission command as an activity and discusses the commander's role in mission command.)

*Why Mission Command

4-14. The Army changed from command and control (C2) to mission command and eliminated the term battle command. This philosophical shift emphasizes the commanders rather than the systems that they employ. (See figure 4-2.) Army C2 and battle command did not adequately address the increasing need for commanders to frame and reframe an environment of ill-structured problems. Framing these problems enables commanders to gain the context of operations by continuously challenging assumptions both before and during execution. Additionally, the old terms inadequately addressed the role of the commander in building teams with joint, interagency, intergovernmental, and multinational partners.

Command and control (C2) and battle command inadequately describe the role of the commander and staff in today's fight. Mission command–

- Emphasizes the centrality of the commander.
- Balances the art of command and the science of control.
- Reinforces the imperative of trust and collaboration with myriad partners over command and control.
- Enables leaders to anticipate and effectively manage transitions.
- Creates an environment of disciplined initiative for more decentralized execution.

Supports the Army's drive to operational adaptability by–
- Requiring a thorough understanding of the operational environment.
- Seeking adaptive teams capable of anticipating and managing transitions.
- Acknowledging that leaders must share risk across echelons to create opportunities.

---

*Figure 4-2. Why mission command?

4-15. Mission command magnifies leadership in land operations. It illuminates the leader's responsibility to understand, visualize, describe, direct, lead, and assess. It provides commanders and staff with a philosophy for operating in an uncertain environment as opposed to trying to create certainty and imposing order and control over a situation. Mission command recognizes that leaders command not only U.S. forces but also diverse international, nongovernmental, and host-nation partners.

4-16. Mission command supports an adaptable Army in operations. An adaptable Army starts with leaders able to adapt. Confronting hybrid threats—combinations of regular, irregular, terrorist, and criminal groups—in a complex operational environment requires such leaders. These Soldiers not only accept but also seek and embrace operational adaptability as an imperative. Mission command enables an operationally adaptive force that has both the authority and resources to operate effectively at all levels, under clear mission orders. Mission command enables operational adaptability in the Army. It requires a thorough understanding of the operational environment, seeks adaptive teams capable of anticipating and managing transitions, and acknowledges that leaders must share risk across echelons to create opportunities.

4-17. Mission command emphasizes the critical contributions of leaders at every echelon. It establishes a mindset among leaders that the best understanding comes from the bottom up, not from the top down. Mission command emphasizes the importance and common operating assessment of context. It highlights how commanders—through disciplined initiative within the commander's intent—transition among offensive, defensive, and stability operations and between centralized and decentralized operations.

4-18. The Army has adopted mission command as the overarching term for both the warfighting function and the philosophy of command. Mission command guides leaders how to think about what Soldiers do to conduct successful operations on land. By emphasizing people as the driving force behind the development of technology, mission command adapts technology to human needs, not humans to technological restrictions. Understanding people, and influencing humans to achieve success in complex operations, is fundamental to how the commander exercises the art of command.

*Mission Command Tasks

4-19. The commander is the central figure in mission command, essential to integrating the capabilities of the warfighting functions to accomplish the mission. Mission command invokes the greatest possible freedom of action to subordinates. It enables subordinates to develop the situation, adapt, and act decisively through disciplined initiative in dynamic conditions within the commander's intent. Mission command focuses on empowering subordinate leaders and sharing information to facilitate decentralized execution.

4-20. The art of command is the creative and skillful exercise of authority through decisionmaking and leadership. Through the art of command, the commander has four tasks in mission command (see figure 4-3). They are:

- Drive the operations process.
- Understand, visualize, describe, direct, lead, and assess.
- Develop teams among modular formations and joint, interagency, intergovernmental, and multinational partners.
- Lead inform and influence activities.

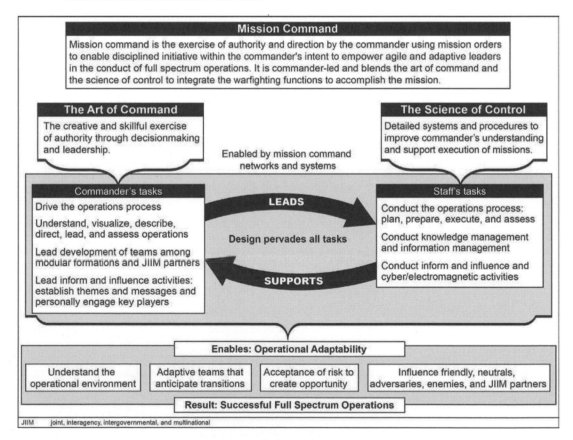

*Figure 4-3. Mission command

4-21. The commander leads the staff's tasks under the science of control. The science of control consists of systems and procedures to improve the commander's understanding and support accomplishing missions. The three staff tasks are:

- Conduct the operations process: plan, prepare, execute, and assess.
- Conduct knowledge management and information management.
- Conduct inform and influence and cyber/electromagnetic activities.

As much as the commander leads the staff's tasks, the staff tasks fully support the commander in executing the commander's tasks.

4-22. *Mission command networks and systems* **is the coordinated application of personnel, networks, procedures, equipment and facilities, knowledge management, and information management systems essential for the commander to conduct operations.** These networks and systems enable the art of command and science of control. Design provides a cognitive tool to help commanders anticipate change and coordinate applications appropriately. It pervades all tasks and assists the commander to lead adaptive, innovative efforts. Design provides the commander and staff with a methodology to better understand complex, ill-structured problems.

4-23. Successful mission command, supported by design, fosters operational adaptability and a greater understanding of the operational environment. *Operational adaptability* **is the ability to shape conditions and respond effectively to a changing operational environment with appropriate, flexible, and timely actions.** Operational adaptability reflects a quality that Army leaders and forces exhibit through critical thinking, their comfort with ambiguity and uncertainty, their willingness to accept prudent risk, and their ability to rapidly adjust while continuously assessing the situation. Commanders enable operationally adaptive forces through flexibility, collaborative planning, and decentralized execution. Operational adaptability results in teams that—

- Understand the operational environment.
- Adapt and anticipate transitions.
- Accept risks to create opportunities.
- Influence friendly, neutrals, adversaries, enemies, and joint, interagency, intergovernmental, and multinational partners.

The ultimate outcome is successful full spectrum operations.

4-24. *Understand the operational environment:* Command is an individual and personal function. It blends imaginative problem solving, motivational and communications skills, and a thorough understanding of the dynamics of operations. Command during operations requires understanding the complex, dynamic relationships among friendly forces, enemies, and the environment, including the populace. This understanding helps commanders visualize and describe their commander's intent and develop focused planning guidance.

4-25. *Adapt and anticipate transitions:* Operational adaptability enables leaders to transition continuously between fundamentally different operations. Major combat operations may evolve to irregular warfare or peace operations. Units may transition from offensive to defensive operations or from defensive to stability operations. Transitions often involve transferring responsibilities to other organizations or authorities, such as from U.S. forces to partner forces, civil authorities, or international organizations. Commanders identify potential transitions during planning and account for them throughout execution. Assessment ensures that commanders measure progress toward such transitions and take appropriate actions to prepare for and execute them.

4-26. *Accept risks to create opportunities*: Operational adaptability assists commanders to create training and organizational climates that promote calculated, disciplined risk-taking focused on winning rather than preventing defeat. A key aspect of mission command includes identifying risks, deciding how much risk to accept, and minimizing the effects of accepted risk by establishing control measures to mitigate those risks. The staff helps the commander identify risks and offers recommendations to mitigate those risks. (See FM 5-19 for doctrine on composite risk management.) Ultimately, the willingness to take prudent risks rests with the commander. However, commanders must be careful not to decentralize all risks. Through collaboration and dialog, commanders at all levels identify where risk exists and at what level of command risk will be mitigated.

4-27. The commander considers how to establish conditions for success in full spectrum operations, protect the force, and shape the operational environment. War gaming enables commanders and staffs to complete a risk assessment for each course of action. They then propose appropriate control measures. They continually assess the risk of adverse reactions from the population and media. Staff officers develop ways to mitigate those risks. Commanders discuss these risks with subordinate leaders. Commanders and subordinates determine what risks the higher commander will accept and what risk will remain with the subordinate commander. Commanders then allocate resources as deemed appropriate to mitigate risks.

4-28. *Influence friendly, neutrals, adversaries, enemies, and joint, interagency, intergovernmental, and multinational partners*: Commanders personally use inform and influence activities to guide actors to make decisions that support the commander's objectives. Commanders directly shape the themes and messages designed to inform domestic audiences and influence foreign friendly, neutral, adversary, and enemy populations. Commanders ensure that themes and messages synchronize with actions to support operations and achieve the desired end state. Commanders consider how their units' actions will affect the environment and influence perceptions among relevant groups. Commanders assume that their enemies and adversaries can adeptly use the information environment. They expect the enemy to actively and aggressively engage in the information environment to gain an operational advantage. The enemy attempts to confuse the general population, distort facts to support their position, or use other means including intimidation and propaganda.

4-29. Subsequent chapters provide greater detail on the taxonomy of mission command. Chapter 5 discusses the art of command and the role of the commander in mission command. Chapter 6 discusses the science of control. It discusses the systems and procedures that support the commander to drive the commander's tasks and integrate the warfighting functions.

MOVEMENT AND MANEUVER

4-30. The *movement and maneuver warfighting function* is the related tasks and systems that move forces to achieve a position of advantage in relation to the enemy. Direct fire is inherent in maneuver, as is close combat. This function includes tasks associated with force projection related to gaining a positional advantage over an enemy. One example is moving forces to execute a large-scale air or airborne assault. Another is deploying forces to intermediate staging bases in preparation for an offensive operation. *Maneuver* is the employment of forces in the operational area through movement in combination with fires to achieve a position of advantage in respect to the enemy in order to accomplish the mission (JP 3-0). Commanders use maneuver for massing the effects of combat power to achieve surprise, shock, and momentum. Effective maneuver requires close coordination with fires. Movement is necessary to disperse and displace the force as a whole or in part when maneuvering. Both tactical and operational maneuver require logistic support. The movement and maneuver warfighting function includes the following tasks:

- Deploy.
- Move.
- Maneuver.
- Employ direct fires.
- Occupy an area.
- Conduct mobility and countermobility operations.
- Employ battlefield obscuration.

The movement and maneuver warfighting function does not include administrative movements of personnel and materiel. These movements fall under the sustainment warfighting function. FM 3-90 discusses maneuver and tactical movement. FM 3-35 discusses force projection.

INTELLIGENCE

4-31. The *intelligence warfighting function* is the related tasks and systems that facilitate understanding of the operational environment, enemy, terrain, and civil considerations. It includes tasks associated with intelligence, surveillance, and reconnaissance operations. The commander drives the intelligence warfighting function. Intelligence is more than just collection. It is a continuous process that involves analyzing information from all sources and conducting operations to develop the situation. The intelligence warfighting function includes the following tasks:

- Support to force generation.
- Support to situational understanding.
- Provide intelligence support to targeting and information capabilities.
- Conduct intelligence, surveillance, and reconnaissance.

*Intelligence, Surveillance, and Reconnaissance

4-32. Knowledge of the operational environment precludes all effective action, whether in the information or physical domains. Knowledge about the operational environment requires aggressive and continuous surveillance and reconnaissance to acquire information. Information collected from multiple sources and analyzed becomes intelligence that provides answers to commanders' information requirements concerning the enemy and other adversaries, climate, weather, terrain, and population. Developing these requirements is the function of intelligence, reconnaissance, and surveillance (ISR). *Intelligence, surveillance, and reconnaissance is an activity that synchronizes and integrates the planning and operation of sensors, assets, and processing, exploitation, and dissemination systems in direct support of current and future operations. This is an integrated intelligence and operations function. For Army forces, this activity is a combined arms operation that focuses on priority intelligence requirements while answering the commander's critical information requirements*. (JP 2-01 contains ISR doctrine.) Through ISR, commanders and staffs continuously plan, task, and employ collection assets and forces. These Soldiers collect, process, and disseminate timely and accurate information, combat information, and intelligence to satisfy the commander's critical information requirements (CCIRs) and other intelligence requirements. When necessary, ISR assets may focus on special requirements, such as information required for personnel recovery operations. It supports full spectrum operations through four tasks:

- ISR synchronization.
- ISR integration.
- Surveillance.
- Reconnaissance.

4-33. ISR synchronization considers all assets—both internal and external to the organization. It identifies information gaps and the most appropriate assets for collecting information to fill them. It also assigns the most efficient means to process the information into intelligence and disseminate it. ISR integration tasks assets to collect on requirements that intelligence reach or requests for information cannot answer or that commanders consider critical. Commanders integrate assets into a single ISR plan that capitalizes on each asset's capabilities. Commanders also synchronize and coordinate surveillance and reconnaissance missions and employ other units for ISR within the scheme of maneuver. Effectively synchronizing ISR with the overall plan positions ISR assets to continue to collect information, reconstitute for branches or sequels, or shift priorities throughout the operation.

*Intelligence, Surveillance, and Reconnaissance Synchronization

4-34. *Intelligence, surveillance, and reconnaissance synchronization is the task that accomplishes the following: analyzes information requirements and intelligence gaps; evaluates available assets internal and external to the organization; determines gaps in the use of those assets; recommends intelligence, surveillance, and reconnaissance assets controlled by the organization to collect on the commander's critical information requirements; and submits requests for information for adjacent and higher collection support.* This task ensures that ISR, intelligence reach, and requests for information result in successful reporting, production, and dissemination of information, combat information, and intelligence to support decisionmaking.

4-35. The intelligence officer, with the operations officer and other staff elements, synchronizes the entire collection effort. This effort includes recommending tasking for assets the commander controls and submitting requests for information to adjacent and higher echelon units and organizations. When these sources do not answer the CCIR and other requirements, ISR synchronization uses intelligence reach to obtain the information.

4-36. ISR synchronization includes screening subordinate and adjacent unit requests for information concerning the enemy, terrain and weather, and civil considerations. When intelligence reach and requests for information do not satisfy a requirement, ISR synchronization develops specific information requirements to facilitate ISR integration. (FM 2-0 discusses intelligence reach.)

4-37. Commanders use ISR synchronization to assess ISR asset reporting. ISR synchronization includes continually identifying new and partially filled intelligence gaps. It also provides recommendations to the operations officer for tasking ISR assets.

*Intelligence, Surveillance, and Reconnaissance Integration

4-38. *Intelligence, surveillance, and reconnaissance integration* **is the task of assigning and controlling a unit's intelligence, surveillance, and reconnaissance assets (in terms of space, time, and purpose) to collect and report information as a concerted and integrated portion of operation plans and orders.** This task ensures planners assign the best ISR assets through a deliberate and coordinated effort of the entire staff across all warfighting functions by integrating ISR into the operation.

4-39. The operations officer, with input from the intelligence officer, develops tasks based on specific information requirements (developed as part of ISR synchronization). Specific information requirements facilitate tasking by matching requirements to assets. The operations officer assigns tasks based on the latest time that information is of value and the capabilities and limitations of available ISR assets. Then the operations officer identifies, prioritizes, and validates intelligence requirements. The staff develops and synchronizes the ISR plan with the overall operation. During ISR integration, the entire staff participates as responsibility for the ISR plan transitions from the intelligence officer to the operations officer. ISR integration is vital in controlling limited ISR assets. During ISR integration, the staff recommends redundancy and mix as appropriate. ISR synchronization and integration result in an effort focused on answering the commander's requirements through ISR tasks translated into orders.

*Surveillance

4-40. *Surveillance* is the systematic observation of aerospace, surface, or subsurface areas, places, persons, or things, by visual, aural, electronic, photographic, or other means (JP 3-0). Surveillance involves observing an area to collect information.

4-41. Wide-area and focused surveillance missions provide valuable information. National and joint surveillance systems focus on information requirements for combatant commanders. They also provide information to all Services for operations across the area of responsibility. The systematic observation of geographic locations, persons, networks, or equipment is assigned to Army intelligence, reconnaissance, and maneuver assets. Changes or anomalies detected during surveillance missions can develop reconnaissance to confirm or deny the change.

*Reconnaissance

4-42. *Reconnaissance* is a mission undertaken to obtain, by visual observation or other detection methods, information about the activities and resources of an enemy or adversary, or to secure data concerning the meteorological, hydrographic, or geographic characteristics of a particular area (JP 2-0).

4-43. Units performing reconnaissance collect information to confirm or deny current intelligence or predictions. This information may concern the terrain, weather, and population characteristics of a particular area as well the enemy. Reconnaissance normally precedes execution of the overall operation and extends throughout the area of operations. It begins as early as the situation, political direction, and rules of engagement permit. Reconnaissance can locate mobile enemy command and control assets—such as command posts, communications nodes, and satellite terminals—for neutralization, attack, or destruction. Reconnaissance can detect patterns of behavior exhibited by people in the objective area. Commanders at all echelons incorporate reconnaissance into their operations.

*Soldier Surveillance and Reconnaissance

4-44. Surveillance is distinct from reconnaissance. Often surveillance is passive and may be continuous; reconnaissance missions are typically shorter and use active means (such as maneuver). Additionally, reconnaissance may involve fighting for information. Sometimes these operations are deliberate, as in a reconnaissance in force; however, the purpose of reconnaissance is to collect information, not initiate combat. Reconnaissance involves many tactics, techniques, and procedures throughout the course of a mission. An extended period of surveillance may be one of these. Commanders complement surveillance with frequent reconnaissance. Surveillance, in turn, increases the efficiency of reconnaissance by focusing those missions while reducing the risk to Soldiers.

4-45. The Soldier is an indispensable source for much of what the intelligence commanders need. Every Soldier is a sensor. Observations and experiences of Soldiers—who often work with the local populace— provide depth and context to information gathered through surveillance and reconnaissance. Commanders train all Soldiers to report their observations, even when not assigned a surveillance or reconnaissance mission. Commanders and staffs emphasize integrating information gathered from Soldiers into intelligence production.

FIRES

4-46. **The *fires warfighting function* is the related tasks and systems that provide collective and coordinated use of Army indirect fires and joint fires through the targeting process.** It includes tasks associated with integrating and synchronizing the effects of these fires with the effects of other warfighting functions. Commanders integrate these tasks into the concept of operations during planning and adjust them based on the targeting guidance. Fires normally contribute to the overall effect of maneuver, but commanders may use them separately for decisive and shaping operations. The fires warfighting function includes the following tasks:

- Decide surface targets.
- Detect and locate surface targets.
- Provide fire support.
- Assess effectiveness.
- Integrate and synchronize cyber/electromagnetic activities.

SUSTAINMENT

4-47. **The *sustainment warfighting function* is the related tasks and systems that provide support and services to ensure freedom of action, extend operational reach, and prolong endurance.** The endurance of Army forces is primarily a function of their sustainment. Sustainment determines the depth and duration of Army operations. It is essential to retaining and exploiting the initiative. Sustainment provides the support for logistics, personnel services, and health service (excluding force health protection, which is a component of the protection warfighting function) necessary to maintain operations until mission accomplishment. Internment, resettlement, and detainee operations fall under the sustainment warfighting function and include elements of all three major subfunctions. FM 4-0 describes the sustainment warfighting function, and FM 4-02 discusses the Army Health System.

Logistics

4-48. *Logistics* is the planning and executing the movement and support of forces. It includes those aspects of military operations that deal with: a. design and development, acquisition, storage, movement, distribution, maintenance, evacuation, and disposition of materiel; b. movement, evacuation, and hospitalization of personnel; c. acquisition or construction, maintenance, operation, and disposition of facilities; and d. acquisition or furnishing of services (JP 4-0). Although joint doctrine defines it as science, logistics involves both military art and science. Knowing when and how to accept risk, prioritizing myriad requirements, and balancing limited resources all require military art. Logistics integrates strategic, operational, and tactical support of deployed forces while scheduling the mobilization and deployment of additional forces and materiel. Logistics includes—

- Maintenance.
- Transportation.
- Supply.
- Field services.
- Distribution.
- Contracting.
- General engineering support.

Personnel Services

4-49. Personnel services are those sustainment functions related to Soldiers' welfare, readiness, and quality of life. Personnel services complement logistics by planning for and coordinating efforts that provide and sustain personnel. Personnel services include—

- Human resources support.
- Financial management.
- Legal support.
- Religious support.
- Band support.

Health Service Support

4-50. The Army Health System is a component of the Military Health System that oversees operational management of the health service support and force health protection missions. The Army Health System includes all mission support services by the Army Medical Department to support health service support and force health protection mission requirements for the Army. Health service support is part of the sustainment warfighting function while force health protection is a part of the protection warfighting function. (Paragraph 4-53 also discusses force health protection.)

4-51. The health service support mission focuses on the mental and physical well-being of Soldiers and, as directed, other personnel. This mission consists of three elements: casualty care, medical evacuation, and medical logistics. Casualty care encompasses Army Medical Department functions to include—

- Organic and area medical support.
- Hospitalization (to include treatment of chemical, biological, radiological, and nuclear patients).
- Dental treatment.
- Behavioral health and neuropsychiatric treatment.
- Clinical laboratory services.
- Medical evacuation (to include en route care and medical regulating).
- Medical logistics (to include blood and blood products).

Health service support closely relates to force health protection. (See paragraph 4-53.)

PROTECTION

4-52. The *protection warfighting function* is the related tasks and systems that preserve the force so the commander can apply maximum combat power. Preserving the force includes protecting personnel (combatants and noncombatants), physical assets, and information of the United States and multinational military and civilian partners. The protection warfighting function facilitates the commander's ability to maintain the force's integrity and combat power. Protection determines the degree to which potential threats can disrupt operations and then counters or mitigates those threats. Emphasis on protection increases during preparation and continues throughout execution. Protection is a continuing activity; it integrates all protection capabilities to safeguard bases, secure routes, and protect forces. The protection warfighting function includes the following tasks:

- Air and missile defense.
- Personnel recovery.

- Information protection.
- Fratricide avoidance.
- Operational area security.
- Antiterrorism.
- Survivability.
- Force health protection.
- Chemical, biological, radiological, and nuclear operations.
- Safety.
- Operations security.
- Explosive ordnance disposal.

4-53. The force health protection mission under the protection warfighting function includes all measures to mitigate health threats and to promote, improve, or conserve the mental and physical well-being of Soldiers. These measures enable a healthy and fit force, prevent injury and illness, and protect the force from health hazards. The measures include the prevention aspects of several Army Medical Department functions, including the following:

- Preventive medicine, including—
  - Medical surveillance.
  - Occupational and environmental health surveillance.
  - Health risk communication.
- Veterinary services, including—
  - Food inspection.
  - Animal care.
  - Prevention of zoonotic diseases (those transmitted from animals to humans, such as plague or rabies).
- Combat and operational stress control (to include behavioral health, warrior resiliency training, and combat operational stress reactions).
- Dental services (preventive dentistry).
- Laboratory services (area medical laboratory support).

COMBINED ARMS

4-54. Applying combat power depends on combined arms to achieve its full destructive, disruptive, informational, and constructive potential. ***Combined arms*** **is the synchronized and simultaneous application of the elements of combat power to achieve an effect greater than if each element of combat power was used separately or sequentially.** Combined arms merges leadership, information, and each of the warfighting functions and their supporting systems. Used destructively, combined arms integrates different capabilities so that counteracting one makes the enemy vulnerable to another. Used constructively, combined arms multiplies the effectiveness and the efficiency of Army capabilities used in stability or civil support.

4-55. Combined arms uses the capabilities of each warfighting function and information in complementary and reinforcing capabilities. *Complementary* capabilities protect the weaknesses of one system or organization with the capabilities of a different warfighting function. For example, commanders use artillery (fires) to suppress an enemy bunker complex pinning down an infantry unit (movement and maneuver). The infantry unit then closes with and destroys the enemy. In this example, the fires warfighting function complements the maneuver warfighting function. *Reinforcing* capabilities combine similar systems or capabilities within the same warfighting function to increase the function's overall capabilities. In urban operations, for example, infantry, aviation, and armor (movement and maneuver) often operate close to each other. This combination reinforces the protection, maneuver, and direct fire capabilities of each. The infantry protects tanks from enemy infantry and antitank systems; tanks provide protection and firepower for the infantry. Attack helicopters maneuver freely above buildings to fire from positions of advantage, while other aircraft help sustain the ground elements. Together, these capabilities form a lethal team built on movement and maneuver. In another example, multiple artillery units routinely mass fires to support a committed artillery battalion (reinforcement). Joint capabilities—such as close air support and special operations forces—can complement or reinforce Army capabilities.

4-56. Army forces are familiar with combined arms operations. Unified actions—those integrating the capabilities of joint forces with those of multinational military and civilian organizations—have become typical as well. This integration requires careful preparation. Successful unified action requires training and exchange of liaison at every level.

4-57. Combined arms multiplies Army forces' effectiveness in all operations. Units operating without support of other capabilities generate less combat power and may not accomplish their mission. Employing combined arms requires highly trained Soldiers, skilled leadership, effective staff work, and integrated information systems. Commanders synchronize combined arms to apply the effects of combat power to the best advantage. The sequence and simultaneity of combined arms actions vary with both the operational or tactical design and in execution. Typically, ISR activities begin soon after receipt of mission and continue throughout preparation and execution. They do not cease after mission accomplishment but continue as needed. Sustainment and protection are conducted constantly but may peak before and after execution. Maneuver and fires complement each other continuously but sometimes precede each other. For example, the commander conducts preparatory lethal fires combined with electronic warfare to isolate and destroy enemy forces on an objective before maneuver forces make contact. Another example is the shifting of fires beyond the immediate vicinity of maneuver units during a pursuit.

4-58. Units achieve combined arms through organizational design and temporary reorganization (tailored and task-organized forces). For example, units organic to brigade combat teams perform all warfighting functions. However, the capabilities organic to the brigade combat team do not include Army aviation, air and missile defense, and Army special operations forces. When required, commanders add these capabilities through force tailoring and task organization. Higher echelons achieve combined arms capabilities by tailoring and task-organizing different brigades and battalions under corps or division headquarters. For example, a division force commander may reinforce four or five brigade combat teams with any number of the modular support brigades and functional brigades.

4-59. Hybrid threats require a combined arms approach emphasizing small-unit capabilities. Hybrid threats also require a mix of forces different from conventional warfare to address the fundamental differences between them. Requirements that characterize counterinsurgency in general, and civil security and civil control in particular, vary significantly among tactical areas of operations. This situation requires releasing intelligence, civil affairs, and information assets typically held at higher headquarters to brigade combat teams and often to battalion task forces or lower. Liaison officers and adjacent unit coordination are essential to integrating and synchronizing Army operations with those of other organizations. Higher headquarters may need to reinforce the mission command capabilities of their subordinates to improve coordination between them and the various organizations in their areas of operations.

FORCE TAILORING

4-60. **Force tailoring is the process of determining the right mix of forces and the sequence of their deployment in support of a joint force commander.** It involves selecting the right force structure for a joint operation from available units within a combatant command or from the Army force pool. Commanders then sequence selected forces into the operational area as part of force projection. Joint force commanders request and receive forces for each campaign phase, adjusting the quantity and Service component of forces to match the weight of effort required. Army Service component commanders tailor Army forces to meet land force requirements determined by joint force commanders. Army Service component commanders also recommend forces and a deployment sequence to meet those requirements. Force tailoring is continuous. As new forces rotate into the operational area, forces with excess capabilities return to the supporting combatant and Army Service component commands.

TASK-ORGANIZING

4-61. **Task-organizing is the act of designing an operating force, support staff, or logistic package of specific size and composition to meet a unique task or mission. Characteristics to examine when** task-organizing the force include, but are not limited to: training, experience, equipage, sustainability, operating environment, enemy threat, and mobility. For Army forces, it includes allocating available assets to subordinate commanders and establishing their command and support relationships. Task-organizing occurs within a tailored force package as commanders organize groups of units for specific missions. It continues as commanders reorganize units for subsequent missions. The ability of Army forces to task-organize gives them extraordinary agility. It lets operational and tactical commanders configure their units to best use available resources. It also allows Army forces to match unit capabilities rapidly to the priority assigned to offensive, defensive, and stability or civil support tasks.

MUTUAL SUPPORT

4-62. Commanders consider mutual support when task-organizing forces, assigning areas of operations, and positioning units. *Mutual support* is that support which units render each other against an enemy, because of their assigned tasks, their position relative to each other and to the enemy, and their inherent capabilities (JP 3-31). In Army doctrine, mutual support is a planning consideration related to force disposition, not a command relationship. (See appendix B.) Mutual support has two aspects—supporting range and supporting distance. (See figure 4-4.) Understanding mutual support and accepting risk during operations are fundamental to the art of tactics.

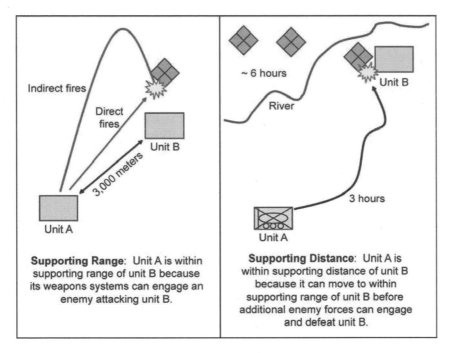

Figure 4-4. Examples of supporting range and supporting distance

4-63. *Supporting range* **is the distance one unit may be geographically separated from a second unit yet remain within the maximum range of the second unit's weapons systems.** It depends on available weapons systems and is normally the maximum range of the supporting unit's indirect fire weapons. For small units (such as squads, sections, and platoons), it is the distance between two units that their direct fires can cover effectively. Visibility may limit supporting range. If one unit cannot effectively or safely fire to support another, the first may not be in supporting range even though its weapons have the required range.

4-64. *Supporting distance* **is the distance between two units that can be traveled in time for one to come to the aid of the other and prevent its defeat by an enemy or ensure it regains control of a civil situation.** The following factors affect supporting distance:

- Terrain and mobility.
- Distance.

- Enemy capabilities.
- Friendly capabilities.
- Reaction time.

When friendly forces are static, supporting range equals supporting distance.

4-65. The command and control capabilities of supported and supporting units affect supporting distance and supporting range. Units may locate within supporting distance, but if the supported unit cannot communicate with the supporting unit, the supporting unit may not be able to affect the operation's outcome. In such cases, the units are not within supporting distance, regardless of their proximity to each other. If the units share a common operational picture, the situation may differ greatly. Relative proximity may be less important than both units' ability to coordinate their maneuver and fires. To exploit the advantage of supporting distance, the units have to synchronize their maneuver and fires more effectively than the enemy can. Otherwise, the enemy can defeat both units in detail.

4-66. Commanders also consider supporting distance in operations dominated by stability or civil support. Units maintain mutual support when one unit can draw on another's capabilities. An interdependent joint force may make proximity less significant than available capability. For example, Air Force assets may be able to move a preventive medicine detachment from an intermediate staging base to an operational area threatened by an epidemic. An additional treatment capability might be moved to the operational area based on the threat to Soldiers and the populace.

4-67. Improved access to joint capabilities gives commanders additional means to achieve mutual support. Those capabilities can extend the operating distances between Army units. Army commanders can substitute joint capabilities for mutual support between subordinate forces. Doing this multiplies supporting distance many times over. Army forces can then extend operations over greater areas at a higher tempo. Joint capabilities are especially useful when subordinate units operate in noncontiguous areas of operations that place units beyond a supporting range or supporting distance. However, depending on them entails accepting risk.

SUMMARY

4-68. The elements of combat power consist of six warfighting functions tied together by leadership and enhanced by information. The commander is at the hub of mission command and essential to integrating the capabilities of all warfighting functions to accomplish the mission through combined arms action. Combined arms generates more combat power than employing arms individually. Army forces are organized for combined arms using force tailoring and task organization. Mutual support used in complementary and reinforcing combinations also multiples the effects of combat power.

This page intentionally left blank.

Chapter 5

The Commander and Mission Command

This chapter discusses how commanders apply the art of command to synthesize and apply this knowledge from all levels across the command. The commander uses design to permeate all aspects of mission command. The commander drives four primary tasks: drive the operations process; understand, visualize, describe, direct, lead, and assess operations; develop teams; and lead inform and influence activities.

*ART OF COMMAND

5-1. *Command* is the authority that a commander in the armed forces lawfully exercises over subordinates by virtue of rank or assignment. Command includes the authority and responsibility for effectively using available resources and for planning the employment of, organizing, directing, coordinating, and controlling military forces for the accomplishment of assigned missions. It also includes responsibility for health, welfare, morale, and discipline of assigned personnel (JP 1). Leaders who command authority strive to do so with firmness, care, and skill.

5-2. Command is considered more art than science because it depends on actions only humans can perform. The art of command is the creative and skillful exercise of authority through decisionmaking and leadership. Enabled by mission command networks and systems, commanders synthesize knowledge from all levels—higher, lower, and lateral—and apply this knowledge across all levels of command. Those in command have authority, decisionmaking skills, and leadership abilities.

5-3. Authority refers to the right and power to judge, act, or command. It includes responsibility, accountability, and delegation. Commanders rely on their education, experience, knowledge, and judgment in applying authority as they decide (plan how to achieve the end state) and lead (direct their forces during preparation and execution). The authority of command provides the basis for control.

5-4. Decisionmaking refers to selecting a course of action as the one most favorable to accomplish the mission. Commanders apply knowledge to the situation thus translating their visualization into action. Decisionmaking includes knowing whether to decide or not, then when and what to decide, and finally, understanding the consequences. Commanders use understanding, visualization, description, and direction to determine and communicate their desired end state.

5-5. Leadership refers to influencing people by providing purpose, direction, and motivation, while operating to accomplish the mission and improve the organization. Commanders lead through a combination of personal example, persuasion, and compulsion. (FM 6-22 discusses leadership.)

DESIGN

5-6. Through collaboration and dialog, commanders use design for visualizing and describing complex operations, and then continually reassessing the situation. *Design* is a methodology for applying critical and creative thinking to understand, visualize, and describe complex, ill-structured problems and develop approaches to solve them (FM 5-0). Commanders who use design possess a greater understanding of the operational environment. With this greater understanding, the commander can provide a clear commander's intent and concept of operations. Such clarity enables subordinate units and commanders to make the effort to take initiative. Mission command requires commanders convey a clear commander's intent and concept of operations.

5-7. Design underpins the commander's tasks in leading innovative, adaptive work and guiding planning, preparation, execution, and assessment in operations. Design requires agile, versatile leaders. Throughout operations, commanders, subordinate commanders, staffs, and other partners collaborate and dialog actively, sharing and questioning information, perceptions, and ideas to better understand situations and make decisions. Effective collaboration includes continuous dialog that leads to increased understanding of the situation, including the current problems.

5-8. Three distinct elements collectively produce a design concept. Together, they constitute an organizational learning methodology that corresponds to three questions that must be answered to produce an actionable design concept to guide planning:

- Framing the operational environment—what is the context in which design will be applied?
- Framing the problem—what problem is the design intended to address?
- Considering operational approaches—what broad, general approach may solve the problem?

5-9. Depending on the situation—to include the complexity of the problem—commanders conduct design before, in parallel with, or after the military decisionmaking process (MDMP). When faced with an ill-structured problem or when developing initial plans for extended operations, commanders often initiate design before the MDMP. This sequence helps them better understand the operational environment, frame the problem, and develop an operational approach to guide more detailed planning.

5-10. When commanders conduct design in parallel with the MDMP, members of the staff conduct mission analysis as the commander and other staff members engage in design activities. Knowledge products—such as results from intelligence preparation of the battlefield and running estimates—help inform the design team about the operational environment. Commanders may direct some staff members to focus their mission analysis on certain areas.

5-11. In time-constrained conditions requiring immediate action or if the problem is well structured, commanders may conduct the MDMP and publish an operation order without conducting design. As time becomes available during execution, commanders may then initiate design to help refine their commander's visualization and the initial plan developed using the MDMP. However, even if commanders do not conduct design at the outset of planning, they continually assess during execution for changes in the operational environment that may require them to reframe the problem. (See FM 5-0 for a detailed discussion on design.)

THE ROLE OF THE COMMANDER IN MISSION COMMAND

5-12. ***Mission command is the exercise of authority and direction by the commander using mission orders to enable disciplined initiative within the commander's intent to empower agile and adaptive leaders in the conduct of full spectrum operations. It is commander-led and blends the art of command and the science of control to integrate the warfighting functions to accomplish the mission.** (See Chapter 4 for the definition of mission command as a warfighting function and all of its components.) The role of the commander in mission command is to direct and lead from the beginning of planning throughout execution, and to assess continually. Successful mission command requires the commander's presence and personal leadership. To ensure mission accomplishment in full spectrum operations, the commander—

- Drives the operations process.
- Understands, visualizes, describes, directs, leads, and assesses operations.
- Develops teams among modular formations and joint, interagency, intergovernmental, and multinational partners.
- Leads inform and influence activities. (Chapter 6 has a more detailed discussion of inform and influence activities.)

*DRIVE THE OPERATIONS PROCESS

5-13. Commanders drive the operations process (see figure 5-1). While staffs perform essential functions that amplify the effectiveness of operations, commanders play the central role in the operations process. Commanders blend the art of command and the science of control. Guided by their experience, knowledge, education, intelligence, and intuition, commanders apply leadership to translate decisions into action. (Chapter 6 discusses the operations process.)

UNDERSTAND, VISUALIZE, DESCRIBE, DIRECT, LEAD, AND ASSESS OPERATIONS

5-14. Commanders understand, visualize, describe, direct, lead, and assess operations. They understand the problem. Commanders visualize the end state and the nature and design of the operation. They describe the time, space, resources, purpose, and action. They direct the warfighting functions. Commanders also continually lead and assess.

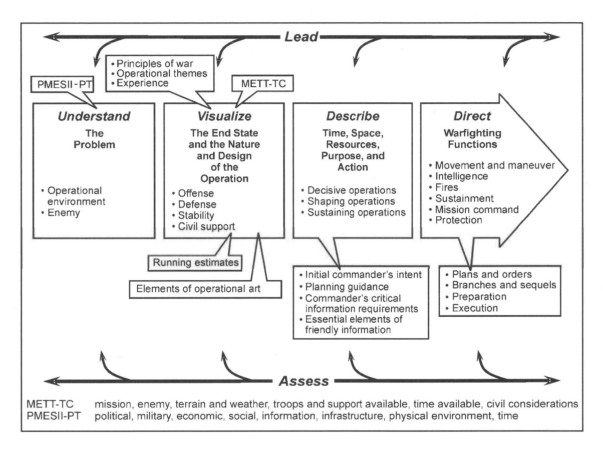

*Figure 5-1. Driving the operations process

5-15. *This process is the Army's model for the exercise of mission command. Commanders apply the methodology of design to gain and maintain a greater **understanding** of the operational environment and support the operations process. They seek to **visualize** the end state and operational approach. They **describe** the visualization to promote a shared understanding. Commanders **direct** action based on situational understanding. They **lead** Soldiers and partners during execution. They **continuously assess** progress of operations and adapt (reframe) as required.

5-16. Commanders conduct (plan, prepare, execute, and assess) operations. They plan to understand a situation, envision a desired future, and, with assistance of their staffs, lay out effective ways of bringing that future about. Commanders guide preparation to help the force and Soldiers improve their ability to execute an operation, and establish conditions that improve friendly forces' opportunities for success. Throughout execution, commanders create conditions for seizing the initiative. Finally, commanders continuously assess the current situation and progress of an operation, and adjust or reframe as needed to ensure objectives are accomplished and success is achieved. Commanders make timely and effective decisions based on applying judgment to available information. It requires knowing both when and what to decide. It also requires commanders to evaluate the quality of information and knowledge. Commanders identify important information requirements and focus subordinates and staff on answering them. They face a thinking, adaptive enemy. Commanders estimate, but cannot predict, the enemy's actions and the course of future events. Once executed, the effects of their decisions are frequently irreversible. Therefore, they anticipate actions that follow their decisions.

5-17. Commanders continuously combine analytic and intuitive approaches to decisionmaking. Analytic decisionmaking approaches a problem systematically. The analytic approach aims to produce the optimal solution to a problem from among the solutions identified. The Army's analytic approach is the MDMP. In contrast, *intuitive decisionmaking* is the act of reaching a conclusion that emphasizes pattern recognition based on knowledge, judgment, experience, education, intelligence, boldness, perception, and character. This approach focuses on assessment of the situation vice comparison of multiple options (FM 6-0). It relies on the experienced commander's and staff member's intuitive ability to recognize the key elements and implications of a particular problem or situation, reject the impractical, and select an adequate solution. (FM 5-0 discusses the MDMP. FM 6-0 discusses analytic and intuitive decisionmaking.)

5-18. The two approaches are not mutually exclusive. Commanders may make an intuitive decision based on situational understanding gained during the MDMP. If time permits, the staff may use a specific MDMP step, such as war gaming, to validate or refine the commander's intuitive decision. In a time-constrained environment, many techniques—such as selecting a single course of action—rely heavily on intuitive decisions. Even in the most rigorous, analytic decisionmaking processes, intuition sets boundaries for analysis.

5-19. *Commanders conduct design to help them with the conceptual aspects of planning to include understanding, visualizing, and describing. After receipt of or in anticipation of a mission, commanders may begin design to understand the operational environment, frame the problem, and develop an operational approach to solve the problem. Using the elements of operational art, commanders visualize the desired end state and a broad concept of how to shape the current conditions into the end state. Commanders describe their visualization through the commander's intent, planning guidance, and concept of operations, clarifying an uncertain situation.

5-20. Commanders continuously lead and assess. Guided by professional judgment gained from experience, knowledge, education, intelligence, and intuition, commanders lead by force of example and personal presence. Leadership inspires Soldiers (and sometimes civilians) to accomplish things that they would otherwise avoid. This often requires risk. Commanders anticipate and accept prudent risk to create opportunities to seize, retain, and exploit the initiative and achieve decisive results. Assessment helps commanders better understand current conditions and broadly describe future conditions that define success. They identify the difference between the two and visualize a sequence of actions to link them.

5-21. *Commanders encourage the leadership and initiative of subordinates through mission command. Commanders accept setbacks that stem from the initiative of subordinates. They understand that land warfare is chaotic and unpredictable and that action is preferable to passivity. They encourage subordinates to accept prudent risks to create opportunities, while providing intent and control that allow for latitude and discretion. They also express gaps in relevant information as commander's critical information requirements (CCIRs). Direction is implicit in command; commanders direct actions to achieve results and lead forces to mission accomplishment.

Understand

5-22. Understanding is fundamental to the role of the commander. It is essential to the commander's ability to establish the situation's context. Understanding involves analyzing and understanding the operational or mission variables in a given operational environment. It is derived from applying judgment to the common operational picture through the filter of the commander's knowledge and experience. Understanding includes physical factors (such as location of forces or population centers), human factors (such as religion or morale), and the relationships among friendly and enemy forces, the local populace and other aspects of the operational environment that potentially represent opportunities and threats to friendly forces.

5-23. To develop a truer understanding of the operational environment, commanders, subordinate commanders, staffs, and other partners collaborate and dialog actively, sharing and questioning information, perceptions, and ideas to better understand situations and make decisions. Competent commanders circulate throughout their areas of operations as often as possible, talking to subordinate commanders and Soldiers conducting operations, while observing for themselves. These individuals have a more finely attuned sense of the local situation, and their intuition may detect trouble or opportunity long before the staff might. Intuition deepens commanders' understanding. It allows them to anticipate potential opportunities and threats, information gaps, and capability shortfalls. Understanding becomes the basis of the commander's visualization.

5-24. Numerous factors determine the commander's depth of understanding. Surveillance and reconnaissance prove indispensable as do actual observation and listening to subordinates. Formulating CCIRs, keeping them current, determining where to place key personnel, and arranging for liaisons also contribute to understanding. Maintaining understanding is a dynamic ability; a commander's situational understanding changes as an operation progresses. Additionally, commanders and their staffs must continually assess the level of confidence they have in their understanding of the situation, and strive to improve upon the degree of understanding. Relevant information fuels understanding and fosters initiative. Knowledge management helps commanders make informed, timely decisions. It brings the relevant information commanders require closer to that which they have. Information management helps commanders develop situational understanding to better frame the problem and assess the situation. It makes relevant information available to the right person at the right time. Greater understanding enables commanders to make better decisions. It allows them to focus their intuition on visualizing the current and future conditions of the environment and describing them to subordinates.

Visualize

5-25. *Commander's visualization* **is the mental process of developing situational understanding, determining a desired end state, and envisioning the broad sequence of events by which the force will achieve that end state.** During planning, commander's visualization provides the basis for developing plans and orders. During execution, it helps commanders determine if, when, and what to decide as they adapt to changing conditions. Commanders and staffs continuously assess the progress of operations toward the desired end state. They plan to adjust operations as required to accomplish the mission.

5-26. Assignment of a mission focuses the commander's visualization. Because military operations are fundamentally dynamic, this visualization must be continuous. Visualizing the desired end state requires commanders to clearly understand the operational environment and analyze the situation. Commanders consider the current situation and perform a mission analysis that assists in their initial visualization. They continually validate their visualization throughout the operation. To develop their visualization, commanders draw on several sources of knowledge and relevant information. These include—

- Elements of operational art appropriate to their echelon.
- Input from the staff and other commanders.
- Principles of war. (See appendix A.)
- Operational themes and related doctrine.
- Running estimates.
- The common operational picture.
- Their experience and judgment.
- Subject matter experts.

Visualization allows commanders to develop their intent and planning guidance for the entire operation, not just the initial onset of action.

5-27. Subordinate, supporting, adjacent, and higher commanders communicate with one another to compare perspectives and visualize their environments. Commanders increase the breadth and depth of their visualizations by collaborating with other commanders. Staff input, as running estimates, focuses analysis and detects potential effects on operations. Commanders direct staffs to provide the information necessary to shape their visualization. Commanders (and staff, if available) translate the commander's visualization into a specific course of action for preparation and execution, focusing on the expected results.

5-28. Commanders consider the elements of operational art as they frame the problem and describe their visualization. (See chapter 7.) However, the utility and application of some elements are often limited at the tactical level. Commanders use the elements that apply to their echelon and situation.

Describe

5-29. After commanders visualize an operation, they communicate their vision to their staffs and subordinates. They describe their shared understanding of the mission and commander's intent. Through collaboration and dialog, commanders ensure subordinates understand the visualization well enough to begin planning. Commanders describe their visualization in doctrinal terms, refining and clarifying it as circumstances require. Commanders express their initial visualization in terms of—

- Initial commander's intent.
- Planning guidance, including an initial concept of operations.
- Information required for further planning (CCIRs).
- Essential elements of friendly information to protect.

Initial Commander's Intent

5-30. Commanders summarize their visualization in their initial intent statement. The initial commander's intent aims to facilitate planning while focusing the overall operations process. Commanders develop this statement. It succinctly describes the commander's visualization of the entire operation listing what the commander wants to accomplish. The initial commander's intent links the operation's purpose with the conditions that define the desired end state. Usually the intent statement evolves as planning progresses and more information becomes available.

5-31. The initial commander's intent statement focuses the staff during the operations process. The staff uses this statement to develop and refine courses of action. These courses of action help establish conditions that define the end state. Planning involves developing lines of effort that link the execution of tactical tasks to end state conditions. A clear initial commander's intent drives this effort.

Planning Guidance

5-32. Commanders provide planning guidance with their initial intent statement. Planning guidance conveys the essence of the commander's visualization. Effective planning guidance is essentially an initial concept of operations that prioritizes each warfighting function. It reflects how the commander sees the operation unfolding. It broadly describes when, where, and how the commander intends to employ combat power to accomplish the mission within the higher commander's intent. Broad and general guidance gives the staff and subordinate leaders' maximum latitude; it lets proficient staffs develop flexible and effective options.

5-33. Commanders use their experience and judgment to add depth and clarity to their planning guidance. They ensure staffs understand the broad outline of their visualization while allowing them the latitude necessary to explore different options. This guidance provides the basis for a detailed concept of operations without dictating the specifics of the final plan. As with their intent, commanders may modify planning guidance based on staff and subordinate input and changing conditions.

Commander's Critical Information Requirements

5-34. A *commander's critical information requirement* is an information requirement identified by the commander as being critical to facilitating timely decisionmaking. The two key elements are friendly force information requirements and priority intelligence requirements (JP 3-0). A CCIR directly influences decisionmaking and facilitates the successful execution of military operations. Commanders decide whether to designate an information requirement as a CCIR based on likely decisions and their visualization of the course of the operation. A CCIR may support one or more decisions. During planning, staffs recommend information requirements for commanders to designate as CCIRs. During preparation and execution, they recommend changes to CCIRs based on assessment. A CCIR is—

- Specified by a commander for a specific operation.
- Applicable only to the commander who specifies it.
- Situation dependent—directly linked to a current or future mission.
- Focused on predictable events or activities.
- Time-sensitive—planners report the answer to a CCIR to the commander immediately by any means available.

5-35. Always promulgated by a plan or order, commanders limit the number of CCIRs to focus the efforts of limited collection assets. Typically, commanders identify ten or fewer CCIRs. The fewer the CCIRs, the easier staffs can remember, recognize, and act on each one. This helps staffs and subordinates identify information the commander needs immediately. While most staffs provide relevant information, a good staff expertly distills that information. It identifies answers to CCIRs and gets them to the commander immediately. It also identifies vital information that does not answer a CCIR but that the commander nonetheless needs to know. A good staff develops this acumen through training and experience. Designating too many CCIRs limits the staff's ability to immediately recognize and react to them. Excessive critical items reduce the focus of collection efforts.

5-36. The list of CCIRs constantly changes. Commanders add and delete individual requirements throughout an operation as they need information for specific decisions. Commanders determine their own CCIRs but may select some from staff nominations. Staff sections recommend the most important intelligence and information requirements for the commander to consider as CCIRs. Once approved, a CCIR falls into one of two categories: priority intelligence requirements (PIRs) and friendly force information requirements (FFIRs).

5-37. A *priority intelligence requirement* is an intelligence requirement, stated as a priority for intelligence support, that the commander and staff need to understand the adversary or the operational environment (JP 2-0). PIRs identify the information about the enemy, terrain and weather, and civil considerations that the commander considers most important. Lessons from recent operations show that intelligence about civil considerations may be as critical as intelligence about the enemy. Thus, all staff sections may recommend information about civil considerations as PIRs. The intelligence officer manages PIRs for the commander.

5-38. A *friendly force information requirement* is information the commander and staff need to understand the status of friendly force and supporting capabilities (JP 3-0). FFIRs identify the information about the mission, troops and support available, and time available for friendly forces that the commander considers most important. In coordination with the staff, the operations officer manages FFIRs for the commander.

Essential Elements of Friendly Information

5-39. **An *essential element of friendly information* is a critical aspect of a friendly operation that, if known by the enemy, would subsequently compromise, lead to failure, or limit success of the operation and therefore should be protected from enemy detection**. Although EEFIs are not CCIRs, they have the same priority. An EEFI establishes an element of information to protect rather than one to collect. EEFIs identify those elements of friendly force information that, if compromised, would jeopardize mission success. EEFIs help commanders protect vital friendly information. Their identification is the first step in the operations security process and central to the protection of information. (FM 3-13 addresses the operations security process.) EEFIs are also key factors in formulating military deception operations.

Direct

5-40. Commanders direct all aspects of operations. This direction takes different forms during planning, preparation, and execution. Commanders make decisions and direct actions based on their situational understanding, which they maintain by continuous assessment. They use control measures to focus the operation on the desired end state. Commanders direct operations by—

- Preparing and approving plans and orders.
- Assigning and adjusting missions, tasks, task organization, and control measures based on changing conditions.
- Positioning units to maximize combat power, anticipate actions, or create or preserve maneuver options.
- Positioning key leaders to ensure observation and supervision at critical times and places.
- Adjusting support priorities and allocating resources based on opportunities and threats.
- Accepting risk to create opportunities to seize, retain, and exploit the initiative.
- Establishing themes (and sometimes messages) for inform and influence activities.
- Committing reserves.

Plans and Orders

5-41. Plans and orders are key tools used by commanders in directing operations. Under mission command, commanders direct with mission orders. ***Mission orders* is a technique for developing orders that emphasizes to subordinates the results to be attained, not how they are to achieve them. It provides maximum freedom of action in determining how to best accomplish assigned missions.** Mission orders synchronize subordinates' actions only as required for mission success. Constraints are appropriate when mission success requires closely synchronized action by multiple units. Even then, commanders establish constraints in a manner that least limits individual initiative. Commanders ensure that orders prepared by the staff follow the precepts of mission orders to facilitate decentralized execution and maximum flexibility of subordinates.

5-42. Generally, subordinate commanders exercise full freedom of action within the concept of operations and commander's intent. Higher commanders may impose additional control over subordinates during a particular phase or mission. As soon as conditions allow, subordinates regain their freedom of action. Effective mission orders communicate to subordinates the situation, their commander's intent and mission, and the important tasks of each unit. The commander's intent and concept of operations set guidelines that ensure unity of effort while allowing subordinate commanders to exercise initiative.

5-43. Mission orders stress not only the tasks required of subordinates but also understanding their context and purpose. While clear direction is essential to accomplishing the mission, commanders strike a balance between necessary but minimum direction and overly detailed direction. Subordinates who act first (within the commander's intent) and report later often achieve far more than those who delay action to wait for the commander's confirmation.

Commander's Intent

5-44. **The *commander's intent* is a clear, concise statement of what the force must do and the conditions the force must establish with respect to the enemy, terrain, and civil considerations that represent the desired end state.** The commander's intent succinctly describes what constitutes success in an operation. It includes the operation's purpose and only the most important conditions that define the end state. It links the mission, concept of operations, and tasks to subordinate units. A clear commander's intent facilitates a shared understanding and focus on the overall conditions that represent mission accomplishment. During execution, the commander's intent spurs individual initiative.

5-45. Soldiers two echelons down must easily remember and clearly understand the commander's intent. The shorter the commander's intent, the better it serves these purposes. Typically, the commander's intent consists of three to five sentences. Commanders formulate and communicate their commander's intent to describe the boundaries within which subordinates may exercise initiative while maintaining unity of effort. To avoid limiting subordinates' freedom of action, commanders place only minimum constraints for coordination on them.

5-46. Commanders develop their intent statement. The commander's intent, coupled with mission, directs subordinates toward mission accomplishment, especially when current orders no longer fit the situation and subordinates must decide how to deviate from them. Subordinate leaders, empowered with authority and a clear understanding of the commander's intent and concept, develop the situation, adapt, and act decisively under fluid, dynamic conditions.

Concept of Operations

5-47. **The *concept of operations* is a statement that directs the manner in which subordinate units cooperate to accomplish the mission and establishes the sequence of actions the force will use to achieve the end state. It is normally expressed in terms of decisive, shaping, and sustaining operations.** The concept of operations expands on the commander's intent by describing how the commander wants the force to accomplish the mission. It states the principal tasks required, the responsible subordinate units, and how the principal tasks complement one another. The concept of operations promotes general understanding by stating the task (such as attack) that directly accomplishes the mission (the decisive operation) and the units that will execute it. The concept of operations clearly describes the other units' tasks in terms of shaping and sustaining operations. It may include, for example, the type of support or specific location for providing support. Normally, the concept of operations projects the status of the force at the end of the operation. If the mission dictates a significant change in tasks during the operation, the commander may phase the operation. Small-unit commanders and leaders usually do not describe their concept of operations in terms of decisive, shaping, and sustaining operations; they simply assign tasks to subordinates using main effort as required. (FM 5-0 discusses the concept of operations in detail.)

5-48. The *decisive operation* **is the operation that directly accomplishes the mission. It determines the outcome of a major operation, battle, or engagement. The decisive operation is the focal point around which commanders design the entire operation.** Multiple units may be engaged in the same decisive operation. For example, one task force may follow another on an axis of advance, prepared to assume the attack. Units operating in noncontiguous areas of operations may execute the tasks composing the higher headquarters' decisive operation simultaneously in different locations. Commanders visualize the decisive operation and then design shaping and sustaining operations around it.

5-49. Changing the mission normally changes the decisive operation. This can occur because of a change of phase but is more typical in the conduct of branches and sequels. When Army forces transition to a new operation, through either mission accomplishment or a significant change in the situation requiring reframing, the commander identifies a new decisive operation. Any element of full spectrum operations can be the decisive operation, as can a specific task, such as movement to contact or civil security. The commander determines the decisive operation. In a protracted stability operation, for example, the commander may identify a stability task in a particular area as the decisive operation: "The decisive operation is to provide civil security in Tal Afar. Task Force Roper provides civil security in Tal Afar commencing D+2."

5-50. **A** *shaping operation* **is an operation at any echelon that creates and preserves conditions for the success of the decisive operation.** Shaping operations establish conditions for the decisive operation through effects on the enemy, population (including local leaders), and terrain. Inform and influence activities, for example, may integrate Soldier and leader engagement tasks into the operation to reduce tensions between Army units and different ethnic groups through direct contact between Army leaders and local leaders. Shaping operations may occur throughout the operational area and involve any combination of forces and capabilities.

5-51. Shaping operations may occur before, during, or after the decisive operation begins. Some shaping operations, especially those executed simultaneously with the decisive operation, may be economy of force actions. However, if the force available does not permit simultaneous decisive and shaping operations, the commander sequences shaping operations around the decisive operation. The concept of operations describes how shaping operations contribute to the decisive operation's success, often in terms of the purpose. For example, "Task Force Hammer conducts search and attack operations in area of operations Anvil to neutralize insurgents that threaten Tal Afar. Task Force Rapier secures area of operations Sparrow as a support area for brigade operations."

5-52. **A** *sustaining operation* **is an operation at any echelon that enables the decisive operation or shaping operations by generating and maintaining combat power.** Sustaining operations differ from decisive and shaping operations in that they are focused internally (on friendly forces) rather than externally (on the enemy or environment). They typically address important sustainment and protection actions essential to the success of decisive and shaping operations. However, sustaining operations cannot be decisive themselves. Note that logistic and medical support provided to the civilian population relate to stability and civil support operations (provide essential services); they are not sustaining operations. At the operational level, sustaining operations focus on preparing the force for the operation's next phase. They determine the limit of operational reach. At the tactical level, sustaining operations determine the tempo of the overall operation; they ensure the force can seize, retain, and exploit the initiative.

5-53. Sustaining operations are continuous; commanders do not reiterate routine sustainment requirements in the concept of operations. Rather, the concept of operations emphasizes important changes in sustainment required by the operation. For example, "Brigade support battalion moves to area of operations Sparrow as soon as it is secure and establishes the brigade support area. On order, brigade special troops battalion assumes control of area of operations Sparrow." If there are no significant changes to sustainment, the sustainment paragraph or annexes discuss it.

5-54. The concept of operations identifies a main effort unit if required; otherwise, the priorities of support go to the unit conducting the decisive operation. **The *main effort* is the designated subordinate unit whose mission at a given point in time is most critical to overall mission success. It is usually weighted with the preponderance of combat power.** Designating a main effort temporarily prioritizes resource allocation. When commanders designate a unit as the main effort, it receives priority of support and resources. Commanders shift resources and priorities to the main effort as circumstances and the commander's intent require. Commanders may shift the main effort several times during an operation. Commanders may designate a unit conducting a shaping operation as the main effort until the decisive operation commences. However, the unit with primary responsibility for the decisive operation becomes the main effort upon execution of the decisive operation. For example, "Task Force Hammer is the main effort until D+2."

Lead

5-55. After commanders make decisions, they lead their forces throughout execution. During execution, commanders provide the strength of character, moral courage, and will to follow through with their decisions. When changing decisions, they must know when and what to decide, and when to make other decisions that address changes in the situation. (FM 6-22 discusses leadership actions during execution. Chapter 4 discusses leadership and combat power.)

5-56. Effective leaders have physical presence. Commanders carefully consider where they need to be, balancing the need to inspire Soldiers with that of maintaining an overall perspective of the entire operation. The commander's forward presence demonstrates a willingness to share danger. It also allows them to appraise for themselves the subordinate unit's condition, including leader and Soldier morale. Forward presence allows commanders to sense the human dimension of conflict, particularly when fear and fatigue reduce effectiveness. Then commanders need to lead by example, side-by-side with Soldiers. Commanders cannot let the perceived advantages of improved information technology compromise their obligation to lead by example.

5-57. The commander's will is the one constant that propels the force through the shock and friction of battle. Friction is inherent in all operations. Inevitably, things can and will go wrong. The ability of leaders and Soldiers to concentrate erodes as they reach the limit of their endurance. Against a skilled and resolute enemy, Soldiers may approach that point when fear, uncertainty, and physical exhaustion dominate their thinking. At this point, the commander's strength of will and personal presence provides the moral impetus for actions that lead to victory.

*Assess

5-58. Assessment helps commanders to better understand current conditions and determine how the operation is progressing. The commander maintains overall perspective, comparing the current situation to the one originally envisioned. This requires critical thinking, inspired when possible, by the commander's participation in design. The information that commanders receive from subordinates often shapes how commanders identify, frame, and seek to solve a problem. Commanders use this information to develop indicators to determine progress toward a successful outcome. These indicators may take the form of intermediate objectives that units must accomplish to achieve a desired end state.

5-59. The commander assesses the overall progress against the conditions extant, always asking whether the mission and commander's intent still apply. When assessment reveals a significant variance from the commander's original visualization, commanders reframe the problem and develop an entirely new plan as required. The staff assessment guides how to exercise control and regulate subordinate activities. Mission command requires that staff officers balance their judgment with the subordinate commanders' perspective; assessing progress against their commander's intent first, and then existing control measures.

*DEVELOP TEAMS AMONG MODULAR FORMATIONS AND JOINT, INTERAGENCY, INTERGOVERNMENTAL, AND MULTINATIONAL PARTNERS

5-60. Developing teams within organizations begins early in the operations process. This key activity begins in preparation and continues throughout execution. As part of unified action, the Army conducts operations with joint, interagency, intergovernmental, and multinational partners, as well as nongovernmental organizations. Commanders integrate all their capabilities. Developing teams enables commanders to shape operations before, during, and after operations. Army and joint, interagency, intergovernmental and multinational leaders study and understand the capabilities and limits of each team member. This effort ensures unity of effort. Leaders develop this understanding by training and continuously planning with joint, intergovernmental, interagency, multinational, and nongovernmental partners. Sustained engagement with host-nation governments and security forces enhances the developed understanding. Integrating capabilities during full spectrum operations requires interaction and preparation before commanders commit forces. Integration occurs through training exercises, exchange programs, and training events. Greater collaboration in developing systems and equipment results for all the forces involved.

5-61. The Army transformed from a division-based force to a modular brigade-based force with brigades organized by function. The brigade building blocks of the division make it a modular force task organized to the needs of the mission while creating options to use forces less than full divisions. However, this modular construct creates a challenge for commanders trying to build trust and confidence within subordinate organizations. These organizations are task-organized to meet specific mission requirements and often not habitually associated with a higher headquarters. Often they have not trained with the higher headquarters that employs them. Collaboration and dialog with subordinate organizations can mitigate these potential obstacles to team building. Through collaboration and dialog, commanders gain insight into the needs of subordinate leaders while also sharing their own clear vision and commander's intent.

5-62. By circulating among subordinate units, commanders can assess subordinates' preparation and execution, get to know new units in the task organization, and personally motivate Soldiers. By personally briefing subordinates, commanders gain firsthand appreciation for the situation as well as ensuring subordinate leaders and Soldiers understand the commander's intent. Commanders lead, coach, and mentor subordinate leaders. This assists in establishing close relationships that foster trust and mutual confidence. A subordinate's understanding of the commander's intent, provided through clear and succinct mission orders, drives successful mission command.

5-63. Commanders also visit with other government agencies, intergovernmental organizations, nongovernmental organizations, and the local populace in their areas of operations. With their presence, commanders build personal relationships with civilian leaders. Knowledge gained during these visits enables commanders to maintain situational understanding and continuously update their commander's visualization prior to and during execution. Civilian organizations, including those of the host nation, frequently arrive before and remain after forces depart. Commanders and staffs identify and make contact with those various organizations.

5-64. A challenge in building teams among civilian and military efforts stems from differing capabilities and cultures in the civilian and host-nation organizations compared to those of the headquarters. To help build partnerships, commanders strive to have partners—

- Represented, integrated, and actively involved in planning and coordinating activities.
- Share an understanding of the situation and problems to solve.
- Collectively determine the resources, capabilities, and activities necessary to achieve their goals.
- Work for unity of effort toward achieving common goals.

5-65. As Army forces conduct operations with various joint and other U.S. government agencies, leaders integrate Army and interagency capabilities to accomplish specific operational objectives. Interagency cooperation seeks to balance and combine the capabilities that the Army and those agencies bring to the operation. To effectively integrate complementary interagency capabilities, commanders follow policy guidance and the higher commander's concept of operations. Army leaders apply their understanding of different cultures and agencies involved to place military efforts in context and to serve on civil-military teams.

5-66. Partnering, especially with multinational partners, helps direct efforts toward mission accomplishment. It exceeds an opportunity for exchanging ideas and information. Partnering, and the need to partner, enables successful military operations. Even when no command authority exists, collaboration between commanders and partners affords commanders opportunities to revise their understanding or operational approach so together they can achieve the desired end state. Commanders seek unity of effort through coordination and cooperation even if participants come from different commands or organizations. Achieving unity of effort depends on leaders working with partners. They develop a mutual understanding of the environment and a common commitment to solutions. They address causes of conflict and sources of enemy strength. Achieving unity of effort requires Army leaders to have a high degree of cultural understanding and social skills. Without such understanding and skills, leaders will fail to mediate and collaborate with diverse partners.

5-67. Commanders continuously engage and emphasize strengthening existing relationships with modular formations and joint, interagency, intergovernmental, and multinational partners. Such action remains essential to developing mutual trust and common understanding. To build and strengthen bonds of trust and understanding, commanders sustain efforts to conduct combined training, education, and cultural exchanges. Successful joint and multinational operations often depend on close coordination, constant communication, and addressing issues concerning strategy and operations openly and directly.

*LEAD INFORM AND INFLUENCE ACTIVITIES

5-68. Effective full spectrum operations require commanders to establish, synchronize, and integrate actions with information themes and messages to achieve a desired end state. The integration of actions, themes, and messages aids the commander to provide consistent messages to diverse audiences. In an information-saturated environment, actions, themes, and messages are inextricably linked requiring careful coordination and integration. Information, as an element of combat power, is a critical and sometimes decisive factor in full spectrum operations. Effectively employed, information can shape the operational environment and multiply the effects of friendly successes while countering adversary or enemy information efforts. Commanders establish themes and messages. They personally engage key players, ensuring that the themes and messages are transmitted and received as the commander intends.

5-69. Information theme means a unifying or dominant idea or image that expresses the purposes for an action. A message is a verbal, written, or electronic communication that supports an information theme focused on an audience. It supports a specific action or objective. Accurate, timely, and synchronized themes and messages—delivered to the right audiences and integrated with effective actions—increase the pressure on the enemy. When dealing with friendly and neutral audiences, synchronized and integrated actions, information themes, and messages create significant opportunities to gain support for operations. Influencing behavior among varied and diverse groups enables commanders to deny the enemy safe havens and support bases necessary to mobilize resources and prepare for operations. Influence is as much a product of public perception as a measure of operational success. It reflects the ability of friendly forces to operate within the cultural and societal norms of the local populace while accomplishing the mission. Influence requires legitimacy. Developing legitimacy requires time, patience, and coordinated, cooperative efforts across the operational area. (Chapter 6 has a detailed discussion of inform and influence activities.)

SUMMARY

5-70. Commanders execute mission command to achieve success in full spectrum operations. The role of the commander in mission command is to direct and lead from the beginning of planning throughout execution, and continually assess. The commander is the central figure in mission command. Design permeates all aspects of mission command. Commanders drive the operations process. They understand, visualize, describe, direct, lead, and assess operations in complex, dynamic environments. Commanders lead the development of teams with joint, interagency, intergovernmental, and multinational partners as well as nongovernmental organizations. Commanders establish and synchronize information themes and messages to inform and influences specific audiences. Throughout operations, commanders, subordinate commanders, staffs, and other partners collaborate and dialog actively, sharing and questioning information, perceptions, and ideas to better understand situations and make decisions. Commanders encourage individual initiative through mission orders and a climate of mutual trust and understanding. Guided by their experience, knowledge, education, intelligence, and intuition, commanders apply leadership to translate decisions into action. Commanders synchronize forces and capabilities in time, space, and purpose to accomplish missions.

Chapter 6

The Science of Control

This chapter describes how commanders and staffs apply the science of control to support the commander's tasks. It discusses the staff tasks. This chapter details how staffs conduct the operations process, conduct knowledge management and information management, and conduct inform and influence and cyber/ electromagnetic activities.

6-1.   While command is a personal function, control involves the entire force. **In the context of mission command,** *control* **is the regulation of forces and warfighting functions to accomplish the mission in accordance with the commander's intent.** Commanders require control to direct operations. Aided by staffs, commanders exercise control over all forces in their area of operations. Staffs coordinate, synchronize, and integrate actions, inform the commander, and exercise control for the commander.

6-2.   The control aspect of mission command applies more science than art because it relies on objectivity, facts, empirical methods, and analysis. The science of control includes the detailed systems and procedures to improve the commander's understanding and support execution of missions. Commanders and staffs use the science of control to overcome the physical and procedural constraints under which units operate. Control demands commanders and staffs understand those aspects of operations that they can analyze and measure. These include the physical capabilities and limitations of friendly and enemy organizations and systems. Control also requires a realistic appreciation for time-distance factors and the time required to initiate certain actions. The science of control supports the art of command.

6-3.   When dealing with complex problems, commanders use design to assist them in understanding the operational environment, framing the problem, and developing a broad general approach to its solution. Design pervades all systems and procedures, enabling commanders to better understand complex problems. The commander's visualization and description of what to do to achieve desired conditions must flow logically from what commanders understand and how they have framed complex problems.

SECTION II – THE STAFF TASKS

6-4.   *Three key staff tasks apply to the science of control:
- Conduct the operations process: plan, prepare, execute, and assess.
- Conduct knowledge management and information management.
- Conduct inform and influence and cyber/electromagnetic activities.

These three tasks support the commander's tasks and, although discussed in this chapter on control, complement the commander's tasks.

CONDUCT THE OPERATIONS PROCESS

6-5.   **The** *operations process* **consists of the major mission command activities performed during operations: planning, preparing, executing, and continuously assessing the operation. The commander drives the operations process through leadership.** Commanders may perform the activities of the operations process sequentially or simultaneously. These activities are usually not discrete; they overlap and recur as circumstances demand. Commanders use the operations process to help them decide when and where to make decisions, control operations, and provide command presence. (See FM 5-0 for a detailed discussion on the operations process.)

6-6. *Planning, to include design, is synchronized. Throughout the operations process, commanders synchronize forces and warfighting functions to accomplish missions. Synchronization enables units to achieve synergic effects. For example, units must synchronize delivery of fires with target acquisition to produce the desired effects. However, synchronization is not an end in itself. It is useful only as it contributes to the greater effectiveness of the force. Unnecessary synchronization or synchronization for limited gains degrades tempo, impedes initiative, and allows the enemy to act within the friendly force decision process. Excessive synchronization undermines mission command.

6-7. Both design and the military decisionmaking process (MDMP) assist commanders and staffs with the conceptual aspects of planning. Commanders and staffs use design with the MDMP and troop leading procedures to integrate activities during planning. They also develop additional procedures and processes for executing control. Paragraphs 6-32 through 6-73 discuss this support in detail.

PLAN

6-8. *Planning is the process by which commanders (and the staff, if available) translate the commander's visualization into a specific course of action for preparation and execution, focusing on the expected results. Planning begins with analysis and assessment of the conditions in the operational environment, with particular emphasis on the enemy, to determine the relationships among the mission variables. It involves understanding and framing the problem and envisioning the set of conditions that represent the desired end state. Design and the MDMP assist commanders and staffs with the conceptual aspects of planning. Based on the commander's guidance, planning includes formulating one or more supportable courses of action to accomplish the mission. Good plans foster initiative, account for uncertainty and friction, and mitigate risks.

6-9. Commanders and staffs consider the consequences and implications of each course of action. Once the commander selects a course of action, the staff formulates specified tasks to subordinates, required staff actions, and an assessment framework. Planning develops the detailed information required during execution. Examples include setting initial conditions, assigning command relationships, and establishing priorities. Planning does not cease with production of a plan or order. It continues throughout an operation as the order is refined based on changes in the situation. In addition, staffs refine plans for branches and sequels during an operation.

6-10. Whenever possible, commanders employ red teams to examine plans from an opponent's perspective. Red teams provide insight into possible flaws in the plan as well as potential reactions by the enemy and other people in the area of operations. This insight helps the staff improve the plan and develop more effective branches and sequels.

6-11. The scope, complexity, and length of planning horizons differ at the operational and tactical levels. At the operational level, campaign planning coordinates major actions across significant periods. Planners integrate Service capabilities with those of joint, interagency, intergovernmental, and multinational organizations. (JP 5-0 contains doctrine for joint operation planning.) Tactical planning has the same clarity of purpose but typically reflects a shorter planning horizon. Comprehensive, continuous, and adaptive planning characterizes successful operations at both levels.

6-12. The Army uses three doctrinal planning procedures to integrate activities during planning: design, the MDMP, and troop leading procedures. Upon receipt of a mission, commanders may begin design to understand the operational environment, frame the problem, and develop an operational approach to solve the problem. The design concept serves as the foundation for more detailed planning, including the production of plans and orders using the MDMP. In units with a formally organized staff, the MDMP provides structure to help commanders and staffs develop running estimates, plans, and orders. It provides a logical sequence for decisionmaking and interaction between the commander and staff, and it provides a common framework for parallel planning. At the lowest tactical echelons, commanders and leaders follow troop leading procedures. Design, the MDMP, and troop leading procedures hinge on the commander's ability to visualize and describe the operation. They are means to an end; their inherent value lies in the results achieved, not the process. (FM 5-0 discusses design, the MDMP, and troop leading procedures.)

6-13. Planning continues as necessary during preparation and execution. When circumstances are not suited for the MDMP or troop leading procedures, commanders rely on design, intuitive decisionmaking, and direct contact with subordinate commanders to integrate activities.

PREPARE

6-14. *Preparation* **consists of activities performed by units to improve their ability to execute an operation. Preparation includes, but is not limited to, plan refinement; rehearsals; intelligence, surveillance, and reconnaissance; coordination; inspections; and movement.** Preparation establishes conditions that improve friendly forces' opportunities for success. It facilitates and sustains transitions, including those to branches and sequels.

6-15. Preparation requires staff, unit, and Soldier actions. Mission success depends on preparation as much as on planning. Rehearsals help staffs, units, and Soldiers to better understand their roles in upcoming operations, practice complicated tasks, and ensure equipment and weapons function properly. Activities specific to preparation include—

- Revision and refinement of the plan.
- Rehearsals.
- Force tailoring and task-organizing.
- Surveillance and reconnaissance.
- Training.
- Troop movements.
- Precombat checks and inspections.
- Sustainment preparations.
- Integration of new Soldiers and units.
- Subordinate confirmation briefs and backbriefs.

6-16. Several preparation activities begin during planning and continue throughout execution. For example, uncommitted forces prepare for contingencies identified in branches and subsequent events detailed in sequels. Committed units revert to preparation when they accomplish their objectives, occupy defensive positions, or pass into reserve.

EXECUTE

6-17. *Execution* **is putting a plan into action by applying combat power to accomplish the mission and using situational understanding to assess progress and make execution and adjustment decisions.** It focuses on concerted action to seize, retain, and exploit the initiative. Army forces seize the initiative immediately and dictate tempo throughout all operations.

6-18. Commanders use mission command to achieve maximum flexibility and foster individual initiative. Subordinates exercising their initiative can significantly increase the tempo of operations; however, this may desynchronize the overall operation. Desynchronization may reduce commanders' abilities to mass the effects of combat power. Executing even relatively minor, planned actions produces second- and third-order effects throughout the force; these affect the operation's overall synchronization. Nonetheless, under mission command, commanders accept some risk of desynchronization as the price of seizing, retaining, and exploiting the initiative.

6-19. The commander's intent and mission orders focus every echelon on executing the concept of operations. Mission command enables and prompts collaborative synchronization among subordinates. When subordinates exploit opportunities, individual initiative resynchronizes the overall operation continuously. Subordinates' success may offer opportunities anticipated in the concept of operations or develop advantages that make a new concept practical. In either case, the commander's intent keeps the force focused and synchronized. Subordinates need not wait for top-down synchronization. The climate fostered by mission command encourages subordinates to act on information about the enemy, adversaries, events, and trends without detailed direction.

6-20. As commanders assess the operation, they determine when to make decisions. Orders usually identify some decision points; however, unanticipated enemy actions or conditions often present situations that require unanticipated decisions. Commanders act when decisions are required. They do not wait for a set time in the battle rhythm.

6-21. During execution, commanders draw on experience, intellect, creativity, intuition, and education to make rapid decisions. They learn deliberately as the situation develops and make changes based on that learning. Staffs synchronize or resynchronize forces and warfighting functions more quickly during execution than during planning and preparation. They must do this while forces are moving and processes are ongoing.

6-22. During execution, commanders incorporate considerations for the operation's next phase or sequel. They begin to visualize how to transition from the current operation to the next one. Based on their visualization, commanders direct actions to posture the force for the transition. As they visualize the implications of events and their solutions, commanders describe their conclusions to staff and subordinates through updated commander's critical information requirements and planning guidance. The guidance may be to develop a branch or change the main effort to exploit success. Commanders direct adjustments when necessary, primarily through fragmentary orders.

ASSESS

6-23. *Assessment* **refers to the continuous monitoring and evaluation of the current situation, particularly the enemy, and progress of an operation.** Assessment precedes and guides every operations process activity and concludes each operation or phase of an operation. It involves a comparison of forecasted outcomes to actual events. Assessment entails three tasks:

- Continuously assess the enemy's reactions and vulnerabilities.
- Continuously monitor the situation and progress of the operation towards the commander's desired end state.
- Evaluate the operation against measures of effectiveness and measures of performance.

6-24. Staffs monitor the current situation for unanticipated successes, failures, or enemy actions. As commanders and staffs assess the operation, they look for opportunities, threats, and acceptable progress. They accept risks, seize opportunities, and mitigate threats. Throughout the operation, commanders visualize, describe, and direct changes to the operation.

6-25. A *measure of performance* is a criterion used to assess friendly actions that is tied to measuring task accomplishment (JP 3-0). Measures of performance answer the question, "Was the task or action performed as the commander intended?" A measure of performance confirms or denies that a unit has performed a task properly.

6-26. A *measure of effectiveness* is a criterion used to assess changes in system behavior, capability, or operational environment that is tied to measuring the attainment of an end state, achievement of an objective, or creation of an effect (JP 3-0). Measures of effectiveness focus on the results or consequences of actions taken. They answer the question, "Is the force doing the right things, or are additional or alternative actions required?" A measure of effectiveness provides a benchmark against which the commander assesses progress toward accomplishing the mission.

6-27. Staffs analyze the current situation using mission variables and prepare their running estimates. A *running estimate* is the continuous assessment of the current situation used to determine if the current operation is proceeding according to the commander's intent and if planned future operations are supportable (FM 5-0). Staffs continuously assess how new information might impact conducting operations. They update running estimates and determine if adjustments to the operation are required. Commanders empower their staffs to make adjustments within their areas of expertise. This requires staffs to understand the aspects of operations that require the commander's attention as opposed to those delegated to their control.

6-28. Commanders integrate their own assessments and those of subordinate commanders into all aspects of the operations process. Assessment helps commanders refine their situational understanding. It allows them to make informed, rational decisions throughout the entire operation. During planning, assessment focuses on understanding the current conditions in the operational environment and developing relevant courses of action. During preparation and execution, it emphasizes evaluating progress toward the desired end state, determining variances from expectations, and determining the significance (threat or opportunity) of those variances.

6-29. Planners primarily use the common operational picture, observations of commanders, and running estimates for assessing the operation against the concept of operations, mission, and commander's intent. The commander's visualization forms the basis of the commander's personal decisionmaking methodology throughout the operation. Running estimates provide information, conclusions, and recommendations from the perspective of each staff section. They help to refine the common operational picture and supplement it with information not readily displayed.

6-30. During assessment, commanders may decide to reframe after realizing the desired conditions have changed, are not achievable, or cannot be attained through the current operational approach. Reframing provides the freedom to operate beyond the limits of any single perspective. Conditions change during execution. Commanders and staff expect such change because forces interact within the operational environment. Recognizing and anticipating these changes is fundamental to design and essential to an organization's ability to learn.

6-31. Commanders avoid excessive analysis when assessing operations. Committing valuable time and energy to developing elaborate and time-consuming assessments squanders resources better devoted to other operations process activities. Effective commanders avoid burdening subordinates and staffs with overly detailed assessment and collection tasks. Generally, the echelon at which a specific operation, task, or action is conducted should be the echelon at which it is assessed. This provides a focus for assessment at each echelon. It enhances the efficiency of the overall operations process.

SUPPORT TO THE OPERATIONS PROCESS

6-32. Throughout the operations process, commanders and staff develop additional procedures and processes for executing control. They may execute these simultaneously. Commanders and staff also produce products that provide enough control to ensure subordinates execute within the commander's intent.

Integrating Processes

6-33. Certain integrating processes occur during all operations process activities (see figure 6-1, page 6-6). Commanders synchronize these processes with each other and integrate them into the overall operation:
- Intelligence preparation of the battlefield. (For joint and functional component commanders, this is intelligence preparation of the operational environment. See JP 2-0.)
- Targeting. (See FM 3-60.)
- Intelligence, surveillance, and reconnaissance synchronization.
- Composite risk management. (See FM 5-19.)
- Knowledge management.

Continuing Activities

6-34. The following activities continue during all operations process activities. Commanders synchronize these activities with one another and integrate them into the overall operation:
- Intelligence, surveillance, and reconnaissance.
- Security operations.
- Protection.
- Liaison and coordination.
- Terrain management.
- Information management.
- Airspace command and control.

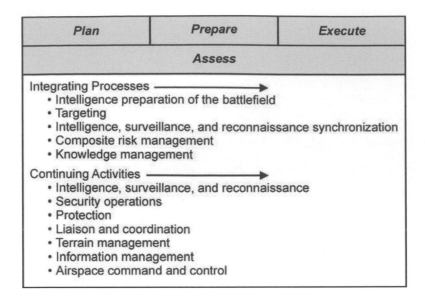

Figure 6-1. Operations process expanded

*Mission Command Networks and Systems

6-35. Commanders cannot exercise mission command alone except in the smallest organizations. Thus, commanders perform these functions through mission command networks and systems. (Chapter 4 defines mission command networks and systems.) An effective mission command system enables commanders to conduct operations that accomplish the mission decisively.

6-36. A commander's mission command system begins with people. No amount of technology can reduce the importance of the human dimension. (FM 6-22 discusses the human dimension.) Therefore, commanders base their mission command systems on human characteristics more than on equipment and procedures. Effective mission command systems required trained personnel; the best technology cannot support mission command without them.

6-37. Networks are key enablers to successful operations. Commanders capitalize on networks to extend the connectivity of higher levels to staff and subordinates. This connectivity supports operational adaptability without sacrificing coordination or unity of effort. Commanders ensure that all units have access to, understand, and communicate information across friendly networks. Electronic long-distance sensor, collector, and transmitter networks provide actionable information across the battlefield. To enable mission command, leaders and Soldiers access networks to create, process, and integrate information. Network systems provide synthesized information so leaders can make informed decisions without being overburdened. Commanders use these systems to communicate with joint, interagency, intergovernmental, and multinational partners on multiple networks.

6-38. Procedures govern actions within a mission command system to make it more effective and efficient. Procedures are standard, detailed steps that describe how to perform specific tasks. Adhering to procedures minimizes confusion, misunderstanding, and hesitation as commanders make frequent, rapid decisions to meet operational requirements.

6-39. Equipment and facilities provide sustainment and a work environment for the other elements of a mission command system. Facilities vary in size and complexity. At the lowest echelon, commanders may use their command post or vehicle as the facility. At the highest echelons, facilities consist of large and complex buildings. Units equip facilities with current and emerging technologies that provide timely, accurate, and reliable information to commanders.

6-40. To respond to a rapidly changing operational environment and develop creativity, innovation, and adaptation, information must become knowledge. Knowledge must permeate the Army. This requires both art and science. Knowledge management generates knowledge products and services among commanders and staffs. It supports collaboration and the conduct of operations while improving organizational performance. Information management combines information systems and information processes to distribute, store, display, and protect knowledge products and services. (Paragraph 6-81 discusses information management.)

6-41. Agile and adaptive Soldiers are the single most important element of any mission command system. Their actions and responses—everything from fire and maneuver techniques to the disciplined observation of rules of engagement—control operations. Soldiers also assist commanders and exercise control on their behalf. Staffs perform many functions that help commanders exercise mission command:

- Provide relevant information and analysis.
- Maintain running estimates and make recommendations.
- Prepare plans and orders.
- Monitor operations.
- Control operations.
- Assess the progress of operations.

FORMS OF CONTROL

6-42. Control allows commanders to adjust operations to conform to their commander's intent as conditions change. Staffs provide their greatest support in assisting the commander with control. Commanders use two forms of control—procedural and positive. Commanders balance the two forms based on the situation.

6-43. *Army procedural control* **is a technique of regulating forces that relies on a combination of orders, regulations, policies, and doctrine (including tactics, techniques, and procedures)**. Army procedural control requires no intervention by the higher headquarters once it is established.

6-44. *Army positive control* **is a technique of regulating forces that involves commanders and leaders actively assessing, deciding, and directing them.** It may restrict Soldiers since commanders directly monitor operations and intervene, directing specific actions to better synchronize subordinates' operations. Excessive use of Army positive control can rapidly become detailed command.

6-45. The definitions of individual control measures provide Army procedural control without requiring detailed explanations. For example, boundaries, the most important control measure, designate the area of operations assigned to or by a commander. Commanders know they have full freedom of action within their area of operations.

6-46. Army positive control may best apply when units require detailed directions to sequence actions or coordinate the activities with nearby forces. A river crossing illustrates this situation. In exercising Army positive control, commanders may use digital information systems to assess without requesting information explicitly or continuously from subordinates. Positive control supplements mission command when necessary.

CONTROL MEASURES

6-47. Commanders exercise Army procedural and Army positive controls through control measures. **A** *control measure* **is a means of regulating forces or warfighting functions**. Control measures are established under a commander's authority; however, commanders may authorize staff officers and subordinate leaders to establish them. Commanders use control measures to assign responsibilities, require synchronization between forces, impose restrictions, or establish guidelines to regulate freedom of action. Commanders use control measures to coordinate subordinates' actions. The control measures can be permissive or restrictive. Permissive control measures allow specific actions to occur; restrictive control measures limit the conduct of certain actions.

6-48. Control measures help commanders direct by establishing responsibilities and limits that prevent subordinate units' actions from impeding one another. They foster coordination and cooperation between forces without unnecessarily restricting freedom of action, decisionmaking, and individual initiative.

6-49. Control measures may be detailed (such as a division operation order) or simple (such as a checkpoint). Control measures include, but are not limited to—

- Laws and regulations.
- Planning guidance.
- Delegation of authority.
- Specific instructions to plans and orders and their elements, including—
    - Commander's intent.
    - Unit missions and tasks.
    - Commander's critical information requirements.
    - Essential elements of friendly information.
    - Task organization.
    - Concept of operations.
    - Target lists.
    - Rules of engagement.
    - Service support plans.
    - Graphic control measures.
    - Unit standing operating procedures that control actions as reporting and battle rhythm.
- Information requirements.

6-50. Certain control measures belong to the commander alone—the commander's intent, unit mission statement, planning guidance, commander's critical information requirements (CCIRs), and essential elements of friendly information (EEFIs). Commanders cannot delegate these control measures. Unit standard operating procedures specify many control measures. An operation plan or order modifies and adds additional measures for a specific operation. Commanders, assisted by their staffs, modify control measures to account for the dynamic conditions of operations.

6-51. Some control measures are graphic. **A *graphic control measure* is a symbol used on maps and displays to regulate forces and warfighting functions**. Graphic control measures are always prescriptive. They include symbols for boundaries, fire support coordination measures, some airspace control measures, air defense areas, and minefields. Commanders establish them to regulate maneuver, movement, airspace use, fires, and other aspects of operations. In general, all graphic control measures relate to easily identifiable natural or manmade terrain features. (FM 1-02 portrays and defines graphic control measures and discusses rules for selecting and applying them.)

MISSION VARIABLES: THE FACTORS OF METT-TC

6-52. METT-TC is a memory aid that identifies the mission variables: Mission, Enemy, Terrain and weather, Troops and support available, Time available, and Civil considerations. It is used in information management (the major categories of relevant information) and in tactics (the major variables considered during mission analysis). Mission analysis describes characteristics of the area of operations in terms of METT-TC, focusing on how they might affect the mission. (FM 6-0 discusses METT-TC in more detail.)

6-53. The *mission* is the task, together with the purpose, that clearly indicates the action to be taken and the reason therefore (JP 3-0). Commanders analyze a mission in terms of specified tasks, implied tasks, and the commander's intent two echelons up. They also consider the missions of adjacent units to understand their relative contributions to the decisive operation. Results of that analysis yield the essential tasks that—with the purpose of the operation—clearly specify the actions required. This analysis also produces the unit's mission statement—a short description of the task and purpose that clearly indicates the action to be taken and the reason for doing so. It contains the elements of who, what, when, where, and why. Mission command requires that commanders clearly communicate—and subordinates understand—the purpose for conducting an operation or a task.

6-54. When assigning missions, commanders ensure each subordinate's mission supports the decisive operation and the higher commander's intent. They identify the purpose for each task assigned, nesting unit missions with one another and with the decisive operation. (FM 5-0 discusses the nested concept.) Under mission command, commanders articulate each subordinate's mission in words that foster individual initiative.

6-55. The second variable to consider is the *enemy*. Relevant information regarding the enemy may include the following:

- Dispositions (including organization, strength, location, and mobility).
- Doctrine (or known execution patterns).
- Personal habits and idiosyncrasies.
- Equipment, capabilities, and vulnerabilities.
- Probable courses of action.

Analysis of the enemy includes not only the known enemy but also other threats to mission success. Such threats might include multiple adversaries posing with a wide array of political, economic, religious, and personal motivations.

6-56. To understand threat capabilities and vulnerabilities, commanders and staffs require detailed, timely, and accurate intelligence. Of all relevant information, intelligence is the most uncertain. Commanders use surveillance and reconnaissance to collect the most important threat-related information and process it into intelligence.

6-57. *Terrain and weather* are natural conditions that profoundly influence operations. Terrain and weather are neutral; they favor neither side unless one is more familiar with—or better prepared to operate in—the physical environment. Terrain includes natural features (such as rivers and mountains) and manmade features (such as cities, airfields, and bridges). Terrain directly affects how commanders select objectives and locate, move, and control forces. It also influences protective measures and the effectiveness of weapons and other systems. Effective use of terrain reduces the effects of enemy fires, increases the effects of friendly fires, and facilitates surprise. Terrain appreciation—the ability to predict its impact on operations—is an important skill for every leader. For tactical operations, commanders analyze terrain using the five military aspects of terrain, expressed in the memory aid, OAKOC: **O**bservation and fields of fire, **A**venues of approach, **K**ey and decisive terrain, **O**bstacles, **C**over and concealment.

6-58. Climate and weather affect all operations. Climate means the prevailing pattern of temperature, wind velocity, and precipitation in a specific area measured over a period of years. Climate is a more predictable phenomenon than weather and better suited to operational-level analysis. Planners typically focus analysis on how climate affects large-scale operations over a geographically diverse area. In contrast, weather describes the conditions of temperature, wind velocity, precipitation, and visibility at a specific place and time. It applies better to tactical analysis, where its effect on operations is limited in scale and duration. Climate and weather affect conditions and capabilities of Soldiers and weapons systems, including mobility, obstacle emplacement times, and munitions performance. Effective commanders use climate and weather to their advantage.

6-59. The fourth mission variable is *troops and support available*. This refers to the number, type, capabilities, and condition of available friendly troops and support from joint, interagency, multinational, host-nation, commercial (via contracting), and private organizations. It also includes support provided by civilians. Commanders and staffs maintain information on friendly forces two echelons down. They track subordinate readiness—including training, maintenance, logistics, and morale. Commanders provide subordinates with the mix of troops and support needed to accomplish their missions. When assigning or allocating troops to subordinates, commanders and staffs consider differences in mobility, protection, firepower, equipment, morale, experience, leadership, and training.

6-60. Commanders and staffs consider available troops and support when determining the resources required to accomplish a mission—a troop-to-task analysis. If commanders determine they lack sufficient resources, they request additional support. When they lack the resources needed to execute simultaneous operations, commanders execute sequential operations.

6-61. The next mission variable is *time available*. Controlling and exploiting time drives initiative, tempo, and momentum. By exploiting time, commanders can exert constant pressure, control the relative speed of decisions and actions, and exhaust enemy forces. Upon receipt of a mission, commanders assess the time available for planning, preparing, and executing it. This includes the time required to assemble, deploy, and maneuver units to where they can best mass the effects of combat power. Commanders also consider how much time they can give subordinates to plan and prepare their own operations. Parallel and collaborative planning helps optimize available time. (FM 5-0 discusses parallel and collaborative planning.)

6-62. Commanders relate time to the enemy and conditions. As part of this analysis, commanders consider time in two contexts: First, they estimate how much time friendly forces have to accomplish the mission relative to enemy efforts to defeat them. Second, they consider the time needed to accomplish their objectives or to change current conditions into those of the desired end state. Analyzing the time available helps commanders determine how quickly and how far in advance to plan operations. The more time the commander and staff take, the more time the enemy has. The time spent perfecting a plan may work to the enemy's advantage; the additional time provided to enemy forces often offsets the minor gains a slightly improved plan gives friendly forces.

6-63. Commanders consider the time available relative to the situation. Success depends on preventing the situation from deteriorating further. Ultimately, good plans executed sooner produce better results than perfect plans executed later.

6-64. Finally, understanding the operational environment requires understanding *civil considerations*. *Civil considerations* reflect the influence of manmade infrastructure, civilian institutions, and attitudes and activities of the civilian leaders, populations, and organizations within an area of operations on the conduct of military operations (FM 6-0). Commanders and staffs analyze civil considerations in terms of the categories expressed in the memory aid ASCOPE: <u>A</u>reas, <u>S</u>tructures, <u>C</u>apabilities, <u>O</u>rganizations, <u>P</u>eople, and <u>E</u>vents.

6-65. Civil considerations help commanders understand the social, political, and cultural variables within the area of operations and their affect on the mission. Understanding the relationship between military operations and civilians, culture, and society is critical to conducting full spectrum operations. (FM 3-05.40 contains additional information on civil considerations.) These considerations relate directly to the effects of the other instruments of national power. They provide a vital link between actions of forces interacting with the local populace and the desired end state.

6-66. Civil considerations are essential to developing effective plans for all operations—not just those dominated by stability or civil support. Full spectrum operations often involve stabilizing the situation, securing the peace, building host-nation capacity, and transitioning authority to civilian control. Combat operations directly affect the populace, infrastructure, and the force's ability to transition to host-nation authority. The degree to which the populace is expected to support or resist Army forces also affects the design of offensive and defensive operations.

6-67. Commanders and staffs use personal knowledge, area studies, and the intelligence and civil affairs running estimates to assess social, economic, and political factors. Commanders consider how these factors may relate to potential lawlessness, subversion, or insurgency. Their goal is to develop their understanding to the level of cultural awareness. At this level, they can estimate the effects of friendly actions and direct their subordinates with confidence. Cultural awareness improves how Soldiers interact with the populace and deters their false or unrealistic expectations. They have more knowledge of the society's common practices, perceptions, assumptions, customs, and values, giving better insight into the intent of individuals and groups.

AREA OF OPERATIONS

6-68. One of the most important control measures is the area of operations. The Army or land force commander is the supported commander within an area of operations designated by the joint force commander for land operations. Within their areas of operations, commanders integrate and synchronize maneuver, fires, and interdiction. To facilitate this integration and synchronization, commanders have the authority to designate targeting priorities and timing of fires.

6-69. Commanders consider a unit's area of influence when assigning it an area of operations. An *area of influence* is a geographical area wherein a commander is directly capable of influencing operations by maneuver or fire support systems normally under the commander's command or control (JP 3-16). The area of influence normally surrounds and includes the area of operations. Understanding the area of influence helps the commander and staff plan branches to the current operation in which the force uses capabilities outside the area of operations. An area of operations should not be substantially larger than the unit's area of influence.

6-70. Ideally, the entire area of influence encompasses the area of operations. An area of operations that is too large for a unit to control can allow sanctuaries for enemy forces and may limit joint flexibility. Assigning areas of operations to subordinate commanders maximizes decentralized execution by empowering those commanders to exercise initiative. Mission command authorizes commanders to create any effects necessary to accomplish the mission (consistent with the rules of engagement) within their areas of operations. However, commanders cannot create effects outside their areas of operations without permission from the commander assigned the area of operations in which those effects will occur. Further, commanders must control all parts of their area of operations not assigned to subordinates. Assignment of an area of operations includes authority to perform the following:

- Terrain management.
- Intelligence collection.
- Civil affairs activities.
- Air and ground movement control.
- Clearance of fires.
- Security.

6-71. Subordinate unit areas of operations may be contiguous or noncontiguous. (See figure 6-2.) A common boundary separates contiguous areas of operations. Noncontiguous areas of operations do not share a common boundary; the concept of operations provides procedural control of elements of the force. **An *unassigned area* is the area between noncontiguous areas of operations or beyond contiguous areas of operations. The higher headquarters is responsible for controlling unassigned areas within its area of operations.** Designating an unassigned area only indicates that the area is not assigned to a subordinate. Unassigned areas remain the responsibility of the controlling headquarters.

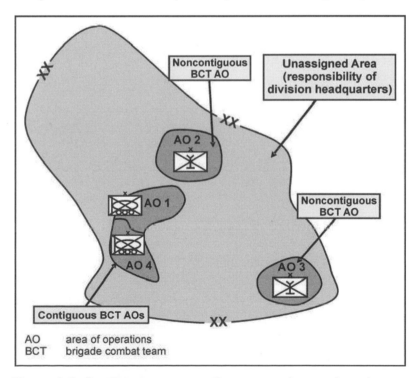

Figure 6-2. Contiguous, noncontiguous, and unassigned areas

COMMON OPERATIONAL PICTURE

6-72. The *common operational picture* is a single display of relevant information within a commander's area of interest tailored to the user's requirements and based on common data and information shared by more than one command. An *area of interest* is area of concern to the commander, including the area of influence, areas adjacent thereto, and extending into enemy territory to the objectives of current or planned operations. This area also includes areas occupied by enemy forces who could jeopardize the accomplishment of the mission (JP 2-03). The area of interest for stability or civil support operations may be much larger than that associated with offensive and defensive operations.

6-73. The availability of a common operational picture facilitates mission command. The common operational picture lets subordinates see the overall operation and their contributions to it as the operation progresses. This knowledge reduces the level of control higher commanders need to exercise over subordinates. The common operational picture features a scale and level of detail that meets the information needs of that commander and staff. It varies among staff sections and echelons. Separate echelons create a common operational picture by collaborating, sharing, and refining relevant information. To the extent permitted by technology, the common operational picture incorporates as much information from running estimates as possible.

*CONDUCT KNOWLEDGE MANAGEMENT AND INFORMATION MANAGEMENT

6-74. Staffs apply the science of control to support the commander's tasks by conducting knowledge management and information management.

*KNOWLEDGE MANAGEMENT

6-75. *Knowledge management* is the art of creating, organizing, applying, and transferring knowledge to facilitate situational understanding and decisionmaking. Knowledge management supports improving organizational learning, innovation, and performance. Its processes ensure that knowledge products and services are relevant, accurate, timely, and useable to commanders and decisionmakers. Knowledge management has three major components:

- People—those inside and outside the organization who create, organize, share, and use knowledge, and the leaders who foster an adaptive, learning environment.
- Processes—the methods to create, capture, organize, and apply knowledge.
- Technology—information systems that help collect, process, store, and display knowledge. Technology helps put knowledge products and services into organized frameworks.

6-76. Knowledge management enables commanders make informed, timely decisions despite the uncertainty of operations. It enables effective collaboration by linking organizations with Soldiers requiring knowledge. Knowledge management enhances rapid adaptation in dynamic operations. Analyzing and evaluating information creates knowledge. Since a wide range of knowledge might affect operations, the commander's information requirements may extend beyond military matters. Defining these requirements is an important aspect of knowledge management. Commanders define their information requirements with their CCIRs. The CCIRs focus development of knowledge products. (See FM 6-01.1 for a discussion on knowledge management.)

6-77. Commanders and staffs assess knowledge management effectiveness by considering whether it lessens the fog of war. Knowledge management narrows the gap between relevant information commanders require and that which they have. Developing a knowledge management plan enables leaders to—

- Address knowledge and information flow.
- Develop criteria for displaying the common operational picture.
- Access and filter information from sources normally found outside the military or the organization.
- Support developing situational awareness and situational understanding.

- Enable rapid, accurate retrieval of previously developed knowledge to satisfy new requirements.
- Route products to the right individuals in a readily understood format.
- Keep information from overwhelming commanders and staffs.

6-78. Staff responsibility for knowledge management begins with the chief of staff. Depending on the complexity of the situation, it may require dedicated personnel.

*SITUATIONAL AWARENESS

6-79. Commanders begin their visualization with situational awareness. *Situational awareness* **means immediate knowledge of the conditions of the operation, constrained geographically and in time**. More simply, it is Soldiers knowing what is currently happening around them. Situational awareness occurs in Soldiers' minds. It is not a display or the common operational picture; it is the interpretation of displays or the actual observation of a situation. On receipt of mission, commanders develop their situational awareness. They base it on information and knowledge products, such as the common operational picture and running estimates.

*SITUATIONAL UNDERSTANDING

6-80. During mission analysis, commanders apply judgment to their situational awareness to arrive at situational understanding. *Situational understanding* **is the product of applying analysis and judgment to relevant information to determine the relationships among the mission variables to facilitate decisionmaking.** It enables commanders to determine the implications of what is happening and forecast what may happen. Situational understanding enhances decisionmaking by identifying opportunities, threats to the force or mission accomplishment, and information gaps. It helps commanders identify enemy options and likely future actions, the probable consequences of proposed friendly actions, and the effect of the operational environment on both. Situational understanding based on a continuously updated common operational picture fosters individual initiative by reducing, although not eliminating, uncertainty.

*INFORMATION MANAGEMENT

6-81. *Information management* **is the science of using procedures and information systems to collect, process, store, display, disseminate, and protect knowledge products, data, and information.** Information management disseminates timely and protected relevant information to commanders and staffs. Information management helps commanders develop situational understanding. It also helps them make and disseminate effective decisions faster than the enemy can. Among other aspects, information management includes lower-level mechanical methods, such as organizing, collating, plotting, and arranging. However, information management goes beyond technical control of data flowing across networks. It employs both staff management and automatic processes to provide relevant information to the right person at the right time. Information management centers on commanders and the information they need to exercise mission command. It has two components: information systems and relevant information.

*INFORMATION SYSTEMS

6-82. An information system consists of equipment and facilities that collect, process, store, display, and disseminate information. This includes computers—hardware and software—and communications, as well as policies and procedures for their use. Information systems are the physical dimension of information management. They automatically sort, filter, store, and disseminate information according to the commander's priorities. These capabilities relieve the staff of handling routine data. Information systems—especially when merged into a single, integrated network—enable extensive information sharing. Commanders best use information systems when they determine their information requirements and focus their staffs and organizations on meeting them.

6-83. LandWarNet is the Army's portion of the Global Information Grid. LandWarNet encompasses all Army information management systems and information systems that collect, process, store, display, disseminate, and protect information worldwide. It enables execution of Army command and control processes and supports operations by widely disseminating relevant information. LandWarNet facilitates rapidly converting relevant information into decisions and actions. It allows commanders to exercise mission command from anywhere in their area of operations. (JP 6-0 describes the Global Information Grid.)

*RELEVANT INFORMATION

6-84. *Relevant information* **is all information of importance to commanders and staffs in the exercise of mission command.** To be relevant, information must be accurate, timely, usable, complete, precise, reliable, and secure. Relevant information provides answers commanders and staffs need to conduct operations successfully. The mission variables are the categories of relevant information. (FM 6-0 contains doctrine on relevant information and the cognitive hierarchy. The cognitive hierarchy describes how data become information, knowledge, and understanding.)

6-85. Effective information management identifies relevant information and processes data into information for development into and use as knowledge. Information management then quickly routes information and knowledge products to those who need them. All information given to commanders should be relevant information. That is, commanders should only receive information or knowledge products that they need for exercising mission command. The information commanders receive drives how they visualize the operation. How relevant information fits into the commander's visualization determines its value. In turn, their visualization guides what information commanders seek. Commanders emphasize the most important relevant information they need by establishing CCIRs. Providing the information commanders need to make decisions and maintain an accurate situational understanding requires staffs who understand the commander's intent and know the CCIRs.

INFORMATION CATEGORIES

6-86. Information management places information into one of four categories: specified requirements, implied requirements, gaps, and distractions. Specified requirements are requirements commanders specifically identify. CCIRs, priority intelligence requirements, and friendly force information requirements are categories of specified requirements. Implied requirements are important pieces of information that commanders need but have not requested. Effective staffs develop implied requirements and recommend them for specified requirements. These often become priority intelligence requirements or friendly force information requirements. Gaps are elements of information commanders need to achieve situational understanding but do not have. Ideally, analysis identifies gaps and translates them into specified requirements. Intelligence, surveillance, and reconnaissance (ISR) synchronization and integration focus on collecting information to fill gaps. Until a gap is filled, commanders and staffs make assumptions, clearly identifying them as such. This practice is most common during planning. Staffs continually review assumptions and replace them with facts as information becomes available. Distractions include information commanders do not need to know but continue to receive. Distractions contribute to information overload.

6-87. Effective information management keeps commanders and staffs aware of the quality of their information as they use it to build situational understanding. Soldiers processing information use these criteria to evaluate the quality of an element of information:

- Relevance—applies to the current mission, situation, or task.
- Accuracy—conveys the true situation.
- Timeliness—is available in time to make decisions.
- Usability—is portrayed in common, easily understood formats and displays.
- Completeness—provides all necessary data.
- Precision—has the required level of detail.
- Security—affords required protection.

*CONDUCT INFORM AND INFLUENCE AND CYBER/ELECTROMAGNETIC ACTIVITIES

6-88. Under mission command, staffs apply the science of control to support the commander's tasks by conducting inform and influence and cyber/electromagnetic activities. This information task supports and enhances current joint information operations doctrine. It not only focuses on the adversary, but it expands to focus on all audiences within the information environment—friendly, neutral, adversary, and enemy. Information systems are everywhere with pervasive news and opinion media. Such systems expose individual actions that can have immediate strategic implications. Staffs integrate the task—conduct inform and influence and cyber/electromagnetic activities—into the staff process.

6-89. Commanders and staff fully integrate the task into all operations. Commanders, with advice from the staff, guide the integration of the information task with other actions in their concept of operations. Staffs include the information task in the operations process from inception. Mismanagement of the information task increases likelihood chance of information fratricide, where friendly force use of information adversely affects friendly forces.

6-90. Cyber/electromagnetic activities seek to seize, retain, and exploit advantages in and through cyberspace and the electromagnetic spectrum. These activities deny and degrade adversary and enemy use of cyberspace and the electromagnetic spectrum. Cyber/electromagnetic activities protect friendly mission command networks and systems. *Cyberspace* is a global domain within the information environment consisting of the interdependent network of information technology infrastructures, including the Internet, telecommunications networks, computer systems, and embedded processors and controllers (JP 1-02). Cyberspace is essential for mission command of Army forces and for effective inform and influence activities. It is also a venue to attack enemy networks and systems. The *electromagnetic spectrum* is defined as the range of frequencies of electromagnetic radiation from zero to infinity. It is divided into 26 alphabetically designated bands (JP 3-13.1). Modern wireless communications and networks, and hence mission command, depend on the electromagnetic spectrum. The spectrum is also necessary for sensors, self-protection, and precision weapons. Commanders use the electromagnetic spectrum to attack enemy networks and systems.

*INFORM AND INFLUENCE ACTIVITIES

6-91. **Inform and influence activities is defined as the integrating activities within the mission command warfighting function which ensures themes and messages designed to inform domestic audiences and influence foreign friendly, neutral, adversary, and enemy populations are synchronized with actions to support full spectrum operations. Inform and influence activities incorporate components and enablers expanding the commander's ability to use other resources to inform and influence.** When conducting inform and influence activities, commanders determine how these activities affect the populace and their perceptions. (See figure 6-3, page 6-16.) Often commanders influence disparate people to resolve differences peacefully. To do so, commanders understand human behavior and other cultures. Inform and influence activities may involve attacking an enemy's will to fight through defeat mechanisms or to gain support from various partners for friendly actions.

Task: Integrate inform and influence activities that synchronize themes and messages with actions to support operations.

Purpose: To inform domestic audiences and influence foreign friendly, neutral, adversary, and enemy audiences.

Inform	Influence
Task: Conduct inform activities.	**Task:** Conduct influence activities.
Purpose: To provide information to domestic and foreign audiences to accurately describe operations.	**Purpose:** To effectively change attitudes, beliefs, and ultimately behavior of foreign friendly, neutral, adversary, and enemy audiences to support operations.
Public Affairs - Advisor with a statutory responsibility to factually and accurately inform various publics (domestic and foreign) without intent to propagandize or change behavior. Serves as the principal advisor to the commander for media engagement and conduct of media operations. Plans and executes Soldier and community outreach (foreign and domestic).	**Military Deception** - Actions executed to deliberately mislead adversary military decisionmakers as to friendly military capabilities, intentions, and operations, thereby causing the adversary to take specific actions (or inactions) that will contribute to the accomplishment of the friendly mission.

Military Information Support Operations - Operations that convey selected information and indicators to foreign audiences to influence their emotions, motives, objective reasoning, and ultimately the behavior of foreign governments, organizations, groups, and individuals.

Soldier and Leader Engagement - Interactions by Soldiers and leaders to inform or influence perceptions and build relationships with key actors and audiences to encourage them to support U.S. efforts.

Enabler: A military capability or activity that when designated can be used for the purpose of conducting or supporting inform and influence activities; includes combat camera, operations security, civil affairs activities, cyber/electromagnetic activities, and others as designated.

*Figure 6-3. Two lines of effort for inform and influence activities

6-92. Inform and influence activities have into two lines of effort: the inform line of effort and the influence line of effort. These two lines of effort help the commander to accomplish objectives and meet statutory requirements. Each line of effort has a different task, purpose, and effect. These lines of effort may rely on the same capabilities and enablers to accomplish these effects. The dashed line in figure 6-3 indicates that while both lines of effort have different tasks and purposes, they are closely integrated and synchronized for maximum effect. The staff officer for inform and influence activities synchronizes and integrates these lines of effort to ensure unity of effort in words, images, and actions. The element for inform and influence activities, led by the G-7 or S-7, resides in the mission command warfighting function. This element is responsible for integrating the two lines of effort.

6-93. The commander and staff officer for inform and influence activities ensure transparency in themes and messages to the American people. Commanders communicate openly to maintain the Army's trust relationship with the American people. They align themes and messages to inform domestic audiences and influence foreign friendly, neutral, adversary, and enemy populations. Integrating inform and influence activities synchronizes the activities with Army actions to support operations. This integration shapes the operational environment by synchronizing inform and influence activities of higher, adjacent, and lower units as well as of partners. Integrated activities avoid contradictory themes and messages. Contradicting themes and messages may lead to information fratricide and undermine the force's efforts. Poorly defined or ill-timed actions may negatively affect other actions. Thus, commanders aim not to constrain or dictate actions to each line of effort but rather to ensure they synchronize and integrate their efforts with the overall operation.

*Inform Line of Effort

6-94. The inform line of effort provides information to domestic and foreign audiences with accurately described operations. This ensures a thorough understanding of Army, joint, and partner intentions and operations so all participants can make informed judgments about them. Informing does not force or make a decision for the actors but provides them with facts. Providing factual and accurate information counters false information (misinformation or disinformation) disseminated by others. Maintaining transparency and credibility is critical within the inform line of effort. The inform line of effort includes public affairs (at home and abroad), military information support operations (abroad), and Soldier and leader engagements. The inform line of effort enables partners to make their own informed decisions.

*Influence Line of Effort

6-95. The influence line of effort effectively changes attitudes, beliefs, and ultimately behavior of foreign friendly, neutral, adversary, and enemy populations to support operations. Influence guides actors to make decisions that support the commander's objectives. This guidance includes misleading enemy decisionmakers or convincing enemy forces to surrender or cease their efforts. It also includes those actions designed to extend influence to foreign partners and the local populace in an area where Army forces may or may not have a physical presence. Such influence creates and strengthens relationships when Army forces do not have command over partner forces. Successful commanders build relationships on trust and mutual confidence demonstrating how the Army adds value to host-nation objectives. The influence line of effort includes military deception, military information support operations, and Soldier and leader engagement.

*COMPONENTS OF INFORM AND INFLUENCE ACTIVITIES

6-96. A component of inform and influence activities is a military capability or activity specifically designed to influence, inform, or inform and influence select leaders, decisionmakers, and audiences whose behaviors and perceptions are deemed integral to mission success. Commanders are not restricted to just these components when conducting inform and influence activities and may add or subtract enablers as the situation dictates. Enablers that can support inform and influence activities include combat camera, civil affairs activities, cyber/electromagnetic activities, operations security, and other military actions as designated by the commander.

*Public Affairs

6-97. The public affairs officer factually and accurately informs various populations (foreign and domestic) without intent to misinform or change behaviors. As the principal advisor to the commander for media engagement, the public affairs officer conducts media operations and Soldier and community outreach (foreign and domestic). This officer also plans and executes support to public diplomacy by developing information strategies and media facilitation.

6-98. The public affairs officer enables the commander to inform Americans, U.S. Government decisionmakers, and foreign partners. Effective information exchange protects the credibility of the commanders and the Army. This requires care and consideration when synchronizing public affairs with other inform and influence activities. The public affairs officer synchronizes components of public affairs with other inform and influence activities to ensure consistency, command credibility, and operations security.

6-99. The public affairs staff prepare for the following:

- Advising and counseling the commander concerning public affairs.
- Public affairs planning.
- Media engagement.
- Media facilitation.
- Public affairs training.
- Community outreach.
- Communication strategies.

(FM 46-1 and FM 3-61.1 discuss public affairs.)

*Military Information Support Operations

6-100. Military information support operations are planned operations to convey selected information and indicators to foreign audiences. These operations intend to inform, direct, and influence the emotions, motives, objective reasoning, and ultimately the behavior of foreign governments, organizations, groups, and individuals. Commanders focus efforts of military information support operations toward foreign friendly, neutral, adversary, and enemy audiences. Ultimately, commanders want to change each audience's behavior to support friendly operations. Forces for military information support operations are modular and attached to maneuver forces based on mission requirements. Commanders use military information support operations with other inform and influence activities, such as public affairs and military deception.

6-101. Commanders use forces for military information support operations for face-to-face communications or communications in denied areas with the local populace. These forces help commanders solve problems of armed resistance and local interference to military operations while encouraging dialog and cooperation with noncombatants. Effective commanders understand the psychological effects and potential implications of military actions and operations on populations. Knowing the potential impact of military operations facilitates the commander's decisionmaking process. Commanders also use forces for military information support operations to give advice on targeting to maximize effects and minimize adverse impacts and unintended consequences.

6-102. Commanders employ military information support operations even when not in direct contact with specific audiences. They use forces for military information support operations—

- To support combat operations.
- To support special operations.
- For military information support to Department of Defense and other government agencies during peacetime.
- For civil authority information support to lead Federal agencies during domestic disaster relief operations.

6-103. Forces for military information support operations disseminate messages via their resources. These resources consist of other government agencies, contracted media sources, multinational partners, and airborne and seaborne platforms supporting military information support operations. These forces attempt to use as many different dissemination assets as possible to ensure access to the desired and relevant audiences. (See FM 3-05.30.)

*Soldier and Leader Engagement

6-104. Soldier and leader engagement broadly describes interactions that take place among Soldiers, leaders, and audiences in the area of operations. Soldier and leader engagements can occur as impromptu face-to-face encounters on the street or as deliberate as a scheduled meeting. Such engagements can employ other means, such as phone calls or a video-teleconference. These engagements build relationships, inform an audience by providing relevant information, or influence an audience to support objectives. These interactions should be as deliberate as possible; however, not all engagements are planned. Soldiers and leaders cannot account for every situation encountered and should remain flexible and communicate within the bounds of the commander's themes and messages.

6-105. Face-to-face interaction by Soldiers and leaders strongly influences the perceptions of the local populace. Carried out with discipline, professionalism, and cultural sensitivity, day-to-day interactions of Soldiers with the local populace has positive effects. Such interaction amplifies positive actions, counters adversary information, and increases goodwill and support for the friendly mission. Actions in keeping with the commander's themes and messages also reinforce the trust in commander's messages, creating consistency between actions and words.

6-106. Likewise, meetings and other engagements conducted by leaders can be critical to mission success. These leaders work with key communicators, civilian leaders, or others whose perceptions, decisions, and actions affect mission accomplishment. Planned engagements provide the best venue for conveying positive information, assuaging fears, and refuting rumors, lies, and misinformation. Conducted with detailed preparation and planning, meetings and other engagements garner local support for Army operations, providing an opportunity for persuasion, and reducing friction and mistrust.

6-107. Commanders who gain influence with host-nation forces build partner capacity and competence in security force assistance. Gaining influence, even when no command authority exists, depends on collaboration, a mutual understanding of the environment, and a common commitment to solving problems. By developing host-nation relationships, Army forces can widely influence even while creating a small footprint in the area of operations.

*Military Deception

6-108. *Military deception* is those actions executed to deliberately mislead adversary decisionmakers as to friendly military capabilities, intentions, and operations, thereby causing the adversary to take specific actions (or inactions) that will contribute to the accomplishment of the friendly mission (JP 3-13.4). Military deception influences desired behaviors intending to cause adversary decisionmakers to form inaccurate impressions about strength, readiness, locations, and intended missions of friendly forces. Military deception planners target adversary information systems, sensors, and decisionmaking processes so to affect information that reaches the adversary decisionmaker.

6-109. At its most successful, military deception provokes an enemy commander to commit a serious mistake that friendly forces can exploit. However, effective military deception also introduces uncertainty into the enemy's estimate of the situation, and that doubt can lead to hesitation. Military deception is a good means to dislocate an enemy force in time and space.

6-110. Military deception can contribute significantly to the influence line of effort; however, it requires integration into the overall operation beginning with receipt of mission. To achieve maximum effects, military deception requires good operations security, significant preparation, and resources. If added as an afterthought, military deception often proves ineffective. Successful military deception requires a reasonably accurate assessment of the enemy's expectations. While retained as a component of inform and influence activities in this version of FM 3-0, military deception will migrate to another functional area in future editions of FM 3-0. (JP 3-13.4 discusses military deception.)

*ENABLERS OF INFORM AND INFLUENCE ACTIVITIES

6-111. An enabler of inform and influence activities refers to a military capability or activity whose primary purpose, if other than inform and influence activities, can be used for conducting or supporting inform and influence activities. Common enablers include operations security, civil affairs activities, combat camera, and cyber/electromagnetic activities. When properly integrated, enablers enhance inform and influence activities. Commanders consider other activities in addition to this list based on the mission and operational environment.

6-112. Operations security enables commanders to deny adversaries and enemies information that in turn influences their decisionmaking process. Civil affairs activities enhance the relationship between military forces and civil authorities in areas with military forces. Cyber/electromagnetic activities enable and facilitate Army operations by undertaking deliberate actions designed to gain and maintain informational advantages in the information environment. Typically, but not solely, these actions occur through cyberspace operations and electronic warfare. (Paragraphs 6-115 through 6-128 discuss cyber/electro-magnetic activities.)

6-113. *Combat camera* is the acquisition and utilization of still and motion imagery in support of operational and planning requirements across the range of military operations and during joint exercises (JP 3-61). Combat camera generates imagery to support full spectrum operations. Combat camera units provide powerful documentary tools that support public affairs, military information support operations, and Soldier and leader engagement. For example, combat camera units prepare products documenting Army tactical successes that counter enemy propaganda claiming the opposite. (FM 6-02.40 discusses combat camera.)

6-114. The operations process aids the commander and staff in determining if other enablers, not specified above, can support inform and influence activities. For example, commanders can use the positioning of maneuver forces to influence or reinforce a message. Such synchronized military action integrated with associated themes and messages can have a powerful effect. Commanders can destroy certain key targets via fires and maneuver. They also consider constructive means to inform or influence. These could include medical assistance or the use of engineers to restore key civilian infrastructure.

*CYBER/ELECTROMAGNETIC ACTIVITIES

6-115.   The impact of modern electronic and information technologies on human society and military operations increases daily. The electromagnetic spectrum is essential for communication, lethality, sensors, and self-protection. Army forces increasingly depend on cyberspace. Within cyberspace, units use electronics and the electromagnetic spectrum to store, modify, and exchange data via networked systems. Given the Army's dependence on cyberspace as well as the electromagnetic spectrum, commanders fully integrate cyber/electromagnetic activities within the overall operation (see figure 6-4). These activities employ a combined arms approach to operations in a contested cyberspace domain and a congested electromagnetic spectrum. Cyber/electromagnetic activities seize, retain, and exploit advantages in cyberspace and the electromagnetic spectrum. The result enables Army forces to retain freedom of action while denying freedom of action to enemies and adversaries, thereby enabling the overall operation.

Tasks: Conduct cyber/electromagnetic activities as part of combined arms operations.

Purpose: To seize, retain, and exploit an advantage over adversaries and enemies in both cyberspace and across the electromagnetic spectrum, denying and degrading adversary and enemy use of the same, and protecting friendly mission command networks and systems.

Cyberspace Operations	Electronic Warfare
Task: Employ cyber capabilities.	**Task:** Use electromagnetic and directed energy.
Purpose: To achieve objectives in and through cyberspace.	**Purpose:** To control the electromagnetic spectrum or to attack the enemy.
Cyber Situational Awareness - Knowledge of relevant information regarding activities in and through cyberspace and the electromagnetic spectrum.	**Electronic Attack** - Use of electromagnetic energy, directed energy, or antiradiation weapons to attack personnel, facilities, or equipment.
Network Operations - Activities conducted to operate and defend the Global Information Grid.	**Electronic Protection** - Actions taken to protect personnel, facilities, and equipment from any effects of friendly or enemy use of the electromagnetic spectrum.
Cyber Warfare - Extends cyber power beyond the defensive boundaries of the Global Information Grid to deny, degrade, disrupt, destroy, and exploit enemies.	**Electronic Support** - Actions to search for, intercept, identify, and locate or localize sources of intentional and unintentional radiated electromagnetic energy for the purpose of immediate threat recognition, targeting, planning, and conduct of future operations.

Electromagnetic Spectrum Operations - Planning, coordinating, and managing joint use of the electromagnetic spectrum through operational, engineering, and administrative procedures.

Enablers: A capability or activity that can be used for the purpose of conducting or supporting cyber/electromagnetic activities. Includes intelligence, physical attack, law, policy, critical infrastructure protection, and others as designated.

*Figure 6-4. Two lines of effort for cyber/electromagnetic activities

6-116.   Cyber/electromagnetic activities are divided into two lines of effort: the cyberspace operations line of effort and the electronic warfare line of effort. These lines of effort may rely on the same capabilities and enablers to accomplish these effects and must be synchronized and integrated closely to ensure unity of effort in words, images, and actions. The components of the cyberspace operations line of effort integrate with the components of the electronic warfare line of effort and electromagnetic spectrum operations.

*Cyberspace Operations

6-117.   The cyberspace operations line of effort aims to accomplish objectives in and through cyberspace. The components of the cyberspace line of effort include cyber situational awareness, network operations, cyber warfare, and cyber support.

*Electronic Warfare

6-118. *Electronic warfare* is any military action involving the use of electromagnetic and directed energy to control the electromagnetic spectrum or to attack the enemy. Electronic warfare consists of three divisions: electronic attack, electronic protection, and electronic warfare support (JP 3-13.1). The electronic warfare line of effort aims to control the electromagnetic spectrum or to attack the enemy. The components of the electronic warfare line of effort consist of electronic attack, electronic protection, and electronic support.

*COMPONENTS OF CYBER/ELECTROMAGNETIC ACTIVITIES

6-119. Cyber/electromagnetic activities consist of seven components: cyber situational awareness, networks operations, cyber warfare, electronic attack, electronic protection, electronic support, and electromagnetic spectrum operations.

*Cyber Situational Awareness

6-120. Cyber situational awareness is the knowledge of friendly, neutral, adversary, and enemy relevant information regarding activities in and through cyberspace and the electromagnetic spectrum. Soldiers gain this awareness by combining intelligence and operational activity in cyberspace, the electromagnetic spectrum, and the other domains, both unilaterally and through collaboration with our joint, interagency, intergovernmental, multinational, and nongovernmental organizational partners. Cyber situational awareness enables the commander to collect, process, store, display, and disseminates an appropriate level view of networks and systems. This enables an assessment of any changes to the network risk mitigation steps needed due to network degradation. Commanders use cyber situational awareness to—

- Assess enemy and adversary cyber capabilities and intentions.
- Assess friendly, enemy, and adversary cyber vulnerabilities.
- Monitor, protect, and prioritize their networks.
- Assess the operational impact of network disruptions.
- Respond to network outages or attacks.
- Dynamically reallocate network traffic.

*Network Operations

6-121. Network operations install, operate, maintain, and protect LandWarNet, critical infrastructure, key resources, and other specified cyberspace. Units need network operations to ensure operation of mission command networks and systems. (See FM 6-02.71 for details on network operations.)

*Cyber Warfare

6-122. Cyber warfare extends combat power beyond the defensive boundaries of the Global Information Grid to detect, deny, degrade, disrupt, destroy, and exploit enemies. Cyber warfare capabilities target computer networks, telecommunication networks, and embedded processors and controllers in equipment, systems, and infrastructure. Cyber warfare uses cyber exploitation, cyber attack, and cyber defense in a mutually supporting and supported relationship with network operations and cyber support. Cyber warfare accomplishes the following tasks:

- Studies and characterizes the cyber threat.
- Identifies, characterizes, and exploits enemies.
- Contributes to cyber situational awareness.
- Conducts cyber exploitation, attack, and defense.
- Assists attack investigations to determine attribution.

*Electronic Attack

6-123. *Electronic attack* is a division of electronic warfare involving the use of electromagnetic energy, directed energy, or antiradiation weapons to attack personnel, facilities, or equipment with the intent of degrading, neutralizing, or destroying enemy combat capability and is considered a form of fires (JP 3-13.1). Electronic attack has both defensive and offensive capabilities. For example, defensive electronic attack includes efforts to defeat radio-controlled improvised explosive devices. Offensive electronic attack includes—

- Actions taken to prevent or reduce an enemy's effective use of the electromagnetic spectrum, such as jamming and electromagnetic deception.
- Employment of weapons that use either electromagnetic or directed energy as their primary destructive mechanism (lasers, radio frequency weapons, particle beams).
- Offensive and defensive activities, including countermeasures.

*Electronic Protection

6-124. *Electronic protection* is a division of electronic warfare involving actions taken to protect personnel, facilities, and equipment from any effects of friendly or enemy use of the electromagnetic spectrum that degrade, neutralize, or destroy friendly combat capability (JP 3-13.1). Electronic protection includes actions, such as frequency agility in a radio or variable pulse repetition frequency in radar. Electronic protection should not be confused with self-protection. Both defensive electronic attack and electronic protection protect personnel, facilities, capabilities, and equipment. However, electronic protection protects forces from the effects of electronic attack (friendly and enemy). Defensive electronic attack primarily protects forces against lethal attacks by denying enemy use of the electromagnetic spectrum to guide or trigger weapons. To protect friendly capabilities, units—

- Regularly brief force personnel on the electronic warfare threat.
- Ensure that electronic system capabilities are safeguarded during exercises and training.
- Coordinate and deconflict electromagnetic spectrum usage.
- Train on electronic protection active and passive measures.
- Minimize the vulnerability of friendly receivers to enemy jamming (such as reduced power, brevity of transmissions, and directional antennas).

*Electronic Support

6-125. Electronic support is a division of electronic warfare involving actions tasked by, or under the direct control of, an operational commander to search for, intercept, identify, and locate or localize sources of intentional and unintentional radiated electromagnetic energy for the purpose of immediate threat recognition, targeting, planning, and conduct of future operations. Electronic support systems supply information regarding electronic attack, electronic protection, avoidance, targeting, and other tactical employments of forces. Commanders make immediate decisions involving this information. Electronic support systems collect data and produce information or intelligence to—

- Corroborate other sources of information or intelligence.
- Conduct or direct electronic attack operations.
- Initiate self-protection measures.
- Task weapon systems.
- Support electronic protection efforts.
- Create or update electronic warfare databases.
- Support information activities.

FM 3-36 provides Army doctrine for electronic warfare.

*Electromagnetic Spectrum Operations

6-126. Electromagnetic spectrum operations are the conduct of spectrum management, frequency assignments, policy implementation, and host-nation coordination that enables the commander's effective use of the electromagnetic spectrum. (See FM 6-02.70 for detailed information on electromagnetic spectrum operations.)

*ENABLERS OF CYBER/ELECTROMAGNETIC ACTIVITIES

6-127.   An enabler of cyber/electromagnetic activities is called cyber support. Cyber support is supporting activities to enable both network operations and cyber warfare. Cyber support differs from cyber warfare and network operations. Those activities are carried out by multiple organizations and do not require a separate cyber support proponent or lead. Cyber support entails varying intents, conditions, authorities, and levels of effort. Cyber support conducts the following tasks:

- Conduct vulnerability assessment.
- Conduct threat-based security assessment.
- Conduct vulnerability and security remediation.
- Reverse engineering malware.
- Explore cyber aspects of site exploitation.
- Counter intelligence.
- Conduct cyber forensics.
- Coordinate with law enforcement.
- Conduct cyber research, development, test, and evaluation.
- Develop and acquire cyber combat.

*INTEGRATION AND SYNCHRONIZATION OF CYBER/ELECTROMAGNETIC ACTIVITIES

6-128.   Responsibility for integration and synchronization of cyber/electromagnetic activities resides in the electronic warfare element of the fires warfighting function. Unlike the inform and influence activities, cyber/electromagnetic activities do not exist within a distinct staff element. Rather, the cyber/electro-magnetic components operate within an existing electronic warfare workgroup.

SECTION III – SUMMARY

6-129.   Commanders and staffs apply the science of control to accomplish the staff tasks and integrate the warfighting functions. Control permits commanders to counter negative effects during operations. Design pervades all systems and procedures. Commanders, assisted by their staffs, exercise control through the operations process and mission command networks and systems. Commanders turn decisions into effective actions through Army procedural and positive control. Knowledge management and information management support control by transforming information into knowledge to support situational understanding and decisionmaking. Commanders and staffs conduct inform and influence and cyber/electromagnetic activities.

This page intentionally left blank.

Chapter 7

Operational Art

This chapter discusses operational art, the levels of war, and how commanders and staffs apply operational art to understand, visualize, and describe how to establish conditions to achieve a desired end state. Operational art represents a creative approach to dealing with the direction of military forces. It expresses informed vision across the levels of war.

*UNDERSTANDING OPERATIONAL ART

7-1.   *Operational art* is the application of creative imagination by commanders and staffs—supported by their skill, knowledge, and experience—to design strategies, campaigns, and major operations and organize and employ military forces. Operational art integrates ends, ways, and means across the levels of war (JP 3-0).

7-2.   Operational art reflects a holistic understanding of the operational environment and the problem. This understanding enables commanders to develop end state conditions and an operational approach to guide the force in establishing those conditions for lasting success. The *operational approach* is a broad conceptualization of the general actions that will produce the conditions that define the desired end state (FM 5-0). Design (see chapter 5) assists commanders in developing their operational approach. Commanders use a common language to visualize and describe their operational approach.

7-3.   In visualizing an operation, commanders determine which conditions satisfy policy, orders, guidance, and directives. Taken together, these conditions become the end state. Commanders devise and execute plans that complement the actions of the other instruments of national power in a focused, unified effort. To this end, commanders draw on experience, knowledge, education, intellect, intuition, and creativity.

7-4.   Mission command focuses on empowering subordinate leaders and sharing information to facilitate decentralized execution. Effective mission command requires Army leaders at lower levels of command to assume greater responsibility for accomplishing higher headquarters' objectives during operations. (See Chapter 5 for more discussion on mission command.) The ability to exercise operational art provides Soldiers with freedom of action to ensure their efforts contribute to accomplishing those objectives. This ability also allows Army forces to develop the situation as well as adapt and act decisively in dynamic conditions.

THE LEVELS OF WAR

7-5.   The levels of war define and clarify the relationship between strategy and tactical actions. (See figure 7-1, page 7-2.) The levels have no finite limits or boundaries. They correlate to specific levels of responsibility and planning. They help organize thought and approaches to a problem. The levels distinguish between headquarters and the specific responsibilities and actions performed at each echelon. Despite advances in technology, digital information sharing, and the increased visibility of tactical actions, the levels of war remain useful. Decisions at one level always affect other levels.

7-6.   A natural tension exists between the levels of war and echelons of command. This tension stems from different perspectives, requirements, and constraints associated with command at each level of war. Between the levels of war, the horizons for planning, preparation, and execution differ greatly. Operational-level commanders typically synchronize the activities of military and civilian organizations and agencies across large areas. Tactical commanders focus primarily on employing combined arms within an area of operations. They sometimes work with civilian agencies on political, informational, and economic issues. Often, tactical commanders receive missions that divert combat power from tasks that seem more urgent at lower levels. It is a commander's responsibility to recognize and resolve this tension.

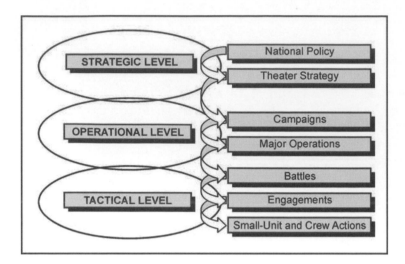

Figure 7-1. Levels of war

7-7. A string of tactical victories does not guarantee success at the operational and strategic levels. Tactical success, while required to set operational conditions, must be tied to achieving the strategic end state. Wars are won at the operational and strategic levels; yet without tactical success, a major operation cannot achieve the desired end state. Commanders overcome this tension through open and continuous dialog, a thorough understanding of the situation across the levels of war, and a shared vision that integrates and synchronizes actions among the echelons.

7-8. Small units, crews, and individuals act at the tactical level. At times, their actions may produce strategic or operational effects. However, this does not mean these elements act at the strategic or operational level. Actions are not strategic unless they contribute directly to achieving the strategic end state. Similarly, actions are considered operational only if directly related to operational movement or the sequencing of battles and engagements. The level at which an action occurs is determined by the perspective of the echelon in terms of planning, preparation, and execution.

STRATEGIC

7-9. The *strategic level of war* is the level of war at which a nation, often as a member of a group of nations, determines national or multinational (alliance or coalition) strategic security objectives and guidance, and develops and uses national resources to achieve these objectives. Activities at this level establish national and multinational military objectives; sequence initiatives; define limits and assess risks for the use of military and other instruments of national power; develop global plans or theater war plans to achieve those objectives; and provide military forces and other capabilities in accordance with strategic plans (JP 3-0).

7-10. *Strategy* is a prudent idea or set of ideas for employing the instruments of national power in a synchronized and integrated fashion to achieve theater, national, and/or multinational objectives (JP 3-0). The President translates national interests and policy into a national strategic end state. Combatant commanders base their theater strategic planning on this end state. To ensure their military strategy aligns with national interests and policy, combatant commanders participate in strategic discourse with the President, Secretary of Defense (through the Chairman of the Joint Chiefs of Staff), and multinational partners. Peacetime military engagement is vital to U.S. strategy and integral to theater security cooperation plans. Strategy involves more than campaigns and major operations. When successful, these plans promote national or multinational goals through peaceful processes. Peacetime military engagement contributes to the ability of multinational forces to operate together.

7-11. National interests and policy define and inform military strategy with a broad framework for conducting operations. A combatant commander's military strategy is thus an instrument that implements national policy and strategy. Successful commanders understand the relationship and links between policy and strategy. They also appreciate the distinctions and interrelationships among the levels of war. This appreciation is fundamental to an informed understanding of the decisions and actions at each level. Without it, commanders cannot sequence and synchronize military and nonmilitary actions toward an end state consistent with national strategy and policy.

OPERATIONAL

7-12. The operational level links employing tactical forces to achieving the strategic end state. At the operational level, commanders conduct campaigns and major operations to establish conditions that define that end state. A *campaign* is a series of related major operations aimed at achieving strategic and operational objectives within a given time and space (JP 5-0). A *major operation* is a series of tactical actions (battles, engagements, strikes) conducted by combat forces of a single or several Services, coordinated in time and place, to achieve strategic or operational objectives in an operational area. These actions are conducted simultaneously or sequentially in accordance with a common plan and are controlled by a single commander. For noncombat operations, a reference to the relative size and scope of a military operation (JP 3-0). Major operations are not solely the purview of combat forces. They are typically conducted with the other instruments of national power. Major operations often bring together the capabilities of other agencies, nations, and organizations.

7-13. Operational art determines when, where, and for what purpose commanders employ major forces. Operational commanders position and maneuver forces to shape conditions in their area of operations for their decisive operation. Commanders exploit tactical victories to gain strategic advantage or reverse the strategic effects of tactical losses.

7-14. Actions at the operational level usually involve broader dimensions of time and space than tactical actions do. Operational commanders need to understand the complexities of the operational environment, look beyond the immediate situation, and consider the consequences of their approach and subordinates' actions. Operational commanders seek to establish the most favorable conditions possible for subordinate commanders by shaping future events.

7-15. Experienced operational commanders understand tactical realities and can establish conditions that favor tactical success. Likewise, good tactical commanders understand the operational and strategic context within which they execute their assigned tasks. This understanding helps them seize opportunities (both foreseen and unforeseen) that contribute to achieving the end state or defeating enemy initiatives that threaten its achievement. Operational commanders require experience at both the operational and tactical levels. This experience gives them the knowledge and intuition needed to understand how tactical and operational possibilities interrelate.

TACTICAL

7-16. Tactics uses and orders the arrangement of forces in relation to each other. Through tactics, commanders use combat power to accomplish missions. The tactical-level commander uses combat power in battles, engagements, and small-unit and crew actions. **A *battle* consists of a set of related engagements that lasts longer and involves larger forces than an engagement.** Battles can affect the course of a campaign or major operation. An *engagement* is a tactical conflict, usually between opposing lower echelons maneuver forces (JP 1-02). Engagements are typically conducted at brigade level and below. They are usually short, executed in terms of minutes, hours, or days.

7-17. Operational-level headquarters determine objectives and provide resources for tactical operations. For any tactical-level operation, the surest measure of success is its contribution to achieving end state conditions. Commanders avoid battles and engagements that do not contribute to achieving the operational end state conditions.

APPLYING OPERATIONAL ART

7-18. Commanders use operational art to envision how to establish conditions that define the desired end state. Actions and interactions across the levels of war influence these conditions. These conditions are fundamentally dynamic and linked together by the human dimension, the most unpredictable and uncertain element of conflict. The operational environment is complex, adaptive, and interactive. Through operational art, commanders apply a comprehensive understanding of it to determine the most effective and efficient methods to influence conditions in various locations across multiple echelons. (See figure 7-2.)

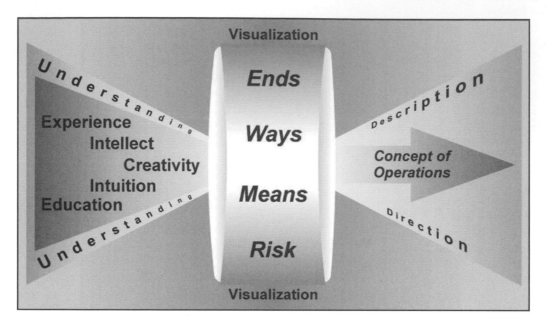

Figure 7-2. Operational art

7-19. Operational art spans a continuum—from comprehensive strategic direction to concrete tactical actions. Bridging this continuum requires creative vision coupled with broad experience and knowledge. Operational art provides a means for commanders to derive the essence of an operation. Without it, tactical actions devolve into a series of disconnected engagements, with relative attrition the only measure of success. Through operational art, commanders translate their concept of operations into an operational design and ultimately into tactical tasks. They do this by integrating ends, ways, and means and by envisioning dynamic combinations of the elements of full spectrum operations across the levels of war. They then apply operational art to array forces and maneuver them to achieve the desired end state.

7-20. Every operation begins with a commander's intent that guides its conduct. In almost all cases, a commander's intent and concept of operations envision all the instruments of national power working toward a common end state. Using operational art, commanders frame their concept by answering several fundamental questions:

- What is the force trying to accomplish (ends)?
- What conditions, when established, constitute the desired end state (ends)?
- How will the force achieve the end state (ways)?
- What sequence of actions is most likely to attain these conditions (ways)?
- What resources are required, and how can they be applied to accomplish that sequence of actions (means)?
- What risks are associated with that sequence of actions, and how can they be mitigated (risk)?

7-21. Commanders understand, visualize, describe, direct, lead, and assess all aspects of operations. Based on a comprehensive analysis of the operational environment, commanders determine the centers of gravity around which to frame the plan.

7-22. When applying operational art, collaboration informs situational understanding. This collaboration involves an open, continuous dialog between commanders that spans the levels of war and echelons of command. This dialog is vital in establishing a common perspective on the problem and a shared understanding of the operational environment's conditions. Effective collaboration enables assessment, fosters critical analysis, and anticipates opportunities and risk. Collaboration allows commanders to recognize and react to changes in the situation.

7-23. Practicing operational art requires a broad understanding of the operational environment at all levels. It also requires practical creativity and the ability to visualize changes in the operational environment. Commanders project their visualization beyond the realm of physical combat. They anticipate the operational environment's evolving military and nonmilitary conditions. Operational art encompasses visualizing the synchronized arrangement and employment of military forces and capabilities to achieve the desired end state. This creative process requires the ability to discern the conditions required for victory before committing forces to action.

7-24. Conflict is fundamentally a human endeavor characterized by violence, uncertainty, chance, and friction. Land operations are inherently tied to the human dimension; they cannot be reduced to a simple formula or checklist. Operational art helps commanders integrate functions and capabilities. It also helps synchronize military actions with actions of other government and civilian organizations. Operational art supports design by providing a conceptual framework for ordering thought when planning operations. Operational art supports the commanders' ability to seize, retain, and exploit initiative and achieve decisive results.

*THE ELEMENTS OF OPERATIONAL ART

7-25. Through operational art supported by design, commanders and staffs develop a broad operational approach and translate it into a coherent, feasible plan for employing forces. This operational approach provides a framework that relates tactical tasks to the desired end state. It provides a unifying purpose and focus to all operations. In applying operational art, commanders and their staffs use a set of intellectual tools to help them think through understanding the operational environment as well as visualizing and describing the operational approach (see figure 7-3). Collectively, this set of tools is known as the elements of operational art. These tools help commanders understand, visualize, and describe complex combinations of combat power and help them formulate their intent and guidance. Commanders selectively use these tools in any operation. However, their application is broadest in the context of long-term operations.

> * End State and Conditions
> * Centers of Gravity
> * Direct or Indirect Approach
> * Decisive Points
> * Lines of Operations/Effort
> * Operational Reach
> * Tempo
> * Simultaneity and Depth
> * Phasing and Transitions
> * Culmination
> * Risk

Figure 7-3. Elements of operational art

7-26. The elements of operational art support the commander in identifying tasks and objectives that link tactical mission to the desired end state. They help refine and focus the operational approach that forms the basis for developing a detailed plan or order. During execution, commanders and staffs consider the elements of operational art as they assess the situation. They adjust current and future operations and plans as the operation unfolds.

END STATE AND CONDITIONS

7-27. The end state is a desired future condition represented by the expressed conditions that the commander wants to exist when an operation ends. Clearly describing the end state requires understanding the operational environment and assessing the friendly, enemy, adversary, and neutral populations. Commanders include end state in their planning guidance and commander's intent. A clearly defined end state promotes unity of effort, facilitates integration and synchronization, and helps mitigate risk.

7-28. Army operations typically focus on achieving the military end state. However, Army operations also contribute to establishing nonmilitary conditions. Sometimes that is their focus. Commanders explicitly describe the end state and its defining conditions for every operation. Otherwise, missions become vague and operations lose focus. Commanders should direct every operation toward a clearly defined, decisive, and attainable end state.

7-29. The end state may evolve as an operation progresses. Commanders may refine guidance, the operational environment's conditions might change, and situational understanding may increase. Therefore, all commanders continuously monitor operations and evaluate their progress. Commanders use formal and informal assessment methods to assess progress in achieving the desired end state and determine whether reframing is required.

CENTERS OF GRAVITY

7-30. A *center of gravity* is the source of power that provides moral or physical strength, freedom of action, or will to act (JP 3-0). This definition states in modern terms the classic description offered by Clausewitz: "the hub of all power and movement, on which everything depends."[3] The loss of a center of gravity ultimately results in defeat. The center of gravity is a vital analytical tool for planning operations. It provides a focal point, identifying sources of strength and weakness.

7-31. Understanding the center of gravity has evolved beyond the term's preindustrial definition. Centers of gravity are now part of a more complex perspective of the operational environment. Today they are not limited to military forces and can be either physical or moral. Physical centers of gravity, such as a capital city or military force, are typically easier to identify, assess, and target. They can often be influenced solely by military means. In contrast, moral centers of gravity are intangible and complex. Dynamic and related to human factors, they can include a charismatic leader, powerful ruling elite, religious tradition, tribal influence, or strong-willed populace. Military means alone usually prove ineffective when targeting moral centers of gravity. Eliminating them requires the collective, integrated efforts of all instruments of national power.

7-32. Center of gravity analysis is thorough and detailed. Faulty conclusions drawn from hasty or abbreviated analyses can adversely affect operations, waste critical resources, and incur undue risk. Thoroughly understanding the operational environment helps commanders identify and target enemy centers of gravity. This understanding encompasses how enemies organize, fight, and make decisions. It also includes their physical and moral strengths and weaknesses. In addition, commanders should understand how military forces interact with other government and civilian agencies. This understanding helps planners identify centers of gravity, their associated decisive points, and the best approach for achieving the desired end state.

DIRECT OR INDIRECT APPROACH

7-33. **The *approach* is the manner in which a commander contends with a center of gravity. The *direct approach* is the manner in which a commander attacks the enemy's center of gravity or principal strength by applying combat power directly against it.** However, centers of gravity are generally well protected and not vulnerable to a direct approach. Thus, commanders usually choose an indirect approach. **The *indirect approach* is the manner in which a commander attacks the enemy's center of gravity by applying combat power against a series of decisive points while avoiding enemy**

---

[3] © 1984. Reproduced with permission of Princeton University Press.

strength. Both approaches use specific combinations of defeat or stability mechanisms depending on the mission. Whether direct or indirect, an effective operational approach achieves decisive results through combinations of defeat and stability mechanisms. As commanders and staffs frame the problem, they determine the appropriate combination of defeat or stability mechanisms to solve it. This begins the process that ends with the plan for an operation that achieves the desired end state.

Defeat Mechanisms

7-34. **A *defeat mechanism* is the method through which friendly forces accomplish their mission against enemy opposition.** A defeat mechanism is described in terms of the physical or psychological effects it produces. Defeat mechanisms are not tactical missions; rather, they describe broad operational and tactical effects. Commanders translate these effects into tactical tasks. Operational art formulates the most effective, efficient way to defeat enemy aims. Physical defeat deprives enemy forces of the ability to achieve those aims; psychological defeat deprives them of the will to do so. Army forces have the most success when applying focused combinations of defeat mechanisms. This produces complementary and reinforcing effects not attainable with a single mechanism. Used individually, a defeat mechanism achieves results proportional to the effort expended. Used in combination, the effects are likely to be both synergistic and lasting. Army forces at all echelons use combinations of four defeat mechanisms:

- Destroy.
- Dislocate.
- Disintegrate.
- Isolate.

7-35. **In the context of defeat mechanisms, *destroy* means to apply lethal combat power on an enemy capability so that it can no longer perform any function and cannot be restored to a usable condition without being entirely rebuilt.** To most effectively destroy enemy capabilities, units use a single, decisive attack. When units cannot mass the necessary combat power simultaneously, commanders apply it sequentially. This approach is called attrition. It defeats the enemy by maintaining the highest possible rate of destruction over time.

7-36. Destruction may not force the enemy to surrender; well-disciplined forces and those able to reconstitute can often endure heavy losses without giving up. Defeat cannot be accurately measured solely in terms of destruction, particularly when criteria focus on narrow metrics, such as casualties, equipment destroyed, or perceived enemy strength. Destruction is especially difficult to assess if friendly forces apply force indiscriminately. The effects of destruction often fade unless combined with isolation and dislocation.

7-37. *Dislocate* **means to employ forces to obtain significant positional advantage, rendering the enemy's dispositions less valuable, perhaps even irrelevant.** It aims to make the enemy expose forces by reacting to the dislocating action. Dislocation requires enemy commanders to make a choice: accept neutralization of part of their force or risk its destruction while repositioning. Turning movements and envelopments produce dislocation. When combined with destruction, dislocation can contribute to rapid success.

7-38. *Disintegrate* **means to disrupt the enemy's command and control system, degrading the ability to conduct operations while leading to a rapid collapse of the enemy's capabilities or will to fight.** It exploits the effects of dislocation and destruction to shatter the enemy's coherence. Typically, disintegration—coupled with destruction and dislocation—follows the loss of capabilities that enemy commanders use to develop and maintain situational understanding. Simultaneous operations produce the strongest disintegrative effects. Disintegration is difficult to achieve; however, prolonged isolation, destruction, and dislocation can produce it.

7-39. **In the context of defeat mechanisms, *isolate* means to deny an enemy or adversary access to capabilities that enable the exercise of coercion, influence, potential advantage, and freedom of action.** Isolation limits the enemy's ability to conduct operations effectively by marginalizing one or more of these capabilities. It exposes the enemy to continued degradation through the massed effects of the other defeat mechanisms. There are two types of isolation:

- Physical isolation, which is difficult to achieve, but easier to assess. An isolated enemy loses freedom of movement and access to support.
- Psychological isolation, which, while difficult to assess, is a vital enabler of disintegration. The most important indicators include the breakdown of enemy morale and the alienation of a population from the enemy.

7-40. Isolation alone rarely defeats an enemy. However, it complements and reinforces other defeat mechanisms' effects. Offensive operations often focus on destroying personnel and equipment. They may use maneuver to dislocate forces. However, these effects multiply when combined with isolating the enemy from sources of physical and moral support.

Stability Mechanisms

7-41. Commanders use stability mechanisms to visualize how to employ the stability element of full spectrum operations. A *stability mechanism* is the primary method through which friendly forces affect civilians in order to attain conditions that support establishing a lasting, stable peace. As with defeat mechanisms, combinations of stability mechanisms produce complementary and reinforcing effects that accomplish the mission more effectively and efficiently than single mechanisms do alone. The four stability mechanisms are—

- Compel.
- Control.
- Influence.
- Support.

7-42. *Compel* means to use, or threaten to use, lethal force to establish control and dominance, effect behavioral change, or enforce compliance with mandates, agreements, or civil authority. The appropriate and discriminate use of lethal force reinforces efforts to stabilize a situation, gain consent, or ensure compliance. Conversely, misusing force can adversely affect an operation's legitimacy. Legitimacy is essential to producing effective compliance. Compliance depends on how the local populace and others perceive the force's ability to exercise lethal force to accomplish the mission.

7-43. **In the context of stability mechanisms,** *control* **means to impose civil order**. It includes securing borders, routes, sensitive sites, population centers, and individuals. It also involves physically occupying key terrain and facilities. Control includes activities related to disarmament, demobilization, and reintegration, as well as security sector reform. (Chapter 3 discusses the security sector.)

7-44. ***In the context of stability mechanisms,*** *influence* **means to alter the opinions and attitudes of a civilian population through inform and influence activities, presence, and conduct.** It aims to change behaviors through nonlethal means. Influence is as much a product of public perception as a measure of success. It reflects the ability of friendly forces to operate within the cultural and societal norms of the local populace while accomplishing the mission. Influence requires legitimacy. Developing legitimacy requires time, patience, and coordinated, cooperative efforts across the operational area.

7-45. **In the context of stability mechanisms,** *support* **means to establish, reinforce, or set the conditions necessary for the other instruments of national power to function effectively.** It requires coordination and cooperation with civilian agencies as they assess the immediate needs of failed or failing states and plan for, prepare for, or execute responses to them. In extreme circumstances, support may require committing considerable resources for a protracted period. This commitment may involve establishing or reestablishing the institutions required for normal life. These typically include a legitimate civil authority, market economy, and criminal justice system supported by government institutions for health, education, and civil service.

Using Defeat and Stability Mechanisms

7-46. Defeat and stability mechanisms complement center of gravity analysis. This analysis reveals the intrinsic vulnerabilities of a given center of gravity. Defeat mechanisms describe ways to isolate or destroy it. For example, a decisive point may be temporarily neutralized by dislocating it. The enemy may commit significant combat power to regain that capability, presenting an opportunity to destroy committed enemy forces. By combining dislocation and destruction, the commander can effectively eliminate the capability. Thus, the effect on the center of gravity is permanent, and friendly forces retain freedom of action and initiative.

7-47. The approach reflects the commander's visualization for applying combinations of defeat and stability mechanisms. An effective approach, direct or indirect, focuses operations toward achieving the end state.

DECISIVE POINTS

7-48. A *decisive point* is a geographic place, specific key event, critical factor, or function that, when acted upon, allows commanders to gain a marked advantage over an adversary or contribute materially to achieving success (JP 3-0). Decisive points are not centers of gravity; they are keys to attacking or protecting them. Decisive points apply at both the operational and tactical levels. At the operational level, they typically provide direct use against a center of gravity. At the tactical level, they tie directly to mission accomplishment.

7-49. Some decisive points are geographic. Examples include port facilities, distribution networks and nodes, and bases of operations. Specific events and elements of an enemy force may also be decisive points. Examples of such events include commitment of the enemy operational reserve and reopening a major oil refinery. A common characteristic of decisive points is their major importance to a center of gravity. A decisive point's importance requires the enemy to commit significant resources to defend it. The loss of a decisive point weakens a center of gravity and may expose more decisive points.

7-50. Decisive points have a different character during operations dominated by stability or civil support. These decisive points may be less tangible and more closely associated with important events and conditions. For example, during operations after Hurricane Andrew in 1992, reopening schools was a decisive point. Other examples include—

- Repairing a vital water treatment facility.
- Establishing a training academy for national security forces.
- Securing an election.
- Quantifiably reducing crime.

None of these examples is purely physical. Nonetheless, any may be vital to establishing conditions for transitioning to civil authority. In an operation dominated by stability or civil support, this transition is typically an end state condition.

7-51. Commanders identify the decisive points that offer the greatest advantage against centers of gravity. Decisive points that enable commanders to seize, retain, or exploit the initiative are crucial. Controlling them is essential to mission accomplishment. Enemy control of a decisive point may exhaust friendly momentum, force early culmination, or allow an enemy counterattack. Decisive points shape the design of operations. They help commanders select clearly decisive, attainable objectives that directly contribute to achieving the end state.

LINES OF OPERATIONS AND LINES OF EFFORT

7-52. Lines of operations and lines of effort bridge the broad concept of operations across to discreet tactical tasks. They link objectives to the end state. Continuous assessment gives commanders the information required to revise and adjust lines of operations and effort. Subordinate commanders reallocate resources accordingly.

7-53. Commanders may describe an operation along lines of operations, lines of effort, or a combination of both. Irregular warfare, for example, typically requires a deliberate approach using lines of operations complemented with lines of effort; the combination of them may change based on the conditions within the operational area. An operational approach using both lines of operations and lines of effort reflects the characteristics and advantages of each. With this approach, commanders synchronize and sequence actions, deliberately creating complementary and reinforcing effects. The lines then converge on the well-defined, commonly understood end state outlined in the commander's intent.

Lines of Operations

7-54. A *line of operations* **is a line that defines the directional orientation of a force in time and space in relation to the enemy and links the force with its base of operations and objectives.** (See figure 7-4.) Lines of operations connect a series of decisive points that lead to control of a geographic or force-oriented objective. Operations designed using lines of operations generally consist of a series of actions executed according to a well-defined sequence. Major combat operations are typically designed using lines of operations. These lines tie offensive and defensive tasks to the geographic and positional references in the operational area. Commanders synchronize activities along complementary lines of operations to achieve the end state. Lines of operations may be either interior or exterior.

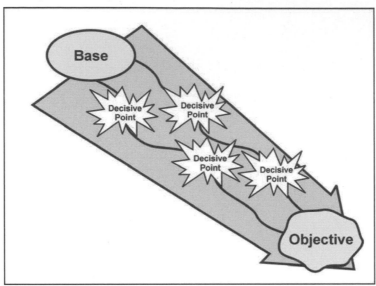

Figure 7-4. Example of a line of operations

7-55. **A force operates on** *interior lines* **when its operations diverge from a central point**. Interior lines usually represent a central position, where a friendly force can reinforce or concentrate its elements faster than the enemy force can reposition. With interior lines, friendly forces are closer to separate enemy forces than the enemy forces are to one another. Interior lines allow an isolated force to mass combat power against a specific portion of an enemy force by shifting capabilities more rapidly than the enemy can react.

7-56. **A force operates on** *exterior lines* **when its operations converge on the enemy**. Operations on exterior lines offer opportunities to encircle ̍ and annihilate an enemy force. However, these operations typically require a force stronger or more mobile than the enemy.

7-57. The relevance of interior and exterior lines depends on the time and space relationship between the opposing forces. Although an enemy force may have interior lines with respect to the friendly force, this advantage disappears if the friendly force is more agile and operates at a higher tempo. (Paragraph 7-71 defines tempo.) Conversely, if a smaller friendly force maneuvers to a position between larger but less agile enemy forces, the friendly force can better defeat them in detail before they can react effectively.

Lines of Effort

7-58. **A** *line of effort* **is a line that links multiple tasks and missions using the logic of purpose—cause and effect—to focus efforts toward establishing operational and strategic conditions.** Lines of effort are essential to long-term planning when positional references to an enemy or adversary have little relevance. In operations involving many nonmilitary factors, lines of effort may form the only way to link tasks, effects, conditions, and the desired end state. Lines of effort help commanders visualize how military capabilities can support the other instruments of national power. They prove particularly invaluable when used to achieve unity of effort in operations involving multinational forces and civilian organizations, where unity of command is elusive, if not impractical.

7-59. Commanders use lines of effort to describe how they envision their operations establishing the more intangible end state conditions. These lines of effort show how individual actions relate to each other and to achieving the end state. Ideally, lines of effort combine the complementary, long-term effects of stability or civil support tasks with the cyclic, short-term events typical of offensive or defensive tasks.

7-60. Commanders at all levels may use lines of effort to develop missions and tasks and to allocate resources. Commanders may designate one line of effort as the decisive operation and others as shaping operations. Commanders synchronize and sequence related actions along multiple lines of effort. Seeing these relationships helps commanders assess progress toward achieving the end state as forces perform tasks and accomplish missions.

7-61. Commanders typically visualize stability and civil support operations along lines of effort. For stability operations, commanders may consider linking primary stability tasks to their corresponding Department of State post-conflict technical sectors. (See Chapter 3 for a discussion on stability tasks.) These stability tasks link military actions with the broader interagency effort across the levels of war. Figure 7-5 provides an example. A full array of lines of effort might include offensive and defensive lines, as well as a line for inform and influence activities. Inform and influence activities typically produce effects across multiple lines of effort.

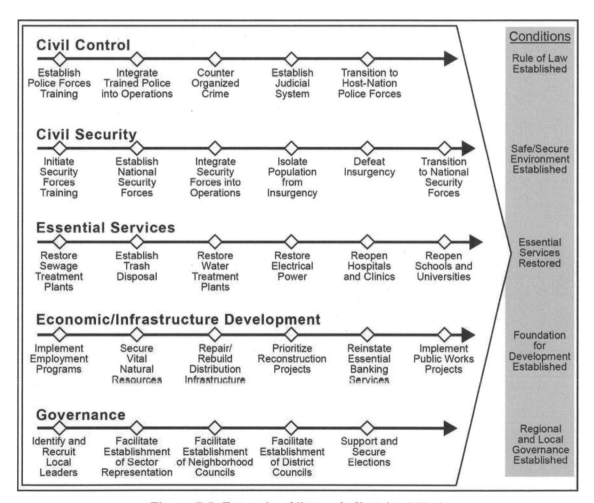

Figure 7-5. Example of lines of effort (stability)

7-62. The five post-conflict technical sectors described in chapter 3 may become lines of effort, as illustrated in figure 7-5. They provide a framework for analyzing an operational environment where stability operations are the major focus. They identify the breadth and depth of relevant civilian agency tasks and emphasize the relationships among them. Using them as lines of effort can help as Army forces in collaborative interagency planning and dialog. Planning and dialog leads to developing lines of effort that synchronize the effects of the instruments of national power. However, the sectors are not themselves lines of effort and are not the default solution for every operation. During a civil support mission, lines of effort normally portray support in response to a disaster or terrorist attack, support to law enforcement, and other support as required.

7-63. As operations progress, commanders may modify the lines of effort after assessing conditions and collaborating with multinational military and civilian partners. Lines of effort typically focus on integrating the effects of military operations with those of other instruments of national power to support the broader effort. Each operation, however, differs. Commanders develop and modify lines of effort to keep operations focused on achieving the end state, even as the situation changes.

Combining Lines of Operations and Lines of Effort

7-64. Commanders use both lines of operations and lines of effort to connect objectives to a central, unifying purpose. Lines of operations portray the more traditional links between objectives, decisive points, and centers of gravity. However, lines of operations do not project the long-term plan beyond defeating enemy forces and seizing terrain. Combining lines of operations and lines of effort allows commanders to include nonmilitary activities in their long-term plan. This combination helps commanders incorporate stability tasks that establish the end state conditions into the operation. It allows commanders to consider the less tangible aspects of the operational environment where the other instruments of national power dominate. Commanders can then visualize concurrent and post-conflict stability activities. Making these connections relates the tasks and purposes of the elements of full spectrum operations with joint effects identified in the long-term plan.

OPERATIONAL REACH

7-65. *Operational reach* is the distance and duration across which a unit can successfully employ military capabilities (JP 3-0). It reflects the ability to achieve success through a well-conceived operational approach. Operational reach is a tether; it is a function of protection, sustainment, endurance, and relative combat power. The limit of a unit's operational reach is its culminating point. (See paragraph 7-85.) It balances the natural tension between endurance, momentum, and protection. The following actions can extend operational reach:

- Forward positioning of forces, reserves, bases, and support capabilities along lines of operations.
- Employing weapons systems with extended ranges, such as missiles.
- Phasing an operation to focus limited resources.
- Leveraging supply discipline, contracting, and host-nation support. Maximizing distribution network efficiency.
- Leveraging joint capabilities.

7-66. Endurance refers to the ability to employ combat power anywhere for protracted periods. It stems from the ability to create, protect, and sustain a force, regardless of the distance from its base and the austerity of the environment. Endurance involves anticipating requirements and making the most effective, efficient use of available resources. Their endurance gives Army forces their campaign capability. It makes permanent the changing effects of other capabilities.

7-67. Momentum comes from seizing the initiative and executing high-tempo operations that overwhelm enemy resistance. Commanders control momentum by maintaining focus and pressure. They set a tempo that prevents exhaustion and maintains sustainment. A sustainable tempo extends operational reach. Commanders maintain momentum by anticipating and transitioning rapidly between primary tasks or—when necessary—the elements of full spectrum operations. Sometimes commanders push the force to its culminating point to take maximum advantage of an opportunity. For example, exploitations and pursuits often involve pushing all available forces to the limit of their endurance to capitalize on momentum and retain the initiative.

7-68. Protection is an important contributor to operational reach. Commanders anticipate how enemy actions might disrupt operations and then determine the protection capabilities required to maintain sufficient reach. Protection closely relates to endurance and momentum. It also contributes to the commander's ability to extend operations in time and space. The protection warfighting function helps commanders maintain the deploying force's integrity and combat power.

7-69. **An *operational pause* is a deliberate halt taken to extend operational reach or prevent culmination.** Commanders may execute an operational pause for several reasons. These may include the force being close to culmination, the decisive operation failing, or the end state changing. In planning an operation, commanders carefully balance initiative, momentum, reach, and culmination to avoid unnecessary operational pauses. In protracted operations, however, they may have to execute operational pauses to extend operational reach. Commanders carefully plan, prepare for, and execute these pauses to prevent losing the initiative. During an operational pause, commanders retain the initiative by using shaping operations to keep pressure on enemy forces. These shaping operations confuse the enemy while friendly forces generate combat power for the decisive operation.

7-70. Commanders and staffs balance operational reach, direct and indirect approaches, and operational pauses to ensure Army forces accomplish their missions before culminating. Commanders continually strive to extend operational reach. They assess friendly and enemy force status, anticipate culmination, and plan operational pauses if necessary. Commanders have studied and reflected on the challenge of conducting and sustaining operations over long distances and times. History contains many examples of operations hampered by inadequate operational reach. Achieving the desired end state requires forces with the operational reach to establish and maintain the end state conditions.

TEMPO

7-71. ***Tempo* is the relative speed and rhythm of military operations over time with respect to the enemy.** It reflects the rate of military action. Controlling tempo helps commanders keep the initiative during combat operations or rapidly establish a sense of normalcy during humanitarian crises. During operations dominated by the offense and defense, commanders normally seek to maintain a higher tempo than the enemy; rapid tempo can overwhelm an enemy's ability to counter friendly actions. During operations dominated by stability and civil support, commanders act quickly to control events. By acting faster than the situation deteriorates, commanders can change the dynamics of a crisis and restore stability. The capability to act quickly enhances flexibility and operational adaptability across the spectrum of conflict.

7-72. Commanders control tempo throughout the conduct of operations. First, they formulate operations that stress the complementary and reinforcing effects of simultaneous and sequential operations. They synchronize those operations in time and space to degrade enemy capabilities throughout the operational area. Second, commanders avoid unnecessary engagements. This practice includes bypassing resistance that appears at times and places commanders do not consider decisive. Third, through mission command they enable subordinates to exercise initiative and act independently. Controlling tempo requires both audacity and patience: audacity initiates the actions needed to develop a situation; patience allows a situation to develop until the force can strike at the decisive time and place. Ultimately, the goal is maintaining a tempo appropriate to retaining the initiative and achieving the end state.

7-73. Army forces expend more energy and resources when operating at a high tempo. Commanders assess the force's capacity to operate at a high tempo based on its performance and available resources. An effective operational design varies tempo throughout an operation to increase endurance while maintaining appropriate speed and momentum. There is more to tempo than speed. While speed can be important, commanders balance speed with endurance.

SIMULTANEITY AND DEPTH

7-74. Simultaneity and depth extend operations in time and space. Simultaneity has two components. Both depend on depth to attain lasting effects and maximum synergy. Simultaneous combinations of offensive, defensive, and stability tasks overwhelm enemy forces and their will to resist while setting the conditions for a lasting, stable peace. Simultaneous actions across the depth of the operational area place more demands on enemy forces than enemy forces can effectively respond to them. Operations combining depth and simultaneity achieve a synergy that paralyzes enemy forces. This prevents them from reacting appropriately, inducing their early culmination. Similarly, stability or civil support tasks—executed in depth with simultaneous defensive and offensive tasks when necessary—establish control of the situation throughout the operational area.

7-75. Simultaneity also refers to the concurrent effects operations produce at the tactical, operational, and strategic levels. Tactical commanders fight the battles and engagements that accomplish objectives in accordance with the operational commander's intent. Operational commanders set the conditions for tactical success in battles within a campaign or major operation. These victories, in turn, create the conditions that define the end state. Because of the complex interaction among the levels of war, commanders cannot be concerned only with events at their respective echelon. Success requires them to understand how their actions affect the operations of commanders at all other echelons.

7-76. ***Depth* is the extension of operations in time, space, and resources**. Operations in depth can disrupt the enemy's decision cycle. These operations contribute to protecting the force by destroying enemy capabilities before the enemy can use them. Commanders balance their forces' tempo to produce simultaneous results throughout their operational area. To achieve simultaneity, commanders establish a higher tempo to target enemy capabilities located at the limit of a force's operational reach.

7-77. Simultaneity and depth are inherent in full spectrum operations. Army forces execute simultaneous operations across vast areas. They force the enemy to react to numerous friendly actions—potential and actual—throughout the operational area. Army forces use combined arms, advanced information systems, and joint capabilities to increase the depth of their operations. The complementary effects produced by executing simultaneous operations in depth overwhelm enemy forces, forcing them to respond piecemeal or not at all.

7-78. Commanders extend the depth of operations through joint integration. When determining an operation's depth, commanders consider their own capabilities, as well as joint capabilities and limitations. They use these capabilities to ensure actions executed at operational depth receive robust and uninterrupted support. Commanders sequence and synchronize operations in time and space to achieve simultaneous effects throughout the operational area.

PHASING AND TRANSITIONS

7-79. **A *phase* is a planning and execution tool used to divide an operation in duration or activity. A change in phase usually involves a change of mission, task organization, or rules of engagement. Phasing helps in planning and controlling and may be indicated by time, distance, terrain, or an event.** The ability of Army forces to extend operations in time and space, coupled with a desire to dictate tempo, often presents commanders with more objectives and decisive points than the force can engage simultaneously. At both the operational and tactical levels, this situation may require commanders and staffs to consider sequencing operations. Sequencing involves integrating capabilities and synchronizing actions. This is accomplished through phasing.

7-80. Phasing is key to arranging complex operations. It describes how the commander envisions the overall operation unfolding. It is the logical expression of the commander's visualization in time. Within a phase, a large portion of the force executes similar or mutually supporting activities. Achieving a specified condition or set of conditions typically marks the end of a phase.

7-81. Simultaneity, depth, and tempo are vital to full spectrum operations. However, they cannot always be attained to the degree desired. In such cases, commanders limit the number of objectives and decisive points engaged simultaneously. They deliberately sequence certain actions to maintain tempo while focusing combat power at the decisive point in time and space. Commanders combine simultaneous and sequential operations to establish the end state conditions.

7-82. Phasing can extend operational reach. Only when the force lacks the capability to accomplish the mission in a single action do commanders phase the operation. Each phase should strive to—
* Focus effort.
* Concentrate combat power in time and space at a decisive point.
* Deliberately and logically accomplish its objectives.

7-83. Transitions mark a change of focus between phases or between the ongoing operation and execution of a branch or sequel. Shifting priorities between the elements of full spectrum operations—such as from offense to stability—also involves a transition. Transitions require planning and preparation well before their execution to maintain the momentum and tempo of operations. The force is vulnerable during transitions, and commanders establish clear conditions for their execution. Transitions may create unexpected opportunities; they may also make forces vulnerable to enemy threats.

7-84. An unexpected change in conditions may require commanders to direct an abrupt transition between phases. In such cases, the overall composition of the force remains unchanged despite sudden changes in mission, task organization, and rules of engagement. Typically, task organization evolves to meet changing conditions; however, transition planning must also account for changes in mission. Commanders attuned to sudden changes can better adapt their forces to dynamic conditions. They continuously assess the situation and task-organize and cycle their forces to retain the initiative. They strive to achieve changes in emphasis without incurring an operational pause.

CULMINATION

7-85. **The *culminating point* is that point in time and space at which a force no longer possesses the capability to continue its current form of operations.** Culmination represents a decisive shift in relative combat power. It is relevant to both attackers and defenders at each level of war. In the offense, the culminating point occurs when the force cannot continue the attack and must assume a defensive posture or execute an operational pause. In the defense, it occurs when the force can no longer defend itself and must withdraw or risk destruction.

7-86. With stability, the culminating point is more difficult to identify. Three conditions can result in culmination:

- Being too dispersed to adequately control the situation.
- Being unable to provide the necessary security.
- Lacking required resources.

7-87. During civil support, culmination is unlikely. However, culmination may occur if forces must respond to more catastrophic events than they can manage simultaneously. That situation results in culmination due to exhaustion.

7-88. Culmination may be a planned event. In such cases, the concept of operations predicts which part of the force will culminate, and the task organization includes additional forces to assume the mission. Culmination is expected and measures are in place to mitigate it. Culmination is typically caused by direct combat actions or higher echelon resourcing decisions. It relates to the force's ability to generate and apply combat power and is not a lasting condition. Tactical units may be reinforced or reconstituted to continue operations.

RISK

7-89. Risk, uncertainty, and chance are inherent in all military operations. When commanders accept risk, they create opportunities to seize, retain, and exploit the initiative and achieve decisive results. Risk is a potent catalyst that fuels opportunity. The willingness to incur risk is often the key to exposing enemy weaknesses that the enemy considers beyond friendly reach. Understanding risk requires calculated assessments coupled with boldness and imagination. Successful commanders assess and mitigate risk continuously throughout the operations process.

7-90. Inadequate planning and preparation recklessly risks forces. It is equally rash to delay action while waiting for perfect intelligence and synchronization. Reasonably estimating and intentionally accepting risk is fundamental to conducting operations and essential to mission command. Successfully applying military force requires commanders who assess the risks, analyze and minimize the hazards, and execute a plan that accounts for those hazards. Experienced commanders balance audacity and imagination with risk and uncertainty to strike at a time and place and in a manner wholly unexpected by enemy forces. This is the essence of surprise. It results from carefully considering and accepting risk. (FMs 3-90 and 6-0 discuss tactical risk.)

7-91. Operational art balances risk and opportunity to create and maintain the conditions necessary to seize, retain, and exploit the initiative and achieve decisive results. During execution, opportunity is fleeting. The surest means to create opportunity is to accept risk while minimizing hazards to friendly forces. A good operational approach considers risk and uncertainty equally with friction and chance. The final plans and orders then provide the flexibility commanders need to take advantage of opportunity in complex, dynamic environments.

SUMMARY

7-92. Operational art is a cognitive aspect of operations supported by design. While the character of conflict changes with time, the violent and chaotic nature of warfare does not. The essence of military art remains timeless. Operational art—the creative expression of informed vision to integrate ends, ways, and means across the levels of war—is fundamental to the Army's ability to seize, retain, and exploit the initiative.

Chapter 8

Strategic and Operational Reach

Army forces require strategic and operational reach to deploy and immediately conduct operations anywhere with little or no advanced notice. Contemporary operations require Army forces that can deploy rapidly and conduct extended campaigns. These operations require Soldiers and units with campaign and expeditionary capabilities. Commanders and organizations require proficiency at force projection, protection, and sustainment. Soldiers require an expeditionary mindset to prepare them for short-notice deployments into uncertain, often austere environments. This chapter discusses how strategic and operational reach affects deploying and employing Army forces. It also addresses principles to maximize the effects of both factors. Strategic and operational reach depend on basing in and near the joint operations area.

STRATEGIC REACH

8-1.   Strategic reach provides the capability to operate against complex, adaptive threats operating anywhere. The distance across which the Nation can project decisive military power is its strategic reach. This multifaceted reach combines joint military capabilities—air, land, maritime, space, special operations, and cyber—with those of the other instruments of national power. Land force capabilities complement those of other Services. Army forces increase the joint force's strategic reach by securing and operating bases far from the United States. However, Army forces depend on joint-enabled force projection capabilities to deploy and sustain them across intercontinental distances. In some cases, land forces use strategic lift to deploy directly to an operational area. In many instances, land operations combine direct deployment with movements from intermediate staging bases located outside the operational area. Access to bases and support depends upon the Nation's diplomatic and economic power as well as its military capabilities.

OPERATIONAL MANEUVER FROM STRATEGIC DISTANCE

8-2.   Operational maneuver from strategic distance combines global force projection with maneuver against an operationally significant objective. (See figure 8-1, page 8-2.) It requires strategic reach that deploys maneuverable landpower to an operational area in a position of advantage. It requires enough operational reach to execute operations decisively without an operational pause. It aims to avoid operational pauses associated with various requirements. Then it can secure and defend a lodgment; develop a base; and receive, stage, and build up forces. Success demands full integration of all available joint means. Thus, it combines force projection with land maneuver to operational depth in an integrated, continuous operation.

8-3.   The most difficult form of operational maneuver from strategic distance projects forces directly from the United States into an operational area. Examples of this operational maneuver from strategic distance include the 1942 invasion of North Africa and the 1992 intervention in Somalia. These operations involved forces projected from the United States with near simultaneous employment. In many cases, operational maneuver from strategic distance requires intermediate staging bases. From these bases, operational maneuver develops using intratheater lift and Army maneuver capabilities. The availability of bases in a region extends the strategic reach of Army forces; bases near the operational area increase opportunities for successful operational maneuver from strategic distance.

8-4.   Today, joint forces combine strategic and operational reach in forcible and unopposed entry operations. These operations originate from outside the operational area, often using intermediate staging bases.

Entry operations conducted across intercontinental distances capitalize on the U.S. dominance of the air and sea. Exploiting these capabilities creates a dilemma for opponents.

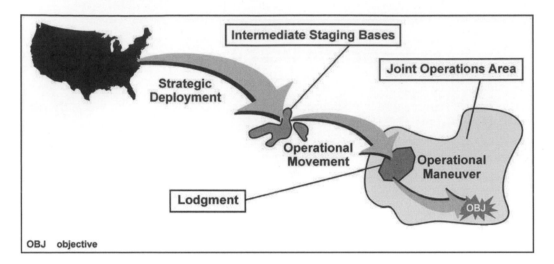

Figure 8-1. Operational maneuver from strategic distance

EXPEDITIONARY CAMPAIGNS

8-5. Expeditionary campaigns are inherently joint operations founded in strategic reach. During crisis response, joint force commanders rely on contingency expeditionary forces to respond promptly. The Army provides ready forces able to operate in any environment—from urban areas to remote, rural regions. The early introduction of credible, capable forces into the operational area is an important strategic factor. This action may quickly convince a potential enemy that further aggression would be too costly. Initial-entry forces need to be interoperable and flexible enough to contend with unforeseen circumstances. Immediately upon arrival, initial-entry forces require enough combat power to establish and protect lodgments and begin simultaneous shaping operations. The ability to fight at the outset is crucial to successfully executing the campaign plan. A tailored force able to dominate situations early enables the joint force commander to seize, retain, and exploit the initiative.

8-6. Expeditionary forces are configured for immediate employment in austere conditions. They do not depend on existing infrastructure; they adapt as the situation evolves. Commanders prepare to transition to sustained operations, assimilate new capabilities into force packages for follow-on operations, or disperse until otherwise required. As a result, the force composition varies throughout the campaign based on the dominant element of full spectrum operations.

8-7. If campaign objectives are not achieved swiftly, the Army provides forces tailored with the combat power and endurance needed for sustained, joint-enabled land operations. Endurance gives the force the ability to employ combat power anywhere for protracted periods. It allows Army forces to preserve the gains of initial operations and complements and reinforces efforts of the other instruments of national power to achieve strategic objectives. It has strategic, operational, and tactical implications. Strategically, endurance requires the Army to sustain the generation and rotation of forces sufficient to meet combatant commanders' requirements. At the operational level, endurance requires Army forces with enough operational reach to complement other joint capabilities throughout a campaign. Tactically, endurance is a function of sustainment and protection. Endurance gives Army forces their campaign capability.

EXPEDITIONARY ARMY FORCES

8-8. Expeditionary forces impose a distinct set of dynamics on Army forces. The Army depends on strategic deployment assets provided by U.S. Transportation Command. Combatant commanders establish priorities to move forces into the operational area. That decision drives allocation of strategic lift and ultimately determines how rapidly Army forces deploy. Although U.S. strategic lift assets exceed those of any other nation, the available lift is rarely sufficient to deploy a large force at one time. Consequently, commanders carefully select elements of the force and the sequence in which they deploy to match operational area conditions. This is force tailoring.

8-9.   The range of possible employment options complicates training. Army forces cannot train for every possible mission; they train for full spectrum operations with emphasis on the most likely mix of tasks. When designated as an expeditionary force for specific missions, Army forces modify training and prepare for that contingency. The volatile nature of crises requires Army forces to simultaneously train, deploy, and execute. Commanders conduct operations with initial-entry forces while assembling and preparing follow-on forces. Commanders carefully consider and accept risk to create opportunity. Such actions help them to seize the initiative during deployment and in the early phases of an operation, even when the situation is not fully developed. Balancing these dynamics is an art mastered through knowledge, experience, and judgment.

8-10. The payoff for mastering expeditionary operations is mission accomplishment. Fast deploying and expansible Army forces give joint force commanders the means to introduce operationally significant land forces into a crisis on short notice. These expeditionary capabilities arm joint force commanders with a preemptive ability to deter, shape, fight, and win. Rapidly deployed expeditionary force packages provide immediate options for seizing or retaining the operational initiative. They complement and reinforce the other Services with modular capability packages that can be swiftly tailored, deployed, and employed.

8-11. Expeditionary capability is more than the ability to deploy quickly. It requires deploying the right mix Army forces to the right place at the right time. It provides joint force commanders with the ability to deter an adversary or take decisive action if deterrence fails. Forward deployed units, forward positioned capabilities, peacetime military engagement, and force projection—from anywhere in the world—all contribute to expeditionary capabilities.

8-12. When deployed, every unit regardless of type generates combat power and contributes to the success of the mission. From the operational and tactical perspectives, commanders ensure deployed Army forces possess sufficient combat power to overwhelm any potential enemy. The art of expeditionary warfare balances the ability to mass the effects of lethal combat systems against the requirements to deploy, support, and sustain units that use those systems. Commanders assemble force packages that maximize the lethality of initial-entry forces. These packages remain consistent with both the mission and the requirement to project, employ, and sustain the force. Commanders tailor follow-on forces to increase both the lethality and operational reach of the entire force.

8-13. Deploying commanders integrate protection capabilities to ensure mission accomplishment and increase the survivability of deployed Army forces. As with the other attributes, lift constraints and time available complicate the situation. Survivability requires astutely assessing operational risk. In many operations, rapid offensive action to seize the initiative may better protect forces than massive defenses around lodgments.

8-14. Generating and sustaining combat power is fundamental to expeditionary warfare. Commanders reconcile competing requirements. Army forces must accomplish joint force commander-assigned missions, yet they require adequate sustainment for operations extended in time and space. Commanders tailor force packages to provide sufficient sustainment capability without amassing a significant sustainment footprint. Wherever possible, commanders augment sustainment capacity with host-nation and contracted support.

FORCE PROJECTION

8-15. Force projection is the military component of power projection. It is a central element of the National Military Strategy. Speed is paramount; force projection is a race between friendly forces and the enemy or situation. The side that achieves an operational capability first can seize the initiative. Thus, it is not the velocity of individual stages or transportation means that is decisive; it is a combat-ready force deployed to an operational area before the enemy is ready or the situation deteriorates further.

8-16. Commanders visualize force projection as one seamless operation. Deployment speed sets the initial tempo of military activity in the operational area. Commanders understand how speed, sequence, and mix of deploying forces affect their employment options. They see how their employment concept establishes deployment requirements. Commanders prioritize the mix of forces on the time-phased force and deployment list to project forces into the operational area where and when required. Singular focus on the land component, to the exclusion of complementary joint capabilities, may result in incorrect force sequencing. Commanders exercise active and continuous command and control during force projection. They couple it with detailed reverse-sequence planning. Thus, the right forces and the right support are available and ready to conduct decisive operations when needed.

8-17. Force projection encompasses five processes: mobilization, deployment, employment, sustainment, and redeployment. These processes occur in a continuous, overlapping, and repeating sequence throughout an operation. Force projection operations are inherently joint. They require detailed planning and synchronization. Sound, informed decisions made early on force projection may determine a campaign's success.

8-18. Each process has its own criteria. Mobilization is the process of bringing the armed forces to a state of readiness in response to a contingency. Deployment is the relocation of forces and materiel to a desired operational area in response to a contingency. It has four supporting components: predeployment activities; fort to port; port to port; and reception, staging, onward movement, and integration. Employment is the conduct of operations to support a joint force commander. Sustainment involves providing and maintaining personnel and materiel required to support a joint force commander. Redeployment is the return of forces and materiel to the home or mobilization station. (JP 4-05 discusses mobilization. JP 3-0 discusses employment. JP 4-0 and FM 4-0 discuss sustainment. FMI 3-35 discusses deployment and redeployment of brigade-sized and larger Army forces. FM 4-01.011 discusses deployment and redeployment of battalion-sized and smaller Army forces.)

8-19. Reception, staging, onward movement, and integration focuses on reassembling deploying units and quickly integrating them into the force. It is the critical link between deploying and employing forces. Effective reception, staging, onward movement, and integration establishes a smooth flow of personnel, equipment, and materiel from ports of debarkation through employment as reassembled, mission-capable forces. A deploying unit is most vulnerable between its arrival and operational employment, so protection is vital.

8-20. Closing the force more rapidly can be achieved by increasing the allocation of strategic lift or by using pre-positioned equipment sets. (FMs 100-17-1 and 100-17-2 discuss pre-positioned operations.) Combatant commanders and Army Service component commands can also facilitate force projection through anticipatory actions. Actions may include positioning equipment or troops in anticipated crisis areas, securing access to ports and airfields, enhancing capabilities of regional forces, and protecting areas critical to force projection.

ENTRY OPERATIONS

8-21. Whenever possible, Army forces seek an unopposed entry, either unassisted or assisted by the host nation. An assisted entry requires host-nation cooperation. In an assisted entry, initial-entry forces are tailored to deploy efficiently and transition quickly to follow-on operations. Reception, staging, onward movement, and integration focuses on cooperating with the host nation to expedite moving units from ports of debarkation to tactical assembly areas. In an unassisted entry, no secure facilities for deploying forces exist. The joint force commander deploys balanced force packages with enough combat power to secure an adequate lodgment and perform reception, staging, onward movement, and integration. Force sequencing for an unassisted entry is similar to that of a forcible entry.

8-22. A *forcible entry* is the seizing and holding of a military lodgment in the face of armed opposition (JP 3-18). Once the assault force seizes the lodgment, it normally defends to retain it while the joint force commander rapidly deploys additional combat power by air and sea. When conditions are favorable, joint force commanders may combine a forcible entry with other offensive operations in a coup de main. This action can achieve the strategic objectives in a simultaneous major operation. The 1989 invasion of

Panama is an example of operational maneuver from strategic distance in a coup de main. (JP 3-18 contains joint doctrine for forcible entry operations.)

8-23. A forcible entry operation can be by parachute, air, or amphibious assault. The Army's parachute assault and air assault forces provide a formidable forcible entry capability. Marine forces specialize in amphibious assault; they also conduct air assaults as part of amphibious operations. Special operations forces play an important role in forcible entry; they conduct shaping operations in support of conventional forces while executing their own missions. These capabilities permit joint force commanders to overwhelm enemy anti-access measures and quickly insert combat power. The entry force either resolves the situation or secures a lodgment for delivery of larger forces by aircraft or ships. The three forms of forcible entry produce complementary and reinforcing effects that help joint force commanders to seize the initiative early in a campaign.

8-24. Forcible entry operations are inherently complex and always joint. Often only hours separate the alert from deployment. The demands of simultaneous deployment and employment create a distinct set of dynamics. Operations are carefully planned and rehearsed in training areas and marshalling areas. Personnel and equipment are configured for employment upon arrival without reception, staging, onward movement, and integration.

OPERATIONAL REACH

8-25. The challenge of conducting and sustaining operations over long distances has been studied and theorized upon since the time of Sun Tzu. History is replete with examples of campaigns plagued with inadequate operational reach. To achieve the desired end state, forces must possess the necessary operational reach to establish and maintain conditions that define success. (See paragraphs 6-74 through 6-79.)

8-26. Extending operational reach is a paramount concern for commanders. Commanders and staffs increase operational reach through deliberate, focused operational design. Operational design balances the natural tension between tempo, endurance, and risk to increase operational reach. A well-designed operation, executed skillfully, extends operational reach several ways, to include—

- Setting the tempo of the operation for greater endurance.
- Phasing the operation to assure its continuation.
- Employing the support of other Service components to relieve land forces of tasks that detract from the decisive operation.

BASING

8-27. A *base* is a locality from which operations are projected or supported (JP 1-02). The base includes installations and facilities that provide sustainment. Bases may be joint or single Service areas. Commanders often designate a specific area as a base and assign responsibility for protection and terrain management within the base to a single commander. Units located within the base are under the tactical control of the base commander. Within large bases, controlling commanders may designate base clusters for mutual protection and command and control.

8-28. Strategic and operational reach initially depend upon basing in the area of responsibility and overflight rights. Both affect how much combat power can be generated in the operational area in a prescribed period. The arrangement and location of forward bases (often in austere, rapidly emplaced configurations) complement the ability of Army forces to conduct sustained, continuous combat operations to operational depth. Though typically determined by diplomatic and political considerations, basing and overflight rights are essential to the commander's ability to maintain or extend operational reach.

8-29. Army forces typically rely on a mix of intermediate staging bases, lodgments (subsequently developed into bases), and forward operating bases to deploy and employ landpower simultaneously to operational depth. These bases establish and maintain strategic reach for deploying forces and ensure sufficient operational reach to extend operations in time and space.

INTERMEDIATE STAGING BASES

8-30. An *intermediate staging base* is a tailorable, temporary location used for staging forces, sustainment and/or extraction into and out of an operational area (JP 3-35). At the intermediate staging base, units are unloaded from intertheater lift, reassembled and integrated with their equipment, and then moved by intra-theater lift into the operational area. The theater army commander provides extensive support to Army forces transiting the base. The combatant commander may designate the theater army commander to command the base or provide a headquarters suitable for the task. Intermediate staging bases are established near, but normally not in, the operational area. They often are located in the supported combatant commander's area of responsibility. For land forces, intermediate staging bases may be located in the operational area. However, they are always established outside the range of enemy fires and beyond the enemy's political sphere of influence.

8-31. Ideally, secure bases will be available in the operational area, but conditions that compel deployment may also negate the availability of a secure lodgment in the operational area. Under these circumstances, an intermediate staging base may serve as the principal staging base for entry operations. In cases where the force needs to secure a lodgment, an intermediate staging base may be critical to success.

8-32. Normally, intermediate staging bases exploit advantages of existing, developed capabilities, serving as efficient transfer points from high-volume commercial carriers to various tactical, intratheater transport means. However, these bases are transshipment points. Using them can increase handling requirements and deployment times and may require infrastructure development to support further deployment. When deciding whether to operate through an intermediate staging base, commanders carefully weigh advantages gained by deploying through the base against operational risks, such as time, lift, and distance, associated with its utilization.

LODGMENTS

8-33. A *lodgment* is a designated area in a hostile or potentially hostile territory that, when seized and held, makes the continuous landing of troops and materiel possible and provides maneuver space for subsequent operations (JP 3-18). Identifying and preparing the initial lodgment significantly influences the conduct of an operation. Lodgments should expand to allow easy access to strategic sealift and airlift, offer adequate space for storage, facilitate transshipment of supplies and equipment, and be accessible to multiple lines of communications. Typically, deploying forces establish lodgments near key points of entry in the operational area that offer central access to air, land, and sea transportation hubs.

8-34. A lodgment rarely possesses the ideal characteristics desired to support ongoing operations. Improving the base capabilities may require early deployment of maintenance, engineering, or terminal operations forces. Contracting, medical, legal, and financial management personnel who arrange access to host-nation capabilities should be among the first to deploy. The requirement for adequate sustainment capability is especially critical in the operation's early stages when building combat power is critical and forces are most vulnerable. Identifying infrastructure requirements during mission analysis is essential to establishing the lodgment and enhancing the responsiveness and sustainability of the force.

8-35. The time required to establish a lodgment depends on the extent and condition of the civil and military infrastructure present in the operational area. In areas where extensive industrial facilities and distribution capabilities exist and are available, commanders can initiate operations without a significant pause. In the absence of these capabilities, the force cannot begin operations until a sufficient base is established and operational. In more austere environments, where initial entry and operations may be severely restricted, acquisition, construction, and sustainment capabilities should arrive early in the deployment flow. This arrival improves the lodgment, generates and moves forces and materiel into forward operating bases, and establishes operational-level sustainment capability to support the deployed force.

FORWARD OPERATING BASES

8-36. **A *forward operating base* is an area used to support tactical operations without establishing full support facilities**. Such bases may be used for an extended time. During protracted operations, they may be expanded and improved to establish a more permanent presence. The scale and complexity of the base, however, directly relates to the size of the force required to maintain it. A large base with extensive facilities requires a much larger security force than a smaller, austere base. Commanders weigh whether to expand and improve a forward operating base against the type and number of forces available to secure it, the expected length of the forward deployment, and the force's sustainment requirements.

8-37. Forward operating bases extend and maintain the operational reach of Army forces, providing secure locations from which to conduct and sustain operations. They not only enable extending operations in time and space; they also contribute to the overall endurance of the force, an essential element of the Army's campaign capability. Forward operating bases allow forward-deployed forces to reduce operational risk, maintain momentum, and avoid culmination.

8-38. Typically, forward operating bases are established adjacent to a regional distribution hub, such as a large airfield (civilian or military), rail terminal, or major highway junction. This facilitates movement into and out of the operational area while providing a secure location through which to distribute personnel, equipment, and supplies. However, forward operating bases may be located in austere locations with limited access to transportation infrastructure. In such cases, units will not likely maintain the base for extended periods.

*SUPPORT AREAS

8-39. When lodgment or a forward operating base expands to include clusters of sustainment, headquarters, and other supporting units, commanders may designate a support area. **A *support area* is a specific surface area designated by the echelon commander to facilitate the positioning, employment, and protection of resources required to sustain, enable, and control tactical operations**. Within a support area, a designated unit such as a brigade combat team or maneuver enhancement brigade provides area security, terrain management, movement control, mobility support, clearance of fires, and required tactical combat forces. This allows sustainment units to focus on their primary function.

SUMMARY

8-40. The Nation requires joint forces with strategic and operational reach. Given the enormous distances that separate the United States from regions in conflict, this imposes serious challenges for the Army. Even within the United States, the distances between Army installations and major cities often span a significant expanse. Above all, the Army must remain versatile, adapting not only to the particular requirements of different areas of responsibility, but also to limitations in strategic and intratheater lift. Available lift will never equal an ideal land force's requirements. Joint force commanders need some landpower deployed very rapidly and capable of seizing a lodgment. They also need follow-on land forces able to persevere for months and years as the campaign progresses. Once deployed, Army commanders develop and protect bases and lines of communications in austere areas. These house not only Soldiers but also joint and multinational forces. With each base, Army forces extend their operational reach throughout the operational area, using landpower to multiply the effectiveness of American military power.

This page intentionally left blank.

Appendix A

Principles of War and Operations

The nine principles of war represent the most important nonphysical factors that affect the conduct of operations at the strategic, operational, and tactical levels. The Army published its original principles of war after World War I. In the following years, the Army adjusted the original principles modestly as they stood the tests of analysis, experimentation, and practice. The principles of war are not a checklist. While they are considered in all operations, they do not apply in the same way to every situation. Rather, they summarize characteristics of successful operations. Their greatest value lies in the education of the military professional. Applied to the study of past campaigns, major operations, battles, and engagements, the principles of war are powerful analysis tools. Joint doctrine adds three principles of operations to the traditional nine principles of war.

OBJECTIVE

Direct every military operation toward a clearly defined, decisive, and attainable objective.

A-1.   The principle of objective drives all military activity. At the operational and tactical levels, objective ensures all actions contribute to the higher commander's end state. When undertaking any mission, commanders should clearly understand the expected outcome and its impact. Combat power is limited; commanders never have enough to address every aspect of the situation. Objectives allow commanders to focus combat power on the most important tasks. Clearly stated objectives also promote individual initiative. These objectives clarify what subordinates need to accomplish by emphasizing the outcome rather than the method. Commanders should avoid actions that do not contribute directly to achieving the objectives.

A-2.   The purpose of military operations is to accomplish the military objectives that support achieving the conflict's overall political goals. In offensive and defensive operations, this involves destroying the enemy and his will to fight. The objective of stability or civil support operations may be more difficult to define; nonetheless, it too must be clear from the beginning. Objectives must contribute to the operation's purpose directly, quickly, and economically. Each tactical operation must contribute to achieving operational and strategic objectives.

A-3.   Military leaders cannot dissociate objective from the related joint principles of restraint and legitimacy, particularly in stability operations. The amount of force used to obtain the objective must be prudent and appropriate to strategic aims. Means used to accomplish the military objective must not undermine the local population's willing acceptance of a lawfully constituted government. Without restraint or legitimacy, support for military action deteriorates, and the objective becomes unobtainable.

OFFENSIVE

Seize, retain, and exploit the initiative.

A-4.   As a principle of war, offensive is synonymous with initiative. The surest way to achieve decisive results is to seize, retain, and exploit the initiative. Seizing the initiative dictates the nature, scope, and tempo of an operation. Seizing the initiative compels an enemy to react. Commanders use initiative to impose their will on an enemy or adversary or to control a situation. Seizing, retaining, and exploiting the initiative are all essential to maintain the freedom of action necessary to achieve success and exploit vulnerabilities. It helps commanders respond effectively to rapidly changing situations and unexpected developments.

A-5. In combat operations, offensive action is the most effective and decisive way to achieve a clearly defined objective. Offensive operations are the means by which a military force seizes and holds the initiative while maintaining freedom of action and achieving decisive results. The importance of offensive action is fundamentally true across all levels of war. Defensive operations shape for offensive operations by economizing forces and creating conditions suitable for counterattacks.

MASS

Concentrate the effects of combat power at the decisive place and time.

A-6. Commanders mass the effects of combat power in time and space to achieve both destructive and constructive results. Massing in time applies the elements of combat power against multiple decisive points simultaneously. Massing in space concentrates the effects of combat power against a single decisive point. Both can overwhelm opponents or dominate a situation. Commanders select the method that best fits the circumstances. Massed effects overwhelm the entire enemy or adversary force before it can react effectively.

A-7. Army forces can mass lethal and nonlethal effects quickly and across large distances. This does not imply that they accomplish their missions with massed fires alone. Swift and fluid maneuver based on situational understanding complements fires. Often, this combination in a single operation accomplishes what formerly took an entire campaign.

A-8. In combat, commanders mass the effects of combat power against a combination of elements critical to the enemy force to shatter its coherence. Some effects may be concentrated and vulnerable to operations that mass in both time and space. Other effects may be spread throughout depth of the operational area, vulnerable only to massing effects in time.

A-9. Mass applies equally in operations characterized by civil support or stability. Massing in a stability or civil support operation includes providing the proper forces at the right time and place to alleviate suffering and provide security. Commanders determine priorities among the elements of full spectrum operations and allocate the majority of their available forces to the most important tasks. They focus combat power to produce significant results quickly in specific areas, sequentially if necessary, rather than dispersing capabilities across wide areas and accomplishing less.

ECONOMY OF FORCE

Allocate minimum essential combat power to secondary efforts.

A-10. Economy of force is the reciprocal of mass. Commanders allocate only the minimum combat power necessary to shaping and sustaining operations so they can mass combat power for the decisive operation. This requires accepting prudent risk. Taking calculated risks is inherent in conflict. Commanders never leave any unit without a purpose. When the time comes to execute, all units should have tasks to perform.

MANEUVER

Place the enemy in a disadvantageous position through the flexible application of combat power.

A-11. Maneuver concentrates and disperses combat power to keep the enemy at a disadvantage. It achieves results that would otherwise be more costly. Effective maneuver keeps enemy forces off balance by making them confront new problems and new dangers faster than they can counter them. Army forces gain and preserve freedom of action, reduce vulnerability, and exploit success through maneuver. Maneuver is more than just fire and movement. It includes the dynamic, flexible application of all the elements of combat power. It requires flexibility in thought, plans, and operations. In operations dominated by stability or civil support, commanders use maneuver to interpose Army forces between the population and threats to security and to concentrate capabilities through movement.

UNITY OF COMMAND

For every objective, ensure unity of effort under one responsible commander.

A-12. Applying a force's full combat power requires unity of command. Unity of command means that a single commander directs and coordinates the actions of all forces toward a common objective. Cooperation may produce coordination, but giving a single commander the required authority is the most effective way to achieve unity of effort.

A-13. The joint, interagency, intergovernmental, and multinational nature of unified action creates situations where the commander does not directly control all organizations in the operational area. In the absence of command authority, commanders cooperate, negotiate, and build consensus to achieve unity of effort.

SECURITY

Never permit the enemy to acquire an unexpected advantage.

A-14. Security protects and preserves combat power. Security results from measures a command takes to protect itself from surprise, interference, sabotage, annoyance, and threat surveillance and reconnaissance. Military deception greatly enhances security.

SURPRISE

Strike the enemy at a time or place or in a manner for which he is unprepared.

A-15. Surprise is the reciprocal of security. It is a major contributor to achieving shock. It results from taking actions for which the enemy is unprepared. Surprise is a powerful but temporary combat multiplier. It is not essential to take enemy forces completely unaware; it is only necessary that they become aware too late to react effectively. Factors contributing to surprise include speed, operations security, and asymmetric capabilities.

SIMPLICITY

Prepare clear, uncomplicated plans and clear, concise orders to ensure thorough understanding.

A-16. Plans and orders should be simple and direct. Simple plans and clear, concise orders reduce misunderstanding and confusion. The situation determines the degree of simplicity required. Simple plans executed on time are better than detailed plans executed late. Commanders at all levels weigh potential benefits of a complex concept of operations against the risk that subordinates will fail to understand or follow it. Orders use clearly defined terms and graphics. Doing this conveys specific instructions to subordinates with reduced chances for misinterpretation and confusion.

A-17. Multinational operations put a premium on simplicity. Differences in language, doctrine, and culture complicate them. Simple plans and orders minimize the confusion inherent in this complex environment. The same applies to operations involving interagency and nongovernmental organizations.

ADDITIONAL PRINCIPLES OF JOINT OPERATIONS

A-18. In addition to these nine principles, JP 3-0 adds three principles of operations—perseverance, legitimacy, and restraint. Together with the principles of war, these twelve make up the principles of joint operations.

PERSEVERANCE

Ensure the commitment necessary to attain the national strategic end state.

A-19. Commanders prepare for measured, protracted military operations in pursuit of the desired national strategic end state. Some joint operations may require years to reach the desired end state. Resolving the underlying causes of the crisis may be elusive, making it difficult to achieve conditions supporting the end state. The patient, resolute, and persistent pursuit of national goals and objectives often is a requirement for success. This will frequently involve diplomatic, informational, and economic measures to supplement military efforts. In the end, the will of the American public, as expressed through their elected officials and advised by expert military judgment, determines the duration and size of any military commitment.

A-20. Army forces' endurance and commanders' perseverance are necessary to accomplish long-term missions. A decisive offensive operation may swiftly create conditions for short-term success. However, protracted stability operations, executed simultaneously with defensive and offensive tasks, may be needed to achieve the strategic end state. Commanders balance their desire to enter the operational area, accomplish the mission quickly, and depart against broader requirements. These include the long-term commitment needed to achieve national goals and objectives.

LEGITIMACY

Develop and maintain the will necessary to attain the national strategic end state.

A-21. For Army forces, legitimacy comes from three important factors. First, the operation or campaign must be conducted under U.S. law. Second, the operation must be conducted according to international laws and treaties recognized by the United States, particularly the law of war. Third, the campaign or operation should develop or reinforce the authority and acceptance for the host-nation government by both the governed and the international community. This last factor is frequently the decisive element.

A-22. Legitimacy is also based on the will of the American people to support the mission. The American people's perception of legitimacy is strengthened if obvious national or humanitarian interests are at stake. Their perception also depends on their assurance that American lives are not being placed at risk needlessly or carelessly.

A-23. Other interested audiences may include foreign nations, civil populations in and near the operational area, and participating multinational forces. Committed forces must sustain the legitimacy of the operation and of the host-nation government, where applicable. Security actions must balance with the need to maintain legitimacy. Commanders must consider all actions potentially competing for strategic and tactical requirements. All actions must exhibit fairness in dealing with competing factions where appropriate. Legitimacy depends on the level of consent to the force and to the host-nation government, the people's expectations, and the force's credibility.

RESTRAINT

Limit collateral damage and prevent the unnecessary use of force.

A-24. Restraint requires careful and disciplined balancing of security, the conduct of military operations, and the desired strategic end state. Excessive force antagonizes those friendly and neutral parties involved. Hence, it damages the legitimacy of the organization that uses it while potentially enhancing the legitimacy of any opposing party. The rules of engagement must be carefully matched to the strategic end state and the situation. Commanders at all levels ensure their personnel are properly trained in rules of engagement and quickly informed of any changes. Rules of engagement may vary according to national policy concerns but should always be consistent with the inherent right of self-defense.

A-25. Restraint is best achieved when rules of engagement issued at the beginning of an operation address a range of plausible situations. Commanders should consistently review and revise rules of engagement as necessary. Additionally, commanders should carefully examine them to ensure that the lives and health of Soldiers are not needlessly endangered. National concerns may lead to different rules of engagement for multinational participants; commanders must be aware of national restrictions imposed on force participants.

Appendix B
Command and Support Relationships

Command and support relationships provide the basis for unity of command and unity of effort in operations. Command relationships affect Army force generation, force tailoring, and task organization. Commanders use Army support relationships when task-organizing Army forces. All command and support relationships fall within the framework of joint doctrine. JP 1 discusses joint command relationships and authorities.

CHAIN OF COMMAND

B-1. The President and Secretary of Defense exercise authority and control of the armed forces through two distinct branches of the chain of command as described in JP 1. (See figure B-1 [taken from JP 1], page B-2.) One branch runs from the President, through the Secretary of Defense, to the combatant commanders for missions and forces assigned to combatant commands. The other branch runs from the President through the Secretary of Defense to the secretaries of the military departments. This branch is used for purposes other than operational direction of forces assigned to the combatant commands. Each military department operates under the authority, direction, and control of the secretary of that military department. These secretaries exercise authority through their respective Service chiefs over Service forces not assigned to combatant commanders. The Service chiefs, except as otherwise prescribed by law, perform their duties under the authority, direction, and control of the secretaries to whom they are directly responsible.

B-2. The typical operational chain of command extends from the combatant commander to a joint task force commander, then to a functional component commander or a Service component commander. Joint task forces and functional component commands, such as a land component, comprise forces that are normally subordinate to a Service component command but have been placed under the operational control (OPCON) of the joint task force, and subsequently to a functional component commander. Conversely, the combatant commander may designate one of the Service component commanders as the joint task force commander or as a functional component commander. In some cases, the combatant commander may not establish a joint task force, retaining operational control over subordinate functional commands and Service components directly.

B-3. Under joint doctrine, each joint force includes a Service component command that provides administrative and logistic support to Service forces under OPCON of that joint force. However, Army doctrine distinguishes between the Army component of a combatant command and Army components of subordinate joint forces. Under Army doctrine, Army Service component command (ASCC) refers to the Army component assigned to a combatant command. There is only one ASCC within a combatant command's area of responsibility. The Army components of all other joint forces are called ARFORs. **An *ARFOR* is the Army Service component headquarters for a joint task force or a joint and multinational force**. It consists of the senior Army headquarters and its commander (when not designated as the joint force commander) and all Army forces that the combatant commander subordinates to the joint task force or places under the control of a multinational force commander. The ARFOR becomes the conduit for most Service-related issues and administrative support. The Army Service component command may function as an ARFOR headquarters when the combatant commander does not exercise command and control through subordinate joint force commanders.

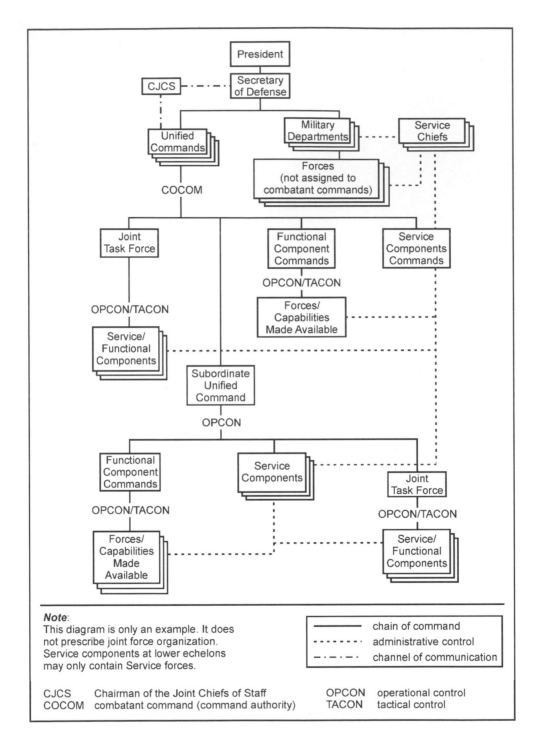

Figure B-1. Chain of command branches

B-4. The Secretary of the Army directs the flow of administrative control (ADCON). (See paragraphs B-25 through B-27.) Administrative control for Army units within a combatant command normally extends from the Secretary of the Army through the ASCC, through an ARFOR, and then to Army units assigned or attached to an Army headquarters within that joint command. However, administrative control is not tied to the operational chain of command. The Secretary of the Army may redirect some or all Service responsibilities outside the normal ASCC channels. In similar fashion, the ASCC may distribute some administrative responsibilities outside the ARFOR. Their primary considerations are the effectiveness of Army forces and the care of Soldiers.

COMBATANT COMMANDS

B-5. The Unified Command Plan establishes combatant commanders' missions and geographic responsibilities. Combatant commanders directly link operational military forces to the Secretary of Defense and the President. The Secretary of Defense deploys troops and exercises military power through the combatant commands. Six combatant commands have areas of responsibility. They are the geographic combatant commands. Each geographic combatant command has (or will have) an assigned ASCC. For doctrinal purposes, these commands become "theater armies" to distinguish them from the similar organizations assigned to functional component commands. The geographic combatant commands and their theater armies are—

- U.S. Northern Command (U.S. Army, North—USARNORTH).
- U.S. Southern Command (U.S. Army, South—USARSO).
- U.S. Central Command (U.S. Army, Central—USARCENT).
- U.S. European Command (U.S. Army, Europe—USAREUR).
- U.S. Pacific Command (U.S. Army, Pacific—USARPAC).
- U.S. Africa Command (U.S. Army, Africa—USARAF) implementation date pending.

In addition to these geographic combatant commands, U.S. Forces Korea is a subordinate unified command of U.S. Pacific Command. It has a theater army also (Eighth Army—EUSA).

B-6. There are four functional combatant commands. Each has global responsibilities. Like the geographic combatant commands, each has an ASCC assigned. These organizations are not theater armies; they are functional Service component commands. The functional combatant commands and their associated ASCCs are—

- U.S. Joint Forces Command (U.S. Army Forces Command—FORSCOM).
- U.S. Strategic Command (U.S. Army Space and Missile Defense Command/Army Strategic Command—SMDC/ARSTRAT).
- U.S. Special Operations Command (U.S. Army Special Operations Command—USASOC).
- U.S. Transportation Command (Military Surface Deployment and Distribution Command—SDDC).

JOINT TASK FORCES AND SERVICE COMPONENTS

B-7. Joint task forces are the organizations most often used by a combatant commander for contingencies. Combatant commanders establish joint task forces and designate the joint force commanders for these commands. Those commanders exercise OPCON of all U.S. forces through functional component commands, Service components, subordinate joint task forces, or a combination of these. (See figure B-2 [taken from JP 1], page B-4.) The senior Army officer assigned to a joint task force, other than the joint force commander and members of the joint task force staff, becomes the ARFOR commander. The ARFOR commander answers to the Secretary of the Army through the ASCC for most ADCON responsibilities.

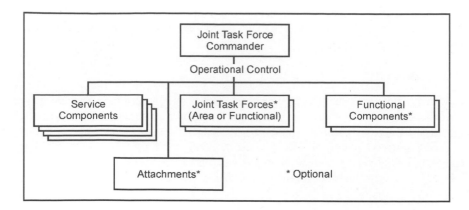

Figure B-2. Joint task force organization options

B-8. Depending on the joint task force organization, the ARFOR commander may exercise OPCON of some or all Army forces assigned to the task force. For example, an Army corps headquarters may become a joint force land component within a large joint task force. (See figure B-3, which shows an example of a joint task force organized into functional components.) The corps commander exercises OPCON of Army divisions and tactical control (TACON) of Marine Corps forces within the land component. As the senior Army headquarters, the corps becomes the ARFOR for not only the Army divisions but also all other Army units within the joint task force, including those not under OPCON of the corps. This ensures that Service responsibilities are fulfilled while giving the joint force commander maximum flexibility for employing the joint force. Unless modified by the Secretary of the Army or the ASCC, Service responsibilities continue through the ARFOR to the respective Army commanders. Army forces in figure B-3 are shaded to show this relationship. The corps has OPCON of the Army divisions and TACON of the Marine division. The corps does not have OPCON over the other Army units but does, as the ARFOR, exercise ADCON over them. The corps also assists the ASCC in controlling Army support to other Services and to any multinational forces as directed.

B-9. When an Army headquarters becomes the joint force land component as part of a joint task force, Army units subordinated to it are normally under OPCON. Marine Corps forces made available to a joint force land component command built around an Army headquarters are normally under TACON. The land component commander makes recommendations to the joint force commander on properly using attached, OPCON, or TACON assets; planning and coordinating land operations; and accomplishing such operational missions as assigned.

B-10. Navy and Coast Guard forces often operate under a joint force maritime component commander. This commander makes recommendations to the joint force commander on proper use of assets attached or under OPCON or TACON. Maritime component commanders also make recommendations concerning planning and coordinating maritime operations and accomplishing such missions.

B-11. A joint force air component commander is normally designated the supported commander for the air interdiction and counterair missions. The air component command is typically the headquarters with the majority of air assets. Like the other functional component commanders, the air component commander makes recommendations to the joint force commander on properly using assets attached or under OPCON or TACON. The air component commander makes recommendations for planning and coordinating air operations and accomplishing such missions. Additionally, the air component commander often has responsibility for airspace control authority and area air defense.

B-12. The joint force commander may organize special operations forces and conventional forces together as a joint special operations task force or a subordinate joint task force. Other functional components and subordinate task forces—such as a joint logistic task force or joint psychological operations task force—are established as required.

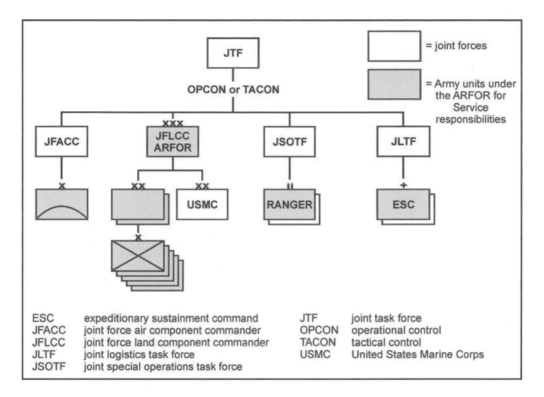

Figure B-3. Example of a joint task force showing an Army corps as joint force land component commander with ARFOR responsibilities

JOINT COMMAND RELATIONSHIPS

B-13. JP 1 specifies and details four types of joint command relationships:

- Combatant command (command authority) (COCOM).
- Operational control.
- Tactical control.
- Support.

The following paragraphs summarize important provisions of these relationships. The glossary contains complete definitions.

COMBATANT COMMAND (COMMAND AUTHORITY)

B-14. COCOM is the command authority over assigned forces vested only in commanders of combatant commands or as directed by the President or the Secretary of Defense in the Unified Command Plan and cannot be delegated or transferred. Title 10, U.S. Code, section 164 specifies it in law. Normally, the combatant commander exercises this authority through subordinate joint force commanders, Service component, and functional component commanders. COCOM includes the directive authority for logistic matters (or the authority to delegate it to a subordinate joint force commander for common support capabilities required to accomplish the subordinate's mission).

OPERATIONAL CONTROL

B-15. OPCON is the authority to perform those functions of command over subordinate forces involving—
- Organizing and employing commands and forces.
- Assigning tasks.
- Designating objectives.
- Giving authoritative direction necessary to accomplish missions.

B-16. OPCON normally includes authority over all aspects of operations and joint training necessary to accomplish missions. It does not include directive authority for logistics or matters of administration, discipline, internal organization, or unit training. The combatant commander must specifically delegate these elements of COCOM. OPCON does include the authority to delineate functional responsibilities and operational areas of subordinate joint force commanders. In two instances, the Secretary of Defense may specify adjustments to accommodate authorities beyond OPCON in an establishing directive: when transferring forces between combatant commanders or when transferring members and/or organizations from the military departments to a combatant command. Adjustments will be coordinated with the participating combatant commanders. (JP 1 discusses operational control in detail.)

TACTICAL CONTROL

B-17. TACON is inherent in OPCON. It may be delegated to and exercised by commanders at any echelon at or below the level of combatant command. TACON provides sufficient authority for controlling and directing the application of force or tactical use of combat support assets within the assigned mission or task. TACON does not provide organizational authority or authoritative direction for administrative and logistic support; the commander of the parent unit continues to exercise these authorities unless otherwise specified in the establishing directive. (JP 1 discusses tactical control in detail.)

SUPPORT

B-18. Support is a command authority in joint doctrine. A supported and supporting relationship is established by a superior commander between subordinate commanders when one organization should aid, protect, complement, or sustain another force. Designating supporting relationships is important. It conveys priorities to commanders and staffs planning or executing joint operations. Designating a support relationship does not provide authority to organize and employ commands and forces, nor does it include authoritative direction for administrative and logistic support. Joint doctrine divides support into the categories listed in table B-1.

Table B-1. Joint support categories

Category	Definition
General support	That support which is given to the supported force as a whole and not to any particular subdivision thereof (JP 1-02).
Mutual support	That support which units render each other against an enemy, because of their assigned tasks, their position relative to each other and to the enemy, and their inherent capabilities (JP 1-02).
Direct support	A mission requiring a force to support another specific force and authorizing it to answer directly to the supported force's request for assistance (JP 3-09.1).
Close support	That action of the supporting force against targets or objectives which are sufficiently near the supported force as to require detailed integration or coordination of the supporting action with the fire, movement, or other actions of the supported force (JP 1-02).

B-19. Support is, by design, somewhat vague but very flexible. Establishing authorities ensure both supported and supporting commanders understand the authority of supported commanders. Joint force commanders often establish supported and supporting relationships among components. For example, the maritime component commander is normally the supported commander for sea control operations; the air component commander is normally the supported commander for counterair operations. An Army headquarters designated as the land component may be the supporting force during some campaign phases and the supported force in other phases.

B-20. The joint force commander may establish a support relationship between functional and Service component commanders. Conducting operations across a large operational area often involves both the land and air component commanders. The joint task force commander places the land component in general support of the air component until the latter achieves air superiority. Conversely, within the land area of operations, the land component commander becomes the supported commander and the air component commander provides close support. A joint support relationship is not used when an Army commander task-organizes Army forces in a supporting role. When task-organized to support another Army force, Army forces use one of four Army support relationships. (See paragraphs B-35 through B-36.)

JOINT ASSIGNMENT AND ATTACHMENT

B-21. All forces under the jurisdiction of the secretaries of the military departments (with exception) are assigned to combatant commands or the commander, U.S. Element North America Aerospace Defense Command (known as USELEMNORAD). The exception exempts those forces necessary to carry out the functions of the military departments as noted in Title 10, U.S. Code, section 162. The assignment of forces to the combatant commands comes from the Secretary of Defense in the "Forces for Unified Commands" memorandum. According to this memorandum and the Unified Command Plan, unless otherwise directed by the President or the Secretary of Defense, all forces operating in the geographic area assigned to a specific combatant commander are assigned or attached to that combatant commander. A force assigned or attached to a combatant command may be transferred from that command to another combatant commander only when directed by the Secretary of Defense and approved by the President. The Secretary of Defense specifies the command relationship the gaining commander will exercise (and the losing commander will relinquish). Establishing authorities for subordinate unified commands and joint task forces may direct the assignment or attachment of their forces to those subordinate commands and delegate the command relationship as appropriate. (See JP 1.)

B-22. When the Secretary of Defense assigns Army forces to a combatant command, the transfer is either permanent or the duration is unknown but very lengthy. The combatant commander exercises COCOM over assigned forces. When the Secretary of Defense attaches Army units, this indicates that the transfer of units is relatively temporary. Attached forces normally return to their parent combatant command at the end of the deployment. The combatant commander exercises OPCON of the attached force. In either case, the combatant commander normally exercises OPCON over Army forces through the ASCC until the combatant commander establishes a joint task force or functional component. At that time, the combatant commander delegates OPCON to the joint task force commander. When the joint force commander establishes any command relationship, the ASCC clearly specifies ADCON responsibilities for all affected Army commanders.

COORDINATING AUTHORITY

B-23. Coordinating authority is the authority delegated to a commander or individual for coordinating specific functions or activities involving forces of two or more military departments, two or more joint force components, or two or more forces of the same Service. The commander or individual granted coordinating authority can require consultation between the agencies involved but does not have the authority to compel agreement. In the event that essential agreement cannot be obtained, the matter shall be referred to the appointing authority. Coordinating authority is a consultation relationship, not an authority through which command may be exercised. Coordinating authority is more applicable to planning and similar activities than to operations. (See JP 1.) For example, a joint security commander exercises coordinating authority over area security operations within the joint security area. Commanders or leaders at any echelon at or below combatant command may be delegated coordinating authority. These individuals may be assigned responsibilities established through a memorandum of agreement between military and nonmilitary organizations.

DIRECT LIAISON AUTHORIZED

B-24. *Direct liaison authorized* is that authority granted by a commander (any level) to a subordinate to directly consult or coordinate an action with a command or agency within or outside of the granting command. Direct liaison authorized is more applicable to planning than operations and always carries with it the requirement of keeping the commander granting direct liaison authorized informed. Direct liaison authorized is a coordination relationship, not an authority through which command may be exercised (JP 1).

ADMINISTRATIVE CONTROL

B-25. *Administrative control* is direction or exercise of authority over subordinate or other organizations in respect to administration and support, including organization of Service forces, control of resources and equipment, personnel management, unit logistics, individual and unit training, readiness, mobilization, demobilization, discipline, and other matters not included in the operational missions of the subordinate or other organizations (JP 1). It is a Service authority, not a joint authority. It is exercised under the authority of and is delegated by the Secretary of the Army. ADCON is synonymous with the Army's Title 10 authorities and responsibilities.

B-26. ADCON of Army forces involves the entire Army. Figure B-4 identifies major responsibilities of the Department of the Army and illustrates their normal distribution between the Army generating force and operating forces. The generating force consists of those Army organizations whose primary mission is to generate and sustain the operational Army's capabilities for employment by joint force commanders. *Operating forces* consist of those forces whose primary missions are to participate in combat and the integral supporting elements thereof (JP 1-02). Often, commanders in the operating force and commanders in the generating force subdivide specific responsibilities. Army generating force capabilities and organizations are linked to operating forces through co-location and reachback.

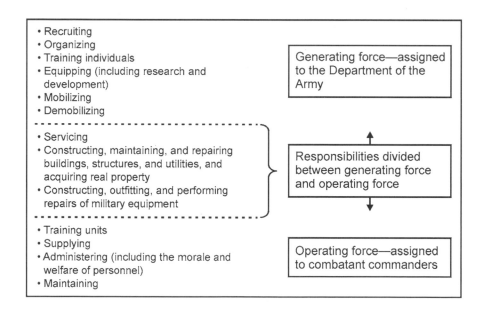

Figure B-4. Normal distribution of Army administrative control responsibilities

B-27. The ASCC is always the senior Army headquarters assigned to a combatant command. Its commander exercises command authorities as assigned by the combatant commander and ADCON as delegated by the Secretary of the Army. ADCON is the Army's authority to administer and support Army forces even while in a combatant command area of responsibility. COCOM is the basic authority for command and control of the same Army forces. The Army is obligated to meet the combatant commander's requirements for the operational forces. Essentially, ADCON directs the Army's support of operational force requirements. Unless modified by the Secretary of the Army, administrative responsibilities normally flow from Department of the Army through the ASCC to those Army forces assigned or attached to that combatant command. ASCCs usually "share" ADCON for at least some administrative or support functions. "Shared ADCON" refers to the internal allocation of Title 10, U.S. Code, section 3013(b) responsibilities and functions. This is especially true for Reserve Component forces. Certain administrative functions, such as pay, stay with the Reserve Component headquarters, even after unit mobilization. Shared ADCON also applies to direct reporting units of the Army that typically perform single or unique functions. The direct reporting unit, rather than the ASCC, typically manages individual and unit training for these units. The Secretary of the Army directs shared ADCON.

ARMY COMMAND AND SUPPORT RELATIONSHIPS

B-28. Army command relationships are similar but not identical to joint command authorities and relationships. Differences stem from the way Army forces task-organize internally and the need for a system of support relationships between Army forces. Another important difference is the requirement for Army commanders to handle the administrative support requirements that meet the needs of Soldiers. These differences allow for flexible allocation of Army capabilities within various Army echelons. Army command and support relationships are the basis for building Army task organizations. A *task organization* **is a temporary grouping of forces designed to accomplish a particular mission**. Certain responsibilities are inherent in the Army's command and support relationships.

ARMY COMMAND RELATIONSHIPS

B-29. Table B-2, page B-10, lists the Army command relationships. Command relationships define superior and subordinate relationships between unit commanders. By specifying a chain of command, command relationships unify effort and give commanders the ability to employ subordinate forces with maximum flexibility. Army command relationships identify the degree of control of the gaining Army commander. The type of command relationship often relates to the expected longevity of the relationship between the headquarters involved and quickly identifies the degree of support that the gaining and losing Army commanders provide.

B-30. *Organic* forces are those assigned to and forming an essential part of a military organization. Organic parts of a unit are those listed in its table of organization for the Army, Air Force, and Marine Corps, and are assigned to the administrative organizations of the operating forces for the Navy (JP 1-02). Joint command relationships do not include organic because a joint force commander is not responsible for the organizational structure of units. That is a Service responsibility.

B-31. The Army establishes organic command relationships through organizational documents such as tables of organization and equipment and tables of distribution and allowances. If temporarily task-organized with another headquarters, organic units return to the control of their organic headquarters after completing the mission. To illustrate, within a brigade combat team (BCT), the entire brigade is organic. In contrast, within most modular support brigades, there is a "base" of organic battalions and companies and a variable mix of assigned and attached battalions and companies. (See appendix C.)

B-32. Army assigned units remain subordinate to the higher headquarters for extended periods, typically years. Assignment is based on the needs of the Army and is formalized by orders rather than organizational documents. Although force tailoring or task-organizing may temporarily detach units, they eventually return to their either their headquarters of assignment or their organic headquarters. Attached units are temporarily subordinated to the gaining headquarters, and the period may be lengthy, often months or longer. They
return to their parent headquarters (assigned or organic) when the reason for the attachment ends. The Army headquarters that receives another Army unit through assignment or attachment assumes responsibility for the ADCON requirements, and particularly sustainment, that normally extend down to that echelon, unless modified by directives or orders. For example, when an Army division commander attaches an engineer battalion to a brigade combat team, the brigade commander assumes responsibility for the unit training, maintenance, resupply, and unit-level reporting for that battalion.

Table B-2. Command relationships

If relation-ship is:	Then inherent responsibilities:							
	Have command relation-ship with:	May be task-organized by:[1]	Unless modified, ADCON responsi-bility goes through:	Are assigned position or AO by:	Provide liaison to:	Establish/maintain communi-cations with:	Have priorities establish-ed by:	Can impose on gaining unit further command or support relationship of:
Organic	All organic forces organized with the HQ	Organic HQ	Army HQ specified in organizing document	Organic HQ	N/A	N/A	Organic HQ	Attached; OPCON; TACON; GS; GSR; R; DS
Assigned	Combatant command	Gaining HQ	Gaining Army HQ	OPCON chain of command	As required by OPCON	As required by OPCON	ASCC or Service-assigned HQ	As required by OPCON HQ
Attached	Gaining unit	Gaining unit	Gaining Army HQ	Gaining unit	As required by gaining unit	Unit to which attached	Gaining unit	Attached; OPCON; TACON; GS; GSR; R; DS
OPCON	Gaining unit	Parent unit and gaining unit; gaining unit may pass OPCON to lower HQ[1]	Parent unit	Gaining unit	As required by gaining unit	As required by gaining unit and parent unit	Gaining unit	OPCON; TACON; GS; GSR; R; DS
TACON	Gaining unit	Parent unit	Parent unit	Gaining unit	As required by gaining unit	As required by gaining unit and parent unit	Gaining unit	TACON;GS GSR; R; DS

Note: [1] In NATO, the gaining unit may not task-organize a multinational force. (See TACON.)

ADCON	administrative control	HQ	headquarters
AO	area of operations	N/A	not applicable
ASCC	Army Service component command	NATO	North Atlantic Treaty Organization
DS	direct support	OPCON	operational control
GS	general support	R	reinforcing
GSR	general support–reinforcing	TACON	tactical control

B-33. Army commanders normally place a unit OPCON or TACON to a gaining headquarters for a given mission, lasting perhaps a few days. OPCON lets the gaining commander task-organize and direct forces. TACON does not let the gaining commander task-organize the unit. Hence, TACON is the command relationship often used between Army, other Service, and multinational forces within a task organization, but rarely between Army forces. Neither OPCON nor TACON affects ADCON responsibilities. To modify the example used above, if the Army division commander placed the engineer battalion OPCON to the BCT, the gaining brigade commander would not be responsible for the unit training, maintenance, resupply, and unit-level reporting of the engineers. Those responsibilities would remain with the parent maneuver enhancement brigade.

B-34. The ASCC and ARFOR monitor changes in joint organization carefully and may adjust ADCON responsibilities based on the situation. For example, if a joint task force commander places an Army brigade under TACON of a Marine division, the ARFOR may switch some or all unit ADCON responsibilities to another Army headquarters, based on geography and ability to provide administration and support to that Army force.

ARMY SUPPORT RELATIONSHIPS

B-35. Table B-3 lists Army support relationships. Army support relationships are not a command authority and are more specific than the joint support relationships. Commanders establish support relationships when subordination of one unit to another is inappropriate. They assign a support relationship when—

- The support is more effective if a commander with the requisite technical and tactical expertise controls the supporting unit, rather than the supported commander.
- The echelon of the supporting unit is the same as or higher than that of the supported unit. For example, the supporting unit may be a brigade, and the supported unit may be a battalion. It would be inappropriate for the brigade to be subordinated to the battalion, hence the use of an Army support relationship.
- The supporting unit supports several units simultaneously. The requirement to set support priorities to allocate resources to supported units exists. Assigning support relationships is one aspect of mission command.

Table B-3. Army support relationships

If relation-ship is:	Then inherent responsibilities:							
	Have command relation-ship with:	May be task-organized by:	Receives sustain-ment from:	Are assigned position or an area of operations by:	Provide liaison to:	Establish/ maintain communi-cations with:	Have priorities established by:	Can impose on gaining unit further command or support relation-ship by:
Direct support[1]	Parent unit	Parent unit	Parent unit	Supported unit	Supported unit	Parent unit; supported unit	Supported unit	See note[1]
Reinforc-ing	Parent unit	Parent unit	Parent unit	Reinforced unit	Reinforced unit	Parent unit; reinforced unit	Reinforced unit; then parent unit	Not applicable
General support–reinforc-ing	Parent unit	Parent unit	Parent unit	Parent unit	Reinforced unit and as required by parent unit	Reinforced unit and as required by parent unit	Parent unit; then reinforced unit	Not applicable
General support	Parent unit	Parent unit	Parent unit	Parent unit	As required by parent unit	As required by parent unit	Parent unit	Not applicable

Note: [1] Commanders of units in direct support may further assign support relationships between their subordinate units and elements of the supported unit after coordination with the supported commander.

B-36. Army support relationships allow supporting commanders to employ their units' capabilities to achieve results required by supported commanders. Support relationships are graduated from an exclusive supported and supporting relationship between two units—as in direct support—to a broad level of support extended to all units under the control of the higher headquarters—as in general support. Support relationships do not alter ADCON. Commanders specify and change support relationships through task-organizing.

OTHER RELATIONSHIPS

B-37. Several other relationships established by higher headquarters exist with units that are not in command or support relationships. (See table B-4, page B-12.) These relationships are limited or specialized to a greater degree than the command and support relationships. These limited relationships are not used when tailoring or task-organizing Army forces. Use of these specialized relationships helps clarify certain aspects of OPCON or ADCON.

Table B-4. Other relationships

Relation-ship	Operational use	Established by	Authority and limitations
Training and readiness oversight	TRO is an authority exercised by a combatant commander over assigned RC forces not on active duty. Through TRO, CCDRs shape RC training and readiness. Upon mobilization of the RC forces, TRO is no longer applicable.	The CCDR identified in the "Forces for Unified Commands" memorandum. The CCDR normally delegates TRO to the ASCC. (For most RC forces, the CCDR is JFCOM and the ASCC is FORSCOM.)	TRO allows the CCDR to provide guidance on operational requirements and training priorities, review readiness reports, and review mobilization plans for RC forces. TRO is not a command relationship. ARNG forces remain under the command and control of their respective State Adjutant Generals until mobilized for Federal service. USAR forces remain under the command and control of the USARC until mobilized.
Direct liaison authorized[1]	Allows planning and direct collaboration between two units assigned to different commands, often based on anticipated tailoring and task organization changes.	The parent unit headquarters. This is a coordination relationship, not an authority through which command may be exercised.	Limited to planning and coordination between units.
Aligned	Informal relationship between a theater army and other Army units identified for use in a specific geographic combatant command.	Theater army and parent ASCC.	Normally establishes information channels between the gaining theater army and Army units that are likely to be committed to that area of responsibility.

Note: [1] See also paragraph B-24.

ARNG	Army National Guard	RC	Reserve Component
ASCC	Army Service component command	TRO	training and readiness oversight
CCDR	combatant commander	USAR	U.S. Army Reserve
FORSCOM	U.S. Army Forces Command	USARC	U.S. Army Reserve Command
JFCOM	Joint Forces Command		

B-38. *Training and readiness oversight* is the authority that combatant commanders may exercise over assigned Reserve Component forces when not on active duty or when on active duty for training. As a matter of Department of Defense policy, this authority includes: a. Providing guidance to Service component commanders on operational requirements and priorities to be addressed in military department training and readiness programs; b. Commenting on Service component program recommendations and budget requests; c. Coordinating and approving participation by assigned Reserve Component forces in joint exercises and other joint training when on active duty for training or performing inactive duty for training; d. Obtaining and reviewing readiness and inspection reports on assigned Reserve Component forces; and e. Coordinating and reviewing mobilization plans (including postmobilization training activities and deployability validation procedures) developed for assigned Reserve Component forces (JP 1).

B-39. Responsibilities for both training and readiness are inherent in ADCON and exercised by unit commanders for their units. Army National Guard forces are organized by the Department of the Army under their respective states. These forces remain under command of the governor of that state until mobilized for Federal service. U.S. Army Reserve forces are assigned to U.S. Army Reserve Command. For Army National Guard units, the combatant commander normally exercises training and readiness oversight through their ASCC; for most, this is U.S. Army Forces Command. The ASCC coordinates with the appropriate State Adjutants General and Army National Guard divisions to refine mission-essential task lists for Army National Guard units. The ASCC coordinates mission-essential task lists for Army Reserve units with the U.S. Army Reserve Command. When Reserve Component units align with an expeditionary force package during Army force generation, U.S. Army Forces Command establishes coordinating relationships as required between Regular Army and Reserve Component units. When mobilized, Reserve Component units are assigned or attached to their gaining headquarters. Most operating force ADCON responsibilities, including unit training and readiness, shift to the gaining headquarters.

B-40. The shift to full spectrum operations and smaller, more versatile units affects how Regular Army forces manage training and readiness. Army force packages for the combatant commanders combine forces from many different parent organizations through Army force generation. The Army assigns or attaches Regular Army forces to various Army headquarters based on factors such as stationing, unit history, and habitual association of units in training. Different Army headquarters may share ADCON to optimize administration and support. For example, U.S. Army Forces Command may attach a BCT to a division headquarters located on a different installation. That division commander has training and readiness responsibilities for the BCT but does not control the training resources located at the BCT's installation. The senior Army commander on the BCT's installation manages training resources such as ranges and simulation centers. At the direction of the Secretary of the Army, the commanders share ADCON responsibilities. If the division headquarters deploys on an extended mission and the BCT remains, training and readiness responsibilities for the BCT shift to another commander. Headquarters, Department of the Army or another appropriate Army authority redistributes ADCON responsibilities for the BCT to a new headquarters. When the BCT deploys to a geographic combatant command, ADCON passes to the gaining theater army unless modified by the Secretary of the Army. (FMs 7-0 and 7-1 discuss training responsibilities.)

B-41. Alignment is informal relationship between a theater army and other Army units identified for use in the area of responsibility of a specific geographic combatant command. Alignment helps focus unit exercises and other training on a particular region. This may lead to establishment of direct liaison authorized between the aligned unit and a different ASCC. Any modular Army force may find itself included in an expeditionary force package heading to a different combatant command. Therefore, Army commanders maintain a balance between regional focus and global capability.

REGULATORY AUTHORITIES

B-42. Regulations, policies, and other authoritative sources also direct and guide Army forces, Army commands, direct reporting units, ASCCs, and other Army elements. The Army identifies technical matters, such as network operations or contracting, and assigns responsibilities for them to an appropriate organization. These organizations use technical channels established by regulation, policy, or directive. Commanders may also delegate authority for control of certain technical functions to staff officers or subordinate commanders. (FM 6-0 discusses technical channels.)

B-43. The primary regulation governing the missions, functions, and command and staff relationships, including ADCON, of the subordinate elements of the Department of the Army is AR 10-87. This regulation prescribes the relationships and responsibilities among Army forces, Army commands, direct reporting units, and ASCCs. It includes channels for technical supervision, advice, and support for specific functions among various headquarters, agencies, and units. Other regulations and policies specify responsibilities in accordance with Department of Defense directives and U.S. statutes.

This page intentionally left blank.

Appendix C

The Army Modular Force

This appendix provides an overview of Army modular organizations. In 2003, the Army implemented a fundamental shift toward a brigade-based force. The ongoing transformation of the Army will result in stand-alone division and corps headquarters. Brigade combat teams, modular support brigades, and functional brigades will be pooled for use as part of expeditionary force packages that enhance the flexibility and responsiveness of the Army. The combined arms brigade combat teams become the centerpiece for Army maneuver. They will attach to a higher echelon headquarters—a division, corps, or theater army—as part of a force-tailored formation based on operational requirements.

BACKGROUND

C-1. Today's operational environment requires responsive Army forces tailored to individual combatant commanders' needs. The highly integrated organization of the Army's divisions in the late 1990's made it difficult to deploy divisional units apart from their divisional base and keep the rest of the division ready for other missions. Coupled with the increasing need to employ land forces at the outset of a campaign, the Army needed to reorganize around smaller, more versatile formations able to deploy more promptly.

C-2. No single, large fixed formation can support the diverse requirements of full spectrum operations. To meet the requirements of the geographic combatant commanders, the Army has developed the capability to rapidly tailor and task-organize expeditionary force packages. A force package may consist of any combination of light, medium, and heavy forces; it can blend Regular Army, Army National Guard, and U.S. Army Reserve units and Soldiers.

C-3. The nature of modern land operations has changed in geography and time. In general, operations have become increasingly distributed in space while more simultaneous in time. At the tactical and operational levels, subordinate units routinely operate in noncontiguous areas of operations. This contrasts sharply with the contiguous and hierarchical arrangement of land forces in operations prevalent in the past. More agile forces, improvements in command and control, and continuing integration of joint capabilities at lower echelons all contribute to these changes.

C-4. The other prominent shift in capability came with the introduction and proliferation of satellite-based communications and other advanced information systems for command and control. Command and control of widely dispersed formations no longer entirely relies on terrestrial, line-of-sight communications. When separated by hundreds of miles, today's commanders can still communicate with subordinates and maintain a common operational picture. The Army is only beginning to realize the benefits of these advances. It continues to leverage technology and reshape processes to best integrate new capabilities.

C-5. Tactical operations continue to evolve into distributed, noncontiguous forms. Army forces need versatile and deployable headquarters suited for contingencies and protracted operations. The Army provides the majority of land component command headquarters and joint task force headquarters for contingency operations. The complexity of counterinsurgency campaigns, such as those in Afghanistan and Iraq, require Army headquarters to function as joint and multinational platforms. While dealing with complex issues, the headquarters deploy, evolve, and tailor their compositions as the campaign progresses. As recent natural disasters showed, Army headquarters often provide the command and control element for Regular Army, Army National Guard, and U.S. Army Reserve elements that respond to disasters of all types.

C-6. To meet joint requirements, the Army reorganized its operating forces beginning in 2003. Today, the Army can provide land combat power tailored for any combination of offensive, defensive, and stability or civil support operations as part of an interdependent joint force. Brigades are the principal tactical units for conducting operations. To provide higher echelon command and control, the Army fields a mix of tactical and operational headquarters able to function as land force, joint, multinational, and Service component command headquarters. The headquarters mix is not a rigid hierarchy and does not require a standard array of forces. Each headquarters provides a menu of capabilities to best match the combatant commander's requirements.

C-7. The combatant commanders' requirements are determined by the National Military Strategy, the Joint Strategic Capabilities Plan (as specified in the "Forces for" portions), and operational requirements. The strategic Army role of providing forces to meet global requirements is called force generation. As part of force generation, the Department of the Army establishes manning, training, and readiness cycles; assigns forces to headquarters; and manages modernization. Strategic organization establishes goals for force generation cycles based on Regular Army, Army National Guard, and U.S. Army Reserve manning and readiness cycles.

DIVISION ECHELON AND ABOVE

C-8. The Army of Excellence structure for headquarters and large formations has evolved into three modular headquarters organizations. The Army Service component command focuses on combatant command-level landpower employment. It supports joint, interagency, intergovernmental, and multinational forces within a combatant commander's area of responsibility. The corps provides a headquarters that specializes in operations as a land component command headquarters, as a joint task force for contingencies, or as an intermediate tactical headquarters within large groupings of land forces. The division is optimized for tactical control of brigades during land operations. All three headquarters are modular entities designed to use forces tailored for specified joint operations. All three are also stand-alone headquarters unconstrained by a fixed formation of subordinate units. While three types of modular headquarters exist, the Army forces they control are organized for two broad echelons—theater and tactical. Each set consists primarily of brigades.

THEATER ARMY HEADQUARTERS COMMANDS

C-9. The doctrinal name for the Army Service component command of a geographic combatant command is theater army. The theater army is the primary vehicle for Army support to Army, joint, interagency, intergovernmental, and multinational forces operating across the area of responsibility. When the combatant commander acts as the joint force commander during major combat operations, the theater army may provide the land component commander and headquarters. In that case, it exercises operational control (OPCON) over land forces deployed to a joint operations area. The theater army headquarters continues to perform area of responsibility-wide functions in addition to its operational responsibilities. These functions include reception, staging, onward movement, and integration; logistics over-the-shore operations; and security coordination. (Figure C-1 shows an example of a theater army headquarters organized as a land component command.) When required, the theater army can provide a headquarters able to command and control a joint task force for contingencies with other Service augmentation.

C-10. As the Army Service component command, the theater army exercises administrative control (ADCON) over all Army forces in the area of responsibility unless modified by the Department of the Army. This includes forces assigned, attached, or OPCON to the combatant command. The Army Service component command provides Army support to designated theater-level forces. It also provides this support to joint, interagency, intergovernmental, and multinational elements as the combatant commander directs. The Army Service component command integrates Army forces into execution of theater security cooperation plans as well. It has several theater-level formations associated with it.

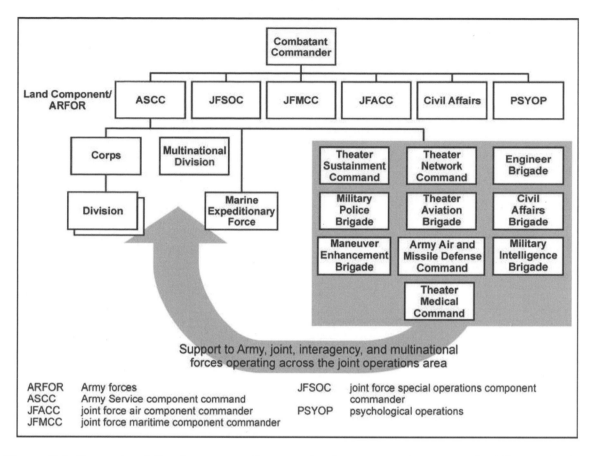

Figure C-1. Example of theater army acting as a land component command while continuing Army support

THEATER-LEVEL FORMATIONS

C-11. An array of theater-level forces may be assigned, attached, or OPCON to a theater army headquarters. Each theater army headquarters normally has organizations providing theater-level capabilities aligned with it or under its control. These organizations include—

- Theater sustainment command.
- Military intelligence brigade.
- Theater network command or brigade.
- Regionally focused civil affairs brigade or planning team.
- Regionally focused medical command.
- Regionally focused air and missile defense command.

C-12. When the theater army is the land component command for major combat operations, several functional commands may augment it. These commands can include—

- Engineer.
- Military police.
- Criminal investigation.
- Aviation.

These commands consist of units from the Regular Army, Army National Guard, and U.S. Army Reserve.

C-13. Several functional brigades are also available to support theater-level operations. They may be task-organized under theater-level functional commands or be directly subordinate to the theater army. When required, the theater army may task-organize functional brigades to corps or divisions. Examples of functional brigades include the following:

- Civil affairs.
- Engineer.
- Theater aviation.
- Military police.
- Chemical, biological, radiological, and nuclear.
- Air and missile defense.
- Medical.

CORPS

C-14. Large land forces require an intermediate echelon between the divisions that control brigade combat teams (BCTs) and the theater army serving as the land component command. Other factors requiring an intermediate headquarters may include—

- The mission's complexity.
- Multinational participation.
- Span of control.

C-15. When required, a corps may become an intermediate tactical headquarters under the land component command, with OPCON of multiple divisions (including multinational or Marine Corps formations) or other large tactical formations. (See figure C-2.) The theater army headquarters tailors the corps headquarters to meet mission requirements. The corps' flexibility allows the Army to meet the needs of joint force commanders for an intermediate land command while maintaining a set of headquarters for contingencies.

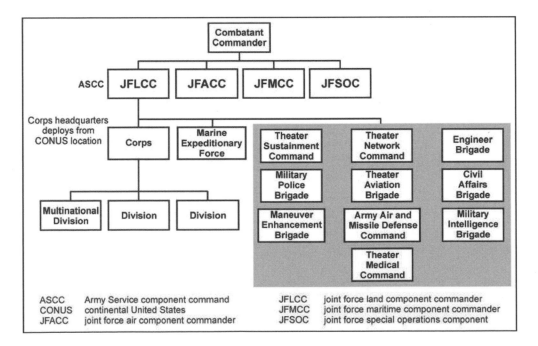

Figure C-2. Corps as an intermediate land force headquarters

C-16. The corps is also a primary candidate headquarters for joint operations. It can rapidly transition to either a joint task force or land component command headquarters for contingency or protracted operations. It can deploy to any area of responsibility to provide command and control for Army, joint, and multinational forces. The corps does not have any echelon-specific units other than the organic corps head-quarters. It can control any mix of modular brigades and divisions, as well as other Service or multinational forces. When used as a land component or as an intermediate tactical headquarters, the corps may also be designated as the ARFOR, with ADCON responsibility for all Army forces subordinate to the joint task force. (Appendix B discusses ARFOR and ADCON responsibilities.)

C-17. When directed, a corps trains as a joint headquarters for contingency operations. With minimum joint augmentation, this headquarters can initiate operations as a joint task force or land component command for contingencies. For sustained operations in this role, a corps is augmented according to an appropriate joint manning document. The corps can also serve as a deployable base for a multinational headquarters directing protracted operations.

DIVISION

C-18. Divisions are the Army's primary tactical warfighting headquarters. Their principal task is directing subordinate brigade operations. Divisions are not fixed formations. They exercise command and control over any mix of brigades and do not have any organic forces beyond their headquarters elements. Their organic structure includes communications network, life support, and command post elements. These provide significant flexibility. With appropriate joint augmentation, a division can be the joint task force or land component command headquarters for small contingencies. The headquarters staff has a functional organization. It also includes organic joint network capability and liaison teams.

C-19. Divisions can control up to six BCTs in major combat operations. They can control more BCTs in protracted stability operations. A division force package may include any mix of heavy, infantry, and Stryker BCTs. In addition to BCTs, each division controls a tailored array of modular support brigades and functional brigades.

C-20. Division headquarters normally have four BCTs attached for training and readiness purposes. However, these brigades may or may not deploy with the division as part of an expeditionary force package. Since divisions have no organic structure beyond the headquarters, all types of brigades may not be present in an operation. In some operations, divisions may control multiple support brigades of the same type. They may also control functional groups, battalions, or separate companies; however, these are normally task-organized to a brigade. The important point is that division organizations vary for each operation. However, for major combat operations, divisions should have at least one of each type of support brigade attached or OPCON to it. (Figures C-3 and C-4, page C-6, illustrate two possible division organizations. Many more combinations are possible.)

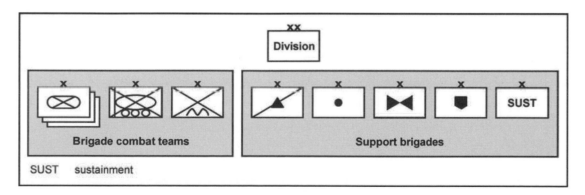

Figure C-3. Example of tailored divisions in offensive operations

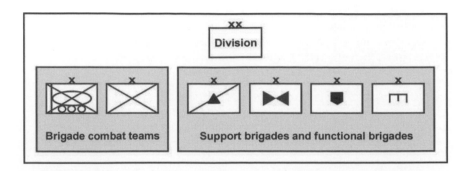

Figure C-4. Example of tailored divisions in defensive operations

BRIGADE COMBAT TEAMS

C-21. As combined arms organizations, BCTs form the basic building block of the Army's tactical formations. They are the principal means of executing engagements. Three standardized BCT designs exist: heavy, infantry, and Stryker. Battalion-sized maneuver, fires, reconnaissance, and sustainment units are organic to BCTs.

C-22. BCTs are modular organizations. They begin as a cohesive combined arms team that can be further task-organized. Commands often augment them for a specific mission with capabilities not organic to the BCT structure. Augmentation might include lift or attack aviation, armor, cannon or rocket artillery, air defense, military police, civil affairs, psychological operations elements, combat engineers, or additional information systems assets. This organizational flexibility allows BCTs to function across the spectrum of conflict.

C-23. The Army plans to convert BCTs to very advanced combined arms formations equipped with the family of future combat systems. These highly modernized brigades will consist of three combined arms battalions, a non-line-of-sight cannon battalion, reconnaissance surveillance and target acquisition squadron, brigade support battalion, brigade intelligence and communications company, and a headquarters company. The brigade combat teams equipped with future combat systems will improve the strategic and operational reach of ground combat formations without sacrificing lethality or survivability. Well before the future combat systems brigades join the operating forces, the Army will field some advanced systems to the current force.

HEAVY BRIGADE COMBAT TEAM

C-24. Heavy BCTs are balanced combined arms units that execute operations with shock and speed. (See figure C-5.) Their main battle tanks, self-propelled artillery, and fighting vehicle-mounted infantry provide tremendous striking power. Heavy BCTs require significant strategic air- and sealift to deploy and sustain. Their fuel consumption may limit operational reach. However, this is offset by the heavy BCT's unmatched tactical mobility and firepower. Heavy BCTs include organic military intelligence, artillery, signal, engineer, reconnaissance, and sustainment capabilities.

INFANTRY BRIGADE COMBAT TEAM

C-25. The infantry BCT requires less strategic lift than other BCTs. (See figure C-6.) When supported with intratheater airlift, infantry BCTs have theaterwide operational reach. The infantry Soldier is the centerpiece of the infantry BCT. Organic antitank, military intelligence, artillery, signal, engineer, reconnaissance, and sustainment elements allow the infantry BCT commander to employ the force in combined arms formations. Infantry BCTs work best for operations in close terrain and densely populated areas. They are easier to sustain than the other BCTs. Selected infantry BCTs include special-purpose capabilities for airborne or air assault operations.

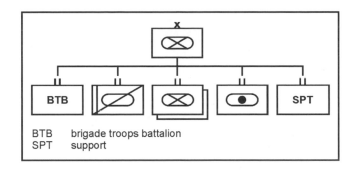

Figure C-5. Heavy brigade combat team

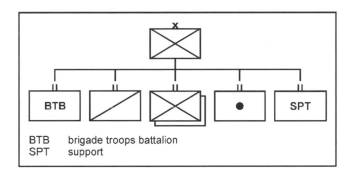

Figure C-6. Infantry brigade combat team

STRYKER BRIGADE COMBAT TEAM

C-26. The Stryker BCT balances combined arms capabilities with significant strategic and intratheater mobility. (See figure C-7.) Designed around the Stryker wheeled armored combat system in several variants, the Stryker BCT has considerable operational reach. It is more deployable than the heavy BCT and has greater tactical mobility, protection, and firepower than the infantry BCT. Stryker BCTs have excellent dismounted capability. The Stryker BCT includes military intelligence, signal, engineer, antitank, artillery, reconnaissance, and sustainment elements. This design lets Stryker BCTs commit combined arms elements down to company level in urban and other complex terrain against a wide range of opponents.

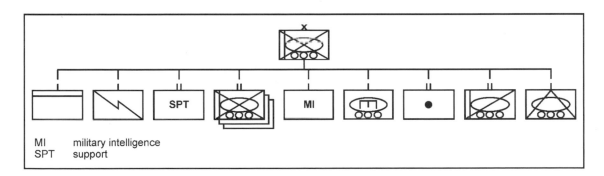

Figure C-7. Stryker brigade combat team

MODULAR SUPPORT BRIGADES

C-27. Five types of modular support brigades complement the BCTs: the battlefield surveillance brigade, fires brigade, combat aviation brigade, maneuver enhancement brigade, and sustainment brigade. These brigades provide multifunctional capabilities to deployed forces. More than one type of support brigade may be task-organized to a division or corps (except for sustainment brigades, which provide general or direct support to a division or corps). In turn, commands may make these brigades available to other Service components of the joint force. Support brigades have the organic expertise to command and control various unit types. Theater armies tailor them by adding functional battalions to or subtracting them from the organic command and control headquarters. The signal and maintenance capabilities of a support brigade headquarters also allows the higher headquarters to task-organize them to a corps, headquarters of another Service, or joint headquarters.

C-28. The number and type of subordinate units vary among the different types of brigades. Four types of support brigades operate as part of a division-sized expeditionary force: the battlefield surveillance brigade, fires brigade, combat aviation brigade, and maneuver enhancement brigade. They are normally assigned, attached, or placed OPCON to a division. Normally, the theater army attaches the sustainment brigade to the theater sustainment command. This brigade provides either general or direct support to forces under the divisions. For a major combat operation, the higher headquarters normally task-organizes one of each type of the five support brigades to a division headquarters.

BATTLEFIELD SURVEILLANCE BRIGADE

C-29. The battlefield surveillance brigade has military intelligence, reconnaissance and surveillance, and requisite sustainment and communications capabilities. (See figure C-8.) The headquarters and headquarters company provides command and control of brigade operations. The military intelligence battalion provides unmanned aircraft systems, signals intelligence, human intelligence, and counterintelligence capabilities. The reconnaissance and surveillance battalion provides reconnaissance and surveillance capabilities, including mounted scout platoons and mobile long-range surveillance teams. The brigade support company provides sustainment for the brigade. The network company provides a communications backbone. This allows the battlefield surveillance brigade to communicate throughout the division area of operations as well as with support assets associated with Army Service component command- and national-level intelligence agencies. Battlefield surveillance brigades can be tailored for the mission before deployment or task-organized by the higher headquarters once deployed. Typical augmentation includes—

- Ground reconnaissance.
- Manned and unmanned Army aviation assets.
- Military intelligence assets, including human intelligence, aerial exploitation, and other national-level assets.
- Armored, infantry, and combined arms units.

C-30. The battlefield surveillance brigade conducts intelligence, surveillance, and reconnaissance (ISR) operations. This capability lets the division commander focus combat power, execute current operations, and prepare for future operations simultaneously. Battlefield surveillance brigades are not designed to conduct guard or cover operations. Those operations may entail fighting to develop the tactical situation; they require a BCT or aviation brigade.

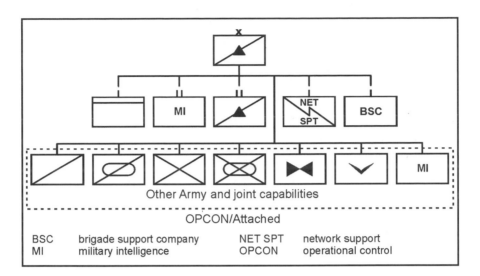

Figure C-8. Battlefield surveillance brigade

FIRES BRIGADE

C-31. Fires brigades are normally assigned, attached, or OPCON to a division. However, they may be OPCON to a task force, land component command, or other Service or functional component. (See figure C-9.) Fires brigades are task-organized based on their assigned tasks.

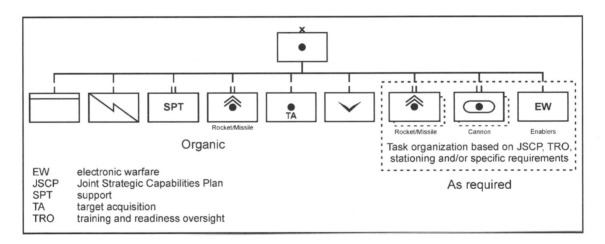

Figure C-9. Fires brigade

C-32. Organic fires brigade assets include a Multiple Launch Rocket System battalion, headquarters battery, and target acquisition battery. Brigades may be task-organized with additional Multiple Launch Rocket System and cannon battalions, counterfire radars, and joint information operations assets. The brigade's higher headquarters usually assigns the brigade missions in terms of target sets to engage, target priorities, or effects to achieve. The situation may also require the brigade to control joint fires assets.

C-33. A fires brigade's primary task is conducting strike operations. This task requires placing ISR and electronic attack capabilities OPCON to the brigade headquarters. Alternatively, the battlefield surveillance brigade can retain control of ISR assets and provide targeting information to the fires brigade through a support relationship.

C-34. Fires brigades perform the following tasks:
- Conduct strike operations.
- Support BCTs and other brigades.
- Conduct joint missions separate from the division.
- Conduct fire support missions for the division and brigades, including counterfire and attacks on specific targets in the division's area of operations.

COMBAT AVIATION BRIGADE

C-35. Most of the Army's aviation combat power resides in multifunctional combat aviation brigades. These organizations can be task-organized based on the mission. They include various types of organizations, with manned and unmanned systems. Combat aviation brigades are organized to support divisions, BCTs, and support brigades. (See figure C-10.) They specialize in providing combat capabilities to multiple BCTs. However, they can be task-organized to support a theater army or corps acting as a joint task force or land component command.

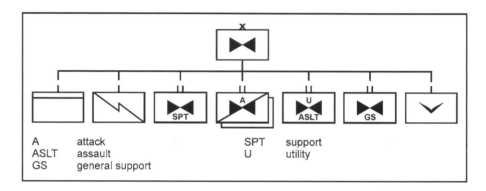

Figure C-10. Combat aviation brigade

C-36. Based on priorities and missions, a combat aviation brigade coordinates operational details directly with supported organizations. Combat aviation brigades typically conduct the following missions:
- Attack.
- Reconnaissance.
- Security.
- Movement to contact.
- Air assault.
- Air movement.
- Aerial casualty evacuation.
- Personnel recovery.
- Command and control support.

SUSTAINMENT BRIGADE

C-37. Sustainment brigades normally have a command relationship with a theater sustainment command and provide general or direct support to divisions and brigades. In major combat operations, the sustainment brigade may be under OPCON of or provide direct support to a division. Sustainment brigades have a flexible organization designed to be task-organized to meet mission requirements. (See figure C-11.) They have a command and staff structure able to control operational- or tactical-level sustainment.

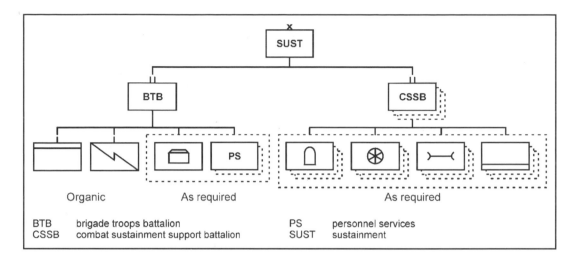

Figure C-11. Sustainment brigade

C-38. The higher headquarters usually reinforces the sustainment brigade with several different modular sustainment elements. The types and quantities of these attachments depend on the mission and the number, size, and type of organizations requiring support.

C-39. A sustainment brigade's only organic unit is its brigade troops battalion. This battalion provides command and control for assigned and attached personnel and units. It directs sustainment operations for the brigade headquarters.

MANEUVER ENHANCEMENT BRIGADE

C-40. Maneuver enhancement brigades command and control forces that provide protection and other support to the force. They are tailored with the capabilities required for each operation. More than one brigade may be assigned to a division or corps. (See figure C-12.) Commands may also attach these brigades directly to the theater army to serve in the theater army area of operations or joint security area.

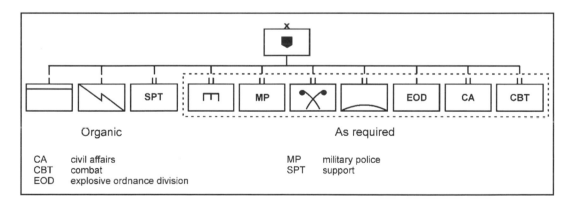

Figure C-12. Maneuver enhancement brigade

C-41. Maneuver enhancement brigades are designed to control the following types of organizations:
- Engineer.
- Military police.
- Chemical, biological, radiological, and nuclear.
- Civil affairs.

- Air and missile defense.
- Explosive ordnance disposal.
- Tactical combat force (when given an area security mission).

C-42. Typical missions for maneuver enhancement brigades are to—
- Conduct area security operations.
- Construct, maintain, and sustain lines of communications.
- Provide mobility and countermobility support.
- Provide vertical, runway, and road construction.
- Conduct chemical, biological, radiological, and nuclear defense throughout the area of operations.
- Conduct limited offensive and defensive tasks.
- Conduct some stability tasks.
- Conduct consequence management operations.

C-43. Maneuver enhancement brigades are organized and trained to conduct selected area security missions, including route and convoy security operations. They are not designed to screen, guard, or cover. A maneuver enhancement brigade may be assigned a support area encompassing the supporting and sustainment organizations and main supply routes of the supported command, typically a division. This mission does not supplant unit local security responsibilities. Units remain responsible for self-protection against level I threats. (JP 3-10 and FM 3-90 discuss area security and protection, including threat levels and tactical combat forces. FMI 3-0.1 discusses support areas.)

C-44. Maneuver enhancement brigades can employ a maneuver battalion as a tactical combat force when the situation requires. With a tactical combat force, the brigade executes limited offensive and defensive tasks against level II or III threats. Tactical combat forces may include not only ground maneuver but also aviation and fires assets. However, commanders should employ a BCT when the situation requires a tactical combat force of two or more ground maneuver battalions.

FUNCTIONAL BRIGADES

C-45. Functional brigades, like the modular support brigades, have a modular subordinate structure that may vary considerably among brigades of the same type. Unlike the modular support brigades, functional brigades typically operate under theater army control and depend on theater-level elements for signal and other support. The theater army may task-organize them to corps or division headquarters. Types of functional brigades include—
- Engineer.
- Military police.
- Chemical, biological, radiological, and nuclear.
- Air and missile defense.
- Signal.
- Explosive ordnance disposal.
- Medical.
- Intelligence.

MODULAR ARMY FORCES CONTROLLED BY OTHER SERVICES

C-46. Other Service headquarters may control modular Army brigades directly. A division or corps headquarters is not necessary. Figure C-13 illustrates a maneuver enhancement brigade OPCON to a Marine expeditionary force. The theater army, with its assigned commands, continues to exercise ADCON over the brigade. The theater army also provides Army capabilities, such as network operations, in support of the Marine expeditionary force. Other examples include placing fires brigade equipped with a Multiple Launch

Rocket System OPCON to the joint force air component commander or a tailored sustainment brigade in general or direct support to a joint special operations task force.

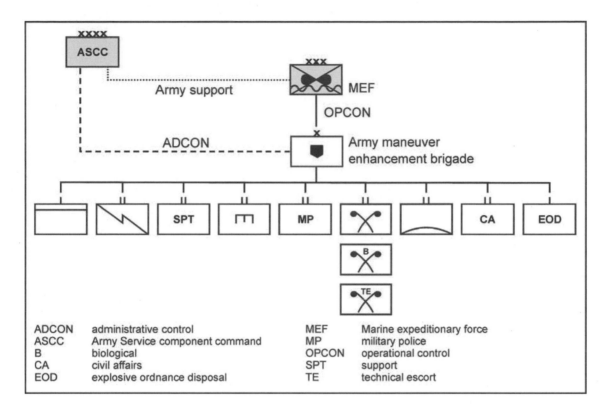

Figure C-13. Maneuver enhancement brigade OPCON to a Marine expeditionary force

This page intentionally left blank.

Appendix D

The Role of Doctrine and Summary of Changes

This appendix discusses the role of doctrine in full spectrum operations and describes the major doctrinal changes contained in this manual.

THE ROLE OF DOCTRINE

D-1. Army doctrine is a body of thought on how Army forces intend to operate as an integral part of a joint force. Doctrine focuses on how to think—not what to think. It establishes the following:

- How the Army views the nature of operations.
- Fundamentals by which Army forces conduct operations.
- Methods by which commanders exercise command and control.

D-2. Doctrine is a guide to action, not a set of fixed rules. It combines history, an understanding of the operational environment, and assumptions about future conditions to help leaders think about how best to accomplish missions. Doctrine is consistent with human nature and broad enough to provide a guide for unexpected situations. It is also based upon the values and ethics of the Service and the Nation; it is codified by law and regulations and applied in the context of operations in the field. It provides an authoritative guide for leaders and Soldiers but requires original applications that adapt it to circumstances. Doctrine should foster initiative and creative thinking.

D-3. Doctrine establishes a common frame of reference including intellectual tools that Army leaders use to solve military problems. It is a menu of practical options based on experience. By establishing common approaches to military tasks, doctrine promotes mutual understanding and enhances effectiveness. It facilitates communication among Soldiers and contributes to a shared professional culture. By establishing a commonly understood set of terms and symbols, doctrine facilitates rapid dissemination of orders and fosters collaborative synchronization among units. It establishes the foundation for curricula in the Army Education System.

D-4. Army doctrine forms the basis for training and leader development standards and support products. Training standards provide performance baselines to evaluate how well a task is executed. Together, doctrine, training, and resources form the key to Army readiness. Doctrine consists of—

- Fundamental principles.
- Tactics, techniques, and procedures.
- Terms and symbols.

FUNDAMENTAL PRINCIPLES

D-5. Fundamental principles provide the foundation upon which Army forces guide their actions. They foster the initiative needed for leaders to become adaptive, creative problem solvers. These principles reflect the Army's collective wisdom regarding past, present, and future operations. They provide a basis for incorporating new ideas, technologies, and organizational designs. Principles apply at all levels of war.

TACTICS, TECHNIQUES, AND PROCEDURES

D-6. Principles alone are not enough to guide operations. Tactics, techniques, and procedures provide additional detail and more specific guidance, based on evolving knowledge and experience. Tactics, techniques, and procedures support and implement fundamental principles, linking them with associated applications. The "how to" of tactics, techniques, and procedures includes descriptive and prescriptive methods and processes. Tactics, techniques, and procedures apply at the operational and tactical levels.

D-7. *Tactics* is the employment and ordered arrangement of forces in relation to each other (CJCSI 5120.02A). Effective tactics translate combat power into decisive results. Primarily descriptive, tactics vary with terrain and other circumstances; they change frequently as the enemy reacts and friendly forces explore new approaches. Applying tactics usually entails acting under time constraints with incomplete information. Tactics always require judgment. For example, a commander may choose to suppress an enemy with fires delivered by the majority of the force while maneuvering a small element to envelop the enemy's position. In a general sense, tactics concerns the application of the various primary tasks associated with those elements of full spectrum operations discussed in FM 3-0. (When revised, FM 3-07 will detail tactical tasks associated with stability operations. A field manual addressing the primary civil support tasks is under development. FM 3-90 will address the primary tasks for offensive and defensive operations.)

D-8. Employing a tactic usually requires using and integrating several techniques and procedures. *Techniques* are nonprescriptive ways or methods used to perform missions, functions, or tasks (CJCSI 5120.02A). They are the primary means of conveying the lessons learned that units gain in operations. Commanders base the decision to use a given technique on their assessment of the situation.

D-9. *Procedures* are standard, detailed steps that prescribe how to perform specific tasks (CJCSI 5120.02A). They normally consist of a series of steps in a set order. Procedures are prescriptive; regardless of circumstances, they are executed in the same manner. Techniques and procedures are the lowest level of doctrine. They are often based on equipment and are specific to particular types of units.

TERMS AND SYMBOLS

D-10. Doctrine provides a common language for professionals to communicate with one another. Terms with commonly understood definitions comprise a major part of that language. Symbols are the language's graphic representations. Establishing and using words and symbols with common military meanings enhances communication among professionals. It makes a common understanding of doctrine possible. Definitions for military terms are established in joint publications, field manuals, and field manuals-interim. The field manual or field manual-interim that establishes an Army term's definition is the proponent publication for that term. Terms are listed in JP 1-02 and FM 1-02. FM 1-02 is also the proponent field manual for symbols. Symbols are always prescriptive. Effective command and control requires terms and symbols that are commonly understood, regardless of Service.

EFFECTS AND ARMY DOCTRINE

D-11. Army forces conduct operations according to Army doctrine. The methods that joint force headquarters use to analyze an operational environment, develop plans, or assess operations do not change this. During operations, joint force headquarters provide direction to senior Army headquarters. Army headquarters then perform the military decisonmaking process (MDMP) to develop its own plan or order. (FM 5-0 describes the MDMP.)

D-12. Army forces do not use the joint systems analysis of the operational environment, effects-based approach to planning, or effects assessment. These planning and assessment methods are intended for use at the strategic and operational levels by properly resourced joint staffs. However, joint interdependence requires Army leaders and staffs to understand joint doctrine that addresses these methods when participating in joint operation planning or assessment or commanding joint forces. (JPs 3-0 and 5-0 establish this doctrine.)

D-13. Describing and assessing operations in terms of effects does not fundamentally change Army doctrine. Army operations remain purpose based and conditions focused. The fundamentals of full spectrum operations and mission command include the idea of focusing efforts toward establishing conditions that define the end state. Achieving success in operations requires commanders to gauge their progress continually. Assessing whether tasks are properly executed cannot accomplish this alone. Rather, commanders assess an operation's progress by evaluating how well the results of executing various tasks contribute to creating end state conditions.

SUMMARY OF MAJOR CHANGES

D-14. The following paragraphs summarize the major doctrinal changes made by this field manual.

CHAPTER 1 – THE OPERATIONAL ENVIRONMENT

D-15. Chapter 1 makes the following changes:

- Replaces the dimensions of the operational environment with the variables established in JP 3-0 (political, military, economic, social, information, infrastructure) plus physical environment and time (**PMESII-PT**). Together, these make up the *operational variables*. The factors of a specific situation bounded by assignment of a mission remain mission, enemy, terrain and weather, troops and support available, time available, civil considerations (**METT-TC**). Together, these are called the *mission variables*.
- Lists areas of **joint interdependence**.
- Incorporates the **Soldier's Rules** established in AR 350-1.

CHAPTER 2 – THE CONTINUUM OF OPERATIONS

D-16. Chapter 2 makes the following changes:

- Establishes the **spectrum of conflict** as a way to describe the level of violence in the operational environment.
- Establishes **operational themes** as a means to describe the character of the predominant major operation within a land force commander's area of operations. The operational themes also provide a framework for categorizing the various types of operations described in joint doctrine.

CHAPTER 3 – FULL SPECTRUM OPERATIONS

D-17. Chapter 3 makes the following changes:

- States the Army's **operational concept** and describes its place in doctrine.
- Describes the Army's role in homeland security.
- Changes the approach to **stability operations**. Stability operations are considered coequal with offensive and defensive operations. They are now discussed in terms of five tactical tasks.
- Rescinds **support operations** as a type of operation. Establishes **civil support operations** as an element of full spectrum operations conducted only in the United States and its territories.
- Uses **lethal** and **nonlethal** as broad descriptions of actions. Rescinds the terms *kinetic* and *nonkinetic*.

CHAPTER 4 – COMBAT POWER

D-18. Chapter 4 makes the following changes:

- Replaces the **battlefield operating systems** with the **warfighting functions** (movement and maneuver, intelligence, fires, sustainment, command and control, and protection).
- Retains the fundamental of **combat power** but changes the **elements of combat power** to the six warfighting functions tied together by leadership and information.
- Rescinds the terms *combat arms, combat support,* and *combat service support.* Uses the appropriate warfighting function to describe unit types and functions.
- Rescinds the *tenets of operations*. The warfighting functions and elements of combat power perform the function of this fundamental.

CHAPTER 5 – COMMAND AND CONTROL

D-19. Chapter 5 makes the following changes:

- Modifies the definition of **command** for the Army. The definition now includes leadership.
- Prescribes a new definition of **battle command**.
- Prescribes a new definition of **commander's visualization**.
- Prescribes a new definition of **commander's intent**.
- Adds *understand* to the commander's role in battle command (described in FM 3-0 [2001] as visualize, describe, direct, assess, and lead).
- Rescinds the *operational framework* construct, including its subordinate constructs of *battle-space* and *battlefield organization*. (**Area of operations** is retained.) Retains **decisive**, **shaping**, and **sustaining operations** (formerly the purpose-based *battlefield organization*) and **main ef-fort** as ways commanders describe subordinates' actions in the concept of operations.
- Prescribes the term **unassigned area** to designate areas between noncontiguous areas of opera-tions or beyond contiguous areas of operations. The higher headquarters is responsible for con-trolling unassigned areas in its area of operations.
- Rescinds the terms *deep, close,* and *rear areas*. Uses **close combat** to describe operations in what used to be called the close area.
- Eliminates *linear* and *nonlinear* as ways to describe the array of forces on the ground. Army doctrine now describes force arrays as occupying either contiguous or noncontiguous areas of operations.
- Describes how the operations process includes several **integrating processes** and **continuing activities** that commanders and staffs synchronize throughout operations.
- Replaces the term *criteria of success* with the joint terms **measure of effectiveness** and **meas-ure of performance**.

CHAPTER 6 – OPERATIONAL ART

D-20. Chapter 6 makes the following changes:

- Introduces **problem framing** as fundamental to operational art.
- Incorporates **risk** as an element of operational design.
- Prescribes the terms **defeat mechanism** and **stability mechanism**. Establishes individual defeat and stability mechanisms.
- Prescribes the term **line of effort** to replace the term *logical line of operations*.

CHAPTER 7 – INFORMATION SUPERIORITY

D-21. Chapter 7 makes the following changes:

- Adds **knowledge management** as a contributor to information superiority.
- Prescribes the following terms:
  - **Intelligence, surveillance, and reconnaissance (ISR)**.
  - **ISR integration**.
  - **ISR synchronization**.
  - **Command and control warfare**.
  - **Information engagement**.
- Describes how Army forces uses five information tasks to shape the operational environment:
  - Information engagement.
  - Command and control warfare.
  - Information protection.
  - Operations security.

- ■ Military deception.
- ● Adopts the term **situational awareness**.

CHAPTER 8 – STRATEGIC AND OPERATIONAL REACH

D-22. Chapter 8 describes the strategic and operational reach (formerly known as strategic responsiveness) that have been developed since FM 3-0 (2001) was published.

APPENDIX A – PRINCIPLES OF WAR AND OPERATIONS

D-23. Appendix A adds the following joint principles of operations to the principles of war: perseverance, legitimacy, and restraint.

APPENDIX B – COMMAND AND SUPPORT RELATIONSHIPS

D-24. Appendix B discusses administrative control and how it applies to tailored and task-organized Army forces. It also explains how headquarters share administrative control.

APPENDIX C – THE ARMY MODULAR FORCE

D-25. Appendix C describes the modular organizations developed since FM 3-0 (2001) was published.

TERMS AND DEFINITIONS

D-26. The following tables list changes to terms for which FM 3-0 is the proponent field manual. Army terms that also have a joint definition are followed by *(Army)*. Terms for which the Army and Marine Corps have agreed on a common definition are followed by *(Army/Marine Corps)*. The tables do not show changed terms when the changes are minor, for example, changing the term from plural to singular.

Table D-1. New Army terms

Army positive control	enemy	intelligence, surveillance, and reconnaissance synchronization	movement and maneuver warfighting function
Army procedural control	fires warfighting function		
civil support[1]	forward operating base	intelligence warfighting function	operational theme
combat power (Army)	graphic control measure	irregular warfare	protection warfighting function
command and control warfare	influence[2]	knowledge management	situational awareness
command and control warfighting function	information engagement	landpower	stability mechanism
compel	information protection	line of effort[3]	support (Army)
defeat mechanism	intelligence, surveillance, and reconnaissance integration	line of operations (Army)	supporter
disintegrate			sustainment warfighting function
dislocate			unassigned area
			warfighting function

Notes:
[1] Replaces support operations and uses the joint definition with Army primary tasks.
[2] Adds a second definition to an existing term.
[3] Replaces logical line of operations.

Table D-2. Modified Army definitions

assessment (Army)	culminating point (Army)	intelligence, surveillance, and reconnaissance	preparation
battle command			running estimate
close combat	decisive operation	isolate[3]	situational understanding
combined arms	defensive operations	main effort	stability operations[4]
commander's intent (Army)	destroy[3]	mission command	supporting distance
commander's visualization	essential element of friendly information	mission orders	supporting range
common operational picture	force tailoring	neutral	sustaining operation
concept of operations (Army)	full spectrum operations	offensive operations	task-organizing[5]
control (Army)[1,2]	information management	operations process	tempo (Army/Marine Corps)
control measure	initiative (individual)	phase (Army/Marine Corps)	urban operations
	initiative (operational)	planning	

Notes:
[1] New definition for use in command and control context.
[2] Added second definition for use as a stability mechanism.
[3] New definition for use in operational art context.

[4] The Army uses the joint definition and assigns Army-specific tasks to this element of full spectrum operations.
[5] Army definition added to joint definition as an addendum.

Table D-3. Rescinded Army definitions

agility[1]	combat service support[2]	offensive information operations (Army)	rear area
assigned forces[1]	combat support[2]	operational fires[1]	subordinates' initiative[5]
asymmetry[1]	deep area	operational framework	support operations[6]
battlefield organization	defensive information operations (Army)	operational picture	versatility[1]
battlespace	force protection (Army)[3]	protection (Army)[4]	logical lines of operations[7]
close area			
combat arms			

Notes:
[1] Army doctrine will follow joint definitions and common English usage.
[2] Army doctrine will not use this term; joint doctrine will continue to use this term.
[3] Activities incorporated into the protection warfighting function.

[4] Replaced by protection warfighting function.
[5] Replaced by individual initiative.
[6] Replaced by civil support operations.
[7] Replaced by lines of effort.

ADDENDUM TO THE ROLE OF DOCTRINE AND SUMMARY OF CHANGES

SUMMARY OF MAJOR CHANGES

D-27. The following paragraphs summarize the major doctrinal changes made by this field manual from the 2008 version.

Chapter 1 – The Operational Environment

D-28. Chapter 1 adds a discussion of hybrid threats.

Chapter 2 – The Continuum of Operations

D-29. Chapter 2 makes the following changes:
- Eliminates graphics to illustrate the continuum of operations.
- Expands and clarifies the discussion of major combat operations.

Chapter 3 – Full Spectrum Operations

D-30. Chapter 3 makes the following changes:
- Moves the discussion of mission command from the section within the operational concept to chapters 4, 5, and 6 to consolidate and emphasize mission command.
- Adds the discussion of stability operations now includes security force assistance.
- Modifies the discussion of civil support tasks from three tasks to four.

Chapter 4 – Combat Power

D-31. Chapter 4 makes the following changes:
- Replaces the command and control warfighting function with mission command warfighting function.
- Introduces the four commander's tasks of mission command: drive the operations process; understand, visualize, describe, direct, lead, and assess operations; develop teams among modular formations and joint, interagency, intergovernmental, and multinational partners; and lead inform and influence activities.
- Introduces the three staff tasks of mission command: conduct the operations process, conduct knowledge management and information management, and conduct inform and influence and cyber/electromagnetic activities.
- Adds integrate and synchronize cyber/electromagnetic activities as a fires warfighting task.
- Modifies the discussion of health service support under the sustainment warfighting function.
- Adds health risk communication as a measure under force health protection in the protection warfighting function.

Chapter 5 – The Commander and Mission Command

D-32. Chapter 5 makes the following changes:
- Changes the title of the chapter to The Commander and Mission Command.
- Moves the discussions of control and the operations process to chapter 6.
- Describes how design assists the commander in better understanding the operational environment.
- Prescribes a new definition for *mission command*.
- Discusses the four commander's tasks of mission command.

- Describes how building teams enables commanders to shape operations before, during, and after operations.
- Rescinds the term *battle command*.
- Rescinds the term *command and control warfare* and the discussion of command and control warfare.
- Describes how the commander uses assessment in operations.

Chapter 6 – The Science of Control

D-33. Chapter 6 is a new chapter. It makes the following changes:

- Changes the title of the chapter to The Science of Control.
- Describes the three staff tasks of mission command.
- Eliminates the *five information tasks* and replaces them with the task of inform and influence and cyber/electromagnetic activities. The joint construct of information operations focuses on adversaries and is based on capabilities. The previous version of FM 3-0, *Operations*, and the 2003 FM 3-13, *Information Operations*, used a similar definition and construct. In 2008, FM 3-0 revised how the Army viewed information operations using five information tasks located in separate warfighting functions. This change accounts for the difference between land operations and those conducted in the other domains. For example, the joint construct of information operations had nothing that focused the efforts of multiple contributors on getting out effective messages to friendly or neutral audiences, which are now accounted in the task of inform and influence activities. The new construct also recognizes the growing importance of a new function that addresses the cyber/electromagnetic arena. As an interim measure, responsibility for integration and synchronization of cyber/electromagnetic activities resides in the electronic warfare element of the fires warfighting function. The concepts and functions of cyber/electromagnetic activities will mature and be refined.
- Rescinds the term *psychological operations* and replaces the term with *military information support operations*.

Chapter 7 – Information Superiority (Deleted)

D-34. Chapter 7, Information Superiority, is deleted. Discussion of inform and influence and cyber/electromagnetic activities is moved to chapter 6.

Chapter 7 – Operational Art

D-35. Chapter 7 (previously chapter 6) makes the following changes:

- Introduces design as a methodology that supports the application of operational art.
- Modifies the definition of operational approach to align with FM 5-0.
- Replaces elements of *operational design* with elements of *operational art*.

Chapter 8 – Strategic and Operational Reach

D-36. Chapter 8 adds a discussion of and defines *support area*.

Appendix A – Principles of War and Operations

Appendix B – Command and Support Relationships

Appendix C – The Army Modular Force

TERMS AND DEFINITIONS

D-37. Table D-4 lists changes to terms for which Change 1 of FM 3-0 is the proponent field manual.

*Table D-4. Army terms for change 1

New terms	Modified terms	Rescinded terms
approach	control[3]	battle command
hybrid threat	direct approach	command and control warfare[6]
inform and influence activities	indirect approach	command and control warfighting function[7]
mission command networks and systems[1]	mission command	information engagement
mission command warfighting function[2]	operational approach[4]	information protection
operational adaptability	operations process[3]	information system
persistent conflict	relevant information[3]	
	running estimate[4]	
	support area[5]	

Notes:
[1] Replaces command and control warfare.
[2] Replaces command and control warfighting function.
[3] Modified definition for use in mission command context.
[4] FM 5-0 is now proponent.
[5] FM 3-0 is now proponent instead of FMI 3-0.1.
[6] Replaced by mission command warfare.
[7] Replaced by mission command warfighting function.

This page intentionally left blank.

Source Notes

These are the sources used, quoted, or paraphrased in this publication. They are listed by page number. Where material appears in a paragraph, both page and paragraph number are listed.

xi   "Stability operations are a core...": DODD 3000.05, *Military Support for Stability, Security, Transition, and Reconstruction (SSTR) Operations* (Washington, DC: Department of Defense, 28 Nov 2005), paragraph 4.1 (page 2).

1-15   "War is thus an act...": Carl von Clausewitz, *On War*, Michael Howard and Peter Paret, eds. (Princeton: Princeton University Press, 1984), 75 (hereafter cited as Clausewitz).

1-17   "Everything in war...": Clausewitz, 119, 120.

1-19   para 1-90. AR 350-1, *Army Training and Leader Development* (Washington DC: Headquarters, Department of the Army, 3 Aug 2007), 80–81. Paragraph 4-18b establishes the Soldier's Rules. < http://www.army.mil/usapa/epubs/pdf/r350_1.pdf > (accessed 10 Jan 2008).

7-6   para 7-30. "the hub of all power...": Clausewitz, 595–596.

This page intentionally left blank.

Glossary

The glossary lists acronyms and terms with Army, multi-Service, or joint definitions, and other selected terms. Where Army and joint definitions are different, *(Army)* follows the term. Terms for which FM 3-0 is the proponent manual (the authority) are marked with an asterisk (*). The proponent manual for other terms is listed in parentheses after the definition.

SECTION I – ACRONYMS AND ABBREVIATIONS

ADCON	administrative control
AR	Army regulation
ARFOR	*See* ARFOR under terms.
ASCC	Army Service component command
BCT	brigade combat team
CBRNE	chemical, biological, radiological, nuclear, and high-yield explosives
CCIR	commander's critical information requirement
CJCSI	Chairman of the Joint Chiefs of Staff instruction
COCOM	combatant command (command authority)
DA	Department of the Army
DODI	Department of Defense instruction
EEFI	essential element of friendly information
FFIR	friendly force information requirement
FM	field manual
ISR	intelligence, surveillance, and reconnaissance
JP	joint publication
MDMP	military decisonmaking process
METT-TC	*See* METT-TC under terms.
NATO	North Atlantic Treaty Organization
OPCON	operational control
PIR	priority intelligence requirement
PMESII-PT	*See* PMESII-PT under terms.
TACON	tactical control
U.S.	United States
WMD	weapons of mass destruction

SECTION II – TERMS

administrative control

(joint) Direction or exercise of authority over subordinate or other organizations in respect to administration and support, including organization of Service forces, control of resources and equipment, personnel management, unit logistics, individual and unit training, readiness, mobilization, demobilization, discipline, and other matters not included in the operational missions of the subordinate or other organizations. (JP 1)

adversary

(joint) A party acknowledged as potentially hostile to a friendly party and against which the use of force may be envisaged. (JP 3-0)

alliance

(joint) The relationship that results from a formal agreement (for example, treaty) between two or more nations for broad, long-term objectives that further the common interests of the members. (JP 3-0)

antiterrorism

(joint) Defensive measures used to reduce the vulnerability of individuals and property to terrorist acts, to include limited response and containment by local military and civilian forces. (JP 3-07.2)

*approach

The manner in which a commander contends with a center of gravity.

area of influence

(joint) A geographical area wherein a commander is directly capable of influencing operations by maneuver or fire support systems normally under the commander's command or control. (JP 3-16)

area of interest

(joint) area of concern to the commander, including the area of influence, areas adjacent thereto, and extending into enemy territory to the objectives of current or planned operations. This area also includes areas occupied by enemy forces who could jeopardize the accomplishment of the mission. (JP 2-03)

*ARFOR

The Army Service component headquarters for a joint task force or a joint and multinational force.

*Army positive control

A technique of regulating forces that involves commanders and leaders actively assessing, deciding, and directing them.

*Army procedural control

A technique of regulating forces that relies on a combination of orders, regulations, policies, and doctrine (including tactics, techniques, and procedures).

*assessment

(Army) The continuous monitoring and evaluation of the current situation, particularly the enemy, and progress of an operation.

base

(joint) A locality from which operations are projected or supported. (JP 4-0)

*battle

A set of related engagements that lasts longer and involves larger forces than an engagement.

campaign

(joint) A series of related major operations aimed at achieving strategic and operational objectives within a given time and space. (JP 5-0)

center of gravity

> (joint) The source of power that provides moral or physical strength, freedom of action, or will to act. (JP 3-0)

civil considerations

> The influence of manmade infrastructure, civilian institutions, and attitudes and activities of the civilian leaders, populations, and organizations within an area of operations on the conduct of military operations. (FM 6-0)

civil support

> (joint) Department of Defense support to US civil authorities for domestic emergencies, and for designated law enforcement and other activities. (JP 3-28)

*close combat

> Warfare carried out on land in a direct-fire fight, supported by direct, indirect, and air-delivered fires.

coalition

> (joint) An ad hoc arrangement between two or more nations for common action. (JP 5-0)

coalition action

> (joint) A multinational action outside the bounds of established alliances, usually for single occasions or longer cooperation in a narrow sector of common interest. (JP 5-0)

combat camera

> (joint) The acquisition and utilization of still and motion imagery in support of operational and planning requirements across the range of military operations and during joint exercises. (JP 3-61)

combating terrorism

> (joint) Actions, including antiterrorism and counterterrorism, taken to oppose terrorism throughout the entire threat spectrum. (JP 3-26)

*combat power

> (Army) The total means of destructive, constructive, and information capabilities that a military unit/formation can apply at a given time. Army forces generate combat power by converting potential into effective action.

*combined arms

> The synchronized and simultaneous application of the elements of combat power to achieve an effect greater than if each element of combat power was used separately or sequentially.

command

> (joint) The authority that a commander in the armed forces lawfully exercises over subordinates by virtue of rank or assignment. Command includes the authority and responsibility for effectively using available resources and for planning the employment of, organizing, directing, coordinating, and controlling military forces for the accomplishment of assigned missions. It also includes responsibility for health, welfare, morale, and discipline of assigned personnel. (JP 1)

commander's critical information requirement

> (joint) An information requirement identified by the commander as being critical to facilitating timely decision-making. The two key elements are friendly force information requirements and priority intelligence requirements. (JP 3-0)

*commander's intent

> (Army) A clear, concise statement of what the force must do and the conditions the force must establish with respect to the enemy, terrain, and civil considerations that represent the desired end state.

*commander's visualization

> The mental process of developing situational understanding, determining a desired end state, and envisioning the broad sequence of events by which the force will achieve that end state.

*common operational picture

(Army) A single display of relevant information within a commander's area of interest tailored to the user's requirements and based on common data and information shared by more than one command.

*compel

To use, or threaten to use, lethal force to establish control and dominance, effect behavioral change, or enforce compliance with mandates, agreements, or civil authority.

*concept of operations

(Army) A statement that directs the manner in which subordinate units cooperate to accomplish the mission and establishes the sequence of actions the force will use to achieve the end state. It is normally expressed in terms of decisive, shaping, and sustaining operations.

consequence management

(joint) Actions taken to maintain or restore essential services and manage and mitigate problems resulting from disasters and catastrophes, including natural, man-made, or terrorist incidents. (JP 3-28)

contractor

A person or business that provides products or services for monetary compensation. A contractor furnishes supplies and services or performs work at a certain price or rate based on the terms of a contract. (FM 3-100.21)

*control

(Army)*1. In the context of mission command, control is the regulation of forces and warfighting functions to accomplish the mission in accordance with the commander's intent. (FM 3-0) 2. A tactical mission task that requires the commander to maintain physical influence over a specified area to prevent its use by an enemy. (FM 3-90) 3. An action taken to eliminate a hazard or reduce its risk. (FM 5-19) *4. In the context of stability mechanisms, to impose civil order. (FM 3-0) [See JP 1-02 for joint definitions.]

*control measure

A means of regulating forces or warfighting functions.

counterdrug activities

(joint) Those measures taken to detect, interdict, disrupt, or curtail any activity that is reasonably related to illicit drug trafficking. This includes, but is not limited to, measures taken to detect, interdict, disrupt, or curtail activities related to substances, materiel, weapons, or resources used to finance, support, secure, cultivate, process, or transport illegal drugs. (JP 3-07.4)

counterinsurgency

(joint) Comprehensive civilian and military efforts taken to defeat an insurgency and to address any core grievances. (JP 3-24)

counterterrorism

(joint) Actions taken directly against terrorist networks and indirectly to influence and render global and regional environments inhospitable to terrorist networks. (JP 3-26)

*culminating point

(Army) That point in time and space at which a force no longer possesses the capability to continue its current form of operations.

cyberspace

(joint) A global domain within the information environment consisting of the interdependent network of information technology infrastructures, including the Internet, telecommunications networks, computer systems, and embedded processors and controllers. (JP 1-02)

*decisive operation

The operation that directly accomplishes the mission. It determines the outcome of a major operation, battle, or engagement. The decisive operation is the focal point around which commanders design the entire operation.

decisive point

(joint) A geographic place, specific key event, critical factor, or function that, when acted upon, allows commanders to gain a marked advantage over an adversary or contribute materially to achieving success. (JP 3-0) [Note: In this context, adversary also refers to enemies.]

*defeat mechanism

The method through which friendly forces accomplish their mission against enemy opposition.

*defensive operations

Combat operations conducted to defeat an enemy attack, gain time, economize forces, and develop conditions favorable for offensive or stability operations.

*depth

(Army) The extension of operations in time, space, and resources.

design

A methodology for applying critical and creative thinking to understand, visualize, and describe complex, ill-structured problems and develop approaches to solve them. (FM 5-0)

*destroy

In the context of defeat mechanisms, to apply lethal combat power on an enemy capability so that it can no longer perform any function and cannot be restored to a usable condition without being entirely rebuilt.

*direct approach

The manner in which a commander attacks the enemy's center of gravity or principal strength by applying combat power directly against it.

direct liaison authorized

(joint) That authority granted by a commander (any level) to a subordinate to directly consult or coordinate an action with a command or agency within or outside of the granting command. Direct liaison authorized is more applicable to planning than operations and always carries with it the requirement of keeping the commander granting direct liaison authorized informed. Direct liaison authorized is a coordination relationship, not an authority through which command may be exercised. (JP 1)

*disintegrate

To disrupt the enemy's command and control system, degrading the ability to conduct operations while leading to a rapid collapse of the enemy's capabilities or will to fight.

*dislocate

To employ forces to obtain significant positional advantage, rendering the enemy's dispositions less valuable, perhaps even irrelevant.

electromagnetic spectrum

(joint) The range of frequencies of electromagnetic radiation from zero to infinity. It is divided into 26 alphabetically designated bands. (JP 3-13.1)

electronic attack

(joint) A division of electronic warfare involving the use of electromagnetic energy, directed energy, or antiradiation weapons to attack personnel, facilities, or equipment with the intent of degrading, neutralizing, or destroying enemy combat capability and is considered a form of fires. (JP 3-13.1)

electronic protection

(joint) A division of electronic warfare involving actions taken to protect personnel, facilities, and equipment from any effects of friendly or enemy use of the electromagnetic spectrum that degrade, neutralize, or destroy friendly combat capability. (JP 3-13.1)

electronic warfare

(joint) Any military action involving the use of electromagnetic and directed energy to control the electromagnetic spectrum or to attack the enemy. Electronic warfare consists of three divisions: electronic attack, electronic protection, and electronic warfare support. (JP 3-13.1)

electronic warfare support

(joint) A division of electronic warfare involving actions tasked by, or under the direct control of, an operational commander to search for, intercept, identify, and locate or localize sources of intentional and unintentional radiated electromagnetic energy for the purpose of immediate threat recognition, targeting, planning, and conduct of future operations. (JP 3-13.1)

end state

(joint) The set of required conditions that defines achievement of the commander's objectives. (JP 3-0)

*enemy

A party identified as hostile against which the use of force is authorized.

engagement

(joint) A tactical conflict, usually between opposing, lower echelon maneuver forces. (JP 1-02)

*essential element of friendly information

(Army) A critical aspect of a friendly operation that, if known by the enemy, would subsequently compromise, lead to failure, or limit success of the operation and therefore should be protected from enemy detection.

*execution

Putting a plan into action by applying combat power to accomplish the mission and using situational understanding to assess progress and make execution and adjustment decisions.

*exterior lines

A force operates on exterior lines when its operations converge on the enemy.

*fires warfighting function

The related tasks and systems that provide collective and coordinated use of Army indirect fires and joint fires through the targeting process.

*force tailoring

The process of determining the right mix of forces and the sequence of their deployment in support of a joint force commander.

forcible entry

(joint) The seizing and holding of a military lodgment in the face of armed opposition. (JP 3-18)

foreign humanitarian assistance

(joint) Department of Defense activities, normally in support of the United States Agency for International Development or Department of State, conducted outside the United States, its territories, and possessions to relieve or reduce human suffering, disease, hunger, or privation. (JP 3-29)

foreign internal defense

(joint) The participation by civilian and military agencies of a government in any of the action programs taken by another government or other designated organization to free and protect its society from subversion, lawlessness, and insurgency. (JP 3-22)

*forward operating base

(Army) An area used to support tactical operations without establishing full support facilities.

friendly force information requirement

(joint) Information the commander and staff need to understand the status of friendly force and supporting capabilities. (JP 3-0)

*full spectrum operations

The Army's operational concept: Army forces combine offensive, defensive, and stability or civil support operations simultaneously as part of an interdependent joint force to seize, retain, and exploit the initiative, accepting prudent risk to create opportunities to achieve decisive results. They employ synchronized action—lethal and nonlethal—proportional to the mission and informed by a thorough understanding of all variables of the operational environment. Mission command that conveys intent and an appreciation of all aspects of the situation guides the adaptive use of Army forces.

*graphic control measure

A symbol used on maps and displays to regulate forces and warfighting functions.

*hybrid threat

A hybrid threat is the diverse and dynamic combination of regular forces, irregular forces, and/or criminal elements all unified to achieve mutually benefitting effects.

*indirect approach

The manner in which a commander attacks the enemy's center of gravity by applying combat power against a series of decisive points while avoiding enemy strength.

*individual initiative

The willingness to act in the absence of orders, when existing orders no longer fit the situation, or when unforeseen opportunities or threats arise.

*influence

In the context of stability mechanisms, to alter the opinions and attitudes of a civilian population through inform and influence activities, presence, and conduct.

*inform and influence activities

The integrating activities within the mission command warfighting function which ensure themes and messages designed to inform domestic audiences and influence foreign friendly, neutral, adversary, and enemy populations are synchronized with actions to support full spectrum operations. Inform and influence activities incorporate components and enablers expanding the commander's ability to use other resources to inform and influence.

information environment

(joint) The aggregate of individuals, organizations, and systems that collect, process, disseminate, or act on information. (JP 3-13)

*information management

(Army) The science of using procedures and information systems to collect, process, store, display, disseminate, and protect knowledge products, data, and information.

insurgency

(joint) The organized movement of subversion and violence by a group or movement that seeks to overthrow or force change of a governing authority. Insurgency can also refer to the group itself. (JP 3-24)

*intelligence, surveillance, and reconnaissance

(Army) An activity that synchronizes and integrates the planning and operation of sensors, assets, and processing, exploitation, and dissemination systems in direct support of current and future operations. This is an integrated intelligence and operations function. For Army forces, this activity is a combined arms operation that focuses on priority intelligence requirements while answering the commander's critical information requirements.

*intelligence, surveillance, and reconnaissance integration

The task of assigning and controlling a unit's intelligence, surveillance, and reconnaissance assets (in terms of space, time, and purpose) to collect and report information as a concerted and integrated portion of operation plans and orders.

*intelligence, surveillance, and reconnaissance synchronization

The task that accomplishes the following: analyzes information requirements and intelligence gaps; evaluates available assets internal and external to the organization; determines gaps in the use of those assets; recommends intelligence, surveillance, and reconnaissance assets controlled by the organization to collect on the commander's critical information requirements; and submits requests for information for adjacent and higher collection support.

*intelligence warfighting function

The related tasks and systems that facilitate understanding of the operational environment, enemy, terrain, and civil considerations.

interagency coordination

(joint) Within the context of Department of Defense involvement, the coordination that occurs between elements of Department of Defense, and engaged US Government agencies for the purpose of achieving an objective. (JP 3-0)

intergovernmental organization

(joint) An organization created by a formal agreement (for example, a treaty) between two or more governments. It may be established on a global, regional, or functional basis for wide-ranging or narrowly defined purposes. Formed to protect and promote national interests shared by member states. (JP 3-08)

*interior lines

A force operates on interior lines when its operations diverge from a central point.

intermediate staging base

(joint) A tailorable, temporary location used for staging forces, sustainment and/or extraction into and out of an operational area. (JP 3-35)

intuitive decisionmaking

The act of reaching a conclusion which emphasizes pattern recognition based on knowledge, judgment, experience, education, intelligence, boldness, perception, and character. This approach focuses on assessment of the situation vice comparison of multiple options. (FM 6-0)

*irregular warfare

(Army) A violent struggle among state and nonstate actors for legitimacy and influence over a population.

*isolate

In the context of defeat mechanisms, to deny an enemy or adversary access to capabilities that enable the exercise of coercion, influence, potential advantage, and freedom of action.

joint combined exchange training

(joint) A program conducted overseas to fulfill US forces training requirements and at the same time exchange the sharing of skills between US forces and host nation counterparts. Training activities are designed to improve US and host nation capabilities. (JP 3-05)

*knowledge management

The art of creating, organizing, applying, and transferring knowledge to facilitate situational understanding and decisionmaking.

*landpower

The ability—by threat, force, or occupation—to gain, sustain, and exploit control over land, resources, and people.

law of war

(joint) That part of international law that regulates the conduct of armed hostilities. (JP 1-02)

leadership

The process of influencing people by providing purpose, direction, and motivation, while operating to accomplish the mission and improve the organization. (FM 6-22)

*line of effort

A line that links multiple tasks and missions using the logic of purpose—cause and effect—to focus efforts toward establishing operational and strategic conditions.

*line of operations

(Army) A line that defines the directional orientation of a force in time and space in relation to the enemy and links the force with its base of operations and objectives.

lodgment

(joint) A designated area in a hostile or potentially hostile territory that, when seized and held, makes the continuous landing of troops and materiel possible and provides maneuver space for subsequent operations. (JP 3-18)

logistics

(joint) The planning and executing the movement and support of forces. It includes those aspects of military operations that deal with: a. design and development, acquisition, storage, movement, distribution, maintenance, evacuation, and disposition of materiel; b. movement, evacuation, and hospitalization of personnel; c. acquisition or construction, maintenance, operation, and disposition of facilities; and d. acquisition or furnishing of services. (JP 4-0)

*main effort

The designated subordinate unit whose mission at a given point in time is most critical to overall mission success. It is usually weighted with the preponderance of combat power.

major operation

(joint) A series of tactical actions (battles, engagements, strikes) conducted by combat forces of a single or several Services, coordinated in time and place, to achieve strategic or operational objectives in an operational area. These actions are conducted simultaneously or sequentially in accordance with a common plan and are controlled by a single commander. For noncombat operations, a reference to the relative size and scope of a military operation. (JP 3-0)

maneuver

(joint) The employment of forces in the operational area through movement in combination with fires to achieve a position of advantage in respect to the enemy in order to accomplish the mission. (JP 3-0)

measure of effectiveness

(joint) A criterion used to assess changes in system behavior, capability, or operational environment that is tied to measuring the attainment of an end state, achievement of an objective, or creation of an effect. (JP 3-0)

measure of performance

(joint) A criterion used to assess friendly actions that is tied to measuring task accomplishment. (JP 3-0)

METT-TC

A memory aid used in two contexts: 1. In the context of information management, the major subject categories into which relevant information is grouped for military operations: mission, enemy, terrain and weather, troops and support available, time available, civil considerations. (FM 6-0) 2. In the context of tactics, major variables considered during mission analysis (mission variables). (FM 3-90)

military deception

(joint)Those actions executed to deliberately mislead adversary decision makers as to friendly military capabilities, intentions, and operations, thereby causing the adversary to take specific actions (or inactions) that will contribute to the accomplishment of the friendly mission. (JP 3-13.4)

mission

(joint) task, together with the purpose, that clearly indicates the action to be taken and the reason therefore. (JP 3-0)

*mission command

(Army) The exercise of authority and direction by the commander using mission orders to enable disciplined initiative within the commander's intent to empower agile and adaptive leaders in the conduct of full spectrum operations. It is commander-led and blends the art of command and the science of control to integrate the warfighting functions to accomplish the mission.

*mission command networks and systems

The coordinated application of personnel, networks, procedures, equipment and facilities, knowledge management, and information management systems essential for the commander to conduct operations.

*mission command warfighting function

Develops and integrates those activities enabling a commander to balance the art of command and the science of control.

*mission orders

A technique for developing orders that emphasizes to subordinates the results to be attained, not how they are to achieve them. It provides maximum freedom of action in determining how to best accomplish assigned missions.

*movement and maneuver warfighing function

The related tasks and systems that move forces to achieve a position of advantage in relation to the enemy.

multinational operations

(joint) A collective term to describe military actions conducted by forces of two or more nations, usually undertaken within the structure of a coalition or alliance. (JP 3-16)

mutual support

(joint) That support which units render each other against an enemy, because of their assigned tasks, their position relative to each other and to the enemy, and their inherent capabilities. (JP 3-31)

*neutral

(Army) A party identified as neither supporting nor opposing friendly or enemy forces.

noncombatant evacuation operations

(joint) Operations directed by the Department of State or other appropriate authority, in conjunction with the Department of Defense, whereby noncombatants are evacuated from foreign countries when their lives are endangered by war, civil unrest, or natural disaster to safe havens or to the United States. (JP 3-0)

nongovernmental organization

(joint) A private, self-governing, not-for-profit organization dedicated to alleviating human suffering; and/or promoting education, health care, economic development, environmental protection, human rights, and conflict resolution; and/or encouraging the establishment of democratic institutions and civil society. (JP 3-08)

*offensive operations

Combat operations conducted to defeat and destroy enemy forces and seize terrain, resources, and population centers. They impose the commander's will on the enemy.

operating forces

(joint) Those forces whose primary missions are to participate in combat and the integral supporting elements thereof. (JP 1-02)

*operational adaptability

The ability to shape conditions and respond effectively to changing threats and situations with appropriate, flexible, and timely actions.

operational approach

A broad conceptualization of the general actions that will produce the conditions that define the desired end state. (FM 5-0)

operational art

(joint) The application of creative imagination by commanders and staffs—supported by their skill, knowledge, and experience—to design strategies, campaigns, and major operations and organize and employ military forces. Operational art integrates ends, ways, and means across the levels of war. (JP 3-0)

operational concept

See full spectrum operations.

operational environment

(joint) A composite of the conditions, circumstances, and influences that affect the employment of capabilities and bear on the decisions of the commander. (JP 3-0)

*operational initiative

The setting or dictating the terms of action throughout an operation.

*operational pause

(Army) A deliberate halt taken to extend operational reach or prevent culmination.

operational reach

(joint) The distance and duration across which a unit can successfully employ military capabilities. (JP 3-0)

*operational theme

The character of the dominant major operation being conducted at any time within a land force commander's area of operations. The operational theme helps convey the nature of the major operation to the force to facilitate common understanding of how the commander broadly intends to operate.

*operations process

The major mission command activities performed during operations: planning, preparing, executing, and continuously assessing the operation. The commander drives the operations process through leadership.

organic

(joint) Those assigned to and forming an essential part of a military organization. Organic parts of a unit are those listed in its table of organization for the Army, Air Force, and Marine Corps, and are assigned to the administrative organizations of the operating forces for the Navy. (JP 1-02)

other government agency

(joint) Within the context of interagency coordination, a non Department of Defense agency of the United States Government. (JP 1)

peace building

(joint) Stability actions, predominately diplomatic and economic, that strengthen and rebuild governmental infrastructure and institutions in order to avoid a relapse into conflict. (JP 3-07.3)

peace enforcement

(joint) The application of military force, or the threat of its use, normally pursuant to international authorization, to compel compliance with resolutions or sanctions designed to maintain or restore peace and order. (JP 3-07.3)

peacekeeping

(joint) Military operations undertaken with the consent of all major parties to a dispute, designed to monitor and facilitate implementation of an agreement (cease fire, truce, or other such agreement) and support diplomatic efforts to reach a long-term political settlement. (JP 3-07.3)

peacemaking

(joint) The process of diplomacy, mediation, negotiation, or other forms of peaceful settlements that arranges an end to a dispute and resolves issues that led to it. (JP 3-0)

peace operations

(joint) A broad term that encompasses multiagency and multinational crisis response and limited contingency operations involving all instruments of national power with military missions to contain conflict, redress the peace, and shape the environment to support reconciliation and rebuilding and facilitate the transition to legitimate governance. Peace operations include peacekeeping, peace enforcement, peacemaking, peace building, and conflict prevention efforts. (JP 3-07.3)

*peacetime military engagement

All military activities that involve other nations and are intended to shape the security environment in peacetime. It includes programs and exercises that the United States military conducts with other nations to shape the international environment, improve mutual understanding, and improve interoperability with treaty partners or potential coalition partners. Peacetime military engagement activities are designed to support a combatant commander's objectives within the theater security cooperation plan.

*persistent conflict

The protracted confrontation among state, nonstate, and individual actors that are increasingly willing to use violence to achieve their political and ideological ends.

*phase

(Army/Marine Corps) A planning and execution tool used to divide an operation in duration or activity. A change in phase usually involves a change of mission, task organization, or rules of engagement. Phasing helps in planning and controlling and may be indicated by time, distance, terrain, or an event.

*planning

The process by which commanders (and the staff, if available) translate the commander's visualization into a specific course of action for preparation and execution, focusing on the expected results.

*PMESII-PT

A memory aid for the varibles used to describe the operational environment: political, military, economic, social, information, infrastructure, physical environment, time (operational variables).

*preparation

Activities performed by units to improve their ability to execute an operation. Preparation includes, but is not limited to, plan refinement; rehearsals; intelligence, surveillance, and reconnaissance; coordination; inspections; and movement.

priority intelligence requirement

(joint) An intelligence requirement, stated as a priority for intelligence support, that the commander and staff need to understand the adversary or the operational environment. (JP 2-0) [Note: In this context, adversary also refers to enemies.]

procedures

(joint) Standard, detailed steps that describe how to perform specific tasks. (CJCSI 5120.02)

*protection warfighting function

The related tasks and systems that preserve the force so the commander can apply maximum combat power.

raid

(joint) An operation to temporarily seize an area in order to secure information, confuse an adversary, capture personnel or equipment, or to destroy a capability. It ends with a planned withdrawal upon completion of the assigned mission. (JP 3-0) [*Note:* In this context, adversary also refers to enemies.]

reconnaissance

(joint) A mission undertaken to obtain, by visual observation or other detection methods, information about the activities and resources of an enemy or adversary, or to secure data concerning the meteorological, hydrographic, or geographic characteristics of a particular area. (JP 2-0)

recovery operations

(joint) Operations conducted to search for, locate, identify, recover, and return isolated personnel, human remains, sensitive equipment, or items critical to national security. (JP 3-50)

*relevant information

All information of importance to commanders and staffs in the exercise of mission command.

rules of engagement

(joint) Directives issued by competent military authority that delineate the circumstances and limitations under which United States forces will initiate and/or continue combat engagement with other forces encountered. (JP 1-04)

running estimate

The continuous assessment of the current situation used to determine if the current operation is proceeding according to the commander's intent and if planned future operations are supportable. (FM 5-0)

sanction enforcement

(joint) Operations that employ coercive measures to interdict the movement of certain types of designated items into or out of a nation or specified area. (JP 3-0)

*shaping operation

An operation at any echelon that creates and preserves conditions for the success of the decisive operation.

security force assistance

(Army) The unified action to generate, employ, and sustain local, host-nation, or regional security forces in support of a legitimate authority. (FM 3-07)

show of force

(joint) An operation designed to demonstrate US resolve that involves increased visibility of US deployed forces in an attempt to defuse a specific situation that, if allowed to continue, may be detrimental to US interests or national objectives. (JP 3-0)

*situational awareness

Immediate knowledge of the conditions of the operation, constrained geographically and in time.

*situational understanding

The product of applying analysis and judgment to relevant information to determine the relationships among the mission variables to facilitate decisionmaking.

*stability mechanism

The primary method through which friendly forces affect civilians in order to attain conditions that support establishing a lasting, stable peace.

stability operations

(joint) An overarching term encompassing various military missions, tasks, and activities conducted outside the United States in coordination with other instruments of national power to maintain or reestablish a safe and secure environment, provide essential governmental services, emergency infrastructure reconstruction, and humanitarian relief. (JP 3-0)

strategic level of war

> (joint) The level of war at which a nation, often as a member of a group of nations, determines national or multinational (alliance or coalition) strategic security objectives and guidance, and develops and uses national resources to achieve these objectives. Activities at this level establish national and multinational military objectives; sequence initiatives; define limits and assess risks for the use of military and other instruments of national power; develop global plans or theater war plans to achieve those objectives; and provide military forces and other capabilities in accordance with strategic plans. (JP 3-0)

strategy

> (joint) A prudent idea or set of ideas for employing the instruments of national power in a synchronized and integrated fashion to achieve theater, national, and/or multinational objectives. (JP 3-0)

strike

> (joint) An attack to damage or destroy an objective or a capability. (JP 3-0)

*support

> (joint) The action of a force that aids, protects, complements, or sustains another force in accordance with a directive requiring such action. (JP 1) *(Army) In the context of stability mechanisms, to establish, reinforce, or set the conditions necessary for the other instruments of national power to function effectively.

*support area

> A specific surface area designated by the echelon commander to facilitate the positioning, employment, and protection of resources required to sustain, enable, and control tactical operations.

*supporter

> A party who sympathizes with friendly forces and who may or may not provide material assistance to them.

*supporting distance

> The distance between two units that can be traveled in time for one to come to the aid of the other and prevent its defeat by an enemy or ensure it regains control of a civil situation.

*supporting range

> The distance one unit may be geographically separated from a second unit yet remain within the maximum range of the second unit's weapons systems.

surveillance

> (joint) The systematic observation of aerospace, surface, or subsurface areas, places, persons, or things, by visual, aural, electronic, photographic, or other means. (JP 3-0)

*sustaining operation

> An operation at any echelon that enables the decisive operation or shaping operations by generating and maintaining combat power.

*sustainment warfighting function

> The related tasks and systems that provide support and services to ensure freedom of action, extend operational reach, and prolong endurance.

synchronization

> (joint) The arrangement of military actions in time, space, and purpose to produce maximum relative combat power at a decisive place and time. (JP 2-0)

tactics

> (joint) The employment and ordered arrangement of forces in relation to each other. (CJCSI 5120.02)

*task organization

> (Army) A temporary grouping of forces designed to accomplish a particular mission.

*task-organizing

(Army) The act of designing an operating force, support staff, or logistic package of specific size and composition to meet a unique task or mission. Characteristics to examine when task-organizing the force include, but are not limited to: training, experience, equipage, sustainability, operating environment, enemy threat, and mobility. For Army forces, it includes allocating available assets to subordinate commanders and establishing their command and support relationships.

techniques

(joint) Nonprescriptive ways or methods used to perform missions, functions, or tasks. (CJCSI 5120.02)

*tempo

The relative speed and rhythm of military operations over time with respect to the enemy.

terrorism

(joint) The calculated use of unlawful violence or threat of unlawful violence to inculcate fear; [these acts are] intended to coerce or to intimidate governments or societies in the pursuit of goals that are generally political, religious, or ideological. (JP 3-07.2)

training and readiness oversight

(joint) The authority that combatant commanders may exercise over assigned Reserve Component forces when not on active duty or when on active duty for training. As a matter of Department of Defense policy, this authority includes: a. Providing guidance to Service component commanders on operational requirements and priorities to be addressed in Military Department training and readiness programs; b. Commenting on Service component program recommendations and budget requests; c. Coordinating and approving participation by assigned Reserve Component forces in joint exercises and other joint training when on active duty for training or performing inactive duty for training; d. Obtaining and reviewing readiness and inspection reports on assigned Reserve Component forces; and e. Coordinating and reviewing mobilization plans (including post-mobilization training activities and deployability validation procedures) developed for assigned Reserve Component forces. (JP 1)

*unassigned area

The area between noncontiguous areas of operations or beyond contiguous areas of operations. The higher headquarters is responsible for controlling unassigned areas within its area of operations.

unconventional warfare

(joint) A broad spectrum of military and paramilitary operations, normally of long duration, predominantly conducted through, with, or by indigenous or surrogate forces who are organized, trained, equipped, supported, and directed in varying degrees by an external source. It includes, but is not limited to, guerrilla warfare, subversion, sabotage, intelligence activities, and unconventional assisted recovery. (JP 3-05)

unified action

(joint) The synchronization, coordination, and/or integration of the activities of governmental and nongovernmental entities with military operations to achieve unity of effort. (JP 1)

*urban operation

A military operation conducted where manmade construction and high population density are the dominant features.

*warfighting function

A group of tasks and systems (people, organizations, information, and processes) united by a common purpose that commanders use to accomplish missions and training objectives.

This page intentionally left blank.

References

Field manuals and selected joint publications are listed by new number followed by old number.

REQUIRED PUBLICATIONS

These documents must be available to intended users of this publication.

FM 1-02 (101-5-1). *Operational Terms and Graphics*. 21 September 2004.

JP 1-02. *Department of Defense Dictionary of Military and Associated Terms*. 8 November 2010.

RELATED PUBLICATIONS

These documents contain relevant supplemental information.

JOINT AND DEPARTMENT OF DEFENSE PUBLICATIONS

Most joint publications are available online: <http://www.dtic.mil/doctrine/new_pubs/jointpub.htm>.
Most CJCS directives are available online: <http://www.dtic.mil/cjcs_directives/index.htm>.

CJCSI 5120.02. *Joint Doctrine Development System*. 4 December 2009.

DODI 3000.05. *Stability Operations*. 16 September 2009.

JP 1. *Doctrine for the Armed Forces of the United States*. 14 May 2007.

JP 1-04. *Legal Support to Military Operations*. 1 March 2007.

JP 2-0. *Joint Intelligence*. 22 June 2007.

JP 2-01. *Joint and National Intelligence Support to Military Operations*. 7 October 2004.

JP 2-03. *Geospatial Intelligence Support to Joint Operations*. 22 March 2007.

JP 3-0. *Joint Operations*. 17 September 2006.

JP 3-05. *Doctrine for Joint Special Operations*. 17 December 2003.

JP 3-06. *Joint Urban Operations*. 8 November 2009.

JP 3-07.2. *Antiterrorism*. 24 November 2010.

JP 3-07.3. *Peace Operations*. 17 October 2007.

JP 3-07.4. *Joint Counterdrug Operations*. 13 June 2007.

JP 3-08. *Interagency, Intergovernmental Organization, and Nongovernmental Organization Coordination During Joint Operations* (2 volumes). 17 March 2006.

JP 3-09.3. *Close Air Support*. 8 July 2009.

JP 3-10. *Joint Security Operations in Theater*. 3 February 2010.

JP 3-13. *Information Operations*. 13 February 2006.

JP 3-13.1. *Electronic Warfare*. 25 January 2007.

JP 3-13.4. *Military Deception*. 13 July 2006.

JP 3-16. *Multinational Operations*. 7 March 2007.

JP 3-18. *Joint Forcible Entry Operations*. 16 June 2008.

JP 3-22. *Foreign Internal Defense*. 12 July 2010.

JP 3-24. *Counterinsurgency Operations*. 5 October 2009.

JP 3-26. *Counterterrorism*. 13 November 2009.

JP 3-28. *Civil Support*. 14 September 2007.

JP 3-29. *Foreign Humanitarian Assistance.* 17 March 2009.

JP 3-31. *Command and Control for Joint Land Operations.* 29 June 2010.

JP 3-35. *Deployment and Redeployment Operations.* 7 May 2007.

JP 3-40. *Combating Weapons of Mass Destruction.* 10 June 2009.

JP 3-41. *Chemical, Biological, Radiological, Nuclear, and High-Yield Explosives Consequence Management.* 2 October 2006.

JP 3-50. *Personnel Recovery.* 5 January 2007.

JP 3-57. *Civil-Military Operations.* 8 July 2008.

JP 3-61. *Public Affairs.* 25 August 2010.

JP 3-68. *Noncombatant Evacuation Operations.* 22 January 2007.

JP 4-0. *Joint Logistics.* 18 July 2008.

JP 4-05. *Joint Mobilization Planning.* 22 March 2010.

JP 5-0. *Joint Operation Planning.* 26 December 2006.

JP 6-0. *Joint Communications System.* 10 June 2010.

ARMY PUBLICATIONS

Most Army doctrinal publications are available online: <http://www.apd.army.mil/>. Army regulations are produced only in electronic media and available at the same link.

AR 10-87. *Army Commands, Army Service Component Commands, and Direct Reporting Units.* 4 September 2007.

AR 12-1. *Security Assistance, Training, and Export Policy.* 23 July 2010.

AR 34-1. *Multinational Force Compatibility.* 6 January 2004.

AR 350-1. *Army Training and Leader Development.* 18 December 2009.

FM 2-0 (34-1). *Intelligence.* 23 March 2010.

FM 3-05.30/MCRP 3-40.6. *Psychological Operations.* 15 April 2005.

FM 3-05.40 (41-10). *Civil Affairs Operations.* 29 September 2006.

FM 3-05.202 (31-20-3). *Special Forces Foreign Internal Defense Operations.* 2 February 2007.

FM 3-05.401. *Civil Affairs Tactics, Techniques, and Procedures.* 5 July 2007.

FM 3-06. *Urban Operations.* 26 October 2006.

FM 3-07. *Stability Operations.* 6 October 2008.

FM 3-07.1. *Security Force Operations.* 1 May 2009.

FM 3-13 (100-6). *Information Operations: Doctrine, Tactics, Techniques, and Procedures.* 28 November 2003.

FM 3-16. *The Army in Multinational Operations.* 20 May 2010.

FM 3-24. *Counterinsurgency.* 15 December 2006.

FM 3-28. *Civil Support Operations.* 20 August 2010.

FM 3-35. *Army Deployment and Redeployment.* 21 April 2010.

FM 3-35.1. *Army Pre-Positioned Operations.* 1 July 2008.

FM 3-36. *Electronic Warfare in Operations.* 25 February 2009.

FM 3-50.1. *Army Personnel Recovery.* 10 August 2005.

FM 3-60. *The Targeting Process.* 26 November 2010.

FM 3-61.1. *Public Affairs, Tactics, Techniques and Procedures.* 1 October 2000.

FM 3-90. *Tactics.* 4 July 2001.

FM 3-100.21 (100-21). *Contractors on the Battlefield.* 3 January 2003.

FM 4-0. *Sustainment.* 30 April 2009.

FM 4-02. *Force Health Protection in a Global Environment.* 13 February 2003.

FM 5-0. *The Operations Process.* 26 March 2010.

FM 5-19 (100-14). *Composite Risk Management.* 21 August 2006.

FM 6-0. *Mission Command: Command and Control of Army Forces.* 11 August 2003.

FM 6-01.1. *Knowledge Management Section.* 29 August 2008.

FM 6-02.40. *Visual Information Operations.* 10 March 2009.

FM 6-02.70. *Army Electromagnetic Spectrum Operations.* 20 May 2010.

FM 6-02.71. *Network Operations.* 14 July 2009.

FM 6-22 (22-100). *Army Leadership.* 12 October 2006.

FM 7-0. *Training for Full Spectrum Operations.* 23 February 2011.

FM 27-10. *The Law of Land Warfare.* 18 July 1956.

FM 46-1. *Public Affairs Operations.* 30 May 1997.

OTHER PUBLICATIONS

National Military Strategy of the United States of America. Washington, DC: U.S. Government Printing Office, 2004.

Title 10, United States Code, Armed Forces.

Section 162, Combatant Commands: Assigned Forces; Chain of Command.

Section 164, Commanders of Combatant Commands: Assignment; Powers and Duties.

Title 32, United States Code, National Guard.

von Steuben, Baron Friedrich Wilhelm. *Regulations for the Order and Discipline of the Troops of the United States.* Philadelphia: Styner and Cist, 1779.

WEB SITES

United Nations Department of Public Information Nongovernmental Organization Web site. <http://www.un.org/dpi/ngosection/dpingo-directory.asp>

SOURCES USED

These sources are quoted or paraphrased in this publication.

Clausewitz, Carl von. *On War.* Edited by Michael Howard and Peter Paret. Princeton: Princeton University Press, 1984.

Gates, Robert M. (Secretary of Defense). "Landon Lecture." Speech given at Kansas State University, Manhattan, Kansas, 26 November 2007. <http://www.defenselink.mil/speeches/speech.aspx?speechid=1199> (accessed 28 December 2010).

Tsouras, Peter G., ed. *The Greenhill Dictionary of Military Quotations.* London: Greenhill, 2000.

PRESCRIBED FORMS

None

REFERENCED FORMS

DA Form 2028. *Recommended Changes to Publications and Blank Forms.*

Index

Entries are by paragraph number.

Entries are by paragraph number.

Entries are by paragraph number.

Entries are by paragraph number.

Entries are by paragraph number.

Entries are by paragraph number.

Entries are by paragraph number.

By order of the Secretary of the Army:

GEORGE W. CASEY, JR.
General, United States Army
Chief of Staff

Official:

JOYCE E. MORROW
Administrative Assistant to the
Secretary of the Army
0803814

DISTRIBUTION:

Active Army, Army National Guard, and U.S. Army Reserve: To be distributed in accordance with the initial distribution number 110502, requirements for FM 3-0.

PIN: 079091-000